Authentic Human Sexuality
An Integrated Christian Approach

By Judith K. Balswick *and* Jack O. Balswick

SECOND EDITION

IVP Academic
An imprint of InterVarsity Press
Downers Grove, Illinois

InterVarsity Press
P.O. Box 1400, Downers Grove, IL 60515-1426
World Wide Web: www.ivpress.com
E-mail: email@ivpress.com

2nd edition©2008 by Judith K. Balswick and Jack O. Balswick
1st edition©1999 by Judith K. Balswick and Jack O. Balswick

InterVarsity Press ® *is the book-publishing division of InterVarsity Christian Fellowship/USA* ®*, a movement of students and faculty active on campus at hundreds of universities, colleges and schools of nursing in the United States of America, and a member movement of the International Fellowship of Evangelical Students. For information about local and regional activities, visit intervarsity.org.*

All Scripture quotations, unless otherwise indicated, are taken from the Holy Bible, New International Version ®. NIV ®. *Copyright ©1973, 1978, 1984 by International Bible Society. Used by permission of Zondervan Publishing House. All rights reserved.*

Design: Cindy Kiple
Images: David Sanger/Getty Images

ISBN 978-0-8308-2883-8

Printed in the United States of America ∞

Library of Congress Cataloging-in-Publication Data

Balswick, Judith K.
  Authentic human sexuality: an integrated christian approach /
  Judith K. Balswick & Jack O. Balswick.—2nd ed.
      p. cm.
  Includes bibliographical references.
  ISBN 978-0-8308-2883-8 (pbk.: alk paper)
  1. Sex. 2. Sexual ethics. 3. Sex—Religious aspects—Christianity.
  I. Balswick, Jack O. II. Title.
  HQ21.B166 2008
  261.8'357—dc22

                                                                                              2008008859

P	21	20	19	18	16	15	14	13	12	11	10	9	8
Y	24	23	22	21	20	19	18	17	16	15			

Contents

Preface

We are grateful for the positive response to the first edition of *Authentic Human Sexuality*, especially since it has been used as a source for courses taught at Christian seminaries and colleges. While keeping the overall organization of the first edition, we accomplish three significant changes in this second edition. First, theological writings and social science research on issues of human sexuality have been updated (see the references at the back of the book and the suggestions "For Further Reading" at chapter ends). Second, we have added depth to our theological model of sexual relationships by utilizing a trinitarian theology of relationship. In an effort to define what it means to develop an authentic sexuality, we find a foundational starting point in trinitarian theology. Being created in God's image gives us reason to look to God as a model of how to express ourselves in relationship to others. Third, we have included a new chapter on sexual development throughout the human life span.

Significant relational aspects of human sexuality are found in biblical stories such as the Song of Songs and are developed in characters like Abraham, Sarah and Hagar; Jacob, Leah and Rachel; Rebekah and Isaac; and David and Bathsheba. Throughout the Old Testament the relationship between the children of Israel and Yahweh illustrates how movement toward or rejection of God's way leads to fulfillment or distortion in human relationships. Jesus revolutionized what it means to be male and female in caring relationships. The apostle Paul and other New Testament writers provide further instruction to singles and married on how to be in relationship. Drawing upon a scriptural foundation, our Christian theology addresses what it means to be created as sexual beings and how our sexuality leads to meaningful and authentic sexuality. This serves as a basis for various topics on sexuality.

The book is divided into four parts. In part one, "The Origin and Formation of Sexuality," we look into the multitude of factors (historical, sociological and cultural) that contribute to human sexuality. This sets the stage for chapter two, "An Interactive Developmental Model" of human sexuality, which brings in biological and sociocultural factors in the context of a developmental framework. Chapter three, "Principles of Authentic Sexuality," offers unique principles and biblical perspectives on sexuality and spirituality. In chapter four, "Sexual Being in Relationship," we build a biblical foundation of purpose and meaning that is based on the *image Dei*. We use trinitarian theology as a model for two essential dimensions of being created as sexual beings: differentiation and connection. We then consider how our sexuality leads to meaningful relationships through interdependence and unity. The biblical accounts of covenant, grace, empowerment and intimacy provide the theology of authentic sexual relationships. Chapter five presents the specific biopsychosociological forces the influence the formation of sexual orientation, including various explanations of homosexuality. Chapter six examines biblical references to homosexuality and describes various ministry approaches to homosexuality.

Part two, "Authentic Sexuality," extends the theological model presented in chapter three and addresses a variety of relationships. Chapter seven brings out the unique dynamics of sexual intimacy and singleness, while chapter eight pays particular attention to the emerging practice of premarital cohabitation, noting concerns and citations. Chapter nine offers a biblical perspective on maximizing marital sexual fulfillment, and chapter ten looks at some of the common causes of extramarital sex and the serious consequences it has on a relationship.

In part three, "Inauthentic Sexuality," we examine several inauthentic forms of human sexuality. Chapter eleven sees sexual harassment as the uninvited eroticizing of a relationship. Sexual abuse of children, the topic of chapter twelve, is discussed as a violation deep within the child's soul. Chapter thirteen focuses on two forms of sexualized power—rape and other sexual violence—seeing them as destructive forces that emerge out of a violent world. Chapters fourteen and fifteen investigate two particularly self-defeating and devastating forms of inauthentic sexuality: pornography and sexual addiction.

The nature of our modern electronic mass society determines that issues of authentic human sexuality transcend individual, familial and localized community boundaries. Part four offers a final chapter, "The Sexually Authentic Society," which examines the importance of developing societal structures capable of promoting and sustaining authentic sexuality. It challenges the Christian community to be intentional and proactive in bringing salt and light to a world in desperate need for theology that gives meaning and rightful understanding to human sexuality.

Figures

PART ONE

The Origin and Formation of Sexuality

1

Sexuality

A Historical, Sociocultural Context

Few contemporary issues generate as much heat and conflict in society, and within the church, as those having to do with human sexuality. Controversy continues over homosexuality, including debates over causation, legitimization and the ability to change orientation. Subtle and not-so-subtle sexual messages and innuendos in the media—television, music, movies and so forth—generate controversy over the issue of free speech versus censorship. The easy access and sheer amount of pornography that even a child can access on the Internet yields consequences that we do not yet fathom. Increased rates of sexual compulsion have resulted in a number of therapeutic and twelve-step programs addressing sexual addiction as a new dimension of their addiction programs. Reports show that three out of four single adults will engage in sexual intercourse before they reach age 20, one out of two will cohabit before marriage, and 25 percent of men and 15 percent of women will have engaged in extramarital sex. Also disturbing are the high rates of uninvited and nonconsensual sex that are reported, especially by women, ranging from sexual harassment to sexual abuse, rape and other violent sex crimes.

It would be a mistake to think that Christians less than members in society at large struggle with issues of sexual morality and behavior. Sexual indiscretions by leaders within the Christian community serve as a reminder that no one is immune from failures in this area. Although Christians may have a solid biblical foundation that provides a meaningful theology of authentic human sexually, it is more difficult to live consistently by that value system.

In writing this book, our starting point is to acknowledge that, as part of a fallen creation, all human beings struggle with their sexual nature and come short of the sexual wholeness that God intended. This recognition means that we approach this topic with humility and compassion. We must balance *truth* and *mercy* as we develop biblical guidelines, principles and models for dealing with authentic human sexuality. While boldly asserting the truth of Scripture in building a foundation for sexual morality and behavior, we do so with an attitude of mercy and grace as extended to us in Christ Jesus. The vigor with which some condemn the sexual shortcomings of others is not only nonproductive; it is also hypocritical. Here we remind ourselves of William Shakespeare's observation that we can "protest too much!" as a way of denying sexual sin in our lives (*Hamlet*, act 3, scene 2, line 230). We must be careful to acknowledge the beam in our own eye, before we cast stones at others (Mt 7:1-5; Jn 8:7). On the other hand, it behooves the Christian community to join against the devastating ills of our postmodern society, which seems to tolerate every type of inauthentic sexuality. This "anything and everything goes" mentality leaves people without clarity and vision about how to develop authenticity in their sexual lives.

Although we could use terms like *normal, functional* or *healthy* sexuality, our focus in this book is *authentic* sexuality. So, what exactly do we mean by authentic sexuality? A simple definition of *authentic* is to be real, genuine, believable and trustworthy. We describe sexuality as something that is authentic (real, congruent, integrated), as opposed to something inauthentic (a counterfeit version of the real thing, incongruent, distorted). Our presupposition is that God intends for our sexuality to be a genuine, believable and trustworthy part of ourselves. To be authentic in our sexuality means that we affirm the sexual in ourselves as an integral part of our total being. In this way we embrace what God has created and declare with God, "It is very good!" (Gen 1:31).

Though our sexuality is created as God's perfect design, we are also excruciatingly aware of the distortions that have occurred through the consequences of sin, fallen nature and deviation from God's original design. This good gift of sex has been perverted and corrupted in our secular world, which is why it is such a struggle for most people. Inauthentic sexuality, a consequence of our fallen condition, leaves us open to unreal, false, convoluted and unreliable messages about sexuality and sexual behaviors. This happens through the interplay of societal attitudes and beliefs, sociocultural structures, biological and psychological factors, as well as individual choice and human agency. In short, authentic sexuality has to do with human beings seeking to live as sexual beings according to God's design and purpose.

The purpose of this book is to consider biological, psychological and sociocultural factors as we bring a biblical focus to authentic human sexuality. Due to the complex factors contributing to sexual development and barriers hindering it, our task of defining authentic sexuality is far from simple. Human sexuality must be understood in terms of a variety of influences that include biology, sociology, psychology, theology, gender, emotions, behaviors, attitudes and values. These multiple layers present multidimensional levels at which authentic human sexuality has an interactive and interpersonal dimension. While authentic human sexuality at the *individual* level is most obvious, it incorporates *relational, communal, societal* and even *global* levels. In this chapter we begin at the individual level by addressing the relationship between sexuality and gender; then we provide a historical-sociocultural context for understanding the development of authentic human sexuality.

SEXUALITY AND GENDER

The term *sex* is used to refer to either *sexuality* or *gender;* although the two concepts are closely related, they are separate constructs. *Gender* or *gender role* refers to one's gender identity as defined by a particular culture. This includes such things as manner of talk, movement, expression, style of dress, as well as gender-based attitudes and interests, stereotypes and behavioral expectations. Given the changes in gender roles in recent years, we focus here on the relationship between sexuality and gender.

The sexual revolution that began in the first half of the twentieth century was followed in later years by a revolution in redefining gender roles. The combination of these two revolutionary changes has multiplied the complexity of understanding sexual development in modern societies. Until the 1960s it was generally assumed that little girls would naturally grow up to be women, with certain well-defined "feminine" roles and identities, and little boys would grow up to be men, with corresponding roles and identities. Social sciences helped us realize that sexual scripts determined much of what was assumed to be "natural" cultural distinctions of male and female.

From the time they are newborn babies, the traditional script for boys was physical courage, toughness, competitiveness, strength, control, dominance and aggressiveness; whereas girls were scripted to be gentle, expressive, responsive, sensitive and compliant. The discovery that much of the expressed difference between males and females is learned rather than genetic has challenged traditional definitions of masculinity and femininity. Rather than giving a detailed account of current changes in gender roles, we shall limit our comments here to the aspects of gender redefinition most directly related to sexuality.

The fact that females were regarded as "less sexual" than males, social scientists discovered, was largely due to the greater sexual restraints placed on females when compared to males. As little girls grew up, parents took a more protective stance toward their daughter's sexuality. Girls were cautioned to show modesty in their clothes, to keep their dresses down and their breasts covered, and to guard themselves against sexual advances. These messages were generalized and reinforced by society at large.

On the other hand, messages that boys received from their parents and society were much less restrictive. Boys were given more freedom to uncover their bodies and to explore themselves physically. As boys grew into puberty, they often became part of adolescent male subculture, where they were encouraged to make sexual advances toward girls as a sign of their masculinity. This message about sexuality is reflected in the language of the adolescent male subculture even today. The boy who fails to "score" can be in danger of having his sexuality called into question. By the time adulthood is reached, males have traditionally been conditioned to be sexually active, while females have been culturally conditioned to resist sexual stimuli and advances.

It is also through culture that males and females come to learn which symbols and objects to associate with sexual meaning and stimuli. The following story, told by a female missionary on her first term in the mission field, illustrates the cultural basis for sexual arousal. While walking through a rural village for the first time, she realized that the men of the village were whistling at her. Since she was modestly attired and the women in the village were bare-breasted, she was quite surprised by this reaction. Later, an experienced missionary explained to her that men in this culture found plump legs to be a sexual stimulus. This demonstrates how a culture defines its sex symbols and corresponding response to these symbols.

The extent to which human sexual responsiveness is culturally conditioned can also be detected through the change in women's bathing suits over the last hundred years. During Victorian times men and women were not permitted to bathe together on a public beach. Around the turn of the century, when mixed bathing finally became more acceptable, bathing suits covered the body down to the ankles and wrists. During the twentieth century, bathing suits have steadily shrunk, exposing ever-increasing expanses of anatomy.

Increased exposure of the body has also diminished the sexual stimulus of various body parts. While a bare knee could have caused quite a stir around the turn of the century, it is not the focus of erotic attention today. To emphasize this point, suppose a young man living at the turn of the century were placed in a time capsule and transported to a typical bathing beach in the United States today. A man conditioned to sexual conventions of the 1890s would be totally shocked, to say the least! Thus, a person's sexual response can be understood in part by social and cultural conditioning.

Since the changes brought about by the sexual and gender revolutions, social scientists have increasingly tried to decipher how much of the difference in sexuality between males and females is biologically hardwired and how much is a result of sociocultural factors. A leader in this field, Eleanor Maccoby (1998), suggests that assessing the role of biology in human sex differences is based on four kinds of evidence: (1) the age at which sex differences emerge, (2) the consistency of sex differences across cultures and over time, (3) the consistency of sex differences across species, and (4) the relationship of physiological factors such as sex hormones and brain structures to behaviors that show sex differences such as aggression.

Based upon these criteria, it is possible to offer some summary observations on male/female differences in sexuality. Research on differing hormonal levels in both women and men indicates a relationship to sexual arousal and sexual passivity/aggressiveness. Though there are biologically produced differences among women and among men, there are also *normative* (as in average) differences *between* men and women. The bottom line is that a proportion of the difference in sexuality between men and women is based on biological as well as sociocultural factors. Oliver and Hyde's (1993) meta-analysis of 177 individual studies of sex differences boil the differences down to a summary statement: Men's attitudes and behaviors are characterized as more nonrelational sexuality and female sexuality as more relational. For instance, men are found to masturbate more than women, hold more sexually permissive attitudes, regard casual intercourse positively, be more sexually promiscuous, and have a higher incidence of homosexuality.

These differences between men and women are also found in sexual attitudes. A study of over 16,000 people in 52 countries found that men more than women have a desire for multiple sexual partners (Schmitt 2003). In a later study based on over 14,000 persons in 48 countries, Schmitt (2006) reports that men more than women had *unrestricted attitudes* that permitted more promiscuous relationships, while women more than men had *restricted attitudes* that tended to prefer committed and monogamous sexual relationships.

This type of evidence has led to a book by Levant and Brooks titled *Men and Sex: New Psychological Perspectives* (1997). Based on their premise that the major developmental task facing men is *integrating sexuality within a relational context,* they write about this as a common struggle for men. As they define it, nonrelational sexuality is "the tendency to experience sex primarily as lust without any requirements for relational intimacy or emotional attachment" (p. 1).

There are the two major explanations of the origin of male nonrelational sexuality. *Evolutionary psychology* refers to natural selection as the culprit, reasoning that males are physiologically programmed for nonrelational sexuality (Buss and Schmitt 1993; Archer 1996). This theory suggests that men and women employ different strategies in selecting mates, based on the assumption that creatures act in ways that will best assure that their genes will be passed on in the future gene pool of a species. Men are sexually promiscuous since dispersing sperm to a number of women maximizes the continuance of their genes. Women, however, are "discreet shoppers" since they only have so many eggs and must carefully mate with a man who will stay with them and thus increase the probability that their offspring will survive.

The differences between evolutionary psychology and the biblical perspective in regard to the origin of male-female differences are critiqued by Mary Stewart Van Leeuwen (2002). In contrast to the biblical worldview, "evolutionary psychology has no basis for sorting out what is created from what is fallen in human behavior" (p. 146). Since evolutionary psychology seeks to replace the biblical ideal "with a thoroughly materialist worldview, [it] is not the foundation on which to build a sexual ethic, either for men or for women" (Van Leeuwen, 2002:147). While evolutionary psychology can be opposed for theological reasons, it can also be refuted on the basis of psychological theory and research. Moore and Travis (2000:48) report, "There is no evidence that promiscuous men have more offspring than men who invest heavily in the nurturing of their children." Based on their cross-cultural comparisons of thirty-seven cultures, Eagly and Wood (1999:408) conclude that evidence "supports the social structural account of sex differences in male preference."

Alternatively, *social constructionists* admit to some biological basis for differences between males and females in sexuality, but they argue that nonrelational sexuality is in large part a reflection of how male sexuality is culturally defined within traditional gender ideology (Chodorow 1999; Pleck 1995; Maccoby 1998). Social constructionists contend that gender-role socialization has a differential effect on male and female psychosexual development. Socialization patterns allow for the expressing of feelings in girls but discourage it in boys; this can result in males having greater difficulty in distinguishing between their sexual feelings and emotional feelings. This socialization pattern may also account for a male's greater vulnerability to nonrelational forms of sex, while a female's sexuality and desire is tied much more to romantic or love-based relationality (Balswick 1990; Pollack 1998).

Gilbert Bilezikian (2006) and Mary Stewart Van Leeuwen (1990) bring out a theological explanation for gender differences in sexuality. Their beginning point is to draw upon the differential participation of Adam and Eve in the Genesis account of the fall. Genesis 3:6 indicates that whereas Adam and Eve both disobeyed God when eating the forbidden fruit, each sinned in a distinctive way. For her part, Eve went beyond God's command and transgressed God's directive of dominion accountability when she willfully refused to submit to God's dominion. Adam sinned by disobeying God when he chose his relationship with Eve over relationship with God, violating the bounds of relationship accountability.

Consequences of Eve's and Adam's sins were expulsion from the Garden of Eden, struggle with pain in childbirth and work, difficulty in raising children, making a living, and eventual death. There were also personal and relational consequences of their particular sins. For overstepping God's boundary of dominion, Eve's punishment was that she would now have to endure being dominated by the man: "Your desire will be for your husband, and he will rule over you" (Gen 3:16). For overstepping God's boundary and choosing Eve over God, Adam would blame her and seek to dominate her rather than be in a relationship of respect and mutuality. The curse for Adam was that his decision to dominate would thwart closeness and intimacy with his mate. As a result of both their sin, there would be a propensity in males to dominate and in females to submit, making it difficult to achieve person-centered intimate connection in relationships.

Although a nonrelational orientation to sexuality may be rooted in the Fall, it is a condition that has been reinforced by sociocultural structures throughout the developmental process.

This interpretation of the Genesis account can be recognized in expressions of the nonrelational/relational aspects of sexuality. Men more than women struggle with integrating their sexuality into a personal, relational context. Nonrelational sexuality can be recognized in a person's inability to experience a deep emotional connection during sexual encounters with a partner. Sexual expression is more focused on the pleasure and less on the person. Serious forms of nonrelational sexuality include repetitive infidelity, compulsive womanizing, obsession with pornography, sex via phone or computer, strip shows, "gentlemen's clubs," prostitution, sexual addictions, sexual harassment, rape and child molestation (Levant and Brooks 1997:14-15).

While women also struggle with nonrelational sex, the greater tendency is to be so relationally focused that there is failure to keep appropriate personal and sexual boundaries in relationships.

THE HISTORICAL-SOCIOCULTURAL CONTEXT OF SEXUALITY

We use the concept *sociocultural* to encompass all life experiences—psychological, social and cultural—and their collective effect on the formation of human sexuality. The primary importance of sociocultural influence is in defining what sexuality means for the individual. Human beings are unique among all living creatures due to language capacity and therefore the ability to assign meaning to human behavior. A person does not learn the meaning of sexual behavior in a vacuum, but rather in a sociocultural context.

Sexuality is learned within a specific family, tribe, community and society. Since individuals are members of a number of social groupings, the messages about sexuality can vary widely. In pluralistic industrial societies, the messages can also be highly contradictory. Consistency in the meaning of sexuality within a certain social group or cultural system is hard to achieve because it hinges on how meaning is transmitted, perceived and internalized. We must understand each of these levels as they make a unique and joint contribution to the attitudes and meaning of sexuality. In this section we shall consider the *cultural* level, which provides attitudes, values and beliefs about sexuality; and the *sociological* level, which provides the context of sexuality.

Cultural level: Attitudes, values and beliefs. Prevailing cultural attitudes toward sex play a major role in the formation of sexuality within a person. Thus cultures try to control the expression of sexuality in different ways. In Muslim societies, requiring women to cover most parts of their body is an attempt to control men's sexual impulses. In such cultures all public space is declared to be male space—off-limits to a woman unless a man escorts her. Women themselves are veiled, not so much to protect themselves as to protect men from the irresistible power of female sexuality.

Women are thought to have a natural advantage over men because of their sexuality. If not suppressed, women's sexuality would cause *fitna* (chaos) in society; men would be defenseless before the potential powers of female sexuality. Such cultural beliefs and attitudes powerfully affect the developing sexuality within males and females in such societies. Girls come to internalize a view of their own sexuality as powerful and yet shameful. Boys come to internalize an attitude that they have little self-control over their own sexual impulses.

In his book *Sexuality and the Jesus Tradition* (2005:236), theologian William Loader contrasts this cultural perspective with the attitude Jesus took toward women. Loader says that Matthew 5:28, "But I tell you that anyone who looks at a woman lustfully has already committed adultery with her in his heart," "places responsibility squarely on the shoulders of men for the way they handle their sexual lust and not on women. . . . Jesus did not treat women as dangerous." Loader concludes that "women in the early Jesus movement were welcomed not on the basis of suppressing their sexuality, let alone abandoning or shielding it from men, but as women including their sexuality on the basis that the men who followed Jesus would take responsibility for their sexuality and not reduce women to the level of sexual objects or threats."

Although the method of controlling sexuality in Muslim societies may be flawed, the method used to control sexuality in some Christian societies has been equally flawed. Many have faulted both the Puritan and Victorian cultures for trying to repress sexuality itself. In many respects the consequences have been less than healthy, inhibiting an open and honest acceptance of sexuality. The emergence of a robust underground trade in pornography and prostitution and a strong sexual double standard is generally thought to be in part a result of such repression.

The terms *puritanical* and *Victorian* are still used today to connote an uptight view of sex. Calling one who advocates sexual restraint in modern society a "prude" is an example. However, when taking into account the standards of seventeenth-century European culture, we believe the Puritans used biblical restraint along with a healthy view of sexuality. While advocating a clear standard of celibacy for the unmarried and monogamy for married people, they also proposed a liberated view of sexual pleasure in the marriage relationship. Sexual expression between spouses was regarded as good, natural and desirable for both spouses. An example of this comes out of a New England Puritan church record in 1675: A husband confessed that he was planning to abstain from having sex with his wife as a personal repentance for disobeying God. Once the church elders heard this, they pronounced that he had no right to deny his wife sexual pleasure because she, too, had rights to sexual fulfillment. In this case, sexual expression between spouses was not to be withheld for the purpose of repentance because it would deprive the wife of her inalienable right to marital sexual activity (Reiss 1960).

On the other hand, during the Victorian period there were many sexual taboos and repressive messages about sex. During this period of history, anything that appeared to be sexual was covered up. For example, check the bathing attire on the beaches of that era. Not only did people have to cover their arms and legs in public, but also little skirts were placed over the legs of the chairs and sofas. Bare legs, whether on a person or furniture, were a symbol of sexual immodesty.

Also during this time of sexual restraint, the *double standard* became the norm for how men and women were to express themselves sexually. It was generally agreed that since men had sexual needs, they were allowed to find a "bad" woman (prostitute) to take care of their sexual passions, but they would be socially allowed to marry only a "good" woman (virgin). At this point, men also kept mistresses to meet their sexual desires. This was a loud and clear message to both men and women that sex was not to be desired by pure or proper women, but was a passion in men that needed to be tolerated.

This double standard held until the first half of the twentieth century, when it was replaced by the standard of *permissiveness with affection.* This was the beginning of the so-called sexual liberation, often associated as the "roaring [19]20s." This new standard acknowledged that sexual desire and expression should no longer be regarded as pathological for women, but acceptable and desirable for women as well as men. The change in standard did not take place all at once. Differing degrees of relational commitment (progressively having strong feelings of affection for, being in love, or being engaged) were alternative criteria for alternative degrees of sexual intimacy (progressive physical expressions of hugging, kissing, fondling, intercourse). The major change in sexual standards was from a double standard to one in which some degree of sexual expression was accepted between a single man and a single women who shared some degree of commitment. Therefore, when two people loved each other and committed to their relationship, it was permissible to engage in physically erotic expressions of sexuality.

In the years following World War II, there was a period characterized by a preoccupation with sex. This began with the publication of the Kinsey reports: *Sexual Behavior in the Human Male* (Kinsey, Pomeroy and Martin 1948) and *Sexual Behavior in the Human Female* (Kinsey, Pomeroy and Martin 1953). About the same time, Hugh Hefner left his job as a copyeditor at *Fortune* magazine and started a publication known as *Playboy* magazine. The sexual freedom of this era took "expression with affection" one step further by promoting the idea that it was permissible to have affection for a number of partners, not just the person you would marry. In addition, this second sexual liberation introduced the premarital sexual standard of *permissiveness without affection.* This set the stage for expressing sex as a recreational activity.

In the name of sexual liberation, sex became a glorified object, devoid of the meaning associated with personal commitment and intimacy. C. S. Lewis (1960) writes about this in a hypothetical illustration of a society overly focused on sex: Suppose there is a place in which people pay good money to enter a room to view a covered platter sitting on a table. Then, at the assigned time and to the beat of the drums, someone slowly lifts the cover of the platter to expose what is underneath. There, before the lustful and expectant eyes of the many spectators, is a luscious pork chop! One would begin to wonder what was so desperately wrong with the eating habits of such a society. Lewis's point is well taken! We must ask, What are we to make of a society that has such a preoccupation with sex?

In many modern societies, sex has even been taken a step further. Now the platter is no longer covered! In many ways, there is a *saturation with sex.* Sex is boldly presented as front-page news, no longer hidden at the bottom of the last page. We hear it over the radio in popular music, are bombarded with it in the advertising media, and find it expressed as a major theme in movies and daytime soap operas. How much further can a society go before the pendulum swings back?

By 1980 we saw some backlash to this overexposure to sex in a trend toward a *new virginity.* Feminists began to question what came along with their newfound sexual freedom. Many felt that their relational perspective and desire for emotional intimacy had been sabotaged in the process. Many college women even began to wear large red buttons declaring NO to casual sex as a protest to this dehumanizing trend.

At about the same time, cable TV channels also found a sharp drop-off in their late-night X-rated movie audiences. Raw, explicit sex had lost its appeal as a shock and stimulus, and some people were beginning to rebel against sex being depicted as entertainment and recreation. The "free sex" morality was also reexamined in the light of the AIDS epidemic. The fear of sexually transmitted diseases (STDs) caused many to reexamine these promiscuous sex standards. Promotion of safe-sex practices became widespread. Monogamy resurged as a more-sane way to express sexuality in today's world.

Yet the current scene is still a mixed bag. While we have witnessed conservative Christian young people marching on Washington and making purity pledges, the rate of sexual intercourse among junior and senior high school students is increasing. We hear that monogamy is the norm, yet extramarital affairs are on the rise. Prominent celebrities in the media advocate the safe-sex message, yet many confess to making exceptions in their personal sexual encounters. On one hand we are encouraged by the message that mature sex has to do with responsible emotional and physical intimacy with one's lifetime partner, yet many are engaging in casual sex or struggling with sexual addictions of one kind or another. As youth are exposed to the incongruent contemporary sexual attitudes, they seem to be growing up in an absurd and confusing world.

This points to the need for current cultural attitudes to be understood in light of past attitudes toward sexuality. The predominant cultural attitudes held in the United States have changed over several historical periods, but the cultural memory is still present today. The current cultural climate reflects the tension between *sexual repression*, a term used to describe sexual attitudes from past history, and *sexual liberation*, the trend in our modern world to eliminate the "hang-ups" developed during these earlier periods.

Every society must find ways to control or restrain rampant sexual impulses that lead to indiscriminate sexual acting out. Great efforts are spent to protect innocent victims (children, women, elderly) from sexual crimes. This is certainly a major tension and issue in contemporary society. In the Sermon on the Mount, Jesus says that sexual lusting must be met with the willingness to pluck out one's eye or sever one's hand (Mt 5:28-30). Christians need to pay serious attention and give utmost support toward societal attempts to control sexual perversions.

Sociological level. The cultural meaning of sexuality resides within and is filtered through a variety of social structures. In two books, *Journey into Sexuality* (1986) and *An Insider's View of Sexual Science Since Kinsey* (2006), Ira Reiss presents a sociological explanation of sexuality. He makes the assumption that sexuality is learned in a societal context. People learn about sexuality the same way they learn about friendship or love relationships. Sexual learning is especially potent, he suggests, because of the bonding created between persons when physical pleasure and personal self-disclosure accompany the sexual encounter. This partner bonding is what most societies wish to support. Sexual bonding not only promotes the formation of kinship ties but also helps to form gender-role concepts.

Based upon cross-societal evidence, Reiss suggests that in all societies

sexuality is linked to three elements of the social structure: *marital jealousy, gender role power* and *ideology* (beliefs about what is normal). Marital
jealousy serves as a "boundary-maintenance mechanism" that aims at protecting relationships that society views as important. Powerful people in
social structures will be more likely than those less powerful to be jealous
of their partners and to react with greater violence and aggression. This is
where gender-role power comes in. Usually those who are in power have
control over what the society views as important. Thus, since sexuality
is viewed as important by the powerful, males will tend to demand and
possess greater sexual rights than females, since males usually have more
power.

Reiss's notion on marital jealousy may need to be reformulated in light of
some recent social science findings. William Jankowiak (2006) has studied societies in which polygamy exists. His studies have included polygamous Mormon families as well as other non-Western societies. In plural
marriages, to his surprise, he found nearly universal evidence of *emotional*
jealousy, but not *sexual* jealousy. He concluded that human beings are not
so much sexually monogamous as emotionally monogamous. Or to put it
another way, sexual desire may not be monogamous, but emotional love is.
Jankowiak's conclusions are in line with the strong biblical based *relational*
aspect of marriage that we will present in chapter nine.

Ideology, the third element, refers to the shared societal beliefs about
sexual normality and human nature. Sexual ideologies are subtypes of
the general ideology in a society and revolve around two dimensions:
(1) overall gender equality and (2) the relative sexual permissiveness
allowed to each gender. For example, North American societies tend to
promote partner equality and therefore emphasize the importance of mutual foreplay and orgasm during sexual intercourse, while such concepts
are less common in societies that fail to value equality between the sexes.

Understanding the importance of Reiss's writings in developing our
concept of authentic sexuality is crucial. He not only gives a sociological
explanation of sexuality but also tries to develop a sexual morality. Reiss
believes that we should hesitate to label as *abnormal* (or in our words, *inauthentic*) any sexual act that can be found as an accepted act in another
culture. Only sexual acts found to be unacceptable in all cultures will be
deemed abnormal. In other words, Reiss argues that *what is, is right!* He
states, "There may well be other scientific bases for defining a sexual act

the standard (of) the world [handwritten annotation]

as abnormal, but until it is clearly established as such by scientific evidence and reasoning, we had better not use such labels freely if we are to avoid the politicization of theory" (Reiss 1986:239). This is a good example of how a person with a naturalistic worldview makes moral decisions. Although it is important for Christians to be informed by what is defined as normative in nature and nurture, we take the Holy Scripture as an ultimate guide for moral values.

The sociologist rightly observes that in all societies, customs provide boundary mechanisms around important relationships in order to preserve them. Upholding marriage as the place to engage in sexual intercourse and bear children organizes and provides stability in a society, even if it is accomplished simply by means of jealousy norms taught to group members in a particular culture. The more-powerful members learn to maximize their control of that which is sanctioned by their group. Hence, when one gender is more powerful, it is more likely that this gender possesses greater sexual rights and privileges. Sociological explanations deemphasize the role of biology in explaining sexuality. Most sociological theories see biological tendencies as malleable by recognizing that sociocultural factors are able to shape tendencies in culturally preferred directions.

One must distinguish between Reiss's sociological analysis of the formation of human sexuality and the values inherent in his interpretation of that analysis. One can accept normative behavior by studying all cultures without accepting carte blanche the value premise that what is, is right. We look for values based on a biblical understanding of sexuality. In addition, the social scientist tends to use culture as the normalizing base, while the biological scientist tends to use biophysical structure. In our view, God is the Creator of all things, and we dare not place a limit on the means (nature and/or nurture) by which God chooses to bring about authentic sexuality. In the following chapter we trace the development of sexuality as it takes place within the individual life span, which will lay the foundation for describing authentic human sexuality.

For Further Reading

Reiss, I. 2006. *An insider's view of sexual science since Kinsey.* Lanham, Md.: Rowman & Littlefield.

2

Human Sexuality

An Interactive Developmental Model

Human sexuality does not arrive fully formed, but rather develops as an interactional process. Therefore, an adequate explanation of human sexuality must take into account both individual developmental and relational aspects. We use the term *interactive* to refer to the biological, sociocultural and theological factors that mutually affect and are affected by each other simultaneously throughout one's life span. First, we will describe the more deterministic models that give partial explanations of human sexuality. Then we will present the more complex interactive explanation.

PARTIAL EXPLANATIONS OF SEXUALITY

Three alternative models of human sexuality are visually illustrated in figure 2.1. The three arrows in figure 2.1 leading from nature to human sexuality, from God to human sexuality, and from nurture to human sexuality represent single-factor explanations of human sexuality. We believe each one alone is an incomplete explanation because it fails to acknowledge the contribution of the other two. When one attempts to explain human sexuality through an exclusive set of explanations, it becomes a shortsighted "deterministic" explanation. Determinism is an explanatory approach that attributes a "one-and-only" causality. Determinism is sometimes referred to as "nothing-buttery," since it proposes that nothing but the one factor is necessary and sufficient to explain a phenomenon (MacKay 1974).

As represented in figure 2.1, *biological determinism* explains human sexuality purely in natural (physiological and genetic) terms, *social determinism* attributes the development of human sexuality solely to sociocultural factors, and *theistic determinism* claims that human sexuality is simply part of God's creation and not dependent on either sociocultural or biological factors. The latter is a type of naive theistic determinism. We believe that each of the deterministic positions yields a limited understanding of human sexuality and fails to provide an adequate grasp of authentic sexuality. Even though each approach explains an important aspect of human sexuality, when taken alone, the explanation is partial.

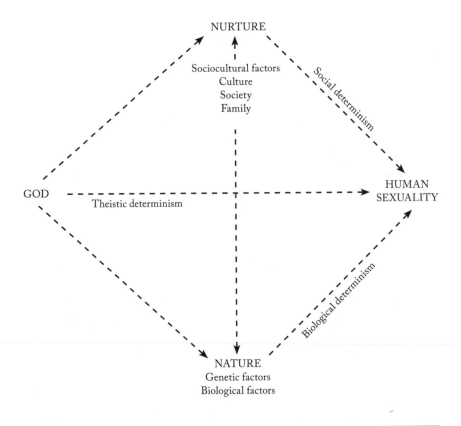

Figure 2.1 Explanations of human sexuality

A holistic understanding of human sexuality is much more complex than what is allowed in any of the single-factor approaches. The arrows between the three explanatory factors represent a more complete explanation of human sexuality. Starting at the extreme left of figure 2.1, we recognize that God can act either directly or indirectly as the author and Creator of human sexuality. We depict God acting indirectly by the arrows pointing from God but then *through* nature and nurture to human sexuality. The two-way vertical arrow between biological and sociocultural factors is meant to recognize the fact that biological and sociocultural factors mutually affect and are affected by each other. Such explanations represent more adequate explanations of human sexuality. God, in infinite power and wisdom, has chosen to use sociocultural and biological factors to bring forth the fullness of one's sexuality.

One should not be uneasy about evidence that points to the influence of sociocultural and biological factors, thinking that this undermines the role of God as the Creator of human sexuality. Rather, God has chosen to work through both biological and sociocultural factors in the formation of human sexuality. A wide range of sociocultural and biological considerations influences the formation of any individual's sexuality. At the same time we solidly believe that God takes a direct role through biblical teachings that help us live out authentic sexuality in our heart's desires, minds and attitudes and through our behavior. We will elaborate on this in the following chapter.

As an aside, let us observe the relationship between one's theological position and the relative importance one gives to sociocultural and biological explanations of human sexuality. For example, people holding a more conservative theological position tend to emphasize biological factors to explain male/female gender differences but focus on environmental factors when it comes to explanations about homosexuality. Persons with liberal theologies tend to do just the opposite. They deemphasize genetic explanations for gender differences but embrace genetic explanations regarding homosexual orientation. It is important to recognize how one's theology influences an acceptance or rejection of social and biological explanations of sexuality.

AN INTERACTIVE DEVELOPMENTAL MODEL

Given the complexity of human sexual development, we present figure

2.2 as a graphic illustration of the *continuous interactive* process between biology and sociocultural factors as they affect sexual formation and development. At the center of the figure, the stages of human development are represented from top to bottom. At each stage of human development, both biological and sociocultural variables play a significant role in sexual development. Even before a child is born (prenatal stage), there are important interactive affects (represented by the top horizontal dotted line) between genes, hormones and the mother's womb as the holding environment. The vertical and diagonal dotted lines represent the idea that both biological factors and sociocultural factors affect the biological and sociocultural makeup of the individual in subsequent developmental stages and within each interaction (horizontal dotted line) with each other.

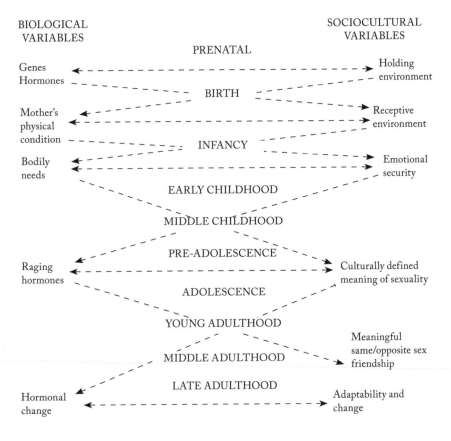

Figure 2.2. An interactive developmental theory of authentic human sexuality

Figure 2.2 gives approximations of the biopsychosocial dynamics of human sexual development and is not meant to be a description of stage-specific development. We point to psychosocial considerations such as meeting basic bodily needs and providing emotional security during infancy as important to a child's sexual development. Emerging from pre-adolescence into adolescence, increased hormonal levels and culturally defined messages about the meaning of sex contribute to the adolescent's sexual development. Sexually promiscuous teenage boys, for example, not only share in common permissive home backgrounds but also higher testosterone levels than those who are less promiscuous. In addition, hormonal levels not only affect the rate of sexual involvement, but engaging in sexual activities increases hormonal levels.

A good example of this interactive effect between biology and sociocultural factors is the accumulated research regarding the brain's impact on sexuality. In response to erotic arousal, the brain organizes bodily reactions that eventually lead to sexual satisfaction or lack of it. Incoming sensual stimuli are encoded in the cortex of the brain, and the hypothalamus determines whether the stimuli are painful or pleasurable. Once this is determined, the message is sent to the pituitary gland, which controls outgoing messages to the adrenal glands in the female and male gonads. If the pituitary gland receives the incoming sexual stimuli as pleasurable, it commands the necessary hormones to begin the sexual arousal process. However, if the message indicates pain, the pituitary gland will close down the sexual arousal system. Needless to say, the brain, as a biological sex organ, is greatly influenced and responsive to the social environment. Once again, the social and biological influences interacting together make it difficult to separate the effect of each.

Developmental theorists sometimes argue for critical periods, a concept that refers to a fixed chronological age in human development during which certain behaviors optimally emerge. What happens at one stage of sexual development influences the cumulative effects of what happens at subsequent stages. However, rather than taking place in fixed stages, sexual development emerges along a number of paths as influenced by a combination of factors. Therefore while accepting the idea that there are approximate periods during which developmental tasks become central, oscillation theory suggests that "transitions occur not as step functions, where discontinuous leaps are made from one level of functioning to another, but rather through an oscillation between levels of functioning (Breunlin 1988:140). This leaves more room for unique responses of individuals as they are impacted by sociocultural factors.

Although the concept of stage development can help us understand regular age-related patterns of sexual development, oscillation theory allows for a more flexible ebb and flow for unique individuals between these stages. Some move from one stage to another so smoothly that it does not make sense to speak of separate life-cycle stages, while others struggle more or even become stuck in a given stage. During early sexual transitions, depending on biological and sociocultural input, some individuals may experience a major crisis that affects later development. The point is that there are predictable patterns of sexual development as well as a great variability in the developmental paths different individuals take.

SEXUAL FORMATION IN THE PRENATAL STAGE

Four different criteria can be used to define the sexuality of an individual, as illustrated in figure 2.3. First, *natal sex* has to do with the physical and biological features at birth that determine whether the baby is male or female. Second, *sexual identity* refers to a person's sexual self-concept, the view one has of oneself as a sexual person. Third, *sexual orientation* refers to the direction of one's erotic attraction, which can be the opposite sex (heterosexual), the same sex (homosexual) or both sexes (bisexual). And fourth, *gender* or *gender role* refers to one's gender identity as defined by a particular culture. This includes such things as gender-based attitudes and interests, stereotypes and behavioral expectations.

In the vast majority of cases, there is consistency among all four dimensions of sexuality, resulting in a clearcut definition of gender. However, for some there is inconsistency between the four dimensions, a lack of congruence that causes confusion about gender. For example, some babies are born with either full or partial male and female genitalia (hermaphrodites).

Examples can be given for each and every one of the combinations of the four dimensions of sexuality. There are people whose natal sex is male, but who are female in sexual identity, gender role and sexual orientation. Others are male in terms of natal sex and sexual identity, but female in gender role and sexual orientation, and so forth. In appropriate sections of the book, we address some of the issues posed by such sexual incongruence.

Human sexuality begins at conception. The sperm, carrying either an X or Y sex chromosome, joins the ovum, which contains an X-chromosome, to create a male (XY) or female (XX). If all of the biological details are in order, the child is born some nine months later, anatomically and genetically male or female.

Nature is not always consistent, however, and we must consider aberrations at the prenatal stage that interfere with the normal sexual developmental process. The extra Y-chromosome or X-chromosome, for example, results in striking forms of sexual abnormalities. For instance, males who are born with an XYY-chromosomal makeup, when compared to normal XY males, have an extra dose of maleness. As adults, these men tend to be taller, more muscular, more impulsive, and have higher activity levels. Some might be tempted to put a positive spin on these supermale qualities; nevertheless, a higher percentage of XYY than XY males have been convicted of committing violent and aggressive crimes.

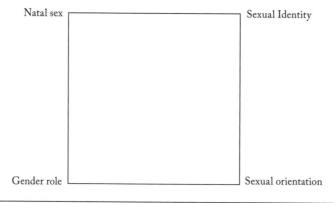

Figure 2.3. Four dimensions of sexuality

On the other hand, males born with an XXY-chromosomal makeup (Klinefelter's syndrome) as adults will be shorter and less muscular; have smaller testicles and underdeveloped pubic, facial and body hair; and experience lower sexual arousal. These males tend to be more timid and passive in general behavior, and in most cases cannot produce sperm.

In females a chromosomal abnormality known as Turner's syndrome results from the absence of an X-chromosome (XO). Characteristics include abnormal ovarian development, failure to menstruate, infertility, and the lack of secondary sexual characteristics, such as enlarged breasts.

In addition, females with Turner's syndrome are often short in stature and predisposed to heart and kidney defects (Orten 1990). This brief summary of some of the effects of abnormal Y- or X-chromosomal makeup points to the significance of their impact on one's sexuality.

Similarly, the presence of too much or too little of the wrong kind of hormones can be a cause of abnormal prenatal sexual development. Two conditions that may result from hormonal abnormalities are hermaphroditism and pseudohermaphroditism. Hermaphroditism is a rare condition in which an individual is born with full or partial genital or reproductive organs of both sexes. Characteristics may include the presence of one ovary and one testicle, feminine breasts or a vaginal opening beneath the penis. Although the internal reproductive systems are usually mixed and incomplete, hermaphrodites are generally genetically female (XX) and capable of menstruating. They may be reared as either male or female, depending largely on external appearance of the genitalia.

Pseudohermaphroditism, more common than hermaphroditism, refers to individuals born with the gonads (internal reproductive glands) matching the sex chromosomes but genitals resembling the opposite sex. In females a condition known as androgenital syndrome can occur when the fetus is exposed to high levels of androgen. This causes the clitoris to enlarge and the labia to fuse together, producing a genitalia resembling the male scrotum. These particular individuals are referred to as female pseudohermaphrodites because they are genetically female (XX), yet are generally reared as males due to the outer appearance. During adolescence the female raised as a male may notice lack of facial hair growth, failure of the voice to deepen, and enlargement of the breasts.

A hormonal abnormality that can result in male pseudohermaphroditism is called testicular feminization syndrome (TFS). This condition is characterized by the lack of male genitals in individuals who are genetically male (XY). Although there are normal levels of androgen, the fetal tissues do not respond to the male hormones, and thus female external genitals are formed. While the newborn infant resembles a female externally, the testes are embedded in the abdomen. Parents are often unaware of this hormonal abnormality until the child reaches adolescence and fails to menstruate.

These abnormalities lead to a less-than-normal physiological sexual system. It is not always so easy, as we shall see in the following section, for these individuals. The medical professionals, parents, and/or individuals themselves will usually make decisions for corrective surgery and hormone therapy.

INFANT SEXUALITY

Although not fully developed as sexual beings, all children experience sexual impulses from the moment of birth. Evidence shows that involuntary physical responses such as penile erection in males and vaginal lubrication may consistently occur during infancy (Friedrich et al. 1991). In fact, the infant's body is responsive to caressing, fondling, stroking and skin-to-skin touch. The obvious smiles and pleasurable sounds a baby makes in reply to such interaction indicate positive responses. The mouth is a center of pleasure for infants as they receive nurture and comfort from their mother's breast. Later, as children develop motor skills, they begin to explore their entire body, taking in pleasurable feelings through self-touch. While these experiences of touch are quite different from adult erotic stimulation, children are born with a capacity for receiving pleasure and a potential for full sexual maturity.

Before the development of sexual awareness, it is difficult to distinguish sexuality from emotional bonding. Babies need to be hugged and cuddled and shown much physical touch. Bodily touch as well as parental acceptance of the infant's body is important at this stage (Orbach 2004). When an infant is deprived of a sufficient amount of physical touch and nurturance, there is a danger of not developing secure emotional bonding. In the worst case scenario is the report of *marasmus* (wasting away) for orphaned children who were not cuddled, and it eventually culminated in infant death.

Ambiguous genitalia. In the vast majority of cases *natal sex*—the physical and biological features at birth that determine whether the baby is male or female—is clearly defined. In a small minority of cases, however, ambiguous genitalia and/or an imbalanced hormonal system leads to sexual ambiguity.

Gender ambiguity occurs among more females than males since there is a strong link between androgen receptivity and the disorder. Embryos that have a high level of insensitivity to androgens while in the uterus are more likely to develop ambiguous genitals (Alderson, Madill and Balen 2004). There are two types of *androgen insensitivity syndrome:* complete

(CAIS), where there is a normal vulva, clitoris, and vaginal opening with a short or dimple-like vagina; and partial (PAIS), where the infant shows ambiguous secondary sex characteristics such as an enlarged clitoris often mistaken for a penis. Such persons, although exhibiting the female XX genotype, are generally male (XY) phenotype.

Ford and Beach (1951) reported ethnographic evidence that many societies provided culturally acceptable ways to sanction persons born with ambiguous sexuality. In many traditional societies, before the emergence of a modern scientific understanding of the human body, creative means are found to deal with sexual ambiguity. Such individuals are often given a "special" status, such as guardian of the communities' spirit. In other societies, individuals are permitted to live with the ambiguity and asked to make a decision once an appropriate age is reached (Chau and Herring 2002).

Sex reassignment. As driven by expert medical opinion in Western medicine, a common solution to sexual ambiguity until recently has been *gender reassignment*. Since it is easier to surgically alter ambiguous genitalia to correspond to female genitalia, most parents were counseled to take this option. The theory behind sex reassignment was that sexuality is *not* hardwired but emerges through cultural socialization.

In recent years the practice of sex reassignment has increasingly been challenged. In the words of one major critic of sex reassignment, Milton Diamond (1997), the doctor looks between the child's legs rather than the ears. If things look good physiologically, they conclude that they have done a good job. At this point in time, such logic is being seen as ludicrous.

The "John/Joan" case is perhaps the most well-known story of sex reassignment gone wrong. Due to a surgical accident at age 2 that severed John's penis, he was reassigned and raised as a girl alongside his twin brother (Money 1975). When this case was uncovered many years later in a follow-up study, "Joan" had rejected her female identity, undergone surgery to construct a penis and was living as a married man with adopted children (Colopinto 2000). John tells of never feeling like a girl. When he was an adolescent, his parents revealed the truth to him, and then he changed back to his male identity. He reports being tormented throughout his life by the way his sex assignment was handled by the medical professionals and the secrecy behind it. Although he finally felt congruent as a man, the emotional turmoil ended when he committed suicide at age 38.

The practice of sex reassignment is being challenged by researchers who have done longitudinal followed-up studies on infants who have gone through reassignment surgery. Reiner and Gearhart (2004) report on their study of sixteen boys (XY) born with ambiguous genitalia, surgically altered to resemble female genitalia. In each case, the parents raised these children as girls based on the assumption that the XY genetic makeup was subordinate to being culturally socialized as a female. It is significant that eight of the children rejected their reassigned sex and insisted that they were boys. Of the remaining eight, three had unclear or undeclared gender identities, and five were satisfied with their assigned female identity. Nearly all of the children showed an interest in typically masculine activities like football, baseball, wrestling and hunting. These findings suggest that prenatal exposure to testosterone plays a strong role in contributing to later male gender identity.

In most cases, medical experts in consultation with parents assume the task of assigning the gender after a careful exploration of known biological and hormonal factors. Traditional wisdom assumes that children need to be assigned a gender identification in order for parents and others to relate to them in appropriate personal and sociocultural ways. Therefore medical professionals make a determination accompanied by appropriate surgical and hormonal procedures to provide congruence with the sex assignment. Sex assignment is usually done soon after birth because its proponents argue that it makes life easier for these children.

An alternative view challenges this practice, believing that it is important to wait until later before performing surgery. It is thought that parents and others should be able to relate to these children as intersexuals until later developmental processes clarify gender more concretely. By implication, this view argues for the demedicalization of sexuality (such as assigning and then surgically altering abnormal sexual characteristics) and the acceptance of what nature has created. From a religious perspective, intersexuals would need a supportive community while they eventually define themselves and live life as the sexual beings God created them to be. It is a challenging problem, especially since gender role, sexual orientation and sexual identity are intervening influences through the life cycle (Brown and Warne 2005).

YOUNG CHILDREN

Children born with a normal physiological package proceed through predictable physiological growth stages. At about age 2, for instance, children show affection for others and an interest in gender differences and sexual body parts. Although much of this is curious exploration, young children seem to derive pleasure out of wrestling and tumbling together, hugging and even kissing each other. In a preschool setting, it is not unusual to observe children engaging in mutually satisfying touch. During these early years, it is unclear what meaning children attribute to such actions. Since sexual behavior is socially learned through the use of language, we can only assume that this early "sexual behavior" is primarily a physical response, a rehearsal of sorts. With the acquisition of language, children come to have a more complex understanding of the erotic meaning of these activities.

At age 2, sexualized behavior increases dramatically, reaching a peak between three and five years old, then decreasing until puberty (Friedrich et al. 1991). Most children between the ages of 2 and 6 are openly curious about their bodies and their genitals. This is also a time when children typically engage in sexual exploration games, talk freely about sexual things, and are quite preoccupied with private body parts and functions. Recognizing children's openness about sexual matters at this age, parents can use this as an opportunity to normalize their two- to six-year-olds' interest in sex. What is needed is acceptance and affirmation of their bodies and bodily functions. At this developmental stage, parents can easily communicate that every body part and function is a miracle of God's creation. Parents can help children properly respect their own bodies and those of others by indicating appropriate behaviors in public and private, like bathroom etiquette practices, touching genitals in private rather than in public, and so forth.

This is an ideal time for parents to build on the natural curiosity about sex to answer questions in a calm and direct way. Children quickly pick up on parental attitudes that reflect discomfort with the topic. They can easily get the message that sex is bad or dirty instead of a good part of being human created by God. Young children do not want elaborate explanations on sex, but they do need parents who are affirming of their bodies and comfortable answering questions. Failing to communicate positive attitudes about their bodies and sex at this point in life will inhibit their questions when they reach latency. So, do not let this opportunity pass by. Affirming acceptance will set the stage for further questions that come at later stages of life. The best predictor of a child emerging into adulthood with a healthy psychosexual self is an emotionally and sexually secure environment that embraces the sacredness of sex as a part of God's good creation.

Unfortunately, there are a variety of ways in which even young children can be harmed by a sexually polluted social environment that portrays sex in a variety of exploitive and dehumanizing ways. The greatest danger for young children, however, is a sexually polluted home environment. Sexual abuse is the topic of chapter thirteen, so at this point we simply acknowledge the devastating impact this has on children. Sexual, verbal and physical abuse of young children can create an emotional wound that lasts a lifetime, interfering with the development of a healthy psychosexual self. Exposing children to a sexualized environment where pornography is readily available, boundaries are disrespected, and children are undermined warps the child's sexual development. Some parents sexualize their children by imputing adult symbols of sexuality onto them, such as beauty contests where children are taught to compete with their looks and bodies in a sexually provocative way.

Children need positive messages about sex as something good and natural. When parents show affection for each other, children learn that love is a wonderful aspect of marriage. It helps them feel secure about their parents' relationship. Yet the erotic dimension of the parents' relationship is appropriately kept private. The special relationship behind the bedroom door is a spousal boundary that is exclusive to the marital relationship.

We can derive some wisdom about healthy childhood sexual development from developmental theorist Erik Erikson. According to Erikson (1968), children begin life in the *trust versus mistrust* stage (age 0-1). Children begin life with a need for trust (unconditional love), and when deprived of a secure and loving environment, they will have difficulty trusting others. Such an early deficiency could constrict one's ability to integrate sex and love in adult relationships. During the next developmental stage of *autonomy versus shame* (ages 1-3), a child needs to achieve a balance between connection and separateness in relationship with others. The amount of tolerance shown regarding sexual topics and behavior during this stage can contribute to the child's capacity to develop a separate psychosexual self.

During the *initiative versus guilt* stage (ages 4-6), children take on responsibility for specific tasks that are commonly gender-stereotyped activity. Parents tend to encourage physically oriented tasks for boys and a tough-natured mindset, while girls are given nurturing tasks and less likely to be affirmed for physical activities. In a like manner, during the *industry versus inferiority* stage (ages 6-11), boys develop greater mastery in the external world of objects and things, while girls pay more attention to interpersonal relationships. Perhaps these differences account for later difficulties in boys knowing how to engage emotionally and in girls for lack of assertiveness.

Parents who create expectations of exaggerated masculinity for their boys or exaggerated femininity for their girls are dampening the God-intended wholeness of being human. Along with being aggressive and tough, boys need to be taught that gentleness, sensitivity and emotional expressiveness are also important male traits corresponding to what the Bible refers to as the fruit of the Spirit (Gal 5:22-23). Male inability to establish a deep emotional connection is identified by many wives as a barrier to a more fulfilling sexual relationship. Correspondingly, girls need to value being active, strong and self-assertive, along with other traits that culture identifies as masculine, so that they emerge with a differentiated self. Thus Lisa McMinn (2000) writes of *Growing Strong Daughters*.

In a summary of current research, Firestone, Firestone and Catlett (2006) note several parent/child intereactions that had a negative effect on the child's sexual development. Harsh attitudes toward a child's body and developing sexuality lead to distorted views of about sexuality and the human body (pp. 49-50). Especially distructive to children's sexual development is the opposite-sex parent's setting up competition between the child and the child's same-sex parent. Parents' exploitive use of the child to fulfill their emotional and/or sexual needs has the damaging effect of "emotional incest." Parents who sexualize the relationship with their child, even when there is no sexual activity involved, causes a distortion in the child's mind (p. 59-62).

LATENCY

Among most children, excessive sexual preoccupation and sexual self-stimulation will subside when the child reaches latency. Freud assigned the term "latency" to children between the ages of 7 and 12, connoting the lack of sexual interest at this age. Recent evidence shows, however, that "children's interest in and expression of sexuality remains lively throughout this period, even though it may not be overt" (Hyde 1994:314). Latency is a stage when children show less overt interest in the opposite sex and are more disposed to bond with members of their own sex. This same-sex bonding period may be instrumental for each sex internalizing gender-appropriate stereotypes. During latency, boys begin to internalize an image of masculine behavior such as boisterous humor, athletic enthusiasm, physical and verbal aggression. Boys are also socialized to be tough, competitive, self-reliant and emotionally stoic. In the same-gendered world of latency, boys learn to reject and avoid "feminine" traits like tenderness, compassion, sentimentality, gentleness, verbal affection, softheartedness and the like. Correspondingly, the world of girls during latency affirms the very characteristics that boys are taught to reject: tenderness, gentleness, verbal affection and connection with peers. They do not want to be labeled "tomboys" and therefore may decline competitive activities like sports. These gender traits acquired in latency will be perpetuated as masculine and feminine sexual behavior in later development. Expectations soon become self-fulfilling prophecy. Children who emerge from latency with rigid sex-role stereotypes are the ones who are most likely to exhibit problematic sexual interactions.

By the time most children begin school, they have developed a sense of appropriateness about the body, touching and sex, even exhibiting modesty about undressing in front of others (Sandnabba et al. 2003). After the uninhibited four-year-old freely ran around the house naked after taking a shower, the parents may be surprised that the same child when seven has become modest and discreet. Though sexual play may decline during latency, children during this age have simply learned to keep sexual interests more hidden from their parents and others. Parents are wise to view sexuality as an integral part of their children at all periods of their development.

PREADOLESCENT

With the emergence of modern culture, preadolescence, the later part of latency (ages 10-12), has come to be identified as a separate developmental stage in between latency and adolescence. The sexual awakening is occurring during this stage as preadolescents are now consuming the sexually charged material in the mass media, originally directed toward adolescent viewing. In her provocatively titled article "Mommy's Little Angel, Daddy's Little Girl: Do You Know What Your Pre-Teens Are Doing?" Joan Atwood (2006) gives evidence that preadolescence may be a time of lost innocence. Based on reports from over 1,300 preteen girls, Atwood concludes that these girls are "well versed in sexual terms and behavior," and "girls overwhelmingly report that their parents are unaware of their sexual chatting on the Internet, even though it occurred regularly throughout the day." Atwood concludes that because girls this age do not think about the consequences of their sexual behavior, they are "at risk for pregnancy and sexual transmitted diseases, including HIV, not to mention the concomitant psychological effects" (p. 447).

Since most mothers are the primary caregivers, girls have the advantage of learning an appropriate gender and sexual role from their same-sex parent. Thus a warm, affectionate, caring mother can go a long way toward securing a healthy sexual identity for a girl. Mothering behavior that interferes with a daughter's developing needs for independence, autonomy and differentiation limits a daughter's healthy sexual development. This might take the form of overprotectiveness, intrusiveness that violates the daughter's emotional and physical boundaries, or overinvolvement in the daughter's relationship with others. As the daughter moves toward sexual maturity, some mothers may exhibit feelings of jealousy, envy or even hostility. This is exacerbated when a mother has a less-than-satisfactory relationship with her husband or other men. In some cases, mothers become overinvolved in their daughter's dating relationships, perhaps in an effort to fulfill unmet emotional and sexual needs by vicariously identifying with a daughter's blossoming romance.

Fathers play a positive role in their daughter's sexual development when they cultivate a warm relationship that affirms their femininity. Being physically and emotionally present and supportive is indeed important. One study reported that a daughter is at special risk for early sexual activity and teenage pregnancy when a father is absent (Ellis et al. 2003).

In their quest to achieve a masculine identity, preadolescent boys are equally vulnerable to some of the worst popular culture portrayals of what it means to be a real man: sexually aggressive, emotional inexpressive, and all that goes into being a *real stud*.

Firestone, Firestone and Catlett (2006) observe that although both fathers and mothers have a major influence on their adolescent's developing sexuality, the role of same-sex parenting is especially important. Healthy sexual development among boys is facilitated by a tender, loving and affectionate relationship with their father. In their behavior toward their wife and other women, fathers serve as a powerful role model for how a man is to treat and relate to women (pp. 89-102).

On the other hand, adolescent male sexuality is adversely influenced by a cold and distant relationship with the father. When these fathers interact, they tend to be controlling, competitive, possessive, harsh and punitive. According to Firestone, Firestone and Catlett (2006:92), "The anxiety and insecurity from these early childhood experiences with their fathers are perpetuated in men's adult relationships." Defenses formed to cope with their pain and hurt interferes with a son's capacity to achieve real intimacy in adult sexual relating.

Mothers are also important to a son's developing sexuality. An emotionally warm, attuned mother provides a safe and protective environment for her son's healthy sexual development. Mothering can fall short of this ideal if she is overprotective, controlling and sexually seductive and nurtures emotional closeness with her son at the expense of her marital relationship. On the other hand, it is also damaging when the mother is rejecting, unavailiable or emotionally withholding.

ADOLESCENCE: WHEN HORMONES ARE RAGING

The most dramatic change in sexual development comes during puberty (ages 11-15), a concept that comes from the Latin *puber,* meaning "of ripe age." One might rightly say that the hormones are raging at this stage, with a surge in the body's production of testosterone in boys and estrogen in girls. Sexual changes include the maturation of the testicles in boys and ovaries in girls. Growth spurts at the physical level are most notable in secondary sex characteristics: pubic and facial hair, deepening of voice and testicular enlargement for boys; breast development, widening of hips and pubic hair for girls. Internal organs of both sexes undergo further development, and sexual maturation culminates in girls when menstruation begins around age 12 or 13.

Puberty, which typically begins about two years earlier in girls than in boys, is the beginning of adolescence, a developmental stage that is as much socially constructed as it is a separate physiological developmental stage. In the past, adulthood was defined as beginning immediately after puberty; in modern times the teenage years have been relegated to an extended time of dependence. It is a time of life characterized by *stress and strain* and confusions. It is hard to grow up in a society that sometimes treats them like children (not driving and voting) and other times like adults (paying for events). Much of the struggle has to do with their developing sexuality. The sexually charged popular culture's messages about sex are portrayed in thousands of commercials for jeans, bras, deodorant, hair care, cologne, perfume, telling adolescents how to be sexy by what they wear, spray on, or do. The commercialization of sex finds its most vulnerable target among teens.

In addition, adolescent males and females are trying to decipher societal codes of what it means to be a male or female. It is a period of high risk-taking behavior, including sexual risks. Although this can be partly understood within a sociocultural context (behavior intentionally aimed at demonstrating one's own manhood or womanhood), research suggests that the adolescent is not fully developed to the point of taking the consequences of behavior seriously (Giedd 1999; Spear 2000).

As a stage of *sexual awakening*, adolescence is accompanied by popular culture's eagerness to disseminate commercially driven messages about male and female sexuality. The explicitness of promiscuous sex in the media blurs the distinction between appearance and reality. In a policy statement, the American Academy of Pediatrics (2001) announced, "In film, television, and music, sexual messages are becoming more explicit in dialogue, lyrics and behavior. In addition, these messages contain unrealistic, inaccurate, and misleading information that young people accept as fact. . . . The average American adolescent will view nearly 14,000 sexual references per year, yet only 165 of these references deal with birth control, self-control, abstinence, or the risk of pregnancy or STDs" (Media and Sexual Learning section, p. 191). The desensitization effect upon youth results in a belief that engaging in multiple sexual relationships is expected and acceptable.

While adolescent boys are working through male identity issues, females at this age are primarily focused on relational intimacy. Boys develop a sense of identity and self-worth based on their status within an identifiable peer group. Achieving status within the peer group is a competitive process whereby males establish themselves in a pecking order. High ranking is given to hegemonic or "alpha" males, which include the

sexually desirable characteristics of physical strength, athletic capacity
and success in attracting girls. Adolescent males are so preoccupied with
finding their "male" identity through physical prowess, aggressiveness and
dominance that they have little time for developing intimacy skills.

When an adequate masculine identity fails to take root, adolescent
males primarily focus on the physical, making them more likely to coerce
girls into having sex. Girls, on the other hand, generally expect commitment and investment in the relationship to be the basis for having sex
(Eyre, Read and Millstein, 1997). The greater the identity diffusion and
relational isolation, the greater the likelihood that depersonalized sexual
exploitation and promiscuity will characterize an adolescent male's sexual
encounters. Significantly, Tubman, M. Windle and R. Windle (1996) discovered that adolescent boys were twice as likely as adolescent girls to
have sex with multiple partners. In a study of thirteen- to sixteen-year-
old boys, Udry (1988) found testosterone levels to be related to the sexual
activities of coitus, masturbation and feeling sexually "turned on." The
decision to refrain from sexual activities was determined by sociological
factors such as living in an intact home, parent's educational level and
church attendance.

Erik Erikson acknowledges that adolescence is a time when persons
work out identity and intimacy skills. Identity must be established during
adolescence so that one can successfully move into intimate connection at
the young adult stage. The high rate of failure in teenage marriage may
point to insufficient development in identity (girls) and intimacy (boys),
unfinished tasks for teens.

EMERGING ADULTHOOD

Developmental psychologists have coined the term *emerging adulthood*
to represent the stage of life characteristic of modern societies that falls
between adolescence and adulthood. The popularity of the TV program
Friends, with its themes of sex and interpersonal relationships between
single adults, typifies this stage of sexual development.

Typically, males who emerge from adolescence with a coherent, integrated sense of self may be deficient in intimacy skills. Females, on the
other hand, are more likely to have developed intimacy skills and may need
to focus more on defining a solid self. Only when these two tasks are fully
developed are persons prepared to make long-term unconditional commit-

ments in a relationship. Even in committed relationships, however, men are not immune from intimacy struggles. Young women base relational intimacy on verbal communication and emotional sharing; young men are likely to feel intimate just by engaging in activities together. The fear of commitment in relationships and/or inadequacies in emotional relating can keep men at a nonrelational level. Doubting their ability to sustain a long-term committed relationship, they may have a tendency to sexualize friendships and mistakenly equate sexual involvement with intimacy.

Characteristics of such men are a preoccupation with body sex rather than the person-centered sex. It is no accident that men's magazines such as *Playboy* are aimed at these men. *Playboy* teaches insecure males how to be resourceful and shrewd so they can interact with women with a certain detachment by "playing it cool." The playboy is taught to be a skilled manipulator of women, knowing when to turn the lights down, what CD to play, which drinks to serve, and what topics of conversation to pursue. The playboy is not supposed to lose his heart to the woman, but to remain above it all by not relating to her as a person. In his view, she is a nonrelational sex object, with whom he never shares his emotions or heart. The playboy treats women as a commodity to be consumed. The playboy's relationship with women represents the culmination of the marketing-oriented personality, in which a person learns to exploit. Sexuality is reduced to a packageable item that can be handled, with no demands placed on the man. The woman is reduced to a playmate, a playboy accessory. A successful conquest is one in which the bed is shared, but the man emerges free of any personal involvement or investment. When playtime is over, the playmate can be easily discarded.

While young women may be less vulnerable to nonrelational sexuality, they may be more vulnerable to becoming caught up in unhealthy relationships with men who cause them much pain. Books such as *Women Who Love Too Much* (Norwood 1985) and *Men Who Hate Women and the Women Who Love Them* (Forward and Torres 1986) began to appear in the 1980s, exemplifying this theme. Such books help women develop a stronger sense of self so they will not fall for men who exploit them.

Levinson (1978) suggests that a low level of identity integration and a low level of intimacy skills can result in young adults becoming "stuck" in adolescent-type sexual encounters. The tragedy is that some people never do develop relational skills. Emerging adulthood is a time when males and females need to develop the twin tasks of intimacy skills and a strong sense of self.

MIDDLE ADULTHOOD

Hopefully, a strongly defined self and well-developed relational skills are in place by the time one enters middle adulthood. Most have established deeply satisfying relationships with both same-sex and opposite-sex friends and become part of a vital support community. Single and married adults embrace their sexuality and find meaningful ways to express themselves as sexual beings. This is also a time of settling into work or career, establishing a home, developing significant relationships, marriage and/or having children. Among single adults, while some are content with their single status, others are still hoping for future marriage. Meaning comes from their relationships with God, family, friends and faith community. Besides meaningful work/career, many find ways of serving others through community and ministry opportunities.

Erik Erikson (1982) has described the developmental challenge of middle adulthood (ages 30-45) as the conflict of *generativity versus stagnation*. Generativity develops out of a concern for the future of humankind, in which persons invest themselves in other people. A truly generative individual (differentiated) looks beyond personal ambition and gratification, seeking the well-being of others. Persons who fail to resolve generativity become stagnated, lacking any deep connection or relatedness with others.

Erikson also considered ego integration to be the primary development task of the latter stage of middle adulthood (age 45+). This involves bringing the various parts of one's life structure into a consistent and integrated whole. Persons with high ego integration live with a confidence that their life has significance. Sexuality is well integrated into their total being, and their life has meaning. Those who lack the needed inner resources, perhaps because of a series of failures, experience "ego despair." Being lonely and lacking the capacity to establish a meaningful relationship is often part of that despair.

A false cure for the despair can be the distraction of "sexual excitement" that is sought through a variety of nonrelational means, such promiscuous sex, consumption of pornography, or extramarital affairs. The desire for sexual expression is not wrong, but the means of finding it is. The danger in ego despair is to "externalize" problems, to see the despair as emanating from outside rather than from within. A single woman may be in despair about not having found a marital partner and resort to Internet sex or chat rooms to alleviate her loneliness. The false cure does not satisfy her longing for a real life relationship. Personal inadequacy may be projected upon others. For example, a husband may blame his lack of sexual enthusiasm on his wife, not realizing that he gives little in the way of emotional expressiveness that would encourage an intimate sexual connection.

Marital midlife issues. Married persons and single parents in middle adulthood are often highly involved with family life as well as work or career. In terms of their sexuality, the frequency of sexual activity usually declines at this stage (Deveny 2003). In a crosscultural study utilizing data from over 91,000 subjects, Brewis and Myer (2005:499) conclude that "declining coital frequency over time seems [to be] a shared demographic feature of human populations." On the other hand, this research also reports that in many countries coital frequency actually increases with women's age into the thirties. Jacoby (1999) found that differences in generational attitudes toward sexuality might account for much of what was previously assumed to be decline in sexual activity by age. Thus, as the baby boomer generation has aged into their 50s and 60s, their frequency of sexual intercourse tends to decline, but at a more gradual rate than for previous generations.

Since marital sexuality is the topic of chapter nine, here we merely highlight some of the sexual issues that may be encountered during middle adulthood. Although many are secure in long-term commitments of faithfulness in marriage, the high extramarital affairs and divorce rate in modern societies suggest that this is not always the case.

Childbirth is an event that affects the sexual relationship. One study found evidence that pregnancy and giving birth physically alters a woman's body and reduces her level of sexual desire. While giving birth increases some hormones, reduced testosterone also occurs for the mother. In addition to these physical changes, there is the day in and day out demands that a child places on the primary caregiver (usually the mother), which also reduces her interest in sex. The birth of additional children only adds to the problem, since several young children in the home leaves the caregiver too exhausted to respond sexually to her husband. Husbands who lack generative meaning beyond their family life may respond to their wives' lack of enthusiasm for sex by seeking extramarital flirtations or affairs (see chapter ten for a fuller discussion of this).

Typically, husbands and wives in middle adulthood are living busy lives. The dual demands emanating from work and earning a living along with the responsibilities of family life may drain energy away from the marital relationship. Research indicates that a major sexual issue during the settling-down period centers on keeping sexual intimacy alive. Silny (1993:142) reports that most middle-aged men are still highly responsive to sexual stimuli, but less preoccupied with sexual thoughts and fantasies.

Men's midlife issues. Much has been made of especially men transitioning through the midlife crisis period (usually identified as the early 40s). For some men this can be the big shakeup, strongly impacting confidence in his manhood and sexuality. A number of work-related factors have been identified as affecting a man's self-confidence: fear of being overtaken in one's work by a younger person, not being "on time" in the scheme of life, realizing that one will not reach occupation goals, workaholic tendencies and career burnout.

Male menopause is a term coined to refer to a broader period of change in the male life cycle. Male andropause involves hormonal, physiological and chemical changes that occur in men, generally between the ages of 40 and 55. This is a time when men also deal with psychological, interpersonal, social and spiritual dimensions (Carruthers 1997). Hormone replacement is a practice advocated by some to lessen ongoing loss of testosterone, which amounts to 1 percent a year for men past age 21. Besides hormonal changes, a variety of reasons lead to decline: surgeries, medications, health issues, sexual concerns, and financial, work and home-related stressors.

Levinson (1978:209-44) points out four polarities that men may feel about their masculinity and sexuality during this midlife period. First, men in midlife can feel disturbed because of the *young/old* polarity. Men at midlife begin to question if they are still as sexually potent or sexually attractive as when they were young. In an attempt to appear younger or attractive, they dye their gray hair, dress in a sporty style, go on a rigorous weight-lifting routine, buy a flashy car, and so forth. The second polarity is *destruction/creation*. Aware of prostate surgery, impotence and even heart attacks of friends their age, they fear how physical problems may affect their sex lives. Although illness can and does adversely affect an older male's sexual performance, according to Levy (1994:301), "sexual problems, including male impotency . . . usually stem from psychosocial anxiety and apprehension rather than organic causes." It is important that men discover creative ways to express their sexuality and prove that they are not beyond their passionate years.

The *masculinity/femininity* polarity points to middle-aged men who try to sustain a manly appearance of strength and toughness, but at the same time are more open to the sensitive, nurturing and emotional expression. While their masculine side pushes them toward achievement and ambition, their feminine side calls them to be more relational and responsive to the needs of others. Men who are insecure about their masculinity will have difficulty allowing their feminine side to emerge and may resort to a hypermasculinity. Those who are able to get in touch with and embrace their sensitive side can develop a richer, deeper capacity for a more fulfilling sexual and emotional intimacy.

Finally, the *attachment/separateness* polarity points to the need for balance between connection and self-sufficiency. Men who find this balance are capable of deeper emotional attachments because they are not afraid of bonding with their significant other. Men who fail to work through attachment and separation issues (differentiation process) tend to get themselves into sexually enmeshed relationships at one extreme or defensively detached relationships at the other. A differentiated man has a balance of connection and separateness that leads to a healthy interdependency.

Women's midlife issues. In *The Seasons of a Woman's Life* (1996) Levinson identifies four types of *gender splitting* that can affect a woman's sexuality. The *domestic/public* split, pulling a woman in opposite directions, reaches its peak during midlife. Related to this is the *homemaker/provider* split: women are torn between the societal ideal of being a superwife and superhomemaker without compromising advancement in her job or career. In the *women's work/men's work* split, women may desire to do typically defined men's work but feel trapped in doing only women's work. Finally, midlife is a time when women also experience a *femininity/masculinity* split in their individual psyche. Women desire the feminine characteristics of emotional expressiveness, sensitivity and nurturing, but they also desire the stereotypically masculine characteristics of having an adventuresome spirit and achievement orientation. The opposing tugs in each of these polarities places midlife women between two ideals: the *internal tradition* figure and the *antifeminist* figure. The sexuality of women is clearly influenced by these conflict areas.

A primary event in middle age for women is *menopause*, the cessation of menstruation that generally takes place within five or six years of a woman's fiftieth birthday. Following menopause, the loss of progesterone, estrogen and testosterone results in a gradual lowering of sexual desire. Loss of estrogen causes the vagina to become less elastic, and with loss of lubrication intercourse can be painful. After the medical community promoted hormone replacement therapy (HRT) as a way to deal with menopause symptoms, over 50 million American women chose hormone replacement therapy by 2001. However, in 2002 a large-scale study found significant medical repercussions (heart attacks, strokes, blood clots, cancers) for women on HRT, changing the general attitude (National Women's Health Network 2002) about the wisdom of taking hormones. The current medical practice is to be cautious and practice HRT in moderation, avoiding long-term use.

Besides coping with various physiological changes, the best predictor of sexual activity for middle-aged women is a positive attitude and enjoyment of sexual experiences throughout life. Many women are interested in keeping the quality of their sex life intact and keeping it as a vital part of their relationships.

LATE ADULTHOOD

The *transition* into late adulthood for most begins at around age 60 and continues on to retirement, usually around age 65 to 70. Laumann and others (1994) found that no other factor affects frequency of total sexual outlet as much as age. While the downward curve toward decreased sexual activity is a physical reality, it does not mean that sexuality is no longer a vital aspect of later life. Metz and Miner (1998) believe that most sexual difficulties experienced by couples in their sixties stem from cultural and lifestyle changes rather than hormonal change.

In later life stages, a positive self-concept is important for maintaining a satisfying sexual life. Levy (1994:293) writes, "Women . . . are more likely to construct their self-images primarily based on judgments about their appearance; men also consider appearance but give greater weight to sexual performance." Fear of performance adequacy may be the greatest barrier to sexual performance among older men. In their extensive research, Masters and Johnson (1966) reported that older men require more direct stimulation to achieve an erection, ejaculation becomes less forceful, and the penis becomes flaccid more quickly following ejaculation.

A significant number of men experience psychological and social difficulties during their later stages of life. Some of this, such as having a less-potent erection or ejaculation, may be related to hormonal decline, disease, prostate surgery and other health problems. Decline in testosterone due to aging means that a man requires firm, more direct and longer stimulation to produce and sustain an erection. Testosterone replacement as well as Viagra and other medications dealing with potency issues can be helpful. Although testosterone decline can be especially pronounced toward the end of mature adulthood, it is not necessarily associated with decreased desire or sexual satisfaction (Masters, Johnson and Kolodny 1994). A couple knowing how to adjust their sexual involvement as they grow older goes a long way in ensuring continued sexual satisfaction for both spouses.

The decline in sexual activity that begins among persons in their sixties accelerates for those in their seventies. No longer having a sexual partner accounts for much of the decline in activity. In her summary of relevant literature, Levy (1994:302) writes, "Evidence suggests that most older people find sex equally as satisfying or more so than when they were younger, particularly when the social rewards of sex are considered." Increased androgyny among older men may mean that their greater sensitivity and capacity for intimacy yields greater enjoyment for all aspects of sexual lovemaking: kissing, cuddling, hugging, holding, stroking, and so forth. Though the frequency of organism among the elderly declines, lovemaking can extend long into the elderly years.

SUMMARY ON SEXUAL DEVELOPMENTAL STAGES

In this summary, generalizations about sexual stages of life need to be given with several precautions in mind. *First,* the research showing differences in sexual activity by age is cross-sectional rather than cohort (group) data. Ideally, the sexual behavior would be followed throughout a person's life cycle, thus assuring that the changes reported are the result of aging, rather than explainable by differences between cohorts of men exposed to different historical periods. People who are elderly today, for instance, were socialized into adulthood when sexual norms were more conservative than for persons entering young adulthood today. In the Chicago research (Laumann et al. 1994), younger cohorts indicate that they are sexually active earlier, have more partners, and have their first sexual experience outside of marriage earlier than adults who were in their fifties at the time of the research.

Second, although it is easier to demonstrate quantitative age differences about sexual behavior, qualitative rather than quantitative differences may be more meaningful. The norms for frequency of sexual intercourse are set for young persons: when older persons participate less frequently in sex, they are seen as "diminishing" sexually. Research consistently shows that desire for and frequency of coitus declines with aging. However, such evidence focuses only on the quantity and not on the quality of sexual engagement.

Third, individual change in sexuality over the life span is best understood as an interaction between physiological and psychosociocultural factors. Physiological changes do affect an individual's sexuality directly and indirectly, but psychosociocultural attitudes have a powerful impact on physiological factors as well.

Fourth, while it is possible to point to normative differences between people at different stages of life, there is great individual variation between persons within each stage, as well as differences in the timing for entering and exiting stages.

Fifth, the degree of sexual adequacy and health exhibited at an early developmental stage has an influence on the degree of sexual adequacy and health at the following stages. The formation of sexuality is best understood as cumulative, so that healthy and adequate sexual formation at one stage is accumulative over the life span; inversely, sexual inadequacy at one stage, if not corrected, has a cumulative negative impact in later stages.

Sixth, in dealing with persons throughout the life cycle, the major task for Christians in ministry and counseling is to assist them in developing a greater capacity for relational and emotional skills. Although nonrelational sex may be a greater issue for men, it needs to be understood as a potential issue for both men and women within a life-cycle context. The redemption of human sexuality centers on empowering men and women to express their sexuality in the context of an emotionally involved, person-centered, committed relationship.

DEVELOPING MEANING OF SEXUALITY

Of all living creatures, the human infant is dependent upon adult care for the longest period of time. There is an inverse relationship between the young's dependence upon adults within a species and the importance of biological (instinctive) factors in shaping sexual behavior. In other words, there is a positive relationship between the young being dependent upon adults in a species and how socioenvironmental factors shape sexual behavior. Thus we understand human sexual behavior as less directly "determined" by biological factors and more susceptible to influence and modification by social factors. Under control of the human brain, the biological base shares with social factors and the cultural matrix as they blend together to form sexuality. All five senses—touch, sight, smell, taste, sound—are encoded on the cerebral cortex with corresponding cultural meanings.

In various societies, the sight of an exposed ankle is defined as sexually stimulating or not, depending on the learned cultural message. Touch in the form of a caress, a kiss or hug is likewise judged sexually stimulating or not, depending on the culturally assigned meaning. Even human sound, like a deep moan or extended groan, is embedded in a social context that determines if one is experiencing pain or sexual pleasure. In a thousand and one ways, the sexual makeup of any individual is formed in the context of this interaction between the biological factors, the social environment and the cultural context that give meaning to our sexuality. As children develop their sexual maps, they become increasingly complex and sophisticated in the manner in which their senses are categorized in the brain. But also with increased sophistication comes an increased ability to control what senses affect the brain. Moral development determines one's ability to make choices about sexual stimuli and behavior for which negative meaning has been assigned. This realization leads us to be responsible for our actions.

Human agency. Human beings are not merely reactive to biological and sociocultural imprints but are active participants in their own sexual development. Human beings are free to make choices. Freedom and human choice are even championed in one of the strongest empirically based models of personality, *social learning theory*. In his reciprocal determinism model, Albert Bandura (1974) asserts, "Within the social learning framework, freedom is defined in terms of the number of options available to people and the right to exercise them. The more behavioral alternatives and social prerogatives people have, the greater is their freedom of action" (p. 865). This view is consistent with the conclusions we offered in our discussion of figure 2.3, that biological and sociocultural factors can either limit or expand the range of choices for any given individual. The greater the number of choices, the greater the range of freedom within which choices can be made.

From a biblical perspective, human choice is not defined solely by biology, psychology and sociocultural factors but also includes spiritual meaning and implication. Since we, as God's creation, are given free choice, we propose a biblical perspective that embraces but is not solely determined by biological, psychological and psychocultural factors. We recommend the book *Whatever Happened to the Soul? Scientific and Theological Portraits of Human Nature* (Brown, Murphy and Maloney 1998) for an in-depth consideration of these ideas. In the chapter "Brain, Mind, and Behavior," Malcolm Jeeves asserts, "It is at the level of our conscious experience that there is indeterminacy, irrespective of any indeterminacy at the level of the brain" (p. 97). In other words, the essence of human freedom is that it is the person and not the brain that chooses and decides. Though we can explain sexual behavior in terms of brain activity, in doing so we must not explain away the conscious human beings who make and are responsible for the sexual choices they make.

From a Christian perspective, one can best understand sexual choice as a reflection of the meaning of sexuality that one holds as residing in familial and community contexts. Authentic human sexuality ultimately needs to be defined by a biblical understanding. In the following two chapters we develop a biblical approach to the deeper meaning of sexuality and sexual relationships.

AUTHENTIC SEXUAL DEVELOPMENT: A SUMMARY

In providing an overview of the many factors contributing to sexual development, this chapter seeks to provide a foundational understanding upon which to define authentic sexuality within a biblical perspective. As a basis for this task, we offer seven summary principles. These principles can serve as a guide in considering the interplay between biological, sociocultural and biblical contributions to the formation of authentic sexuality in the following chapters.

The evidence is insufficient to make causal statements in explaining the development of authentic and inauthentic sexuality. Both biological and sociocultural factors contribute to rather than *cause* human sexuality. The wisdom within the philosophy of science dictates that to be considered a cause, it must be demonstrated that a factor is both necessary and sufficient for an ultimate explanation.

Biological factors serve as necessary, but not sufficient, contributors to the formation of authentic human sexuality. An adequate male or female biological package is needed in order for an individual to develop an authentic male or female sexuality. However, what is biologically given is not sufficient to ensure or hinder authentic sexual development.

Sociocultural factors serve as the sufficient, but not necessary, contributors to the formation of authentic human sexuality. An adequate biological package and adequate sociocultural factors are necessary to develop authentic sexuality. Defining what is "good enough" is the subject of future chapters.

Authentic or inauthentic sexuality emerges as part of a developmental process. Sexuality emerges from physiological, psychological, sociocultural and spiritual factors that make a unique contribution at strategic points in a person's life.

While biological factors are most crucial in establishing sexuality early in life, sociocultural factors become increasingly significant as the child matures. As children develop the capacity to use language, they correspondingly learn the meaning of sexual attitudes and behavior. An understanding or lack of understanding of spiritual meaning for human sexuality becomes increasingly important as the individual constructs a purposeful life. The meaning of sexuality is gained within a social context; thus it is important for family and community members to live out and communicate God's designed meaning for sexuality and sexual expression.

Social units, such as families, churches, communities and societies, will vary greatly in the degree to which they reflect God's design and meaning for human sexuality. Since all individuals are members of various groups, many of which offer competing definitions and meanings of human sexuality, individuals can internalize contradictory meanings of sexuality. The more these significant membership groups consistently reflect God's ideal for sexuality, the more internally consistent will the development of authentic sexuality be in any one individual member. However, since each individual is a choice-making creature with emotive, volitional and moral values, authentic sexuality emerges from the interplay between the individual and the social environment.

Authentic sexuality and inauthentic sexuality are dichotomous only in a moral sense and should never be used to describe given individuals. Authentic sexuality is not totally represented in any one person. Being part of a fallen creation, all human beings are sexually broken and lack perfect wholeness in some way. In the following chapters we hope to identify authentic sexuality within a Christian theological context and thereby provide a model for moving toward authentic sexuality as it is found and represented in the many arenas of daily life.

FUTHER READING

Balswick, J. O., P. E. King and K. S. Reimer. 2005. *The reciprocating self: Human development in theological pespective.* Downers Grove, Ill.: Inter-Varsity Press.

Brown, W. S., N. Murphy and H. N. Maloney, eds. 1998. *Whatever happened to the soul? Scientific and theological portraits of human nature.* Minneapolis: Fortress.

McMinn, L. 2002. *Growing strong daughters: Encouraging girls to become all they're meant to be.* Grand Rapids: Baker Books. Rev. ed., 2007.

Jones, S., and B. Jones. 1993. *How and when to tell your kids about sex.* Colorado Springs: NavPress. 2nd ed., 2007.

3

Principles of
Authentic Sexuality

The first two chapters dealt with the complexity of factors that contribute to the development of human sexuality. Even more challenging in this chapter is the task of defining authentic sexuality. We will begin with a simple definition of authentic as "something that is genuine or real." Authentic sexuality, then, brings authenticity to ourselves and our relationships as it reflects God's divine intention for who we are and how we are to behave as sexual relational beings.

In our society of competing worldviews, the naturalistic assumption of biological and social scientists is to define authentic sexuality in terms of what *is*. The methodology is to compare and contrast crosscultural ethnographic evidence in order to determine normal as opposed to abnormal sexual behavior. In this case sexuality is determined through crosscultural practices. In summarizing the work of sociologist Ira Reiss (1986, 2006), we see that he uses naturalistic assumptions to propose a sexual morality. Reiss believes that it is improper to label as morally abnormal (inauthentic) any sexual act that is acceptable in any culture. Therefore he limits his definition of inauthentic sexual behavior to only that which is unacceptable in *all* cultures. This naturalistic worldview leads to a morality of sexuality that accepts everything as normal, until a behavior is clearly established by scientific evidence and reasoning as being "abnormal" (Reiss 1986:239).

As you can see, making judgments about what is sexually normal and abnormal becomes tricky since naturalists are only comfortable with a construct that "points" to the normative. In our minds, this takes quite a leap of faith. It seems more accurate to look at social, cultural and biological evidence as well as taking into account attitudes and behaviors as more or less consistent with what *most* people report and experience. As with a bell-shaped curve, some individuals will be closer to the center of the curve, while others are more toward the extremes on any given sexual dimension. Though we should not ignore the reality of cultural norms, neither can we ignore the values inherent in the interpretation of the biological and cultural analysis. However, if restricted to a sexual normality defined only in terms of what is culturally normative, the divine purpose that provides intrinsic meaning to a definition of authentic sexuality is obviously missing.

Without question, we gain an enormous understanding of what is "normative" sexual behavior by studying cultures throughout the world. But we cannot stop here. We must faithfully seek out the biblical meaning and purpose of being created as sexual beings. So at this point we propose six basic biblical principles that we believe lead to authentic sexuality. Principles 1 through 4 deal with creation, principle 5 with the Fall, and principle 6 with redemption and restoration:

1. Human sexuality is established in the differentiation between male and female and in the unity established between them.

2. Sexuality is a good gift, meant to draw persons to deeper levels of knowing self, others and God.

3. Humans are born with an innate capacity for sexual pleasure, and human sexuality can best develop within an emotionally caring, trustworthy family environment.

4. Sexuality and spirituality are intricately connected.

5. After the Fall, sexuality became distorted and in need of redemption.

6. Christ offers restoration and renews our potential for authentic sexuality.

DIFFERENTIATION AND UNITY

The starting point for principle 1 is found in the creative act of God noted in Genesis 1:26-28, 31: "Then God said, 'Let us make humankind in our image, according to our likeness, and let them have dominion.' . . . God created humankind in his image, in the image of God he created them;

male and female he created them. God blessed them, and . . . God saw everything that he had made, and indeed, it was very good" (NRSV). First, we observe the importance of the relational nature of the Godhead in the phrase "Let *us* make humankind in *our* image." In these verses we recognize God's holy work in not only creating humankind but also in creating two distinct human beings, male and female. This places authentic being and sexuality in the context of male and female distinctiveness as well as in their unity and harmony.

Karl Barth (1961) expands this discussion: "Man never exists as such, but always as the human male or the human female. . . . Nor can he wish to liberate himself from the relationship and be man without woman or woman apart from man; for in all that characterizes him as a man he will be thrown back upon woman, or as woman upon man. The female is to the male, and the male to the female, the other man and as such the fellow-man." Paul Jewett (1976) takes a similar position: "Man, as created in the divine image, is Man-in-fellowship. . . . The primary form of this fellowship is that of male and female" (pp. 45-46). Jewett views differentiation as complementarity, correspondence and encounter.

Building on these ideas, Ray Anderson (1982) argues that the created differentiation between male and female reflects a differentiation within the Godhead. He writes, "Human sexuality thus has a correspondence to the Godhead in that it is an encounter with a corresponding but different being. Not the 'mating' but the *meeting* is the essence, but one can't be separated from the other on the creaturely level. Human sexuality is the image of God" (p. 106). Differentiation makes unity a profound possibility.

Phyllis Trible (1987) makes a point that in Hebrew *humankind (hā-'ādām)* in the first line of Genesis 1:27 changes to the singular pronoun *him* and finally to the plural form *them*, reinforcing "sexual differentiation within the unity of humanity" (p. 17; NRSV notes). In noting this shift from singular to plural pronouns, she draws several important conclusions in regard to sexual differentiation: first, *hā-'ādām* (humankind) refers to two creatures, thus disallowing an androgynous interpretation of the term; second, the "singular word *hā-'ādām* with its singular pronoun *'ōtô* shows that male and female are not opposite but rather harmonious sexes"; and third, "the parallelism between *hā-'ādām* and 'male and female' shows . . . that sexual differentiation does not mean hierarchy but rather equality" (pp. 18-19).

The question about whether the man was created first and therefore is in a special position of authority over the woman is still debated in Christian circles today. Genesis 2:18 proclaims that it was not good for man to be alone, so a helper was made for him. This particular verse needs to be interpreted with care and clarity. According to biblical scholars, *helper* in the original language *('ēzer)* refers to God as the helper of humankind fifteen of the sixteen times it is used in the Bible. This verse is the one exception; here it is used to describe the relationship between human beings, Eve and Adam. Trible (1987) asserts that even the most inventive exegete would have to make a huge stretch to conclude that God, as our *'ēzer,* is subordinate to humankind. Therefore, it makes no sense to conclude that subordination of the woman to the man is implied in Genesis 2:18.

Rather, God gives Adam a helper who complements him and corresponds to him in mutuality and equality. Referring to Adam's first words upon seeing Eve, "This is now bone of my bones and flesh of my flesh" (Gen 2:23), Trible comments, "These words speak unity, solidarity, mutuality, and equality. Accordingly, in this poem the man does not depict himself as either prior to or superior to the woman. His sexual identity depends upon her even as hers depends upon him. For both of them sexuality originates in the one flesh of humanity" (1987:99).

In other words, a man finds his identity and meaning in being male, just as a woman finds identity and meaning in being female through their differentiation. Differentiation connotes "unique quality" rather than inequality! What is uniquely different enhances and expands the other. Based upon the Genesis account, and continuing throughout the Old and New Testaments, sex is simply taken for granted, and authentic sexuality is founded on two differentiated persons joining together in a sacred union.

As difficult as it is to develop an explicit theology of sexuality, the scriptural view certainly presents sexuality as basic to our human existence and the very thing that informs our way of being in the world as embodied persons. Sexuality involves a whole array of feelings, thoughts, memories, self-understanding, attitudes and behaviors through which we express ourselves in relationship. As we will see in the next principle, our God-designed sexuality is meant to draw us into authentic relationship through connection, communication and communion.

DEEPER LEVELS OF KNOWING

C. S. Lewis (1963) reminds us that physical pleasure is God's idea, not the devil's. We are created as sexual beings with sexual desire. As observed in chapter one, God not only made our bodies but also equipped them with hormones, a nervous system, physical sensations, thought patterns and a psychological capacity to make connection. We were made for each other! God did not mean for man and woman to be alone; instead, God created them in similar but uniquely different ways so they could engage soul to soul and flesh to flesh! It is exhilarating to find that Adam receives his companion with enthusiasm as one who is mysteriously his equal. In union of body, mind and soul, a relationship is solidified as each expands the other in self-knowledge and understanding. Through the good gift of sex, each discovers more about themselves, the other and their Creator God.

We find it necessary to emphasize the good gift of sex, since sex has so often been viewed in negative ways throughout history. A "sex is bad" perspective can be traced back to Greek philosophy, and Platonic dualism made inroads into the early church. While the spirit was pronounced as good, the flesh was denounced as bad. Sex, especially sexual desire, was considered fleshly and lustful, sinful and base.

Condemnation of sexual pleasure often corresponds with a theology that insists on procreation as the sole purpose of human sexuality. Holding to this view makes it quite impossible to attach sacred meaning to sexual desire and pleasure in and of itself. Theologies that uphold the goodness of the sexual union (Gen 2) emphasize the sealing of the one-flesh relationship. Therefore, because procreation is *not* the exclusive reason for sexual expression, sexual desire and fulfillment between man and woman have divine meaning and purpose as well.

Let us imagine Adam and Eve gazing at each other in the garden, recognizing each other as "bone of my bones and flesh of my flesh" (Gen 2:23). Their sexual nature moves them toward each other for a deeper level of knowing one another in the meeting. Their distinctive differences engage them in an emotional and sexual oneness they cannot find in themselves alone. Trible (1987) explains, "The result of this convergence of opposites is a consummation of union: 'and they become one flesh.' No procreative purpose characterizes this sexual union; children are not mentioned. Hence, the man does not leave one family to start another; rather, he abandons familial identity for the one flesh of sexuality" (p. 104). Out of differentiation, two sexual beings, man and woman, find wholeness and one-flesh communion in their sexual consummation.

Deeply embedded within each one of us is a divine longing for wholeness that sends us reaching beyond ourselves to God and others. Sexual desire helps us recognize our incompleteness as human beings and causes us to seek others to find a fuller meaning in life. Our sexuality generates creative energy and capacity for relationship growth and change. How unfortunate it would be if sexual attraction were only a restless biological urge for sexual release; in that case, we would be deprived of the greater satisfaction of deeper emotional relating.

Authentic sexuality urges us toward a rich sharing of our lives. Physical, emotional and intellectual openness becomes the basis for self-understanding. A communion of trust and intimacy helps us take the necessary steps to get beyond our personal safety zone in order to risk honest expression of who we are. This intimate encounter has potential to move us toward harmony and responsiveness.

The Genesis 2:25 passage describes the man and the woman as naked and not ashamed. Authentic sexual interaction carries no shame, for it is entirely natural and good for the man and woman to respond wholeheartedly to each other. Sexual attraction, desire and engagement are part of God's sovereign plan. The Song of Songs affirms a response and celebration of being naked and not ashamed in mutual vulnerability and harmony. "This couple treat each other with tenderness and respect. Neither escaping nor exploiting sex, they embrace and enjoy it. Their love is truly bone of bone and flesh of flesh, and this image of God as male and female is indeed very good (Gen 1:27, 31). Testifying to the goodness of creation, then, eroticism becomes worship in the context of grace" (Trible 1987:161).

When we are bold enough to believe that God is at the center of our sexuality, we will discover ourselves anew and learn to be responsive and responsible in our relationships. In a similar way, our deep desire for Christ brings us to a deeper level of knowing ourselves. As we honestly examine our deepest cravings, we are forced to consider how to bring our lives into accordance with what we cherish and what God desires of us.

CAPACITY FOR SEXUAL PLEASURE AND THE FAMILY ENVIRONMENT

We have already discussed how children experience sexual feelings from the time they are born. The pleasurable feelings an infant experiences center on being held close, caressed and fondled. The parent's body gives sustenance, security and pleasure. Early on, young children also find pleasure through all their senses: smell, taste, touch, hearing and sight. God has created human beings with a tremendous capacity for taking in pleasure.

How sad it is that parents so often give children negative messages about bodily pleasure at a very early age. The genital area is either considered nonexistent (something to be ignored or avoided) or bad (something disgusting). The child begins to hear a different tone in the parent's voice, giving harsh reprimands and showing disapproval. "Bad boy! Off limits!" "Bad girl! Don't touch!" The shameful message communicated during normal curiosity and inquisitive touch leaves children feeling they have done something improper. What forms within children's minds is the sense that it is wrong to feel the slightest pleasure of a genital nature; so they begin to repress the sexual in themselves.

Larry Friesen writes,

> It is precisely during the age from birth till six that presents the greatest opportunities to acquaint young children with a biblical basis for his or her sexuality. A parent can affirm pleasurable feelings generated by genital touch and the inherent enjoyment of one's sexual response by responding to the behavior in a loving and assuring tone of voice. In this way, a child learns that the pleasurable sexual feelings that are experienced are part and parcel of being an infant and growing child. This also opens up the opportunity to impress upon the child that, because of the sacred and precious nature of the pleasurable feelings, it is of utmost importance that such a treasure should be a private matter between the child and the heavenly Father, who is the giver of the gift. Sexual instructions to a child must be specific, according to the understanding of the child, and imbedded into a deeper acceptance that, from birth, sexual pleasure generated by the genital touch is precisely what the Creator had in mind when He drew the original plan. (1989:322-24)

Receiving a positive message about the nature of pleasurable feelings, along with helpful guidance about appropriate ways and places to express such pleasure, provides security about sexuality.

Perhaps it is difficult for parents to talk to their children openly about sex because negative connotations were attached to sexuality during their own development. If parents are able to affirm sex as a good and integral part of being created in the image of God, their children will be able to do the same. Sexual feelings and desires should be considered as something to protect and embrace rather than as something to deny and reject.

Social scientists believe that human sexuality develops according to learned sexual scripts or cultural definitions of what is acceptable sexual behavior. Basically, people learn about sexuality in the same way they learn about other relationships. Sexual learning is especially potent due to the bonding power created when physical and emotional pleasure accompany the interaction. Think for a moment about the parent-child bonding and the personal pleasure expressed between them. The closeness of bodies— the touching, stroking and nurturing—that takes place in this intimate interaction speaks volumes about love. Freud (1953:182) graphically re- minds us that a baby sinking back satiated from the breast and falling asleep with flushed cheeks and a blissful smile is a prototype of sexual satisfaction in later life.

Object relations theorists look at attachment and bonding experiences as foundational for forming intimate relationships in later life. If there has been a serious disruption in this bonding experience, children often ex- hibit deficits when it comes to knowing how to make significant connec- tions with others. When these basic needs are unmet in childhood, adults are often riddled with fears and unable to trust others. On the other hand, when sufficient attachment occurs, children have confidence in relating to others. A balanced, congruent self is the outcome of being nurtured, accepted and affirmed in a loving family environment.

Sexual health in the home develops through an integration of one's physical, emotional, intellectual, social and spiritual selves. Here we find the four guidelines about personal sexual health proposed by the World Health Organization to be most helpful:

1. One's personal and social behaviors are congruent with one's gender identity and a sense of comfort with a range of sex-role behavior.

2. One has the ability to carry on effective interpersonal relationships with members of both sexes, including the potential for love and long-term commitment.

3. One has the capacity to respond to erotic stimulation in such a way as to make sexual activity a positive, pleasurable aspect of one's experience.

4. One has the maturity of judgment to make rewarding decisions about one's sexual behavior that do not conflict with one's overall value system and beliefs about life. (Maddock 1975:52-53)

These guidelines help us focus on the family as a context in which emotionally loving and supportive interactions help members develop a balanced and harmonious sexual self. A positive sexual identity and sexual value system give children an ability to embrace their sexual selves in ways that help them become congruent and authentic in their sexual attitudes and behaviors. Children certainly learn about the meaning of sexuality within the social context of the family as well as the wider community. The more these social contexts reflect God's ideal for sexuality, the greater the potential for authentic sexuality.

Parents can foster healthy sexuality by regarding sexuality as a vital, God-created good that draws their children into meaningful, caring relationships. In the best of all worlds, the family is the place where children gain a clear grasp of themselves as unique and separate sexual beings who are secure in a deep sense of family belonging. James Maddock defines healthy family sexuality as "the balanced expression of sexuality in the life of the family, in ways that enhance the personal identities and sexual health of individual family members and the organization of the family as a system, functioning effectively within its social and material environment" (1975:63). Maddock and Larson go on to describe the following characteristics of healthy family sexuality:

1. A balanced interdependence among all family members based upon respect for both genders as legitimate and valued, including their physical embodiment and ways of experiencing reality—regardless of perceived similarities and differences between males and females.
2. A balance between boundaries that defines individual family members and maintains suitable physical, psychological and social boundaries relevant to respective ages and stages of the life cycle while supporting appropriate gender socialization and personal erotic development.
3. A balanced (verbal and nonverbal) communication among family members that distinguishes between nurturing, affection and erotic contact while helping all of these to occur between appropriate persons in developmentally suitable ways.
4. Shared sexual values, meanings and attitudes among family members, permitting a balance between shared family goals and activities, on the one hand, and individual decisions and actions, on the other.

5. Balanced transactions between the family and its social and historical environments, reflected in reciprocity between family members' sexual attitudes, meanings and behaviors, those of their families of origin and those of their community. (1995:64)

Healthy sexuality may take different forms in different families, but the end result is a balanced position. Within these characteristics, there is high regard for gender variation, difference in individual development, appropriateness of boundaries to protect personal privacy, meaningful interpersonal closeness, honoring of requests for distance, and open channels of communication and negotiation. Individual and family sexual health go hand in hand. Positive patterns of interaction among family members create a network of shared meaning about sex and serve as a basis for defining behavior between members. The family is a unique unit that carries on the traditions, beliefs and values by interfacing with the larger community of which it is a part.

SEXUALITY AND SPIRITUALITY

We believe that spirituality is not just relevant but also essential to working out an authentic sexuality. Some people are shocked to see "sexuality" and "spirituality" placed next to each other in a sentence, let alone to think of them as intricately related. Most of us have been taught to think of sexuality and spirituality as separate entities or exact opposites that have nothing to do with each other.

In his book *The Erotic Word: Sexuality, Spirituality, and the Bible,* David Carr argues that sexuality and spirituality "are intricately interwoven, that when one is impoverished the other is warped, and that there is some kind of crucially important connection between the journey toward God and the journey toward coming to terms with our own sexual embodiment" (2003:10).

While the Bible affirms sexuality, our civilization has too often engaged either in eroticism-hating sexual oppression or hedonistic, unsatiated sexual obsession. Both these extremes fail to acknowledge the personal and relational meaning at the core of sexual wholeness. A further separation between sexuality and spirituality goes back to ascetic practices. The denial of bodily pleasure was a common rule for spirituality. Sexual desires were historically considered as dangerous temptations that needed to be suppressed. Women were suppressed since they were thought to be a primary source of sexual temptation. Some early church leaders went so far as to consider sexual union as a temporary separation from the Holy Spirit. And as little as a century ago, married people were advised not to have sex too often because intercourse was a disgusting act that had led Adam and Eve astray (Hunt 1959).

Augustine is often faulted for cementing the body/soul dualism within the church. Among the erroneous beliefs that Augustine introduced into the church were that sexual intercourse was disgusting, sexual lust and intercourse were the original sins of Adam and Eve, and the guilt and shame associated with this act passed on through inheritance (Hunt 1959:120). Before his conversion, Augustine lived a sexually promiscuous life, and following his conversion he struggled with sexual desires and involvement, facts that help us understand why he took such a negative view toward sexuality.

Due to historical and cultural factors, it may take a radical shift for many to define desire not as a sin but as a positive force that draws us to others and to God. Is it not true that when we desire, seek and yield to God, we experience times of significant transformation? John 15:5 indicates a mysterious union in which Christ abides within us and we in him, to bring forth much fruit in our lives. Through this sacred encounter, we see ourselves in our Creator's eyes, and we are changed.

The Christian concept of spirituality can likewise be thought of as yielding to and being filled by God's Spirit. The height of Christian spirituality is to be filled by God in such a way that one's own will has conformed to God's will, and desire is an effortless experience of being in harmony (unity) with God's will.

Sexuality and spirituality are also analogous in that each can be approached either from a self-negating or self-affirming stance. According to the biblical account, sexuality is an integral part of the creative act of God. Experientially, sexuality and spirituality may be considered analogous experiences. Sexual fulfillment is meant to be a climactic experience that takes place in a relationship between two people who totally give themselves to each other. According to the biblical account, sexuality is essential in the creative act of God.

We come boldly before God with our whole self. Our desire is to engage, submit, worship, confess, listen, and to be transformed and empowered by God's Spirit. There is no holding back in one's hunger for meditating on

God's Word; there is an eagerness to pour out one's soul, to intercede in prayer for others and to express one's deepest desires to God.

Ironically, it is the lack of desire for God's grace and God's way that stagnates us. Spiritual apathy is what keeps us in a defeated and self-negating place. Those who believe they are unworthy are likely to be victims of life, lacking energy or passion for God, yet expecting God to do miracles in their life. Spirituality out of emptiness is a desperate plea to God to fill up the hole and gaps, while spirituality out of the fullness of God's grace leads to increased riches far beyond our imagination. A passionate seeker of God is one who not only desires growth but also is ready to obey and cooperate with God in the transformation. The impotent lover focuses on self-defeating faults, wallows in self-pity and fears change.

Unless our theology affirms the goodness of desire, we will be reluctant to integrate sexuality with spirituality. Desiring, enjoying and relating to a partner who is made in God's image affirms the sacred meaning embedded in the sexual union. Our desire can lead us to profound places of growth, for it takes courage to open ourselves, recognize our vulnerable places, and be changed as we struggle together in our quest for wholeness.

Each of these systems is capable of influencing a given type of person. In differentiation terms, the self-affirming system produces the well-integrated lover, the self-negating system produces the impotent lover, and the self-centered system produces the addicted lover (Schnarch 1997).

Whether in the sexual or spiritual realm, our desire for God and others propels us to new places of ecstasy. In a spiritual sense, if people hunger for merger with God as a way to satisfy emptiness, they have missed the point. God has created us with the desire to be part of the process; we simultaneously work out our salvation as God works within us to shape our lives. Relationship between desire and grace is a critical step: when we actively long for God to dwell within us, we have the impetus for wholeness. Desire leads to salvation and sanctification. We look for a supernatural connection with the Holy Spirit, who empowers us to do God's will. Sexuality is integral to spiritual wholeness and must not be disparaged or glorified, but be in a balanced place as we seek wholeness.

SEXUALITY IN NEED OF REDEMPTION

How pure and uncomplicated human sexuality would be if it were not for the entrance of sin into the world. God's good gift of sex as described in the first two chapters of Genesis is quickly shattered by what happens in chapter three. Sin puts a damper on things, and we live with the consequences of the Fall. Life is no longer a perfect state or a rosy existence; now there is turmoil and pain to contend with in work, family and relationships between men and women.

Sexuality, a gift of God's perfect design, is now a part of our fallen nature, and we must reckon with this truth. Sexuality suffers the consequences of sin, just as everything else does. There are many ways this good gift of sex has been perverted, distorted and warped. We all are prone to behave in ways that are contrary to God's directives. The Old and New Testaments describe how our fallen condition has disrupted relationships through jealousy, greed, murder, abuse, mistreatment, neglect, coveting and so on.

Mary Stewart Van Leeuwen (1984) puts it like this:

> Our disturbed sexual natures are only one aspect of a disturbed and abnormal universe. Our understanding of this ought to keep us from overrating the seriousness of our sexual struggles. We should be no more surprised by the constancy and diversity of our sexual struggles than we are by our moral struggles regarding work, money, possessions, family obligations, or anything else that the Ten Commandments highlight as areas of life in special need of regulation. . . . None of us is going to live a risk-free morally neutral sexual existence in this culture or any other. The sooner we acknowledge this, the more likely it is that we can give support and counsel to one another in this area of our lives as in others. (p. 10)

We become acutely aware of our need for healing and redemption in our sexual attitudes, behaviors and strivings. We are trying to live out an authentic sexuality in the midst of a world that espouses inauthentic sexuality. Being created as sexual persons demands much more of us than a mere assent to a set of rules about sexual behavior and standards. It involves our very being and how we live in relationship to others. In authentic sexual interaction, we are mutually responsible for building mature relationships that bring forth the best in both. Each of us is responsible for our sexual attitudes, behaviors and interpersonal relationships. When we compartmentalize rather than integrate our sexuality, we risk irresponsibility. It is not something that should be left to chance. We need to intentionally integrate our sexuality and spirituality by carefully assessing our attitudes and behaviors in terms of biblical values. It is an ongoing, challenging task to achieve a level of integration that leads to authentic, person-centered sexuality, but that is what God expects of us, and it is well worth the effort.

RESTORATION AND RENEWAL

This good news of the gospel is hopeful because Christ came to earth not only to redeem us, but also to restore us. The Holy Spirit is given to empower us to live out our broken life in a broken world. We Christians are all in the process of trying to follow Christ and live the kind of person-centered sexual lives that God intended. Van Leeuwen (1984) points out that substantial healing is possible as we work toward that healing place. And when we fall short, we are to share each other's burdens and "bear witness to our allegiance to the One whose incarnation has affirmed the worth of our bodily passions, and in whose resurrection we have the promise of all things made new" (p. 30).

God's grace keeps us reaching toward our all-knowing, loving God. Faith is a lifelong process. We must view ourselves as created in God's image and be constantly mindful of God's indwelling presence as we reach for wholeness. Recognizing we have a unique life to live that is not like any other, we must remain grounded in Christ in our particular life circumstances. We each have sexual wounds and struggles, disappointments and confusion, but God provides the light we need so we do not lose our way on that journey toward sexual authenticity. Our God is a generous guide and comfort, present with us through life's challenges.

When we can look at life with all its ups and downs and trust God to transform us through it all, restoration brings us to new heights of wholeness. When we depend on God and are challenged to go beyond what we in ourselves are capable of doing, we experience how our sexuality leads us to a deeper spirituality. Most of us are quite content to remain in our safe and secure world rather than asking God to examine us so we can be accountable before God in this area.

In *The Mystery of Sexuality* (1972:32), Rosemary Haughton views sexuality as "a mystery at the heart of our familiar selves; it is ourselves as we live with other people we love." Through self-acceptance in Christ, we find our familiar self, that unique, differentiated self created by God to live in relationship with others. Knowing who we are in Christ, sons and daughters of God, leads to a deeper level of knowing how God's image within urges us to be rightly related to others. Therefore, spiritual desire leads to a fullness of God, and sexual desire leads to a full, meaningful life in relationship. As we struggle with the Divine about our sexual nature, we are brought to a deeper knowledge of ourselves. Likewise, the sexual relationship is an important place of self-discovery and growth. Our passion drives us to deeper, intimate encounters. When we not only know who we are but Whose we are, we meet life with a view toward growth and transformation.

We all have needs, deficits and wounds to heal, and our hope lies in the belief that our transcendent God wants to make something new (cf. Is 43:19); this can happen if we are willing to die, over and over, to our old selves. We participate in the event as we obediently put on the new and take off the old so we can become more like Jesus. Substantial healing comes when we take an honest look at ourselves and ask God to correct us and give us courage to change.

FOR FURTHER READING

Carr, D. 2002. *Sexuality, spiriuality, and the Bible*. Oxford: Oxford University Press.

Ellens, J. 2006. *Sex in the Bible: A new consideration*. Paeger.

Trible, P. 1987. *God and the rhetoric of sexuality*. Philadelphia: Fortress.

4

Sexual Beings
in Relationship

God created us as sexual beings! Sexuality is therefore an integral part of being human. When we relate to each other as male and female persons, we do so in the context of our sexuality. We believe the intended purpose of our being created as sexual persons is to draw us into significant and satisfying connection with others. The God-ordained relational longing for emotional bonding is what gives us a sense of belonging and purpose. In our embodied person-to-person interaction with others, there is an element of sexuality present, but this is not to insinuate that all or any of our relating includes an erotic dimension.

We make a distinction between sexual energy and erotic energy in relating to others. Being created as sexual beings means we have physical capacity for erotic sexuality, but generally our sexual energy gives us a vitality for relating to others that goes beyond our erotic instincts. The majority of gratifying relationships in our life are actually nonerotic, such as between parent and child, siblings, same- and opposite-sex friendships, extended family members, signficant others in our work environments, and in the our small and large communities. These relationships deeply enrich and give meaning to our lives.

When it comes to erotic sexual expression, the Scripture teaches that this aspect of being created sexual is reserved for the exclusive love relationship defined as the one-flesh union (Gen 2:24). Moving toward another person in courtship and eventual marriage includes many aspects of relationship intimacy, including erotic desires and expression of love. At this level, sexuality reaches its highest expression in person-centered sex.

In this chapter, we present a theological foundation for understanding what it means to be created as sexual beings in the broader sense of term. Relationship love is an all-inclusive bonding with others that God intends for all persons, single and married, young and old. The overaching theme of being authentic sexual beings in all our relationships is the focus of this chapter.

First, we propose trinitarian theology as a model for human relating. The relationship between the three members of the Holy Trinity—Father, Son and Holy Spirit—is simultaneous distinctiveness and complete unity. Indeed, this divine mystery points to God as one, yet three persons. Both Old and New Testaments indicate ways in which the persons of the Trinity work together for creative, redemptive and transformative purposes to humankind. We believe this is a rich analogy for human relationships: achieving unity while maintaining distinctiveness. As distinctly unique persons, we open ourselves to each other through the encounter, making a place for unity.

This engagement is a reciprocal process of making room in ourselves for others as well as giving ourselves to each other in vulnerable ways that bring a relationship deep meaning. Our sexuality brings energy and enthusiasm to the process of knowing and being known, satisfying our deep longing for belonging, connection and interdependence. Recognizing our common humanity as well as our distinctiveness helps us make vital connections with each other. Our differences actually intrigue us and expand who we are as we encounter each other. Our maleness and femaleness, personality differences, giftedness and unique perspectives bring a dimension to our relationship that enhances our distinctiveness and who we are together.

Relationality is initially seen in the first book of the Old Testament. "'Let us make humankind in our own image, according to our likeness.' . . . So God created humankind in his image, in the image of God he created them; male and female he created them" (Gen 1:26-27 NRSV). Here the reference to the triune Godhead is represented in the plural nouns used in the passage: "Let *us*" and "in *our*." The fact that human beings are created in the image of God gives us incentive to understand just what this means in our relationship to one another.

In his book *Reforming Theological Anthropology: After the Philosophical Turn to Relationality*, F. LeRon Shults (2002) points out the significance of the shift from the traditional view that the *imago Dei* refers to rationality, to the more contemporary view that it refers to *relationality*. While rationality is an important aspect of being created in Gods's image, Stanley Grenz (2001) agrees that *relationality* is the most essential way humans are created in the image of God. He comments, "Let us make humankind in our image" suggests that the "same principle of mutuality that forms the genius for the human social dynamic is present in a prior way in the divine being" (p. 48). In other words, humankind mirrors the image of God. Through biblical and traditional wisdom, trinitarian theology provides a solid basis for understanding human relationships.

Trinitarian theologian Miroslav Volf (1998), rightly points out the limits of using the Trinity as an analogy in human relationships. "Our notions of the triune God are not the triune God, even if God is accessible to us only in these notions. A certain doctrine of the Trinity is a model acquired from salvation history and formulated in analogy to our experience, a model with which we seek to approach the mystery of the triune God, not in order to comprehend God completely, but rather in order to worship God as the unfathomable and to imitate God in our own, creaturely way" (p. 198).

With these limitations in mind, we use trinitarian theology as a model for authentic sexual relationship. Individuals, male and female, are equally directed by God to be fruitful and have dominion over creation. They find ultimate meaning in and through their relationship with God and each other.

In the New Testament, Jesus calls us relate to each other in the same way that he relates to his Father (Jn 15). The eternal love between the Father and Son is to be mirrored in the love we have for each other. The biblical narrative on the life of Jesus provides a nuanced description of trinitarian relationality. The oneness of God is clear. Jesus proclaims that he is one with the Father and that those who have seen him have seen the Father. At the same time, we recognize Jesus (the Son of God) being embodied, born in a manger, living a life of obedience, giving his life for others, and eventually suffering and dying on the cross for our sins. In his deepest agony, Jesus looks to the Father, gives up his will, and prays, "Not my will but yours be done" (Lk 22:42).

The concept of differentiation includes the notion of particularity and unity. In describing *perichōrēsis* (the reciprocal interiority of the trinitarian persons), Miroslav Volf comments: "In every divine person as a subject, the other persons also indwell; all mutually permeate one another, though in so doing they do not cease to be distinct persons. . . . Those who have dissolved into one another cannot exist in one another" (1998:209). In human relationships, it is the distinction (differentiation) rather than fusion (absorption) that leads to vital connection and wholeness. In marital terms, both spouses bring their distinct selves (mutual interiority) as they each make space for the other (mutual permeation) so they can indwell each other (interdependence) and become an entity (union) that transcends themselves.

The dominant chracteristic of trinitarian relationality is love, a love that covenants with Israel, a love that offers up a Son, a love that offers grace and forgiveness, a love that will not let us go, a love that sends the Holy Spirit to abide with us and empower us to follow God's ways. In human relationships we are admonished to love one another as God has loved us. Love is to permeate the entire Christian community as brothers and sisters in Christ relate to each other in unity so that the world may know that we are Christians.

As Miroslav Volf proposes in his excellent book *Exclusion and Embrace* (1996), it is in the putting self aside that we can best open ourselves to others. We must "die to self" in order to embrace the one who is different from us. To do this, however, we must have a clear sense of self. Therefore, having a differentiated sense of self as uniquely created in God's image makes it possible to be responsible for our actions and move toward others. Then we are able to embrace the other and form significant relationships. In chapter nine, "Marital Sexuality," we will write more fully on how a couple creates a differentiated unity in marriage.

Our second biblical analogy for understanding authentic sexuality has to do with the nature of God in relationship with humankind. This is a model we have developed in prior books with a focus on family relationships (Balswick and Balswick 2003, 2006, 2007). We draw on narratives throughout the Bible that describe the relationship between our Creator God and the people of God. Examples are familial terms used in the New Testament of Jesus as groom to the church and in the Old Testament of God as parent to the children of Israel. A relational God establishes a model of human relationships that we incorporate into our theology of authentic sexual relationships. These four relationship themes are covenant (loving and being loved), grace (accepting and being accepted), empowerment (empowering and being empowered) and intimacy (knowing and being known).

Our premise is that authentic sexual relationships are to be *covenantal* rather than contractual, *gracing* rather than shaming, *empowering* rather than controlling, and *intimate* rather than distancing. We specify how each of these relationship principles contributes to authenticity in sexual relationships and contrast how opposite transactions lead to an inauthentic sexual relationship.

COVENANTAL COMMITMENT: TO LOVE AND BE LOVED

The first principle of an authentic sexual relationship is *an unconditional covenant commitment*. Although the concept of covenant has a rich heritage in Christian theology, its biblical meaning has often been eroded by thinking of commitment in contractual terms (McLean 1984:2). The notion of covenant includes contractual arrangements, but it involves much more. The core theme of covenant is an *unconditional commitment*, which goes far beyond a simple social contract. We can best understand this deeper meaning of covenant by looking at the supreme acts of God in the Old and New Testaments. God established a covenant with Noah (Gen 6:18) and again with Abraham and his family in Genesis 17:4-7:

> As for me, this is my covenant with you: You will be the father of many nations. No longer will you be called Abram; your name will be Abraham, for I have made you a father of many nations. I will make you very fruitful; I will make nations of you, and kings will come from you. I will establish my covenant as as an everlasting covenant between me and you and your descendants after you for the generations to come, to be your God and the God of your descendants after you.

First, we see here that God made a unilateral commitment. They had no choice in the matter, nor was the covenant determined by their response. That is, God was *not* saying, "I am going to commit myself to you *if* this is your desire," but God made a promise based entirely on God's sole commitment to them. God initiated and sustained the covenant as an independent action.

Second, although God desired and even commanded a response from

Noah and Abraham, the covenant remained unconditional *regardless of their response*. It had nothing to do with Noah or Abraham keeping their end of the bargain. One might ask, "Was God 'free' to retract the offer if it was not reciprocated?" The answer is a resounding *no!* The covenant that God gave was "an everlasting covenant," and God, being true to Godself, would faithfully carry out the promise.

Third, whereas the covenant was *not* conditional, the benefits or *blessings* of the covenant were conditional. While Noah and Abraham were free to receive or reject the offer, they would reap rewards from receiving what God had to offer. In other words, although the continuation of God's love was not based on their action, the blessings of the covenant were gained or lost depending on their response.

In the book of Hosea this relationship between God and Israel is actually presented in terms of a sexual relationship. Israel is alternatively referred to as a "faithful lover" or as the "adulterer," who prostitutes herself by whoring after other lovers (gods). The breaking of the covenant is actually understood in terms of a similar sexual metaphor in Deuteronomy 31:16: "And the LORD said to Moses: 'You are going to rest with your fathers, and these people will soon prostitute themselves to the foreign gods of the land they are entering. They will forsake me and break the covenant I made with them.'"

Israel is frequently warned *not* to go whoring after other gods (Ex 34:15-16; Lev 17:7; 20:5; Num 15:39; 1 Chron 5:25; 2 Chron 21:13). The book of Judges records how Israel "did not listen even to their judges; for they lusted after other gods and bowed down to them" (Judg 2:17 NRSV); and "As soon as Gideon died, the Israelites relapsed and prostituted themselves with the Baals, making Baal-berith their god" (Judg 8:33 NRSV). The psalmist refers to Israel's behavior in similar terms, "They defiled themselves by what they did; by their deeds they prostituted themselves" (Ps 106:39).

The prophet Ezekiel expressed God's sorrow at Israel's behavior, "I have been grieved by their adulterous hearts, which have turned away from me, and by their eyes, which have lusted after their idols" (Ezek 6:9). Note the strong sexual language in the prophetic warning in Ezekiel 23:29-30, "They will leave you naked and bare, and the shame of your prostitution will be exposed. Your lewdness and promiscuity have brought this upon you, because you lusted after the nations and defiled yourself with their idols."

Faithfulness and unfaithfulness are concepts throughout the Scriptures used to describe covenant or the lack of covenant commitment. The pattern of Israel's unfaithfulness and God's continual response to restore the relationship is clearly seen throughout the book of Hosea: "Go, take to yourself an adulterous wife and children of unfaithfulness, because the land is guilty of the vilest adultery in departing from the LORD. . . . I will betroth you to me forever; I will betroth you in righteousness and justice, in love and compassion. I will betroth you in faithfulness, and you will acknowledge the LORD" (Hos 1:2; 2:19-20).

Embedded throughout the entire Bible are examples of God moving toward the created ones with extended arms. Ultimately, God's faithful commitment is seen in the incarnation event and the sacrifice of Christ on the cross at Golgotha. In this final act of love, God's only begotten Son gave himself for all who would believe. Although God stretches out in every way to pursue with enticing covenant love, humans have the freedom to respond to or reject that love. God never overtakes in the pursuit, but faithfully beckons the created ones to respond to the life-changing love of Jesus.

In the New Testament the marital analogy symbolizes the relationship between Christ and the church. When John the Baptist explains that he is not the Christ but sent to proclaim the one who is, he says, "The bride belongs to the bridegroom. The friend who attends the bridegroom waits and listens for him, and is full of joy when he hears the bridegroom's voice" (Jn 3:29). Also, in response to queries about why Jesus and his disciples did not fast, Jesus answered, "How can the guests of the bridegroom mourn while he is with them? The time will come when the bridegroom will be taken from them; then they will fast" (Mt 9:15).

The nature of the conjugal relationship between Christ and the church is recorded in Ephesians 5:25-27, "Christ loved the church and gave himself up for her to make her holy, cleansing her by the washing with water through the word, and to present her to himself as a radiant church, without stain or wrinkle or any other blemish, but holy and blameless." Revelation 21:2 refers to the church in its perfect condition, "coming down out of heaven from God, prepared as a bride beautifully dressed for her husband." The obvious symbolism is the anticipated union between the bride and groom.

Do you grasp the picture of God in covenant relationship? God reach-

ing out with an everlasting commitment of love and loyalty is a model for
authentic sexual relationships. The desire to love and be loved unconditionally is a God-given human desire. We learn to trust others in the context
of committed, trustworthy relationships whether this is between spouses,
parents and children, friends (both same and opposite sex), other members
of the body of Christ, and ultimately between persons who are members
of the wider human family. Covenant commitment provides the security
and safety in which people can see themselves as worthy of love in ways
that move them to intimate connection. Faithful nurture, protection and
affirmation of one another are basic to deepening covenant commitment.

Unfortunately, some people have never experienced such amazing love
in their human relationships. Instead, they have been sexually injured, exploited, abused or harassed by those who were supposed to be trustworthy.
Quite naturally, this makes it extremely difficult for them to trust others.
Fearful of being reinjured, the best survival tactic is to protect oneself from
further harm or intrusion. So often these persons doubt their lovability or
believe they do not deserve to be loved. Thus, even when starved for love,
they may not be able to receive affection. Those fearing abandonment may
tend to cling to others for dear life, suffocating the partner. Many learn
to defend against further disappointment by remaining fiercely distant,
removed and nonfeeling. Another reaction may be to sexualize relationships by becoming sexually promiscuous in a desperate attempt to find
love. Devoid of covenant love, these encounters lack any joy or emotional
connection, making matters worse.

We believe that the Scriptures support sexual intercourse in the context of a marital covenant precisely to protect individuals from the pain of
conditional love. The sacred boundary of covenant commitment ensures
love that is founded on faithful, trustworthy covenant vows. A marriage
of secure devotion, especially in our postmodern world, is a foundation
that God intends for an erotic sexual union. A solid commitment keeps
spouses from leaving prematurely when the going gets rough. The personal promise to stand firm in one's commitment to the spouse and relationship—no matter what the circumstances—creates a strong bond of
shared trust. This kind of covenant supports the marriage bond, sustains
the relationship and promotes deeper sexual fulfillment.

Covenant commitment safeguards love's highest qualities. Mutual
promises to love and to cherish, in sickness and health, for better or worse,

and until death energize a couple to invest themselves for the long haul. Since the demands of a lifelong relationship are such a challenge in today's society, the support of extended family and community of faith helps sustain a couple through the stresses of life. Even when a mutual covenant is made, spouses will inevitably fail each other and therefore need grace.

GRACE: TO FORGIVE AND BE FORGIVEN

The second principle of authentic sexuality is that *offering grace rather than placing blame or shame leads to healing and renewed hope.* By its very nature, covenant love includes grace. From a human perspective the unconditional love of God makes no sense unless experienced through grace. Grace is a relational word because the goal is to restore connection when there has been a breach due to human failure or sin. It is the promise of grace that holds out hope for relationship reconciliation.

When children are loved unconditionally and fully accepted as sexual beings, they are likely to accept themselves and their bodies without shame. Experiencing a gracing atmosphere in the home means there is assurance that mistakes will be forgiven, and a family member will be able to change and reestablish oneself after a mistake has been made. The incredible experience of being acceptable rather than trying to earn acceptance goes a long way in giving kids a positive message about themselves, their bodies and their sexuality. Those who experience acceptance and forgiveness will have an increased capacity to accept and forgive others as well as themselves. On the other hand, when children do not feel accepted, they come to believe that there is no way to met the expectations of others. Therefore they work harder to compensate for their feelings of inadequacy.

Shame, judgment and secrecy about sexuality are familiar themes for girls and women who have a tendency to be people pleasers and perfectionistic; they succumb to obsessive thinking in order to control their fears. They often view God as expecting perfect behavior, with no room for error, leading to a rigidity in their behaviors. In addition, the media trains girls and women to objectify their bodies rather than accepting them. According to therapist Cissy Brady-Rogers, eating disorders are connected with perfectionistic attempts to feel okay about oneself. Christian women with food and body problems "have lacked healthy models or teaching on how to integrate their sexuality with their Christian faith." The absence of a positive sexual identity and affirmation of the body is especially lacking in Christian circles due to a dualistic thinking that spirit is all good and body/flesh is all bad. She concludes, "Ultimately the Church needs to model and teach an integrated view of the female body that celebrates diversity of beauty and embraces female appetites for both food and sex as necessary and good parts of being created in the image of God" (2007:4).

To fully understand the destructive consequences of shame in sexual relationships, it is necessary to distinguish between shame and guilt. Most of us will agree that guilt is a natural human response occurring when a person does something wrong. Guilt urges one to acknowledge mistakes in order to correct the wrongful behavior. Shame, on the other hand, relays the message that one has not just done something wrong, but deep inside, the person is flawed at the core and therefore can never measure up. Believing one is bad to this extinct leads to a defeatist position since there is no way to ever right the wrong.

Most often sexual woundedness is a direct result of shaming messages about sex. Strict religious values based on unrealistic standards inevitably leave one feeling unacceptable and unredeemable as a sexual person. Since one can never measure up or be forgiven, the person may simply stop trying at all! Shame is a major element in persons who struggle with various sexual addictions. Viewing oneself as sexually flawed becomes a self-defeating rejection of one's sexual self. This deafening message leads to a continuous cycle of shame.

A damaging aspect of shaming sexual messages is their potential to undermine one's sexual self-worth. When a person has been profoundly shamed in this area of life, it is more difficult to develop an authentic sexual self. Although most people enter adulthood with certain degrees of sexual shame, they are not debilitated by it. Eventual acceptance of oneself as a sexual person, with recognition and affirmation of one's unique sexual embodiment, becomes the road to sexual self-esteem.

Differentiated persons are able to develop a solid sexual self and sexual value system that is congruent with their personal beliefs. They live by their convictions with the greatest of ease and at the same time regard others and their value sytem with deepest respect. They are able to take in the glorious truth that Jesus accepts them as embodied, sexual persons and that their sexuality has been declared by God as good. When they fail, they draw on the amazing truth that God forgives and the Holy Spirit empowers them to move forward and correct the mistakes they make.

Relationships lived out in an atmosphere of grace bring vitality, whereas a critical perfectionistic attitude suffocates and constrains the relationship. The grace dimension is clearly evident in the relationship between God and Israel. God is painfully aware of Israel's rejection in Hosea 2:13: "'She decked herself with rings and jewelry, and went after her lovers, but me she forgot,' declares the LORD." In the very next verse, we hear God's compassionate response: "Therefore I am now going to allure her; I will lead her into the desert and speak tenderly to her. There I will give her back her vineyards." Grace culminates with a reaffirmation of God's unconditional commitment: "I will betroth you to me forever; I will betroth you in righteousness and justice, in love and compassion. I will betroth you in faithfulness, and you will acknowledge the LORD" (Hos 2:19-20).

Hosea's marriage paralleled God's relationship with Israel. Gomer, an unfaithful wife, sought out other relationships, yet God asked Hosea to continue to pursue her, to give her his love, his home, his name and even his reputation. Although Gomer continued in unfaithful living, the LORD told Hosea, "Go, show your love to your wife again, though she is loved by another and is an adulteress. Love her as the LORD loves the Israelites, though they turn to other gods and love the sacred raisin-cakes" (Hos 3:1). Hosea entreats Gomer with acceptance and accountability, "You are to live with me many days; you must not be a prostitute or be intimate with any man, and I will live with you" (Hos 3:3). This relationship is a symbolic message that conveys God's action with Israel. The Lord not only loved his covenant people but would take them back. Going astray certainly had its negative consequences, but the Lord's compassion and faithful love continued to show forth in forgiveness and mercy.

Grace is never cheap! Grace is not wishy-washy. Grace is a gift of God in Christ Jesus, freely extended in persistant compassion. In later chapters we will show how sexual trangression, whether it be sexual harassment, unfaithfulness or abuse, not only takes a terrible toll on those who are victimized, but results in deep relationship fractures. There should be no toleration for dehumanizing, demoralizing sexual messages that undermine what God has proclaimed as good. In these cases the depth of the offense takes a process of healing that includes confession (admitting the wrong done), reparation (making amends and taking responsibility) and time for reconciliation to occur. It is always God's ideal for every broken relationship to be restored when possible. (see chapter eleven for a more complete discussion of this issue).

Grace, rightly expressed, leads to personal healing and empowerment.

EMPOWERING: TO EMPOWER AND BE EMPOWERED

The third principle for *an authentic sexual relationship is that personal resources and gifts are used for mutual building up rather than control.*

Covenant is the vow to love faithfully; grace is the ability to accept and forgive; empowerment is the action of using our personal gifts and strengths to affirm and strengthen others. Jesus Christ modeled empowerment. The celebrated message of Jesus was that he had come to empower: "I have come that they may have life, and have it to the full" (Jn 10:10). The apostle John puts it this way: "But to all who received him, who believed in his name, he gave power to become children of God, who were born, not of blood or of the will of the flesh or of the will of man, but of God" (Jn 1:12-13 NRSV).

The empowerment of the Holy Spirit is for personal transformation that leads to becoming all we were created to be, to bring glory to the kingdom of God on earth. In our sinful and powerless condition, God gives us the power to become children of God. The supreme example of empowerment is seen in Jesus, who gave his life for others and chose to serve rather than to be served. Jesus radically redefined the understanding of power in his teaching and actions.

What Jesus taught about power was so central to his mission that it serves as an ideal for all human relationships. In Mark 10:43-45, Jesus says, "Whoever wants to become great among you must be your servant, and whoever wants to be first must be slave of all. For even the Son of Man did not come to be served, but to serve, and to give his life as a ransom for many" (NRSV). Jesus rejects the use of power to control others; he affirms the use of power to serve others, lift up the fallen, forgive, encourage responsibility and maturity.

A simple definition of power is the ability to influence another person. In a very real sense, empowerment is "love in action." It is the intentional process of building the other up to become all that God intented for them to be in their sexuality.

Power is a significant component of sexual relationships. When one

person tries to manipulate or coerce another in sexual matters, it is a violation of power. Inversely, those who feel powerless in relationships may use
sex as a way to gain power by giving sexual favors. A clearly defined and
differentiated person has no desire or need to coerce or manipulate others
in the sexual realm. Rather, a differentiated person chooses to honor and
respect others and their personal sexual value system. Having a sexual
value system congruent with one's behavior, differentiated persons also
honor the value system of others and their boundaries.

Inauthentic sexual behaviors are organized around using power to *control*. For example, as mentioned in chapter two, the popular male image of
the playboy lends itself to control and disempowerment of the female. By
remaining emotionally detached, he is in the powerful position. By oper-
ating in a nonfeeling mode, he treats the woman as an object rather than a
person. By reducing her to a nonperson, he can then let himself control her
for his own means. He manipulatively tells her what she wants to hear, but
the empty words are uttered as a means to his own selfish end.

Those who use sexual power to conquer and manipulate do so to control the outcome for personal pleasure. Such nonrelational messages lead
persons to treat others as a possession over whom they try to exert power.
Since power is promoted in our culture, violence is often part of coercive
relationships. Using brute force or abusive putdowns to get one's way sexually is common. By resorting to such offensive behavior, these persons are
actually revealing their own weakness and low self-esteem. Control over
someone gives a false impression of being powerful, but it points out a
serious weakness. Those who tolerate or accept such coercive actions in a
relationship have little sense of self and lack differentiation. Often boundaries are nonexistent, and there is little if any regard for individual rights
or personal choice.

In our postmodern world, men and women resort to using sexual prowess to get what they want out of a person while remaining sexually detached. They may feel powerful in a stance of undifferentiated independence, but they are sacrificing the deeper satisfaction that comes with
person-centered connection.

When mutual empowerment reigns supreme, both persons are affirmed in their sexuality and personhood. Partners relate to each other as
two distinctly unique people who invite each other into a rhythm of interaction that enhances the relationship. Each person respects and maintains

suitable physical, psychological and social boundaries that keep them mutually responsible for their sexual decisions in relating to each other. Shared meanings, attitudes, beliefs and goals are the foundation of the interdependency they are creating in their relationship. Vulnerability is welcomed, and they gladly open themselves to each other for deeper levels of knowing.

The lovemaking is an essential part of the attachment bond. Sexual activity results in the production of the hormone oxytocin, which produces feelings of relaxation, contentment and a desire to remain connected to the spouse in the continuation of the relationship (Hazen 2003). Valuing the love relationship is vital because of its power to communicate emotional closeness and intimacy.

Two persons sufficiently differentiated will have the greatest potential for developing a meaningful, person-centered relationship. Out of covenant security, gracing acceptance and mutual empowerment, intimacy blossoms.

INTIMACY: TO KNOW AND BE KNOWN

The fourth principle is that *an authentic relationship is meant to deepen one's experience of knowing and being known.* One of the incredible truths of Scripture is that God knows us intricately and desires that we know him more deeply. We are encouraged to share our deepest thoughts and feelings with God in prayer as the Holy Spirit speaks through groanings that are too deep for words (Rom 8:26-27).

Positive bonding is important from the cradle to the grave. Whether a relationship includes an erotic dimension or stays at a nonerotic level, the connection achieved through a reciprocal encounter of sharing deepens one's sense of self and other in the context of the relationship. Knowing someone is there for us and that we matter to them on a day-by-day basis means that we exist in each other's minds. In a secure relationship, there is a demonstration of availability and acceptance, an offering of support and comfort, an expression of love.

Most adults establish a level of intimacy through friendship that is intense and profoundly meaningful throughout their lives. Persons in spiritual disciplines and practices describe a deeply gratifying spiritual intimacy with others in their small-group encounters. This kind of sharing in nonerotic relationships has the same capacity for interaction and interdependency. Knowing and being known is not exclusive to erotic relationships.

In the Garden of Eden, Adam and Eve were naked but felt no shame (Gen 2:25). In this perfect place, they stood before each other and before God, completely open and transparent. Nakedness in this passage must be understood as more than physical. Exposed in every way, they faced each other in their vulnerability and felt absolutely no shame in each other's presence. In this pre-Fall environment, there was no need to hide or cover up; there was no desire to keep secrets, pretend or put on airs to impress each other; there was no reason to play deceptive games or control the other. They were authentic in their identity, in their sexuality, in their relationship.

Genesis 1:27 speaks of differentiation in Adam and Eve's male and female embodiment. A man knows his manhood as distinct in relationship to woman just as the woman knows her womanhood as distinct in relationship to man. It is a complementary, intimate process of becoming known. Differentiation frees them to "leave" and "cleave" (Gen 2:24 KJV). They open themselves wholeheartedly to know themselves through a full expression of that self in relationship.

Genesis 2:24 states, "For this reason a man will leave his father and mother and be united to his wife, and they will become one flesh." The action verb *become* refers to a sexual knowing, but intimacy also entails an emotional and intellectual knowing. It seems that differentiation is predicated on one's ability to leave (father and mother) before he or she can rightly cleave. Modern systems theorists describe this as *developmental differentiation.* One of the factors that contribute to a strong relationship bond is the establishment of a sufficient self. Murray Bowen emphasizes the need for an individual to be *emotionally* differentiated from parents in order to maintain a healthy balance of individuality (separateness) and togetherness (connectedness) in subsequent relationships. In other words, only a differentiated person can be securely attached (Bowen 1978; Kerr and Bowen 1988).

Our wired-in human need to seek out and secure emotional connections, not only as children but also with our partners, provides the bond that sustains our love relationships long after the endorphins of romantic love have subsided. Establishing a secure, emotional connection (bonding) *and* standing secure in one's self and with others (differentiation) are equally essential for a mature sexual relationship to flourish.

In *Constructing the Sexual Crucible,* David Schnarch (1991) defines differentiation as "the process by which a person manages individuality and togetherness in a relationship. . . . Differentiation permits a person to function individually and yet be emotionally involved with others, and to do both simultaneously at profound depth. Differentiation of self is a critical task that ideally precedes adult attempts at intimacy, for it is differentiation that permits one to be intimate rather than 'closed' or fused" (p. 198).

According to Schnarch, a person's capacity for sexual intimacy is directly related to that person's degree of differentiation. Where differentiation is low, sexual intimacy is also low due to fears of being engulfed, entrapped, exploited or abandoned. Satisfying sexual encounters are based on two individuals who are full, not empty, so they can give and receive in mutual ways.

Sexuality and intimacy are intricately connected. Becoming "one flesh" involves knowing and being known in the act of intercourse as well as in the act of melding two lives together through a growing covenant commitment. The mutual giving and receiving in reciprocal vulnerability helps spouses discover the fullness of intimacy.

A crucial ingredient for becoming intimate in a sexual relationship is communication. Humans are unique among living creatures in their ability to communicate elaborately with each other through language, a capacity that makes it possible for them to know and be known intimately. The "bone of my bones and flesh of my flesh" (Gen 2:23) response between Adam and Eve was possible because they could communicate thoughts, feelings, desires and wants in a way that was not possible with other living creatures.

Honest communication is the key to authentic sexual transactions. It is important for partners to freely express and discuss sexual feelings, desires and struggles without feeling shame. Freedom and spontaneity come with being comfortable with one's body and having the ability to respond to touch, nurturance, affection and erotic expression.

Emotional distancing in relationship most likely occurs due to a person's fear of intimacy. Sex becomes a vehicle for meeting sexual needs, but these individuals fail to grasp emotional knowing and being known. The superficial sexual connection leaves them feeling isolated, restless and lonely. With nowhere to turn for interaction and communion at a personal level, some turn to addictions that offer symptom relief. This does not solve but simply perpetuates the problem. Persons who feel unworthy of being known try to hide themselves rather than disclose themselves. The cover-up game of hiding one's self leads one further and further away from the emotional connection that could make a difference.

Adam and Eve responded with blame, shame and fear after disobeying God. "Then the eyes of both of them were opened, and they realized they were naked; so they sewed fig leaves together and made coverings for themselves. Then the man and his wife heard the sound of the LORD God as he was walking in the garden in the cool of the day, and they hid from the LORD God among the trees of the garden" (Gen 3:7-8). It was only after their disobedience that Adam and Eve tried to hide from God, because they felt their nakedness and shame. Shame is always a barrier to intimacy.

Only when sex is woven into a wider fabric of communication between two differentiated lovers can it bring them to the deepest places of knowing. The vulnerability that comes from being open, honest and self-reflective helps the spouses find more of themselves in the context of their union. Sex in and of itself cannot bring one to this deeper level of intimacy. However, sexual intimacy that is based on emotional intimacy carries the relationship to new levels of growth and passion.

Emotionally satisfying sex is best when there is committed love. The capacity for partners to express sexual love for each other is contingent upon their mutual trust and responsible actions of faithfulness. John gives us insight into this in 1 John 4:18: "There is no fear in love. But perfect love drives out fear." God expresses perfect love so we can respond to that love without fear, shame or hiding. This brings us back to the first of our principles: an unconditional love commitment, the cornerstone for God's ideal in sexual relationships.

SUMMARY

We have suggested that a theology of sexual relationships involves four sequential but nonlinear principles: *covenant commitment, gracing, empowering* and *intimacy*. We depict these principles in figure 4.1 as spiraling inward because they deepen authenticity in sexual relationships. Observe that an authentic sexual relationship does not emerge fully developed but is a process of two people intentionally moving into deeper levels in these relationship dimensions.

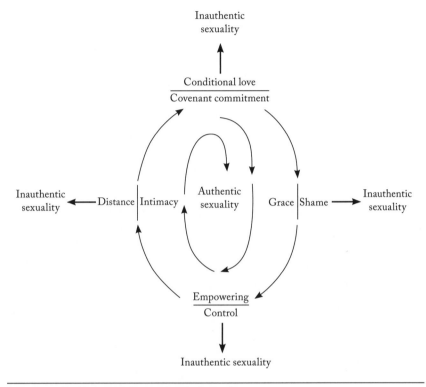

Figure 4.1. Building an authentic sexual relationship

Growth in a sexual relationship can be blocked or retarded at any point when a person is unable or unwilling to follow the biblical relationship principles. We might think of the spiral as a clock spring that unwinds in a counterclockwise direction toward deteriorating levels of couple functioning. The relationship stagnates because one or both partners are unable to risk what it takes to move in the direction of growth, especially if the couple seeks out a quid pro quo (something for something) arrangement that says, "I'll share *if* you share," "I'll forgive *if* you forgive," "I'll make a commitment *as long as* you make one first," or "I'll empower you *when* you empower me." This conditionality is the exact opposite of covenant love. A differentiated person chooses to share and risk vulnerability out of a desire to be known.

A standoff like this may occur at any point or time in the cycle due to broken trust, disappointments, hurt or angry feelings, misunderstanding or a number of things that prevent a forward movement. Pain in one's past may hinder that person's capacity to trust or love unconditionally. It may be that well-kept secrets or shameful behaviors are hindering relationship growth. Insecurity may lead a partner to control the other, or lack of self-esteem may prompt manipulative behaviors. Social conditioning cautions us to protect ourselves by keeping our emotions to ourselves. Most of us constantly struggle with our human tendencies to be conditional in our love, to shame or blame those who fail or disappoint us, to use our resources and power to control or manipulate others, and to disengage or distance ourselves rather than risk personal vulnerability. There are myriad reasons why things go wrong in relationships; this is why it takes courage to step out, take risks, and seek biblical ways of being. It is not a matter of changing the other person, but of being changed by the power of the Holy Spirit so that we act out of the fullness of being differentiated in Christ rather than out of a self-centered emptiness.

A sexual relationship maintains its vitality as it remains dynamic. Thus, we believe that as either partner moves in the direction of commitment, grace, empowering and intimacy—refusing to become sidetracked by contracting, shaming, controlling or distancing—there is great potential for sexual authenticity. May we be strengthened by God's Holy Spirit to move in God's direction of authentic relationship.

FOR FURTHER READING

Balswick, J. K., and J. O. Balswick. 2006. *A model for marriage: Covenant, grace, empowerment, and intimacy.* Downers Grove, Ill.: InterVarsity Press.

———. 2007. *The family: A Christian perspective on the contemporary home.* 3rd ed. Grand Rapids: Baker.

Ellens, J. 2006. *Sex in the Bible: A new consideration.* Westport, Conn.: Paeger.

Volf, M. 1996. *Exclusion and embrace.* Nashville: Abingdon.

5

Homosexuality

The Complexity of Explanations

Being attracted to persons (same or opposite gender) who share similar ideas, feelings, vision and passion for life is one of the great blessings of being authentically human. Most certainly, we experience expressions of love with same-sex persons (siblings, parents and friends) at deep levels of caring. The love between same-gendered persons is often considered a "pure form of love" because it is not complicated by romantic or erotic overtones. Soul-mate friends bring out the truth of who we are by opening us up to express our honest thoughts and secret emotions. For the majority of people, these same-sex relationships do not include an erotic dimension. The purpose of this chapter is to examine same-sex erotic attraction. Before doing this, however, we will point out the four critical criteria that determine one's sexuality.

DIMENSIONS OF SEXUALITY

In chapter two we indicated that natal sex, sexual identity, gender role and sexual orientation are criteria used to understand the complexity of sexual development. While sexual orientation is best understood as only one of these four dimensions of sexuality, it is conventionally used as the reference point in any discussion of homosexuality. The four types of sexual orientation are heterosexual, homosexual, bisexual and transgender. The first three describe individuals who have erotic attraction for the opposite sex, the same sex and both sexes; while *transgender* is an umbrella term used to describe individuals who cross or transcend culturally defined categories of sex and gender. Following are six categories of transgender orientations:

> 1. A transsexual desires and/or has undergone hormone therapy and/or sex reassignment surgery to resolve an extreme conflict between gender identity (basic conviction of being male or female) and sex assignment at birth (natal sex based on male or female anatomy).
> 2. A transvestite likes to wear clothing associated with another sex, for a variety of reasons. Sometimes referred to as cross-dressers, such persons are not dissatisfied with their natal gender and do not desire to change natal gender, sexual identity or sexual orientation, but like to occasionally present themselves as the opposite gender. Some transvestites may be sexually ambiguous in sexual identity or sexual orientation.
> 3. A transgenderist lives in the gender role associated with another sex without going through sex-change surgery.
> 4. A bigendered person identifies as either male and female and has attraction to both genders.
> 5. A drag queen/king is a gay or lesbian who "does drag" by dressing up in women's/men's clothes for exhibitionistic reasons.
> 6. A female/male impersonator mimics the opposite gender for entertainment purposes.

These descriptions indicate how complex it is for some individuals to be aligned on all four dimensions. It is not a clearcut process for them but may take years of struggle to finally find a satisfying and congruent sexual authenticity.

At this point we will focus specifically on homosexuality. We begin with a historical perspective, provide a definition of homosexuality, and summarize various theories that try to explain the causes of homosexuality. We conclude this chapter with an integrative model that includes an interactive process of biopsychosocial and human agency.

HISTORICAL PERSPECTIVE ON HOMOSEXUALITY

Erotic sexual activity between same-sex persons has occurred throughout recorded history. To name just a few, famous persons like Erasmus

(1466-1536), scholar and editor of the Greek New Testament; Leonardo da Vinci (1452-1519), the gifted artist who painted the moving portrait of Christ in *The Last Supper;* James I of England (1566-1625), who commissioned the translation of the Bible that bears his name; Michelangelo (1475-1564), the creator of the beautiful sculpture *The Pietà* and magnificent frescoes on the ceiling of the Sistine Chapel—all these have been counted as having homosexual leanings (Scanzoni and Mollenkott (1978:32-37). Obviously, persons with homosexual orientation (known and unknown) can and do live productive lives and contribute in significant ways to our world.

Throughout the ages the response to homosexuality has ranged from outright condemnation and punishment to tolerance, acceptance and even celebration. The obvious stigmas and sweeping stereotypes attached to homosexuality have created fear, social distance and contempt between homosexuals and heterosexuals.

Not until the 1800s was a distinction commonly made between homosexual orientation (an attraction to the same sex) and homosexual behavior (engaging in sex practices with someone of the same sex). Before that time, homosexuality was categorized as a sin. However, beginning in the twentieth century, this view was replaced by the medical model, in which mental disturbance, homosexuality included, was considered a sickness or mental illness.

Homosexuality was included in the *Diagnostic and Statistical Manual of Mental Illness* (DSM) as a sexual deviance. During the 1970s homosexual groups began to contest this view. The debate continued for about a decade. Later, embarrassed by the lack of a secure scientific explanation, the American Psychiatric Association stopped identifying homosexuality as a mental disorder, removing it from the DSM. The current DSM manual retains dystonic homosexuality as a category only for those who are in conflict about their sexual orientation and desire to change.

By the 1980s the majority of health-care professionals started viewing homosexual orientation as a fact of life rather than a problem to treat. Homosexual orientation and behavior became an acceptable lifestyle rather than a shameful pathology. The homosexual community saw this as an important political victory. No longer was homosexuality diagnosed as a congenital anomaly, a major neurosis, a sexual perversion or a moral deviation. Many therapists today question the appropriateness of putting a homosexual under the psychological duress of working toward changing this orientation. Compassion was felt for those who had tried everything they knew to change, but were unable to solidify or maintain that change over time. This led to a renewed interest in understanding the complex factors that contribute to a homosexual orientation.

HOMOSEXUALITY DEFINED

Arriving at a clear definition of homosexuality is somewhat tricky, since homosexuality can be described as an orientation and/or as a behavior. For instance, those with a homosexual orientation may be erotically attracted to persons of the same sex and never erotically act on that attraction. On the other hand, some persons define themselves as heterosexual in orientation but at times choose to express sexual eroticism through homosexual encounters. Situational homosexuality is a common occurrence for heterosexuals under circumstances where opportunities for heterosexual contact are not possible. For example, there is a high incidence of homosexual behavior reported by inmates in prison. Also, those who define themselves as bisexual are equally attracted to and can be erotically engaged with persons of either the same or the opposite sex.

As you can see, even defining homosexuality becomes complicated. We cannot automatically assume that all persons with homosexual orientation are exclusively attracted to or engage in sexual behavior with the same sex. Nor can we consider persons of predominantly heterosexual orientation to be exclusively sexually involved with the opposite sex. For this reason, sexual attraction is sometimes described along a continuum ranging from exclusively heterosexual at one extreme, attraction to either sex (bisexuality) in the middle, and exclusively homosexual at the other extreme. There can be all kinds of combinations in between. Some will never be attracted to or involved with same-sex persons, and others will never feel the slightest attraction to or engage in sexual behaviors with the opposite sex. Those in between may feel attraction to either gender while never engaging in erotic sexual behaviors; others may engage in sexual behaviors with members of either gender but have a strong preference for heterosexual or homosexual involvement.

The 10 percent solution. You can begin to understand why it is difficult to estimate the exact number of homosexuals in the population. In his groundbreaking study of sexual behavior in the human male and female,

Alfred Kinsey, Pomeroy and Martin (1948, 1953) estimated that approximately 10 percent of the American population was homosexual. However, this figure has been questioned by researchers. In *Kinsey, Sex, and Fraud: The Indoctrination of a People* (Reisman et al. 1990), the authors claim that Kinsey's findings were skewed due to a nonrepresentative sample that included a disproportionate number of subjects from a prison population, thus inflating the percentage.

Lower percentages reported. A host of studies have suggested a much-lower rate in the general population of those who report homosexual behaviors. Remafedi and others (1992), in a study of 34,706 adolescents, discovered that 1 percent of all adolescents and 2.8 percent of eighteen-year-olds had experienced "some" homosexual contact. It seems that youth may engage in same-sex contact as part of sexual experimentation, but not necessarily define themselves as homosexual. In a survey of 3,321 American men aged 20 to 29 (Billy et al. 1993), 2.3 percent reported some homosexual activity over the previous ten years, but only 1.1 percent reported exclusive homosexual activity over those past ten years.

The most comprehensive sex survey since the time of Kinsey has been conducted at the University of Chicago by a group of researchers (Laumann et al.) in 1994. Using the best scientific methodology based on a random sample of nearly 3,500 Americans aged 18-59, they reported their findings in *The Social Organization of Sexuality*. On questions regarding homosexual behavior, they found that 2.7 percent of men and 1.3 percent of women reported having engaged in homosexual sex in the previous year. These questions referred specifically to homosexual behavior and not to homosexual orientation. Undoubtedly there are persons who may have homosexual attractions (orientation) but choose not to act on them. Therefore, it is likely that the percentage with a homosexual orientation is somewhat higher than reported in this study.

Another national survey found that the number of individuals reporting a same-sex sexual experiences increased from 1988 to 1998, but even in 1998 the percentages were low—4.1 percent for men and 2.8 percent for women (Butler 2000). In reviewing the evidence from a number of surveys, King (2005:274) concluded that although many more people have had sexual experiences with individuals of the same sex at one time in their life, "About 3-5% of adult American men and about 1% of adult American women are homosexual."

The available research in other countries estimates that the rate of homosexuality is approximately 2-5 percent. In a survey of 480 British males, Forman and Chilvers (1989) found that 1.7 percent of their subjects had "some" homosexual contact, and less than 1 percent engaged in exclusive homosexual contact. In a random sample of 18,876 men in the United Kingdom, R. Johnson, Nahmins and Madger (1989) found that 6.1 percent reported "some" homosexual contact over their lifetime, yet only 1.1 percent had been sexually active with more than one same-sex partner in the preceding year.

While it is clear that the homosexual population is more concentrated (larger percentages) in major urban areas around the world, in terms of general population, the percentage is relatively small.

EXPLAINING HOMOSEXUALITY

Explanations about homosexuality come from two basic perspectives: one that focuses on psychosocial factors (nurture) and another that focuses on biological factors (nature). Psychosocial explanations of homosexuality can be further divided into social learning theories and neopsychoanalytic theories.

Social learning theories. There are several social learning theory explanations of homosexuality that have common themes. One theory points to a lack of adequate heterosexual experiences during childhood, therefore reckoning that homosexuality develops out of a deprivation of good heterosexual experiences. According to this view, a young person never learns how to adequately relate to persons of the opposite sex and therefore channels one's efforts toward the same sex. A second explanation is an inverted version of this theory. Here it is presumed that homosexuality results from negative experiences one has with members of the opposite sex. In this case, the young person does relate to opposite-sex persons but experiences a series of negative responses in the process. Since erotic attraction for persons of the opposite sex is spurned, they turn to more satisfying experiences with same-sex persons.

A third explanation has to do with early experiences and contact with homosexuals. Proponents of this theory argue that early sexual contact with a homosexual serves to reframe a young person's sexual orientation. However, since there has been no research to corroborate this idea, it seems highly unlikely. Most lesbians, for example, report having heterosexual sex before their first homosexual experience.

A fourth theory looks at homosexuality with a developmental lens in terms of the rate of sexual maturation in adolescents (Storms 1981). Up until about age 12, both boys and girls are in what is termed a homosocial stage, in which they associate quite exclusively with persons of their own sex. Following puberty, each gender becomes much more interested in the opposite sex. The sex drive of most young people emerges *after* they have left their homosocial stage for the heterosocial stage of adolescence. But for some youth, the sex drive emerges earlier. The explanation proposes that when the sex drive emerges while a youth is still in the homosocial stage (twelve and younger), the youth is more likely to develop a homosexual orientation. Proponents of this view explain that there are more male than female homosexuals precisely because the sex drive among males emerges earlier on the average. Thus, there is a greater pool of boys than girls who begin to experience their sex drive during a time when the vast majority of their social relationships are with persons of the same sex.

A fifth social learning theory suggests persons are more likely to have same sex attractions if they have less-gendered socialization in early childhood and preadolescence. Some research has suggested that this might be most true of a younger brother of older sisters or a younger sister of older brothers. Evidence in support of this explanation is offered by Bearman and Bruckner (2002), who compared same- and opposite-sex twins to test this notion. They report that "adoescent males who are opposite-sex twins are *twice as likely* as expected to report same-sex attractions" (p. 1179).

One can easily recognize that the social learning aspect of these various explanations may seem to make some sense, yet the evidence to support these theories is far from conclusive.

Neopsychoanalytic factors. The most popular explanation of homosexuality, psychoanalytic theory, came in the first half of the twentieth century. According to this theory, the origin of same-sex preference is an aberrant psychosexual development that occurs during the genital stage of development at ages 4 to 6. This is a period when children work through the Oedipus or Electra complexes, in which they have an unconscious desire to defeat their same-sex parent in order to gain exclusive access to their opposite-sex parent. Ironically, if the opposite-sex parent encourages this kind of singular attachment, coupled with a cool and distant relationship with the same-sex parent, the child becomes confused about one's own sexual identity and later on has a deep craving for connection with a person of the same sex.

A major effort to test this psychoanalytic theory of homosexuality was conducted by Irving Bieber (1962, 1976). He compared the family patterns of 106 male homosexuals and 100 male heterosexuals who were receiving psychoanalysis. Bieber found that homosexuals, more than heterosexuals, tended to have a dominant, overprotective and overly close mother along with a weak or passive father. Charlotte Wolff (1971) reported similar conclusions in a study of over a hundred nonpatient lesbians and a matched group of heterosexual women. Wolff's major findings show that homosexual more than heterosexual women were reared in families where the mother was rejecting or indifferent and the father was distant or absent. Wolff concluded that in seeking love from other women, lesbians are really seeking the love they failed to get from their mother. She also theorized that lesbians have difficulty relating to men because they were deprived of a warm, loving relationship with their father.

Several psychologists have offered a revised version of classical Freudian explanations of homosexuality. Two influential writers, Elizabeth Moberly (1983a, 1983b) and Leanne Payne (1984), believe that homosexuality is based on certain deficiencies in the parent-child relationship. The primary cause of homosexuality emerges out of deficits in a child's relationship with the child's parent of the same sex. Parents are normal sources of love to their children, so when love is withheld and replaced with hostility and anger, the same-gender child-parent relationship is gravely disturbed. In such situations, children cannot relate to their same-gender parent, resulting in intrapsychic damage at the deepest level. Moberly is careful to point out that the disruption is not merely due to father absence (which she believes rarely results in such severe woundedness) but an *actively destructive* relationship with the same-sex parent who is present in the home.

The damage caused by such disruption is referred to as *defensive detachment.* Defensive detachment emerges in the form of authority problems between parent and child, along with parental resistance to attachment attempts. A son or daughter who needs the security of an authority figure as parent can be overly dependent and at the same time resistant to bonding with that parent. Defensive detachment leads to an ambivalence toward the same-sex parent, which ultimately shows itself in *avoidance-*

approach conflicts. Such conflict can be portrayed as a push-pull interaction. The child has the desire to be close to the parent, yet when closeness is obtained, the child pushes away in fear of being hurt.

Children need to be attached in healthy ways to the parent of the same sex. Among males, defensive detachment blocks the normal identification process with masculinity, resulting in an expressed effeminacy. Among females, the blockage against normal identification with femininity results in an expressed masculinity. Defensive detachment represents an unmet love-need which, when it reemerges, is known as homosexuality.

Proponents of this neopsychoanalytic theory clearly acknowledge that the desire to fulfill this unmet parent love-need is *natural.* There is nothing "unnatural" about it, until the love-need has such a grip on a person that one compulsively seeks to have this need met through erotic means with a same-sex person. The impulse to eroticize the same-sex love-need is sometimes referred to as *cannibal compulsion.* Like the cannibal who desires to eat the flesh of a strong person in order to gain strength, this theory believes that the homosexual male wants to sexually consume the same-sex person who possesses the traits he desires. For this reason, it is argued, homosexual men are attracted to strong, good-looking, self-assured men. This is the image they want to incorporate into themselves. The homosexual, then, has normal needs that he tries to meet through sexual involvement with a same-sex person. However, the lack of fulfillment as a child has now become an abnormal obsession that cannot be fulfilled through sexual encounters alone. All the frantic search for sex never really compensates for the deeper deprivation, which is satisfied only by a secure emotional bonding and affection.

Although proponents of neopsychoanalytic explanations offer a wealth of clinical case studies to support their theory, empirical research to back up these explanations of homosexuality has been lacking: sample sizes are small and nonrandom.

One study compared the family backgrounds of heterosexual and homosexual females in five countries on twelve familial factors that would be relevant to neopsychoanalytic theory (Whitam, Daskalos and Mathy 1995). Of these twelve familial factors—normal family, absent mother/father, warmer parent, stronger parent, hostile father, hostile mother, detached/distant father, detached/distant mother, seductive mother, seductive father, father's attitude toward sex, mother's attitude toward sex—

five were found to be somewhat significant but inconsistent in all five societies. The study concluded that there is "little support for the role of familial factors in the development of female homosexual orientation" (1995:59). Another study comparing samples of homosexual and heterosexual females found no difference in childhood experience of physical or sexual abuse (Steele 1992).

In one of the most comprehensive studies based on interviews with 979 homosexual and 477 heterosexual men and women, Bell, Weinberg and Hammersmith (1981) reported that their data do not support traditional psychoanalytic explanations of homosexuality. Nor does their study support psychosocial explanations of homosexuality that claim lack of adequate heterosexual experiences during childhood, negative experiences with members of the opposite sex, or early experiences and contact with homosexuals.

The most consistent finding in this study was that one-fourth of the gay males in their sample reported a tendency *not* to engage in traditional masculine types of behavior as children. A common response by gay men was a preference for stereotypical girl activities, coupled with the feeling that they did not feel very masculine. The one social psychological factor that seemed to be somewhat important is that homosexual men, more than heterosexual men, reported having a cold and detached relationship with their father. Lesbians reported having engaged in homosexual activity during adolescence, and they also expressed gender nonconformity or dissatisfaction with their gender more often than the heterosexual women in the sample.

Although these studies show no convincing evidence to support these more psychodamic theories, Whitehead (1996) points out that survey-based studies are inadequate to test for the importance of familial contributions to homosexuality. He concludes that "family factors and childhood experiences are still important in the genesis of homosexuality" (p. 322) and can be demonstrated through in-depth, qualitatively based research. The question of research support for neopsychoanalytic theory aside, proponents have developed a commendable redemptive ministry to homosexuals, which we will discuss in the next chapter.

Biological factors. Support for a biological explanation of homosexuality can be categorized as genetic, constitutional, endocrinological or ethological (Herrn 1995). Though no genes have been yet identified, it still is possible to state inferences about the role that genes play in determining sexual orientation. Twin and family studies have demonstrated that genetic factors do explain at least a portion of the variability in sexual orientation.

Beginning in the 1950s, genetic studies reported that identical twins were *usually* of the same sexual orientation (Kallman 1952). This finding was similar to what Buhrich, Bailey and Martin (1991) learned in a study comparing 56 gay men with an identical twin brother and 54 gay men with a nonidentical (fraternal) twin brother. They found that 52 percent of identical twins were themselves gay while only 22 percent of the fraternal twins were gay. In addition, only 11 percent of adoptive brothers of gay men were gay.

Other studies have discovered that homosexuals have a significantly higher proportion of homosexual siblings than heterosexuals (Bailey and Bell 1993), a finding that could be due to either familial or biological influences. Genetic studies appear to indicate that both male and female homosexuality run in families, although it remains unclear whether both run in the same families. Monozygotic, or identical, twins show a higher likelihood of both being homosexual than dizygotic, or nonidentical, twins.

One of the more interesting areas of research is the attempt to show correlations between homosexuality among males and fraternal birth order and handedness. At the time of this writing, both Ray Blanchard and Anthony Bogaert have authored or coauthored a number of articles detailing support for these correlations. Since the results presented are ever changing, we will need to be content with the evidence given in the two latest articles. Blanchard, Cantor, Bogaert, Breelove and Lee (2006:405) report that "the typical positive correlation between homosexuality and greater number of older brothers holds only for right-handed males." At other stages in their research, it was reported that such factors as youngest birth order with biologically related older brothers are part of the mix in predicting homosexuality. Bogaert (2006) interprets the finding that having only biological older brothers predicted men's sexual orientation, regardless of the amount of time reared with these siblings, as meaning that such results "strongly suggest a prenatal origin to the fraternal birth-order effect" (2006:10771). What accounts for this effect is still unknown, although Bogaert speculates that a series of male fetuses somehow results in a hormone transfer in the biological constitution of younger sons.

Bearman and Bruckner (2002:1179) discount these findings by claiming that their own data falsify the hormone transfer hypothesis. Instead, they point to childhood socialization as a better explanation as to why younger brothers of older brothers may have a greater tendency for same-sex attraction.

Hamer (1993) claimed some progress in showing a linkage between DNA markers on the X-chromosome and male sexual orientation. In 2003, Mustanski and Bailey deduced that no specific genes had been identified in either males or females. Though there has been some indication in males that a chromosomal region (not a gene), X_q28, may play a role in male sexual orientation, in females no chromosomal regions have yet been identified as potential indicators of homosexuality. Although further research is needed before any definitive conclusions can be made, they believe that genes are more influential in male sexual orientation than they are in female sexual orientation.

Veniegas and Conley (2000) observe that there has been far less homosexual orientation research done on genetic contributors to females and that there is no conclusive evidence that female homosexual orientation is caused by genes. They state that while there is some reason to believe that male sexual orientation may be linked to genetics, there has been no indication that female sexual orientation is due to biological factors.

In their comprehensive review of biological contributors to homosexuality, Mustanski, Chivers and Bailey (2002) discuss the history of studies of homosexuality and genetic factors. Some of the earliest theories were tested in experiments involving animals. One such theory that has become a bedrock theory of genetic causation of homosexuality is neurohormonal theory. This theory states that homosexuality is due to atypical sex hormone (androgen) levels in utero. Therefore, the fetus receives either too little or too much androgen or testosterone. More specifically, the theory states that male homosexuality is dependent upon low prenatal androgen levels and that female homosexuality depends on high prenatal androgen levels. During the original experiment, variations of androgen were shown to cause female sexual behaviors in male rats and male sexual behaviors in female rats.

Researchers thus postulated that gay men may have decreased levels of circulating androgen levels and that lesbian women may have increased levels of androgen. However, research suggests little or no difference in circulating androgen levels between gay and heterosexual men. The results of experiments involving animals should be taken with reserve since animal studies do not perfectly correlate with nor can be generalized to human behavior. Certain behaviors are specific to the species, such as mounting and lordosis in rats, and humans are far more complex in their sexual behaviors.

Veniegas and Conley (2000) write about the impact of a trend in which public opinion has become more and more open toward homosexuality as a lifestyle that is determined genetically. Over the years, this public opinion most likely leads to increased public acceptance of homosexuality. For instance, Mustanski and Bailey (2003) found an association between the belief that homosexuality is genetically determined with less negative attitudes toward gay people. Still, public opinion is quite varied when it comes to the acceptability of homosexuality, especially for those who view it as a moral and/or religious issue.

LeVay's (1991) research pointed to anatomical differences between certain cells in a portion of the brains (hypothalamus) of homosexuals and heterosexuals that could account for differences in sexual orientation. Researchers question this as a causal factor, however, since many of the homosexuals in the sample had died of AIDS, suggesting that the anatomical differences between gays and straights could very well have been attributed to AIDS.

Bailey and Pillard (1991) speculate that a genetic contribution to homosexuality could range from 30 to 70 percent. In a review of studies on the cause of homosexuality, Rahman and Wilson (2003) conclude that 50-60 percent of sexual orientation is due to genetics. Depending on one's preconceived views, these figures may appear to be rather high or rather low. Inversely, one could speculate that sociocultural factors contribute in the vicinity of 50 percentof the explanations of sexual orientation.

Writing in the *Scientific American,* the psychiatrist William Byne (1994:50) concludes: "Genetic studies suffer from the inevitable confounding of nature and nurture that plagues attempts to study heritability of psychological traits. Investigations of the brain rely on doubtful hypotheses about differences between the brains of men and women. Biological mechanisms that have been proposed to explain the existence of gay men cannot be generalized to explain the existence of lesbians (whom studies have largely neglected)." Byne and Parsons observe "that although recent studies postulate biological factors as the primary basis for sexual orientation, there is no evidence at present to substantiate a biological theory, just as there is no compelling evidence to support any singular psychosocial explanation" (1993:228).

Based on an overview of the current state of the art of biomedical research on homosexuality, Schuklenk and Ristow state that "the cause(s) of homosexuality, is (are) unknown and biomedical research has failed to provide evidence for a possible causation of homosexuality" (1996:5).

A number of researchers contest that although homosexuality may have a biological base, where biological factors are important, they will more likely contribute to general tendencies rather than determine sexual preference. So, if there is a biological precurser that encourages homosexual behavior, it will surely be combined with psychological and cultural factors. In other words, prenatal hormone effects are interactive with postnatal socialization influences.

It seems that DNA research is progressing rapidly, and researchers may have the capacity in the near future to map out sex chromosome in males and females to the point that they will be able to pinpoint which chromosomal regions and genes are connected explicitly to homosexual orientation. Until that day, when it comes to biological indicators, all talk of specifics is merely guesswork and speculation. Though it is possible to look at genetic characteristics that appear to correlate with homosexuality, they cannot completely identify why they are related. At this point, research can only link them to a neurohormonal theory that has not proved to be accurate in testing thus far. It is as if genetic researchers are trying to put two pieces of a puzzle together but are missing the connecting piece and thus can only imagine what that piece might look like. Therefore, it is only when that piece is actually found that the picture will be more conclusive.

One day there will be more complete understanding to what extent and how genetic factors influence homosexuality, but until then it is best to acknowledge what is known and not to pretend to know more than that. While family and twin studies help us consider genetic variables in the equation, we still do not know how big a role genetic variables play. Every theory is just that, *a theory* and not fact. At this point, there is no substantial evidence that neurohormonal theory or any other theory has the answer.

So, we end this speculative discussion on the relationship between genes and sexual orientation by quoting Francis Collins, the director of The National Human Genome Research Institute:

> As gentic predispositions to everything from cancer or diabetes to novelty-seeing behavior or homosexuality are being reported almost daily in the scientific literature, a new and dangerous brand of genetic determinism is subtly invading our culture. Carried to its extreme, this "Genes R Us" mentality would deny the value of social interventions to maximize individual potential, destablize many of our institutions, and even deny the existence of free will. Surely a world in which every aspect of human behavior is hard-wired into our genes cannot comfortably exist with the concept of personal responsibility and free will to try to follow the moral law of right and wrong which people of faith believe has been written into our hearts by a loving and holy God. (Collins 2006)

EXPLAINING HOMOSEXUALITY: AN INTEGRATIVE MODEL

Given the present state of knowledge on sexual orientation, we believe that no one theory or set of explanations, in and of itself, is currently capable of explaining the emergence of homosexuality. This conclusion is presented in an article by J. D. Haynes in a special issue of the *Journal of Homosexuality* on "Sex, cells, and same-sex desire: The biology of sexual preference": "No one theory has proved to be satisfactory" (1995:91).

Whereas twins studies have been used to support a genetic explanation of homosexuality, Bearman and Bruckner (2002) show that although "adolescent males who are opposite-sex twins are twice as likely as expected to report same-sex attraction . . . the pattern of concordance (similarity across pairs) of same-sex preference for sibling pairs does not suggest genetic influence independent of social context" (p. 2279). Beyond considering only genetic and hormonal influences, Bearman and Bruckness argue that "early childhood and preadolescence shapes subsequent same-sex romantic preferences" (p. 2279).

A report on the preliminary results of a national survey of 508 psychiatrists' attitudes concerning the etiology of male homosexuality is likewise inconclusive. Among the twelve theories evaluated, the five highest-ranking theories are biological rather than psychological. Genetic inheritance theory was the highest ranking, followed by prenatal hormone development theory. The highest-ranking psychological theory was the dominant mother theory, followed by the weak father theory (Gallagher, McFalls and Vreeland 1993:1).

Perhaps because of vested interests, it is difficult for many to move beyond single-factor explanations of homosexuality. As the neuroscientist G. Bermant stated in 1995, "Unfortunately, the physical versus mental and nature versus nurture controversies remain alive, well, and mischievous in regard to the correct understanding of human sexuality" (p. 343). Therefore, we approach the topic with a healthy suspicion of any person who claims to know *the* cause of homosexuality. Instead, we promote a model that integrates both biological and psychosocial factors. Along with Bermant, we believe that "sexuality emerges from the interdependencies of biology, awareness, and the facts and artifacts of public life" (1995:343). In an effort to take all of the accumulated evidence into account, we offer the following considerations, which also must be taken as tentative and subject to progressive refinements as additional knowledge is accumulated in the coming years regarding the explanation of sexual orientation.

First, *biology is a necessary contributor and the sociocultural milieu a sufficient contributor.* In chapter one we suggest that biological factors are usually considered *necessary* and sociocultural factors *sufficient* contributors to the formation of human sexuality. We now use this concept to explain homosexual orientation. Byne and Parsons cogently express a similar point of view: "Genes or hormones do not specify sexual orientation per se, but instead bias particular personality traits and therefore influence the manner in which an individual and his or her environment interact as sexual orientation and other personality characteristics unfold developmentally" (1993:236-37). In a similar manner, Paul suggests that any potential biological factors contributing to sexual orientation "must be mediated by a complex sequence of experiences and psychosocial factors" (1993:41).

Using figure 5.1 as a reference point, we suggest that an individual must possess, as a necessary contributor, a genetic or hormonal package, either at birth or through the process of physical maturation, that renders a person susceptible to a homosexual orientation. It will be highly improbable that individuals without this package will ever develop a homosexual orientation because their genetic/hormonal package is loaded in another direction. The genetic or hormonal makeup is therfore considered a necessary condition that needs to be present in order for a homosexual orientation to emerge. At the same time we propose that biological factors are insufficient in and of themselves to produce a homosexual orientation.

What is therefore needed besides a biological predisposition toward homosexuality (the necessary contributing factor) is the presence of psychosocial factors (the sufficient cause). As represented in figure 5.1, the proportion of necessary (biological) contributors to a homosexual orientation is represented from *Low* at the bottom to *High* at the top. The proportion of sufficient (psychosocial) contributors to a homosexual orientation is represented from *Low* at the left to *High* at the right.

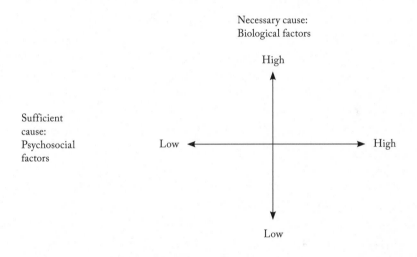

Figure 5.1. **An integrated model of authentic human sexuality**

When there is a high presence of a biological package rendering one susceptible to homosexuality, combined with a high incidence of psychosocial experiences, there is a greater likelihood for a homosexual orientation (upper right corner of fig. 5.1). Persons who are low in biological susceptibility and low in incidence of psychosocial experiences are unlikely to develop a homosexual orientation (lower left corner).

This chart also suggests different "paths" to homosexuality, or possibly even different types of homosexuals. The upper left corner of the figure represents individuals who could potentially be susceptible to a homosexual orientation, but due to psychosocial contributors do not follow through with a homosexual orientation. The lower right corner represents individuals who are exposed to all of the psychosocial conditions that could lead to homosexual orientation, yet they do not have a homosexual orientation because there are insufficient biological-genetic factors.

Daryl Bem (1996) has recently presented a developmental theory of sexual orientation that gives a similar interpretation to the role of biological and sociocultural factors. We present the basic points of his theory in summary form, but recommend a thorough reading of this creative piece of work. We also observe that his theory has been criticized because it does not address or explain lesbian behavior.

Bem's theory is based on an understanding of how a temporal sequence of events leads to the development of sexual orientation. Bem believes that five sequential events act as *causal antecedents* that culminate in a natural erotic/romantic attraction to opposite- or same-sex persons. "The first causal antecedent consists of biological variables such as genes and prenatal hormones that code for childhood temperaments like aggression or activity level" (1996:321). Bem is careful to say that these biological factors do not code for sexual orientation directly but, as we shall see, are the beginning of a chain of sequential events that eventually lead to one's sexual orientation.

Childhood temperaments (the second sequential phase) predispose some children to enjoy active contact and competitive play, which come to be regarded as "male-typical" activity. Other children prefer quiet social interaction and play, which are associated as "female-typical" activities. The sex-typical/atypical activity and playmate preferences lead to the third sequential stage. Children seek out other children who share similar activity preferences. Those who prefer sex-typical activities and same-sex playmates are defined as gender conforming, while children who prefer sex-atypical activities and opposite-sex playmates are referred to as gender nonconforming.

This sets the stage for the fourth important sequential event in the development of sexual orientation. Children who are gender conforming will feel different from opposite-sex peers, "perceiving them as dissimilar, unfamiliar, and exotic" (Bem 1996:321). Correspondingly, gender-nonconforming children will feel different from and even alienated from same-sex peers, perceiving them as dissimilar, unfamiliar and exotic.

When these feelings of dissimilarity and unfamiliarity produce heightened autonomic arousal, the fifth important sequential event occurs. Chronologically, this corresponds to latency, that period of time when male-typical boys feel antipathy when girls are present. Boys who are too much like the unfamiliar and rather strange girls are labeled as "wimps" or "sissies." Female-typical boys feel apprehensive in the presence of other boys. Also, nonconforming girls are ostracized by their female peers because of their "tomboy" behavior. Nonconforming children come to experience a strong sense of fear or anger in the presence of their own gender. Both conforming and nonconforming children experience "heightened, nonspecific autonomic arousal in the presence of peers from whom [they] feel difference" (Bem 1996:321), though among most children this arousal will not be consciously felt.

The sixth event, sexual orientation, is the emergence of erotic/romantic attraction to opposite- or same-sex persons. This occurs when childhood autonomic arousal is transformed into erotic/romantic attraction. In short, the exotic, that which is viewed as different, is transformed into the erotic.

The strength of this model is that it moves discussion beyond a single-factor explanation of homosexuality. Further movement is needed, however, because models such as this are limited by being *linear* and *additive*. Bem's theory, for example, is linear in the sense that biological factors are considered to make important initial contributions to *subsequent* psychosocial factors. This results in overstating the importance and invariance of biological factors as contributors to sexual orientation. In the interactive model of human sexual development that we introduced in chapter one and which we will apply more directly to the development of sexual orientation below, we count the biological and sociocultural variables as ongoing, continuous processes.

An interactive developmental model. We propose that a more adequate explanation of homosexual orientation conceptualizes biological and psychosocial factors as *interactively* related, meaning that they are mutually affecting and being affected by each other simultaneously and continually. Biological factors do not just make their appearance at stage one; rather, the biological organism is continually changing throughout the human life cycle. Temperament and involvement in sex-typical or atypical activity may be formed in childhood, but it is far from fixed and capable of dramatic changes at different stages of life.

We believe it is necessary to have a model recognizing biological variables that "kick in" the same way that the sociocultural variables "kick in" throughout the human developmental process. Therefore, we propose that the effects of biological and sociocultural factors are not additive, but *interactive* in their effect on the development of sexual orientation. These factors both affect and are affected by each other on a continuing basis throughout the human developmental process.

A homosexual orientation emerges as part of a developmental process in which both biological factors and psychosocial factors kick in or fail to kick in at crucial points in the individual life developmental process. Figure 2.2 (see page 31) represents our attempt to graphically illustrate this interactive developmental process.

At conception, genetic factors may contribute to sexual development. During the prenatal period, both congenital conditions (environmental) and endocrinological factors may interact in forming the sexual development of the unborn child. During the early years of life, the quality of the emotional bonding with parents contribute to sexual development. But even here, genetic or hormonal factors may have indirect effects.

As Bem (1996) suggests, due to the genetic/hormonal makeup, a young boy may show signs of gentleness and sensitivity rather than aggressive "masculine" behavior. His father or peers may define him as "effeminate" and try to "correct" this behavior by taunting, teasing or general condemnation of his behavior. This results in the boy feeling rejected and shamed by both father and peers. The effect of this reaction compounds the problem, leading the son to seek fulfillment in his relationships with male friends. Correspondingly, a girl who acts like a tomboy may experience similar treatment. However, we move beyond Bem's "one-way" explanation by considering how psychosocial and biological factors interact with each other throughout the process.

Biological and psychosocial factors contribute both independently and interactively to the nature of a child's sexual development. Sexual abuse during any period of childhood, as well as hormone activation or lack thereof during puberty, can both independently and interactively affect sexual development. By the end of puberty, the bulk of factors contributing to the development of sexual orientation may have played their role, but the interactive effect of biological and psychosocial factors continues throughout an individual's life span.

Human agency. Although the next chapter will focus on a Christian response to homosexuality, before ending our discussion of the factors that contribute to homosexuality, we want to return to the idea of human agency introduced in chapter one. This centers on the question of whether a homosexual orientation is a matter of choosing to have sexual desire for a same-sex person. The short answer is that although a person decides whether or not to act on these desires, a person with a homosexual orientation is *not* responsible for the sexual desire any more than a heterosexual person is responsible for sexual desire directed toward an opposite-sex person.

This is not to say that human beings are merely passive agents and therefore pawns of biological and psychosocial influences. Human beings come to be choice-making creatures through the process of moral development. This primarily involves learning the meaning of sexuality in a social context. As individuals grasp the spiritual meaning of sexuality in terms of being drawn into significant relationships with others, they develop a self-structure that becomes increasingly capable of making choices. As we develop, we are not merely reactive to the forces of environment but also have a capacity to act on our environment and even participate in the creation of that environment. In addition, persons are highly influenced by their religious values, commitment and morality in relating to their Creator. The effect of a personal relationship with the living God and putting Christ at the center of their lives has tremdendous power in determining a person's ultimate choices about their sexuality.

An understanding of the development of sexual orientation, as with the development of any other aspect of the psychosocial self, must acknowledge human agency within that human being. This assumption is made not only by theologians but also by behavioral psychologists. In social learning theory, which is the theoretical offspring of behaviorism, deterministic assumptions are rejected. The major contributor to social learning theory, Albert Bandura, allows for human agency in what he refers to as reciprocal determinism:

> In their transactions with the environment, people are not simply reactors to external stimulation. . . . The extraordinary capacity of humans to use symbols enables them to engage in reflective thought, rather than having to perform possible options and suffer the consequences of thoughtless action. By altering their immediate environment, by creating cognitive self-inducements, and by arranging conditional incentives for themselves, people can exercise some influence over their own behavior. An act therefore includes among its determinants self-produced influences. (1978:345)

We hasten to add that social learning theory does not view human agency as a radical freedom, but more in terms of individuals having choices within a range of possibilities. Bandura concludes, "Within the social learning framework, freedom is defined in terms of the number of options available to people and the right to exercise them. The more behavioral alternatives and social prerogatives people have, the greater is their freedom of action" (1974:865). We believe that a theological discussion of human freedom must take into account the evidence that both biological and sociocultural factors can greatly expand or limit human choices that are framed in terms of human freedom. In that regard, differences in human constitutions, which reflect biological and sociocultural influences, mean that some individuals are more free than others.

We suggest that biological and sociocultural contributors to human sexuality, as applied to an understanding of human sexual development, operate to either increase or decrease the range of choices individuals have in regard to their sexuality. Some individuals are more limited in their range of sexual choices due to the limiting conditions set by biology and social environment. Freedom in making sexual choices can be limited in a variety of ways. Behavioral deficits restrict possible choices and may curtail opportunities in realizing one's possibilities. Growing up in an emotionally cold or hostile social environment can produce internal fears and stringent self-censuring ideas that restrict the effective range of activities and possibilities. We suggest that an array of sexual problems and addictions can be of this sort, and sex therapy or spiritual healing may become an opportunity to restore or expand one's personal choices and freedom.

A truly integrative theory of homosexuality will go beyond biological and psychosocial factors as the only focus. The development of moral character and responsible choice is a crucial aspect of sexual maturity and authenticity for all persons. Although deficiencies in biopsychosocial input present certain challenges and struggles for individuals as they seek sexual congruence and authenticity, everyone must come to grips with the deeper moral and spiritual meaning involved in sexual decision making.

God created human beings as choice-making creatures with the ability to act as well as react. Human beings are not only acted upon; they are also capable of making needed adjustments to biological and sociopsychological constraints. This brings us face-to-face with the more difficult question about how persons with homosexual or bisexual orientations make responsible choices about sexual behavior. In the following chapter we address this more directly and present a Christian response to homosexuality as well.

FOR FURTHER READING

Mustanski, B., and J. Bailey. 2003. A therapist's guide to the genetics of human sexual orientation. *Sexual and Relationship Therapy* 18:429-36.

Mustanski, B., M. Chivers and J. Bailey. 2002. A critical review of recent biological research on human sexual orientation. *Annual Review of Sex Research* 13:89-140.

The Great Debate

6

Homosexuality

A Christian Response

A serious issue being debated in churches today is how the Christian community should respond to homosexuality and homosexual people. Given the complexity of the issues and the competing explanations about the causes of homosexuality, it is not surprising that vastly different positions are taken by Christians within and between denominations. The responses generally reflect a person's understanding of what causes homosexuality along with one's beliefs about what Scripture teaches. Having considered various explanations of homosexuality in the previous chapter, we shall now focus on the specific biblical references relevant to homosexuality. Then we will describe various ministry approaches.

Our interpretation of Scripture about homosexuality is usually intertwined with our view of the biological and social scientific explanations of homosexuality. Personal bias and values are also persuasive factors that enter into the mix. For instance, though conservative Christians often accept biological explanations for gender differences, they tend to reject biological explanations of homosexuality; liberal Christians may reject biological explanations for gender differences but are more prone to accept these explanations for homosexuality. Before elaborating on how a

Christian defends a particular position, we focus on the key references in the Bible concerning homosexuality.

WHAT SCRIPTURE SAYS AND HOW IT IS INTERPRETED

Many biblical passages deal with sexuality in general, but there are only five key specific references to homosexual behavior. The Bible makes no definite statement about homosexuality as an orientation, but only about homosexual behavior. The widely differing ethical positions held within the Christian community center on these few verses, and interpretations are often hotly debated. In presenting the following biblical references, we will limit our comments to contextual observations, reserving exegetical interpretations for the section in the summary on alternative responses to homosexuality.

The earliest scriptural reference to same-gender sexual behavior occurs in the story of Sodom and Gomorrah in Genesis 19, which describes the depravity of this community. God had confided in Abraham that these cities would be destroyed because of their sins. Lot, a godly man, offered his hospitality and therefore his protection to the two angels sent by God to investigate the situation in Sodom and Gomorrah. The wicked men of the city proceeded to surround his house, demanding that these two strangers be released to them to suffer a degrading rape. Lot refused to let his guests undergo the humiliation and violence of this act of homosexual rape. If we allow Scripture to interpret Scripture, we observe that in the four later references about the destruction of Sodom and Gomorrah, homosexuality is not specifically mentioned as the reason for God's judgment. God had been long-suffering over the four hundred years these cities' residents chose to reject God and follow their own ways. They warranted God's judgment and were conquered and destroyed. Ezekiel mentions God's rejection of Sodom and Gomorrah, and the book of Jude refers to the sexual immorality and unnatural lusts of Sodom and Gomorrah. According to discoveries of archaeologists, promiscuity, incest, pedophilia and bestiality were common practices during this time. The homosexual behavior was condemned by God as one of the many sins and should not be elevated to a significance that God does not emphasize. The focus is on the despicable gang rape, shame and humiliation as the condemned sin.

Peter refers to the condemnation of these cities and the ungodly people who inhabited them, speaking of their lawless deeds as well as their indulging in depraved lust and despising authority (2 Pet 2:6-10). God rescued Lot, a righteous man who had endured the torment of living among lawless people with such distorted values. Here is an example where the Lord delivered godly people, punishing the unrighteous for their reprehensible, exploitative acts and holding them accountable until the day of judgment.

In Judges 19 violent rape is described as a despicable evil. By this time in Israel's history, many of them had adopted immoral behaviors (including sex acts) of the Canaanites. God's judgment and comment on this account is not a single condemnation of homosexual behaviors, but of a total moral anarchy in which "every man did what was right in his own eyes" (Judg 17:6; 21:25 RSV).

The Holiness Code in Leviticus addresses same-gender sexual behavior. Leviticus 18:22 reads, "Do not lie with a man as one lies with a woman; that is detestable," and Leviticus 20:13 directs Israel, "If a man lies with a man as one lies with a woman, both of them have done what is detestable." According to the Jewish code, "They must be put to death; their blood will be on their own heads" (Lev 20:13). Although this was a clear and serious judgment, Christians disagree on the application of Levitical law since Christ came to abolish the law. There are other parts of the Holiness Codes that are no longer observed in today's world because of Paul's teachings about our newfound freedom in Christ.

Other passages in the New Testament that may apply to homosexual behavior are lists of various immoral sexual acts. In 1 Corinthians 6:9-10 we read, "Neither the sexually immoral nor idolaters nor adulterers nor male prostitutes nor homosexual offenders nor thieves nor the greedy nor drunkards nor slanderers nor swindlers will inherit the kingdom of God." Some take these words literally, while others believe that the two Greek words, *malakoi* and *arsenokoitai*, from which "male prostitutes," "homosexual offenders" and "perverts" are translated, have imprecise meanings. Some think that this refers specifically to sexual relationships between men and boys, which would be coercive and perverted. First Timothy 1:10 says that the law was made "for adulterers and perverts, for slave traders and liars and perjurers," indicating that it is the power differential of these sexual acts that make them despicable. Taking a power advantage over another is the perversion that is rightly condemned here.

The most noteworthy New Testament reference to same-sex behavior is found in Romans 1:26-27, "God gave them over to shameful lusts. Even their women exchanged natural relations for unnatural ones. In the same way the men also abandoned natural relations with women and were inflamed with lust for one another. Men committed indecent acts with other men, and received in themselves the due penalty for their perversion." These verses quite clearly address homosexual behavior, yet the language of natural and unnatural become part of the debated interpretation. For some theologians, *unnatural* refers to perverse and hedonistic sexual practices, *not* the mutually loving interaction that occurs between same-sex consenting adults. Therefore it is argued that the persons with a homosexual orientation are *not* going against *natural* tendencies. Yet one must then define perverse sexual behaviors for both heterosexual and homosexual people to determine what authentic sexuality means in God's grand design. In the following section, we consider some alternative responses to homosexuality.

Since the Scripture does not address homosexual orientation directly but focuses on homosexual behavior, it behooves Christians to refrain from condemning homosexual orientation as a sin. In terms of homosexual behavior, there are differences of opinion on whether all homosexual behavior would be defined as sin. Some make an exception for homosexuals involved in an exclusive committed and mutually loving relationship. Just as they condemn promiscuous and hedonistic homosexual behaviors in heterosexuals, so would they condemn this as sin for homosexuals. Others believe the Bible teaches that all homosexual behavior is sinful, and therefore all persons must refrain from homosexual erotic activities. As mentioned in previous chapters, one's sexuality as a person with homosexual orientation can be expressed in nonerotic, deeply satisfying friendships, just as is heterosexual relationships. In this next section we present alternative responses to homosexuality.

ALTERNATIVE RESPONSES TO HOMOSEXUALITY

There is a gamut of opinion regarding homosexuality within the Christian community. Here we consider four alternative responses. Figure 6.1 represents a continuum along which these four categories of responses to homosexuality can be understood. We will briefly describe the positions at each of the extremes and then present more detailed descriptions of the two central positions.

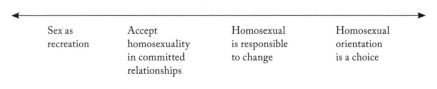

Figure 6.1. Alternative responses to homosxuality

Responses at the extreme. Represented at the extreme left of figure 6.1 is the view that sex is a pleasure to be enjoyed in the same way one enjoys recreation. For both heterosexuals and homosexuals, sexual intercourse is held to be ethical and legitimate if it is between consenting adults. In this position's most extreme form, sex is a desired good in and of itself and there is no need for commitment or even affection between persons. This hedonistic position on homosexuality goes beyond even the most liberal of Christian theologies.

The position at the far right of the figure represents persons who believe that a homosexual orientation (not just behavior) is a personal sin. In this extreme view, every homosexual impulse is an individual choice, and therefore the person is completely responsible for one's sexual orientation as well as sexual behavior. A more tempered view recognizes potential psychosocial contributors to homosexuality, but discounts the magnitude of those influences in the face of the individual responsibility, even for one's formation and development. People holding this view believe that homosexuals should be judged and condemned and even go so far to suggest that the AIDS epidemic is evidence of God's judgment on homosexuality.

Committed gay relationships. The position just left of center contends that homosexual orientation is not a choice but a biological given. Therefore, homosexual erotic expression in a committed, monogamous relationship is affirmed as morally right and good. This is the position generally defended within more liberal Christian theologies. Although most mainline Protestant denominations have not formally adopted this position, nearly all are currently debating the issue. Strongly organized proponents of this position are pressuring denominations to accept this stance under the theme of biblical justice, calling their congregations "reconciling churches."

The injustice experienced by women in patriarchal society and the injustice experienced by gays in a homophobic society are equated as comparable examples of injustices that need to be eradicated. The logical extension of this view is the formal legitimization of same-sex marriages or unions. Some churches have established lifelong commitment ceremonies for gay couples who desire to make such a covenant, sanctioned and supported by their community of believers.

A number of openly gay Christians find acceptance within these local worshiping communities while others choose to worship in a gay church. The Universal Fellowship of Metropolitan Community Church was established in the early 1970s by Reverend Troy Perry, a homosexual Pentecostal minister in Los Angeles. These congregations have spread throughout the United States.

Due to the high view of scriptural authority held by the founders of the gay church, the theology is decidedly more conservative than some more liberal denominations. One major difference between gay churches and other evangelical churches has to do with the interpretation of Scripture when it comes to the promotion and defense of homosexual behavior. The gay church takes great pains to explain its understanding of the key biblical passages on which its morality on homosexuality rests. For example, in response to the creation story, they acknowledge the creation purpose of male and female interaction, but believe that it happens as they are united in a spiritual realm as brothers and sisters in Christ. This is true of unmarried heterosexuals who develop spiritual and emotional connection in the body of Christ as well.

The argument in response to the Sodom and Gomorrah account is that God's judgment was upon the people for the violent rape and inhospitality of the people rather than the specific act of homosexual behavior. Hospitality was viewed as a sacred duty in ancient Hebrew culture; the degrading sexual acts were thus of great offense to God. The intent of these heterosexual men of the city was to sexually rape the strangers to humiliate and shame them. This is a far cry, they argue, from being involved in a loving, mutually expressive homosexual relationship.

Those who accept homosexual behavior between consenting adults generally believe that a person's sexual orientation is determined quite early in life. Thus, sexual expression between same-sex persons is accepted as a normal and essential part of one's life. Since it is "natural" for persons with a homosexual orientation to express themselves sexually with members of the same sex, it would be completely "unnatural" for them to engage in heterosexual union. The scriptural passage in Romans 1 condemning "unnatural" affections between people would therefore not apply to them. They believe this passage condemns persons who are heterosexual by nature but turn against their natural sexual inclinations in sexual behaviors. They further assert that the major thesis in Romans 1 is Paul's declaration that *all* people have sinned and are in need of salvation, rather than the specific issue of homosexuality. They point to Jesus as one who offers grace and acceptance rather than judgment and condemnation.

The gay church condones homosexual erotic expression in compliance with a standard of committed monogamous relationships for both heterosexual and homosexual couples. They believe it is against God's purpose to engage in casual or promiscuous sexual lifestyles. Though the gay church teaches sympathy and care for AIDS victims, they join others in seeing the AIDS epidemic as a tragic result of promiscuous misuse of a God-given sexuality.

Stranger at the Gate describes the depth and sincerity of one person's genuine faith, as well as his tormented experiences while growing up in a society that condemns a Christian with a homosexual orientation. Mel White, a well-known evangelical Christian who grew up in a Christian home, was deeply involved in the church and served as a Youth for Christ leader, seminary professor, producer of evangelistic films, pastor of a large church, and ghostwriter for such people as Billy Graham and Jerry Falwell. After years of struggling to change his sexual orientation, from the time he was a young boy until he was an adult ready to end his life in suicide, Mel writes, "I can't explain why the comfort I find in a gay man's arms is greater than I could find in those of a heterosexual woman. It's not an act of sex. It's an act of love. It's not about sexual gratification. It's about spiritual survival" (M. White 1994:164). After a twenty-five-year marriage, two children and several grandchildren later, White came to the conclusion that one's sexual orientation must be accepted as a gift of God so that one can exercise that gift with integrity, creativity and responsibility. Lila, his former wife, agrees and supports Mel with this testimony: "After all those decades of trying, we discovered that no one can choose or change his or her sexual orientation. Mel had no choice about being a homosexual. Believe me, if he had a choice, I know he would have chosen his marriage, his family and his unique ministry; for Mel's values, like most of the gays and lesbians I know, are the same as mine and my heterosexual friends: love, respect, commitment, nurture, responsibility, honesty, and integrity" (1994:5). Mel laments that so many Christians deny historic, cultural and linguistic evidence that would help them see the meaning of the biblical passages on homosexuality in a different light.

With the formation of the interfaith organization Soulforce, White and other gay Christians have increasingly sought to convince the Christian community that the acceptance of homosexuals is a civil rights issue. Soulforce's strategy for accomplishing this is reflected in its mission statement: "The purpose of soulforce is freedom for lesbian, gay, bisexual, and transgender people from religious and political oppression through the practice of relentless nonviolent resistance" (<http://www.soulforce .org/).

In his book *Religion Gone Bad: The Hidden Dangers of the Christian Right* (2006), White forcefully compares the treatment of homosexuals by the "religious right" to the Nazis' treatment of Jews and homosexuals. Citing both Martin Luther King and Mahatma Gandhi, White argues for a forceful but nonviolent approach to change the hearts of conservative Christians.

Sexual abstinence or change. The position just right of center as represented in figure 6.1 holds the view that although homosexuals are not responsible for their orientation, they are responsible for any acting out of their homosexual impulses. This is the most popular position taken by those from orthodox and evangelical theologies. Christians with a homosexual orientation in this category are commited to changing to a heterosexual orientation through God's transformation of their lives. They may enter marriages and enjoy family life as they believe God intended them to do. On the other hand, those not able to change their orientation sufficiently as gay Christians are to choose sexual abstinence. Just as single heterosexual Christians desire sexual erotic expression and marriage, they must adhere to a standard of abstinence as well.

Some in this centralist position believe that persons with homosexual orientations not only *can* change but must *will* to change. There is strong support in these churches to minister to homosexuals who choose to change their sexual orientation. Most of these ministries have enormous compassion for the brokenness in our world that has contributed to broken sexuality and view healing as a crucial lifelong process. The reality that homosexual orientation is not something that becomes magically converted into a heterosexual orientation means that there must be a purposeful and God-inspired way of moving from one orientation to the other.

Using a developmental model, healing ministries like Living Waters and Exodus usually work toward gradual change, which comes through a prescribed and well-founded structure. Basically, through a small-group and individual-counseling model, along with involvement in a caring community of believers, homosexuals learn about intimacy and authentic sexuality in a supportive, accountable environment.

The view of instant healing from homosexual to heterosexual is considered by this group as misguided. The wounds of guilt and shame heaped upon the homosexual's already-fragile ego and low self-esteem are acknowledged. A responsible ministry involves an open mind and open heart to receive the homosexual person with God's love and mercy.

There are two main approaches for homosexuals who desire change. One is through an individually oriented and small-group reparative psychotherapy, the other through a "redemptive ministry" approach that includes active participation in a vital Spirit-filled community of faith.

Theological writings on homosexuality. Although biblical references to homosexuality are few, given the current debate within the church, the amount of material being written on the topic is voluminous. For a brief but exceptional treatment of the topic, we recommend Richard Hays's chapter on homosexuality in his book *The Moral Vision of the New Testament* (1996). Theologian Jack B. Rogers searches Scripture and finds a place of equality for the homosexual within the church (2005). Theologian Robert Gagnon (2002, 2005, and his helpful website, <http://www.robgagnon.net/>) strongly argues against the type of "concession" that Rogers and others make on the homosexuality issue. The range of issues addressed and biblical basis of Gagnon's writings perhaps provide the best single support of the "sexual abstinence or change" position on homosexuality. A helpful comparision of these two opposing conclusions on homosexuality, both based on Scripture, can be found in Mel White's *What the Bible Says—and Doesn't Say—About Homosexuality* (2002) and a rebuttal by the Wheaton College provost and psychologist Stanton Jones (2006).

SAME-SEX MARRIAGE

One of the hotly debated emergent issues in the church and in society today, even gaining the status of a civil-rights issue, concerns same-sex marriage (Pinello 2006). The issue poses a dilemma for many in and outside the church setting. Even those who oppose homosexual behaviors (erotic expression between same-sex persons) may sympathize with gays who want to form a committed relationship. It is more in keeping with Christian values to be in a lifelong committed relationship rather than engage in the emotional emptiness, to say nothing about the dangers, of promiscuous sexual encounters. What Christian parent whose grown child is openly gay does not want that child to form a deeply meaningful, monogamous same-sex relationship? On the other hand, the moral and ethical concerns about sanctioning marriage between same-sex persons are disconcerting when for centuries and throughout Scripture marriage has been defined as between a man and woman. The ramifications of taking a stand on this issue presents controversy for many.

In their book *What God Has Joined Together? A Christian Case for Gay Marriage*, David Myers and Letha Dawson Scanzoni (2005) present their case for same-sex marriage. Their starting point is a fervent belief in marriage, not only because it is God's ideal but also because strong, loving and healthy relationships make an important contribution at the personal, social and community levels. They reason that attempts to prevent same-sex marriage will have detrimental effects at each of these levels. Granting legal status to same-sex marriage, they claim, will strengthen rather than weaken the institution of marriage. Is this not consonant with the Christian ideal for society? they ask. Myers and Scanzoni point out that the Bible has little to say about same-sex sexual expression, but much to say about promiscuity and exploitation.

Not surprisingly, the work by Myers and Scanzoni elicited an immediate rebuttal to their position. In particular, a well-documented response by Robert Gagnon (2005), nearly as long as the 180-page book, challenges Myers and Sanzoni's position on scriptural, biological and social-scientific grounds. In a briefer response, Albert Mohler (2005), president of Southern Baptist Theological Seminary, warns that Myers and Scanzoni are wrong in normalizing a "love commitment" between same-sex couples. In doing so they seek to place the burden on orthodox Christians to explain why same-sex couples should not be able to "seal" their commitment in socially recognized marriage. Mohler points out that the arguments used by Myer and Scanzoni are based on their assumption that homosexual behavior in itself is not sinful, and their view is therefore based on psychological rather than biblical evidence.

In our view, the Bible solely and consistently refers to marriage as a covenantal (unconditionally committed) relationship between a man and woman. As such, we support a position that reserves the status of marriage for heterosexual union. Based on religious beliefs, anyone can input a sacred status to marriage. But as participants in society, most persons participate in marriage as a secular institution because the legal status of being married is only granted by the state. We find it ironic that millions of heterosexual couples choose to live together without marrying, while many homosexual couples seek to bind their relationship within the context of marriage. So, while many advocate for strict interpretation of marriage by church or state, others would glady grant same-sex individuals the right to form *civil unions* that would assure them of all the civil rights granted to persons in a heterosexual marriage relationship. So, how does one decide to support or oppose these disparate positions?

Compassionate Christians certainly recognize that their brothers and sisters in Christ differ in their view of Scripture and conviction on this matter. In response, some denominations support their gay members by offering marriage-like ceremonies by formally blessing their union. These churches offer their gay members/couples full participation in their leadership, worship and membership. Other denominations simply agree not to make it an issue, recognizing that there are gay couples and members of their congregation who openly worship within their churches. Some denominations welcome the gay person/couple but limit their particaption to nonleader positions in the church. Other denominations openly hold to the position that homosexuality is a sin, and their members are to be obedient to the Scriptures by remaining celibate or by changing their orientation. Most of these churches offer support through prayer and healing ministries for these members.

These issues not only split the church but also major denominations when congregations and leaders cannot agree. Some want to draw strict boundaries clearly defining who are "in" (saved and living according to certain agreed-upon behaviors) and who are outside God's will. Obviously, grace is always extended in Christ, but there are still standards set by the particular church body or denomination, which become the litmus test about a person's status before God.

Christian anthropologist Paul Hiebert (1994) gives an alternative to such boundary criteria for judging others in a complicated world of morality. Instead of declaring a boundary (which differs according to who is doing the drawing) to decide who is "in the inner circle," he reminds us that God is the ultimate judge of every person. So he proposes a model where God's ideal is placed at the center, the source each person seeks, where no boundaries are placed by others. The crucial point is whether persons are moving in the *direction toward* God's will as opposed to *moving away* from God in their lives. The yearning to be who and what God intends for each one is the ultimate test. And since all fall short of God's ideal, everyone must continually examine their own hearts and make every effort to live their lives in congruence with their understanding of God's Word. The biblical truths and the community of faith are there to guide each person toward God's ways.

In Hiebert's model, every person and couple and community must strive toward moving God's way. For example, a homosexual pair may engage in a covenant commitment as life partners, clearly demonstrating grace, empowerment and intimacy in their relationship. They are consciously trying to live according to God's will as they understand Scripture and in the freedom of God's grace.

Perhaps the question for all to consider is whether any of us ever achieve God's complete and perfect ideal. The Scriptures are clear: "None is righteous, no, not one!" (Rom 3:10 RSV). In many aspects of our lives, we may be in tune and move closer to God's way, yet fall short in another aspect of our lives. It becomes an ongoing process, in which each person is consciously determined to move toward God, while acknowledging that the human condition may be a limiting factor as God seeks to draw closer to each of us. Therefore, in our shared state of fallenness and sexual brokenness, we accept and acknowledge each other, who each in their own way and through their own struggles are moving in the direction of God's ideal, as they understand it. At the very least, such a model might help members of the body of Christ to better empathize with those who differ with them on issues like same-sex marriage.

Does homosexuality detrimentally impact a person? The debate over the personal effect of homosexuality upon individuals and society is a controversial topic. Some point to the negative influence the homosexual subculture has on homosexuals, while pro-homosexual persons argue that gays and lesbians are just as adjusted and happy as straights. The evidence is mixed, especially when no distinction is made between the detrimental effects of societal homophobia and the detrimental effects of living within homosexual subcultures. Given the fear and hatred felt by youth who grow up struggling with their sexual identity, it is reasonable to expect a personal cost to their mental well-being, exemplified by the fact that struggling with a homosexual identity is the main cause of suicide among youth. On the other hand, the promiscuous hedonistic lifestyle that is part of the gay community can have profound negative influence on one's personal well-being as well.

A study in Holland based on a sample of over 9,000 respondances found that both male and female homosexuals reported more acute mental health symptoms as well as poorer mental and physical health than heterosexuals in general (Sandfort, Bakker, Vanwesenbeeck and Schellevis 2006). Although the differences were less pronounced, homosexuals also had elevated levels of smoking, alcohol use and drugs when compared to heterosexuals. Since it is difficult to sort out the cause for these differences, we believe it prudent to recognize both societal homophobia and a less-than-wholesome homosexual subcultural lifestyle as contributors to greater personal problems among homosexuals.

REDEMPTIVE MINISTRIES

In this section we draw upon materials from the Desert Stream and Living Waters ministries founded by Andy Comiskey, one of the largest redemptive ministries to homosexuals in the world. Based on a biblical model, their approach emphasizes truth and grace. They focus on striving for God's intended design for heterosexual marriage. Finding the way back to God's truth through Christ's atonement and redemption is the intention.

The creation purpose. The theological starting point is the Genesis 1:27 account of creation: "God created humankind in his image, in the image of God he created him; male and female he created them" (NRSV). A committed heterosexual one-flesh relationship is a sacred expression of humankind being in God's image as male and female. This holy union is a representation of the sacred fullness of God's creation. Therefore same-gender sexual unions fall short of this intended reflection of God's image.

The Fall and redemption. Redemptive ministries have an especially high regard for the mystery reflected in a one-flesh heterosexual union. Because of the Fall, the perfect relationship between man and women was blemished by sin. Adam and Eve sinned against God, which led to alienation and distortion in their relationship. When exposed, they were ashamed, but tried to hide and place blame outside themselves rather than take responsibility for their disobedience against God. One way in which they suffered consequences in their relationship (Gen 3) was to bypass the Creator and go their own way. Men and women need Jesus and the truth of the gospel to find their way back to God.

Through the loving act of God, Jesus seeks to renew a right spirit of truth. In Christ Jesus, homosexuals can reach their full potential through the power of the Holy Spirit to reconcile their lives to God and his purposes. The goal is for homosexuals to develop rightful, nonerotic *same-* and *opposite*-sex relationships according to God's initial creation purpose. Through nonerotic intimate relationships with same-sex friends, the homosexual begins to see new possibilities for genuine connection and love. Whether the person makes a choice for celibacy or eventual heterosexual marriage, one is brought back to a sexual authenticity as God intended.

One of the more controversial aspects of redemptive ministries by gay organizations is the claim that people can change their homosexual orientation to a heterosexual one. Social psychologists recognize two models of change: change in attitude and change in behavior. The debate has to do with whether changing attitudes ultimately changes behavior, or if changing behavior will result in a change of attitudes. A scriptural basis is found in the statement made by Christ: "Where your treasure is, there your heart will be also" (Mt 6:21; Lk 12:34). It seems that Jesus is teaching that one's actions determine their attitudes. Redemptive ministries start with behavior change, believing it eventually changes attitudes and beliefs. It is not a simplistic ministry, but one that includes a variety of healing principles of change in relationships, desires and community.

New relationships. To change a homosexual mindset, one starts by making a clear distinction between homosexual orientation and the homosexual lifestyle. The homosexual must want to change their lifestyle by changing specific behaviors. One must cut off all former homosexual relationships. The homosexual is asked to take responsibility for his or her *behavior,* regardless of what thoughts, desires or feelings he or she might have. Past gender wounds must also be dealt with so that one can grasp a deeper understanding of the gender confusion and make reconciliation. The next important step is to establish nonerotic relationships with straight persons of the same sex. Small-group interaction with people of the same sex can lead to an emotional intimacy, which is believed to be the basic longing that can never be satisfied through sexual encounters. Since homosexuality is viewed as a developmental problem, it is solved through healthy, caring relationships. When the homosexual experiences covenant love with same- and opposite-sex persons in the context of a community of faith, healing takes place, according to this approach.

New desires. Disengaging from homosexual behavior is the initial step that enables one to grow beyond homosexual desires. Change will most likely be a slow process, accompanied by realistic goal setting. When homosexuals break off longstanding relationships, they must be supported through this time of grief and loss. A support group and personal counseling can provide a safe place to deal with the struggles, express feelings, forgive others, face self-hatred and shame, and ask the inevitable "why" questions of God. The battle is fierce, and one must actively draw upon God's power. As Paul tells Timothy, one must *flee* evil, *follow* Christ, and *fight* a fight of faith (1 Tim 6:11-12). Even after the emergence of heterosexual desires, the battle is not over; homosexual thoughts can pop up at the most inopportune moments. The person needs to constantly rely on God for spiritual help and presence to deal with the temptations. Through Bible study, prayer and Christian fellowship, individuals are supported and held accountable.

The ability to resist temptations and follow through on the behavioral commitments comes through reliance on the Holy Spirit. A strong focus of this ministry is to tap into the rich resources in Jesus Christ and to claim the promise given in 2 Corinthians 12:9 that God's strength is made perfect in our weakness. As one finds a new identity in Jesus Christ, there is reason to move away from the homosexual self-image toward God's truth.

The identity as gay or lesbian is often a painful process of discovery. An early awareness of being "different" from peers, along with the fear of being found out, labeled, teased and rejected, keeps people on edge and anxious before declaring themselves homosexual. The thought of being different keeps them from revealing true feelings, and it isolates and distances them from others. Cruel labels like "queer" keep them hiding this aspect of their identity from themselves and others for as long as they can. It is extremely difficult to be congruent or authentic as a sexual being when hiding or pretending to be something you are not.

The research indicates that homosexual youth are two to three times more likely to try suicide because of the tremendous guilt and condemnation of parents, peers and society in general. Knowing how painful the past has been and how difficult it is to trust others, the process of healing takes time and cannot be rushed. A crucial part of the process is spending sufficient time with others who make a covenant to listen with compassion and care as the homosexual reveals struggles, guilt and suffering. Through friendship, compassion and acceptance one finds mercy and hope.

New community. New relationships and a new identity can best be cultivated in a caring community of faith. Engaging a new community is a two-step process. Primarily, one must dispel the myth that a romantic/sexual attraction with a person of the opposite sex is needed to awaken a homosexual from his or her homosexual orientation. The first step is to establish caring relationships with emotionally and spiritually mature straight men and women. The next step is to develop *casual* opposite-sex friendships. Internal healing takes place through small, predictable steps, setbacks and gradual movement forward. Prayer is a strong component of psychological and spiritual healing that takes place in this supportive community of faith, which embraces rather than condemns, giving homosexuals hope of finding authenticity in their sexuality.

THERAPUTIC STRATEGIES

While acknowledging the importance of group and community support, therapeutic approaches place a greater emphasis on understanding the developmental deficits of the past. Individual reparative therapy (Nicolosi 1997) is a means by which "repair" is accomplished through the relationship dynamic established between therapist and client. Built upon neo-Freudian psychology, the therapy focuses on developing emotional connection and intimcy with the therapist along with behavior strategies that change attitudes and modify behaviors. The ability to engage with others in emotionally gratifying connection is an important part of this work.

Sexual identity issues. How are sexual identity issues dealt with in the theraputic community in general? Most secular therapists make the assumption that sexual orientation is a "natural" development. It is important for the client to have a safe place to "put all their cards" on the table, free of *shoulds* or needing to declare a desire to change orientation. The importance of sorting out all the issues concerning one's sexual identity with a nonjudgmental, neutral therapist is the objective. Time to recover from the scars of shame and secrets gives the person a chance to eventually make clear decisions about their future lives. The church has often been part of the external oppression that has been internalized. Since most children try to live up to the expectations of their parents, society and the church, a divided self begins to emerge.

Ex-gays and ex-ex-gays: Evidence for change. What evidence is there that redemptive ministries and/or reparative therapies are effective in changing sexual orientation? Perhaps due to their own failed attempts to change, ex-ex-gays proclaim that such ministries accomplish little. In fact, they pronounce these ministries as naive at best and as a hoax and even dangerous at worst. It is worth noting however, that the former president of the American Psychological Association, Robert Spitzer (2003) reported on a study of 200 persons from Exodus ministry who had been involved in reparative treatment, indicating that 66% of males and 33% of females had changed their homosexual orientation to a hetersexual orientation lasting five years or more. Those ideologically opposed to the possibility of change were quick to criticize Spitzer's research on methodological grounds, that is, nonrepresentative sample, reliance of self-reporting, retrospective design, and so on (Sandfort 2003). It is significant that Simon LeVay, most noted for his research on brain differences in homosexual and heterosexual men concluded that "we should not dismiss out of hand the notion that orienation can be changed" (2003:19).

In their book *Ex-gays? A Longitudinal Study of Religiously Mediated Change in Sexual Orientation* Stanton Jones and Mark Yarhouse (2007) pose and then seek to answer two questions: "Is it ever possible for homosexual persons to change their sexual orientation?" and "Is the attempt to change harmful?" Drawing upon interviews of 73 subjects who had been involved in Exodus ministries (the sample having eroded from an initial sample of 98 over the span of the longitudinal study), Jones and Yarhouse offer a qualified "yes" to the first question and a qualified "no" to the second. They conclude that change *is* possible and that the attempt to change *is not* harmful on the average (p. 367). They emphasize that their study does not guarantee the likelihood of successful change for any particular individual. The authors are careful to describe their findings as showing that "on average, this population had experienced signficant movement away from homosexual orientation and toward heterosexual orientation" rather than a change from being a homsexual in orientation to being a heterosexual in orientation. The evidence pointed to a range of movement along the homosexual-heterosexual continuum, as 15% reported "considerable resolution of homosexual orientation issues and conversion to heterosexual attraction"; 23% had diminished or absent homosexual attraction; 29% reported having experienced no sexual orientation change, but still hopeful of change; 15% experienced no change, had no hope to change and were in a state of confusion because they had not embraced gay identity; and 8% deemed the change process a failure and have embraced gay identity (p. 369)

Interpreting these results invites the proverbial question of whether one views a glass half full or half empty. In his review of the book, Ralph Blair, who is an ex-ex-gay, writes that Jones and Yarhouse too quickly conclude that the attempt to change is not harmful. In following Jones and Yarhouse's logic, he asks, "If but *one* example of 'change' was supposed to have *proved* that change is possible, why is not *one* tragic failure proof of harm?" (2008:1). Blair continues, "But what about all the failed marriages into which 'ex-gays' were pushed and all the self-blame over now abandoned spouses and deprived children? What about all the suicides? What about all the ex- 'ex-gays' who've now thrown out the baby of their Christain faith with the filthy 'ex-gay' bathwater of false Christian promises?" (p. 1).

CONCLUSION

Why such strong emotions? There is no issue in society that generates as much emotion as do issues surrounding homosexuality. Through we try to present a balanced point of view of the issues, we have been accused of compromising the truth when we express compassion for those struggling with sexual identity issues. On the other hand, we are accused of rigidity in defining a biblical point of view when we affirm God's intended ideal of committed heterosexual marriage.

Assessing motives is a perilous task, filled with pitfulls. We think there may be a wide range of reasons behind the strong emotional responses. Some within the Christian community truly believe that the steady march toward a completely secular society must be stopped. Showing strong opposition to the "gay agenda" is thus justified in order to perserve the resemblence of a "Christian society." Perhaps the strongest opposition comes from those who base their beliefs on the very worst stereotypes that have arisen out of raw hatred and fear for those who are different.

Standing for truth and grace means that we must honestly report the research findings. For example, in a recent article, Stacey and Saewyc state that they were "misquoted by a conservative magazine that said lesbian suicide rates were increasing because of gay activism that encouraged youth to come out of the closet; when, in fact, the research study reported that suicide rates were higher *before* coming out of the closet because one had not accepted their orientation" (2006:9). Misreports like these show bias and dishonesty.

Having considered the alternative Christian responses to homosexuality, we now return to the question raised at the conclusion of chapter four: How do homosexual Christians take personal responsibility for their sexual orientation and subsequent behavior? Considering the multiple factors involved in homosexual orientation, by now we hope the reader realizes that this is not a simple matter of *choice*. Such a response is analogous to explaining poverty as the result of a series of bad choices made by poor people. While human agency is an important dimension in understanding any type of human behavior, it is also necessary to consider the profound influence of the biological, psychological and sociological factors involved. When individuals, through little or no determination of their own, receive a biological and sociocultural background rendering them susceptible to homosexuality, their "choice" is much more restricted. On the other hand, persons who receive the biological givens that determine heterosexual orientation, along with a nurturing family and social environment leading to heterosexual congruence, will have an easy, natural inclination toward heterosexuality.

Responsible choice for heterosexuals, bisexuals and homosexuals is made in the context of a supportive family and community who keep us accountable. In this regard, we suggest that there is a *communal* as well as a biopsychosocial dimension to homosexuality. The communal aspect of homosexuality is especially important in understanding why some persons with homosexual orientations choose to express themselves erotically in relationships while others do not.

It is a sociological truism that the greater the availability of a supportive homosexual community, the greater the likelihood that a person with a homosexual orientation will be drawn to homosexual relationships. The homosexual community provides an ideological and plausibility structure that encourages and justifies homosexual activity. On the other hand, a person with a homosexual orientation who chooses celibacy or change will most likely seek a Christian community that encourages, supports and empowers them in that choice.

Though we do not believe that homosexuals are responsible for their orientation, they must decide before God how they will respond and behave. The same is true of heterosexuals, both married and unmarried, who search out a supportive community to help them grapple with various sexual struggles. To be authentic sexual persons, we must address our sexual desires, temptations and behaviors in light of God's Word. In working out a compassionate sexual ethic, the Christian community must be careful not to hold a double standard. If chastity before marriage is the sexual norm, then heterosexuals as well as homosexuals and bisexuals should be asked to abide by that standard.

In the Genesis account the prototype is the male and female becoming "one flesh" for love, intimacy, union and procreation. This persuades us to uphold the heterosexual union as God's intended design for marriages. Our theology of sexuality, then, is based on the premise that God created us to show forth God's image as male and female in relationship. The directive to replenish and subdue the earth (rightful dominion) and to be in authentic relationship (rightful sociability) leads us to a heterosexual norm. In moving together as male and female, married and single, homosexual and heterosexual, in order to promote God's kingdom on earth, we find our holy calling. We firmly believe that the capacity for living in meaningful covenant relationship is a spiritual journey that brings forth God's image.

However, we are also acutely aware of how all of creation was altered after the Fall. Therefore none of us achieves sexual wholeness in accordance with God's highest ideals. Many have been damaged in sexual ways and now struggle with sexual intimacy: some are denied sexual expression even though they long to be married, and others have natural attraction for a same-sex partner. Homosexuals, bisexuals and heterosexuals must strive to find a wholeness in their lives before God in a less-than-ideal world. We all struggle, in our own ways, for sexual authenticity. We believe that God is an essential part of this ongoing process and leads each one on a journey of sexual authenticity. We acknowledge that for many this will be a more painful and difficult road to travel. We grant to all

Christians the privilege of walking through that process with Christ and in the context of a loving community of faith.

A key factor in the development of a healthy, authentic sexuality is the integration of sexual behavior within a biblically based personal value system. We are called to be compassionate and gracious to ourselves and others on that path to wholesome sexuality. We believe the Christian community must model compassion and care for homosexuals, resting in the fact that God is at work in all those who love and desire to serve their Lord.

We acknowledge that some gay Christians may choose to commit themselves to a lifelong, monogamous homosexual union, believing that this is God's best for them. They believe that this reflects an authentic sexuality that is congruent for them and their view of Scripture. Even though we hold to the model of a heterosexual, lifelong, monogamous union, our compassion brings us to support all Christians who pursue God's direction for their lives. A suffering Jesus knows the way and longs to meet those who seek him.

FOR FURTHER READING

Comiskey, A. 1989. *Pursuing sexual wholeness: How Jesus heals the homosexual.* Lake Mary, Fla.: Creation House.

Gagnon, R. 2002. *The Bible and homosexual practice: Texts and hermeneutics* Nashville: Abingdon Press.

Hays, R. 1996. *The moral vision of the New Testament.* San Francisco: HarperCollins. See chap. 16, "Homosexuality," pp. 379-406.

Nicolosi, J. 1997. *Reparative therapy of the male homosexual.* Northvale, N.J.: Jason Aronson.

Payne, L. 1984. *The healing of the homosexual.* Westchester, Ill.: Crossway Books.

Stott, J. 1998. *Same-sex partnerships: A Christian perspective.* Grand Rapids: Baker.

White, M. 1994. *Stranger at the gate.* New York: Simon & Schuster.

Worthen, A., and B. Davies. 1996. *Someone I love is gay: How family and friends can respond.* Downers Grove, Ill.: InterVarsity Press.

PART TWO

Authentic Sexuality

7

Sexuality and Singleness

In 1960 Paul Goodman wrote a book about coming of age in the United States, which he aptly titled *Growing Up Absurd*. Not least among the absurd aspects of growing up is how to behave sexually. Exposed to the electronic media, singles are bombarded with an onslaught of messages enticing them to act out sexual impulses, yet the Christian community continues to uphold the standard of sexual abstinence before marriage.

Asking unmarried singles to control their sexual impulses for longer and longer periods of time is a fairly new phenomenon in our culture. This has been brought about by an earlier-age onset of puberty combined with later-age marriages. Throughout history, young people in most societies married just before their sexual and reproductive capacities were developed. Around the middle 1800s, girls reached menarche between ages 15 and 16 and married around that same age. Today the onset of menarche has dropped to between ages 12 and 13, while the median age at first marriage is 23.6 for women and 26.9 for men. The combination of early hormonal development coupled with a culture that encourages sexual involvement during dating makes it even more difficult for singles to remain celibate before marriage. The early awakening of sexuality through the constant bombardment of messages about sex in modern culture is cause for most singles to consider celibacy an absurd request that is quite impossible to manage during this ten- to twenty-year waiting period before marriage.

We start with the assumption that sexual feelings are extremely powerful, but a person has a clear choice about sexual behaviors. We need to teach teens that it is all right to have sexual feelings and desires, but that they must learn to contain them. The media counter this message by teaching youth that if they have sexual feelings, they should act on them. We need to develop media awareness programs to train teenagers to recognize how they are being manipulated by the media and how they can take constructive steps to counter its destructive messages. One needs only to understand the economics of eroticism to realize why teenagers are among the most manipulated groups in society today. It is enormously profitable for the media to provide sexually titillating and erotically suggestive messages to a large group of voracious consumers whose hormones are raging.

Sadly, many churches and parents turn a deaf ear to this dilemma, refusing to address the difficult questions about sex and singleness. Although rarely articulated, two messages seem to be given to teenagers and singles. Perhaps the most common message is, "Don't ask, don't tell." This response is actually a nonresponse. The other message, "Just say no!" may reflect a stance that ignores the struggle of living in a sexually saturated culture.

Singles need to feel understood as well as receive helpful guidelines in their desire to follow a standard of abstinence. Pretending that young people are not sexual leaves them in a quandary concerning how to be an authentic sexual person in today's world. They need to know how to exist in a singles' subculture that endorses premarital sex, while holding on to the Christian belief in celibacy before marriage. Significantly, the two types of behavior most correlated with teenagers delaying sexual intercourse are religious behaviors such as praying and attending church. The church and biblical teachings are great resources for singles as they develop sound reasons for cultivating person-centered relationships.

In this chapter we present a brief historical outlook on sexual standards, then offer a biblical perspective and give some practical suggestions about how to affirm sexuality while remaining true to biblical standards.

PREMARITAL SEXUAL STANDARDS

There are four recognized premarital sexual standards held in the United States today: *sexual abstinence, double standard, permissiveness with affection,* and *permissiveness without affection.* Although the idea of sexual abstinence continues to be a primary sexual standard when it comes to beliefs about sex before marriage, it is not the actual behavior reported by the majority of singles. The double standard, on the other hand, which accepts sexual intercourse outside marriage for males but not for females, has continued to decline during the past sixty years.

Permissiveness with affection is the most practiced sexual standard when it comes to actual behavior. Many young adults believe that sexual intercourse between two consenting individuals is permissible when they are "in love" and have committed themselves to one another. Society generally accepts this arrangement when couples are in exclusive dating relationships or engaged or living together. However, there is still a societal sanction for legal marriage when a couple decides to have children.

Some confusion comes into play with the "permissiveness with affection" standard. There are those who practice what might be called serial monogamy: they are true to one partner at a time, yet change partners every few years. They have affection for the partner during the sexually exclusive relationship, but they will move on to another partner when they "fall out of love" or become attracted to a new partner. In another scenario, singles report having affection for the partners they have sex with, but that affection may extend to several partners at the same time. As you can see, there is a wide variation in how this standard is interpreted. It can be justified to fit most any situation where there is an intentional relationship.

Permissiveness without affection, although less acceptable as a standard when attitudes are surveyed, has become a fairly common practice in the past thirty years. This view considers sexual intercourse to be a casual, recreational experience between two consenting adults. The recent AIDS epidemic has jolted many into rethinking this standard, due to the serious ramifications of such a promiscuous sexual lifestyle. There are obvious reasons to consider the grave consequences of engaging in sex with many different persons for whom one has no affection, both from a physical and psychological perspective. Because of HIV, relationships from the past may have infected a person with a life-threatening illness in the present. Thus, casual sex for the sake of sexual pleasure has been questioned increasingly in recent years. However, there is not only concern about the increased risk of contracting sexually transmitted diseases but also about the emotional influence of being sexually intimate with a number of different partners for whom there is no affection.

The long-term trend is that youth have become more sexually permissive. It is estimated that today approximately 90 percent of youth have engaged in sexual intercourse by age 20. The sexual lifestyle of many young adults could be described as *serial monogamy*, having sex with a series of partners, but only with one at a time. There is recent evidence to suggest that some youth are making a decision to become less sexually permissive. The number of sexually active teens decreased during the 1990s and early 2000s, according to Grunbaum and others (2002). Also, fewer youth in the 1990s, when compared to youth in the 1980s, believed that it was okay to have premarital intercourse (Ku et al. 1998). The teenage pregnancy and birth rates have also declined during the 1990s (Grunbaum et al. 2002).

It may seem evident, but worth recognizing, that marriage greatly reduces sexual promiscuity. Upon reaching young adulthood (age 26-39) most persons are maintaining a monogamous sexual lifestyle. It is estimated that approximately 80 and 90 percent of sexually active single heterosexual men and women, respectively, report having had only one sex partner with the last year (Laumann et al. 1994).

Hooking up. It is sobering to learn that the recent phenomena of hooking up is a form of nonrelational sex that has become a common part of the sex scene among teenagers. This term usually refers to sexual expression without commitment or any expectation of future attachment. One study reports that "more than one-half of sexually active teens have had sexual partners they are not dating" (Manning, Giodano and Longmore 2006:459). The authors explain that "adolescents having sex outside of the dating context are choosing partners who are friends or ex-girlfriends and/or boyfriends." Still, the researchers found that some teenagers (about one-third) do have hopes that the encounter will lead to a more conventional dating relationship.

The social context of premarital sex. A study of 1,925 seventh- and eighth-grade students revealed that males were more likely than females to have engaged in sexual activity and to hold more permissive attitudes toward sexual involvement (De Gaston, Weed and Jensen 1996). "Females were more committed to abstinence, less permissive in their views of premarital sexuality, less likely to view access to birth control or being in love as a justification for sex, and more likely to view sexual urges as controllable and adolescent sexual activity as an impediment to future goal attainment" (p. 217).

A large sample survey of 26,023 adolescents in 1988 revealed that teens were less likely to become sexually active if they performed better academically, were more religious, did not have suicidal thoughts, came from two-parent families, had a higher socioeconomic standing, lived in a rural area, believed that their parents or other adults cared about their behavior, and had parents who had high expectations of them (Lammers, Ireland, Resnick and Blum 2000).

Although peers have a profound effect on teenagers' sexual behavior, there is evidence that parents also can be influential. Evidence shows that attitudes of parents and peers influence adolescents' sexual attitudes and behavior. De Gaston, Weed and Jensen (1996) found that girls perceived less peer pressure for sex and more support for postponing sex than did boys. Girls were more likely to discuss sex and dating practices with their parents, but also viewed their parents as having more rules and being less approving of their sexuality.

A study of 568 African American adolescent females found that both parental sexual attitudes and quality of parent-adolescent relationships predicted abstinence, after accounting for the variance associated with peer variables (Maguen and Armistead 2006). In a similar vein, a study of over 5,000 Scottish teenagers found that low parental monitoring is predictive of early sexual activity for both sons and daughters. For females, this is also predictive of having more sexual partners and less condom use. In other words, lack of parental monitoring is associated with unsafe sex practices.

An interesting finding by Wright, Williamson and Henderson (2006) was that youth having a lot of spending money also enage in sexual activity earlier. Especially for males, spending money is associated with having more sexual partners. Surprisingly, these researchers also found that the degree of comfort teens feel about talking with their parents about sex did not seem to be related to their sexual behavior.

A study of over 1,000 high school students helps us understand the circumstances under which adolescents experience their first sexual intercourse (De Gaston, Jensen and Weed 1995). When first sexual intercourse occurred, 50 percent of the students were going steady, 25 percent were dating someone they knew well, 20 percent reported that drugs or alcohol were used, and 75 percent were at home or a friend's home. Nearly 50 percent reported that they wished they had waited longer before having sex.

Ninety percent of persons who engage in premarital sex do so in their teenage years. The average age for boys' first sexual experience is sixteen, and for girls it is seventeen. These figures are only one year younger than in 1970. A study of 1,167 high school students revealed that once sexual intercourse activity was initiated, it was persistent for most adolescents (Tubman, M. Windle and R. Windle 1996). Boys were nearly twice as likely as girls to be at high levels of sexual risk by having sex with multiple partners. Repeated intercourse with multiple partners was associated with antisocial behaviors and substance abuse.

The earlier the use of alcohol, cigarettes, marijuana or other illicit drugs, the greater the risk of sexual activity before age 16 for both males and females (Rosenbaum and Kandel 1990). Youth who begin sexual activity at an early age run a higher risk for a premarital birth (Miller and Heaton 1991). The single most powerful predictor of adolescent pregnancy is to have been sexually abused. Sixty percent of children born to adolescent girls are fathered by adults.

Other research indicates a great deal of struggle and sexual conflict in sexual encounters between adolescent males and females. Although a boy is more likely to coerce a girl into having sex by lying or trying to get her drunk or high, girls are more likely to stress the need for commitment and investment in the relationship as a basis for having sex (Eyre, Read and Millstein 1997). A study of English youth also confirmed the use of alcohol as a means of lessening a girl's resistance to having sex. Donovan (1996) reports that young women indicate that alcohol consumption would make them more likely to have sex with somebody for whom they felt attraction. This research supports the traditional assumption about adolescent relationships that girls want romance and boys want sex. This stereotype is challenged by a recent study regarding the meaning of adolescent romantic relationship to boys (Giordano, Longmorre and Manning 2006). Based on over 1,300 interviews, the study found that adolescent boys "report significantly lower levels of confidence navigating various aspects of their romantic relataionships, similar levels of emotional engagement as girls, and greater power and influence on the part of their romantic partners" (p. 260). Chapter thirteen goes into more detail about inauthentic sexual behavior in social dating.

Virginity pledges. In 1990 Richard and Renee Durfield wrote the book *Raising Them Chaste*, which began what has come to be known as the *virginity pledge movement.* Based on their relationships with their own teenage children, the Durfields suggested that along with a "sex talk," parents might give a *key ring* to their child. The key ring was to be worn as a pledge to sexual abstinence and then presented to one's spouse at marriage. This creative suggestion has spawned a number of related programs seeking to promote chastity among single youth. These programs have been praised by some as the answer to preserving chastity, and ridiculed by others as too simplistic a solution to a complex problem. Unfortunately, the debate over the effectiveness of such programs has more often been fueled by ideological differences than by research findings.

According to Bearman and Bruckner (2001), the wisdom gleaned through this first comprehensive study on the effects of virginity pledges is that "critics are wrong when they think it does not work, but they are right when they think it can not work as a universal strategy" (p. 859). This study found that pledges decreased the risk of intercourse substantially, since those taking the pledge were 34 percent less likely to engage in premarital sexual intercourse than among nonpledgers. This was true when researchers controlled for other factors, such as socioeconomic status and closeness to parents, meaning that taking the pledge has a direct and independent effect upon the decision to remain chaste (Bearman and Bruckner 2001).

The best research on the pledge has come from the extensive *National Longitudinal Study of Adolescent Health* in which 14,000 youth responded to surveys given in 1995, 1996 and 2001. Some of the earlier optimism was diminished by the finding that more than half (52%) of those taking the pledge reported having sex within a year (Rosenbaum 2006). This study also reported that responses by adolescents on their sexual experiences were unreliable since more than a fourth of nonvirgins in the first interview, who later took a virginity pledge, indicated in the next inteview that they had never had sex. Rosenbaum questions the accuracy of data on the virginity pledge by concluding that "adolescents who initiate sexual activity are likely to recant virginity pledges, whereas those who take pledges are likely to recant their sexual histories" (2006:1098).

In a positive vein, youth who make a viginity pledge were found to be less likely to experience teen pregnancy, to be less sexually active while in high school and as young adults, to be less likely to give birth out of wedlock, and to have fewer sexual partners (Rector, Johnson, and Marshall 2004). After examining follow-up data from the *National Longitudinal Study of Adolescent Health*, Bruckner and Bearman (2005) tempered the optimistic report given in their previous study by noting that pledgers and nonpledgers had similar rates of sexually transmitted desceases (STDs). Explanations for this are that pledgers were less likely to use contraception the first time they had sex and less likely to undergo STD testing.

A most dramatic finding was that pledgers were *more* likely than nonpledgers to engage in anal and oral sex, sexual behaviors with greater risks of STD. It may be that some youth who take the viginity pledge believe they are honoring their pledge if they abstain from vaginal intercourse. In order for viginity pledges to be most effective, it is necessary to include a full definition and understanding (as some do) of what chastity means. A biblical understanding of chastity must go beyond a "letter of the law" view of what it means to be a "technical virgin" to an understanding that chastity involves the whole person—body, mind and soul.

A related question centers on the effectiveness of "abstinence-only" programs. These programs teach abstinence until mariage, believing that youth should not be encouraged by experts or parents to engage in "safe sex" practices. A five-month follow-up of 2069 middle school students reveals that abstinence-until-marriage interventions increase abstinence beliefs and decrease intentions to have sex and to use condoms. The researchers are hopeful this will result in reducing the prevalence of "casual sex" (Borawski et al. 2005:423). A study by Bersamin, Walker, Walters, Fisher and Grube (2006) found that making a private pledge or promise to oneself to wait to have sexual intercourse or oral sex until one is older is more effective than making a formal virginity pledge. These authors recommend that sexual health programs encourage young people to make an internal, personal commitment to delay the onset of sex, foster sexual norms supportive of delaying sex and be informed that early sexual initiation may threaten future plans.

THE CASE FOR ABSTINENCE

In light of this diversity in sexual standards, Christian singles must decide about a standard for themselves. We will present scriptural support for abstinence as a standard and then ask some critical questions about making sexual choices.

Throughout the Scriptures, sexual intercourse is carefully placed within the context of marriage. This idea is so strong that unmarried persons who engage in intercourse are regarded as entering into a one-flesh union similar to marriage. In 1 Corinthians 6:15-17 the apostle Paul reminds us that when two become one flesh, it is similar to uniting oneself with Christ's spirit. Paul dares to suggest that sexual oneness established between two people is comparable to the unity we are meant to experience with Christ!

Marriage is that time when two persons (1) base their relationship on a mutually shared covenant commitment and (2) consummate their relationship in sexual union. The sealing of the marriage covenant is likened to a sacred mystery in which two individuals become "one flesh" (Gen 2:24; Mt 19:4-6). The act of sexual intercourse carries with it the deeper notion of uniting two persons in the spiritual, emotional, intellectual and physical aspects of their relationship.

Premarital sex is defined as sexual intercourse between unmarried persons who do not share a mutual covenant commitment. This is referred to in the Bible, depending on the translation, as "fornication" or "sexual immorality" (Acts 15:20; 1 Cor 5:1; 6:13, 18; 7:2; 10:8; 2 Cor 12:21; Gal 5:19; Eph 5:3; Col 3:5; 1 Thess 4:3). One could argue that there is no such thing as "premarital intercourse" because the act of intercourse itself, according to the bottom-line position, seals the union, whether or not the couple intends to marry.

An obvious question for couples who forgo marriage but share a covenant commitment is whether they are free to engage in sexual intercourse. Whereas God alone judges the hearts and intentions of any committed couple, it is clear that sexual intercourse is meant to seal their marriage vows as they promise before God to be faithful to each other for a lifetime. On a practical level, merely making a mutual covenant does not automatically imply that the couple should move on to sexual intercourse. In a social-psychological sense, there is a right and wrong time to marry. The right time is when two people are prepared to take their committed love and live together in a responsible, mutually satisfying relationship. A more complete discussion of the wisdom of this position will be given in the next chapter, on cohabitation.

Genesis 2:24 indicates that the right time for marriage is when a couple is able to "leave, unite and cleave" in a newly established union. Until both partners have a sufficient sense of self that allows them to separate from their parents/family of origin, we believe that they are unprepared to enter such a demanding relationship as marriage. Then, when two persons love each other and make a covenant commitment to each other, they are mature enough to consider what is in the best interest of their partner as well as what is in the best interest of the relationship before making decisions about sexual intimacy or when to marry. The uniting of two lives involves a spiritual union that goes far beyond the two of them. It is vowing before God to put Christ at the center as they bind their lives together in the meaningful purposes of work, procreation, family and friendship ties, recreation and service to church and community. Lauren Winner builds a case for the importance of premarital sexual chastity by stressing that sex is communal rather than private—"doing sex in a way that befits the Body of Christ, and that keeps you grounded, and bounded, in the community" (2005:123).

SINGLENESS AND SEXUAL INVOLVEMENT

In this age of tolerance, it is increasingly difficult for Christian singles to simply accept the admonition, "The Bible says it, I believe it, that settles it!" The fact is, when it comes to specific sexual behaviors, the Bible is not so clearcut. This leaves room for various interpretations, increasing the confusion in deciding what the convincing arguments are and whose opinions one chooses to follow. We believe it is more helpful to offer a series of questions that single persons can honestly ask themselves as they develop a moral basis about these gray areas concerning sexual behavior.

Do I have the right reason? Asking the question "What is the right reason?" helps one face some hard facts head-on. Even though pleasure and enjoyment may be a good reason, the potential harm of sexual involvement for a partner, yourself or your particular relationship must also be considered. "Will either of us get hurt by the sexual behaviors we engage in at this time?" "Are we emotionally ready to deepen our relationship at this level?" "Do I have a sufficient self to make a covenant commitment to this person?" "What happens if either of us wants out after we become sexually intimate?" "Will the emotional pain of breaking up after being this involved cause either of us psychological harm?" "What happens if a pregnancy occurs? Will the unborn child be hurt by this choice? Would we be able and willing to care for a child? What would be the effect of putting a child up for adoption? Would we ever consider abortion, and how would that affect us?" "Will being involved sexually at this time hurt our parents, siblings or family in any way?" We could go on and on, but you get the idea.

There are many crucial questions to consider about the level of one's sexual involvement in a relationship before proceeding. Being honest about possible emotional complications keeps denial at bay. Singles, whether young or old, need to ask themselves if they have the right reasons to be involved with a partner sexually, then determine if these reasons are congruent with their psychological development, physical and emotional readiness, and Christian value system.

Will it enrich our relationship? If a couple decides they do have the right reasons for increasing the level of their sexual involvement and are assured that neither of them will be hurt by it, the next step is to consider the influence on the relationship itself. Because they love each other, are deeply committed and believe that good will come out of the mutual decision for increased sexual intimacy, the question here has to do with whether it will enrich their relationship. The point of these questions is to keep the relationship in focus and to assume mutual responsibility for it. "Will sexual expression enhance or take away from our committed love?" "Is it the right time for us to be this involved sexually? For example, how far away is the wedding day?" "Are we committed to the point that we would marry if a pregnancy would occur? How would that affect our relationship?" "Can we trust each other to be faithful throughout the years to our covenant love when we can't postpone our passion now?" "Can we maintain our personal freedom along with paying attention to our partnership commitment?"

We realize that a couple may answer all these questions in the affirmative. Such a response may confirm that they have the right reasons for themselves, each other and the relationship. On the other hand, they may see the need to look more realistically at potential complications if they increase the level of sexual involvement in their relationship at that point in time. Most important, if they have done this honest soul-searching now, keeping unforeseen consequences in full view, they will be at a better place to take responsibility for their decisions.

We know of an unmarried couple who decided to live together because they believed it would enhance their relationship. However, they did not anticipate how difficult it would be for their families when church friends unknowingly asked questions that were too hard to cover up. So the couple stopped going to church. Then they began having difficulty working out finances and blamed each other for not pulling their share of the load. Soon, they were at each other's throats, and neither family was willing to bail them out. Finally, they terminated the living arrangement because they were basically unable to manage their relationship. The breakup was painful, and each suffered emotionally. They were embarrassed about failing at something they were sure they could handle. Each one struggled to work out the relational consequences of being so involved sexually and now to be totally apart. A decision they thought would enhance their relationship actually became its demise. This was a difficult and painful experience for all involved.

Is it the right time? Biblical norms about sexual intercourse are not meant to deprive one of sexual pleasure, but to ensure the sanctity of a mysterious union embedded in a deeply satisfying covenant relationship. We recognize that some Christians have made a full covenant to each other before God and engage in sexual intimacy before marriage. And they seem to do this with few complications. In these cases it precedes marriage that is lasting and fulfilling. However, this is quite a different situation from those who engage in impersonal, indiscriminate sex with a number of different partners without any sense of commitment.

Jennifer and Daniel were in an exclusive relationship for four years. After thoughtful discussion, they finally decided to include intercourse as part of their sexual intimacy with each other. They were secure in their pledge to an exclusive love and eventual marriage. Even though they were not prepared financially to establish a household for at least another year, they felt they were ready for sexual intercourse at this stage in their courtship.

We can certainly have compassion for this couple who believed they made a choice for the right reason, yet the decision was premature due to their financial unsteadiness. Even though they had worked hard to establish independence from their families of origin and had achieved a level of emotional maturity, they remained dependent when it came to money issues. This not only put a strain on their relationship with their parents, who were paying the bills, but also caused tension in their relationship as well. Therefore, instead of enhancing the relationship, the added stress left them estranged from each other and their parents.

Did sexual involvement stymie the future of the relationship? By choosing to engage in sexual intercourse, a couple may shortchange themselves of the total package. For example, intercourse for Jennifer and Daniel diminished their relationship because they were not able to fully enter into all aspects of married life. They ended up living out only part of their dream, so to speak. Emotional bonding occurs through the planning and setting up of a household together. Sexual involvement may help them feel physically close, but focusing on this aspect may disrupt the full meaning of their covenant. So they limp along without the benefit of an all-encompassing relationship.

We believe that sexual intercourse loses its deeper meaning when it is not an integral part of the total life of the couple. The mutual joy, pain, vulnerability and accountability in all aspects of married life deepen the relationship and bring validation to the union. When bonding is limited to the sexual realm, partners are likely to hold back from disclosing all of themselves. This robs them of a daily meshing of their lives through the thick and thin, the essential joys and difficult days of life together. Married life as a total package brings a couple to a higher level of intimacy and commitment.

In another case, Marsha and Gregg had both engaged in sexual intercourse with several partners before they started going steady. Neither had thought very much about their sexual choices or earlier indiscriminate sexual behavior. So, when they came together, it was an automatic assumption that intercourse would be part of their relationship. They engaged in sexual activity for the wrong reason ("It's just the thing people do when they're together") at the wrong time ("We're together because it's convenient"). Neither of them discussed what the sex meant to them, nor did they ask any of the questions about it being for the right reasons, either for themselves or the relationship.

In the absence of a covenant commitment, a crucial piece was missing, leaving a tremendous gap in their sexual union. They each longed for a deeper level of emotional intimacy to match their sexual involvement. Their relationship remained on a fairly superficial level, and they began to feel the same dissatisfaction they did with other partners. Sexual involvement alone does not meet the deeper longings for secure belonging and meaningful covenant commitment.

WRONG REASONS FOR SEXUAL INVOLVEMENT

While some singles, like Jennifer and Daniel, may have believed that they engaged in sex for good reasons, many more have sex for reasons that are wrong—and unhealthy—from the beginning.

Sex used as a substitute for emotional needs. The single life can be one of loneliness and self-doubt. Singles may long for emotional love, but due to low self-esteem, they believe there is nothing in themselves that is lovable. So, they decide to give their bodies as a substitute for what they do not have to offer emotionally. However, the few moments of pleasure never deliver what they truly desire in meeting emotional needs. Sadly, such persons may go from one sexual relationship to another, looking for love in physical terms, only to perpetuate the belief that there is nothing of their personhood that attracts others. Their self-esteem declines even more when they perceive that they are nothing more than a sex object.

Singles who are underdeveloped in relational skills will find it hard to make satisfactory connections and are actually fearful of emotional closeness. They deceive themselves into thinking that physical intimacy equals emotional intimacy. Hiding behind this illusion when a partner asks more of them emotionally, they run in the opposite direction because they cannot deliver something they do not have to give. They are likely to dump that person and become involved in another sexual encounter without ever developing in the emotional realm.

Insufficient ego strength—can't say no! Some persons do not have the ego strength to say *no* to sexual approaches, so they give in even when they do not want to be sexually involved. They do not really enjoy the sexual interaction; however, they are unable to assert themselves, so they tolerate the intrusion. Some may believe they do not have a right to keep sexual boundaries; others fear rejection or ridicule, so they say yes when they want to say no.

When working at a large university, Judy saw how this inability to say no to peers became a tragedy for a college freshman. Dormmates had learned that Dennis was a virgin and began teasing him mercilessly about it. They set him up with a girl for the purpose of "helping him become a real man." There was a big party on the fourth floor that night to celebrate his lost virginity. The dormmates felt triumphant, but Dennis was crushed by his failure to resist their pressure. Extremely guilty about what had happened, he condemned himself harshly for not standing up for what he believed. He was so distraught about going against his personal and religious standards that he attempted suicide the next day. We are saddened about the circumstances that led to the inability of this young man to combat these peer pressures.

When ego strength is underdeveloped, testing a person's sexual values can be a tremendous challenge. Dennis found it especially tough to assert his values in a non-Christian environment. In this case, physical sex with the girl involved proving something to his dormmates rather than coming out of a desire to express affection to someone he loved. The girl was also an innocent victim of this cruel setup. Single persons need to know that they *always* have the right to say no at any time, so they will never feel obligated to anyone.

Using sex to control or coerce. Sex can be used in an effort to control, co-erce or trick a person. Kristin remembers going to the college prom with Chuck and being so "in love" with him that night. They came home at midnight and slow-danced to records in her living room. Kristin felt a nervous, butterfly sensation in her stomach and thought for sure this was a sign of true love. One thing led to another, and soon they were petting heavily, just short of intercourse. The next few weeks Chuck and Kristin spent every waking moment together. Chuck began pushing for more physical involvement just when Kristin wanted to back up a step or two.

That is when Chuck started giving her guilt trips about what she owed him. After all, he said, they had been physically involved, and she was obligated to marry him. His constant pressure made Kristin want to run, but she felt trapped by her earlier behavior. She could not see that if he re-ally loved her, he would not want to badger her into doing things she did not want to do. If he truly cared about her well-being, he would be thrilled that she wanted to complete college and prepare herself for a professional career.

When someone in Kristin's situation pulls away, the coercive partner usually becomes even more desperate, creating ugly, embarrassing scenes in front of others. At this point we can see how the one's pulling away threatens the instability of the one who clings and how that leads to more-forceful attempts at control. This person manipulates out of personal need, not out of love for the other.

Rape and sexual violence are other examples of hostile, coercive sex. Perpetrators have one focus in mind, to satisfy their own needs without regard for the person they victimize. Sex is used to reassure themselves of their adequacy, for they are filled with self-hate, a topic we will discuss in more depth in the chapter on sexual violence. At this point, we simply want to point out the potential danger in the contemporary singles scene, where power and control are used in sexual encounters. Emotionally inadequate males tend to be especially susceptible to coercing their dates into having sex against their will.

Sex for sexual pleasure alone. When sex becomes an idol that supposedly satisfies all needs, persons expect too much too soon from sex. Engaging in sex in order to reduce boredom, pain, loneliness or anxiety is an attempt to escape problems in life. Expecting sex to alleviate these problems leaves one constantly dissatisfied. Trying and trying again for instant cures, this person is continually disillusioned because sexual solutions never satisfy the deeper longings in life.

Sex for the sake of sex is about bodily pleasure without caring who brings the pleasure. It is like having a penis and vagina get together without the persons attached. While it may bring a few minutes of orgasmic sensations, it is devoid of relational meaning. Having sex for pleasure can become such an obsession that one fixates on the external "high" of sex rather then seeing it become a pathway to internal and relational satisfaction. Thinking that it is the sexual pleasure that satisfies, people are desperate to get more of the thing itself, rather than more of the relationship. This person may have little to give, but has a big appetite to take.

Frederick Buechner (1992) makes the following comments about an "anything goes" perspective on sexual behavior. He believes that it is not just a matter of mutual consent or mutual affection or that no one is going to get hurt psychologically, emotionally or spiritually.

> What makes this a tragic situation, I believe, is not so much that by one set of standards or another it is morally wrong, but that in terms of the way human life is, it just does not work very well. Our society is filled with people for whom the sexual relationship is one where body meets body but where person fails to meet person; where the immediate need for sexual gratification is satisfied but where the deeper need for companionship and understanding is left untouched. The result is that the relationship leads not to fulfillment but to a half-conscious sense of incompleteness, of inner loneliness, which is so much the sickness of our time. The desire to know another's nakedness is really the desire to know the other fully as a person. It is the desire to know and to be known, not just sexually but as a total

human being. It is the desire for a relationship where each gives not just of one's own body but of one's own self, body and spirit both, for the other's gladness. (Buechner 1992:264)

SINGLENESS AND PHYSICAL AFFECTION: SOME GUIDING PRINCIPLES

What can couples do when they want to show affection and express themselves sexually while remaining true to the biblical standard of celibacy before marriage? We believe that celibacy does not mean sexual *inactivity*. Quite the contrary, it is important for singles to express themselves in wholesome ways as authentic sexual persons. The capacity to respond to others in a positive, pleasurable way is congruent with a healthy sexuality. Physical expression requires self-awareness, knowledge, discipline and a godly value system.

Christians in the New Testament were told, "Greet one another with a holy kiss" (Rom 16:16). Admittedly, the holy kiss is not clearly defined, but this verse at least alludes to the fact that people can appropriately express affection for each other with physical contact. It is difficult to set up hard and fast rules of premarital sexual involvement due to the many factors that enter into such a decision, such as age and maturity, level of commitment, length of engagement, and the closeness to the marriage ceremony.

At this point we offer some guiding principles in the area of dating, courtship and sexual expression. We reason that it is natural and good for single persons to physically express their affection to the one they love. People need to be affirmed and touched by others. Lack of touch actually makes us "skin hungry" because touching is a basic human need and an important means of communicating acceptance, love and care toward others. Children, for example, are unusually free to express themselves through touch and ask for touch from others. Unfortunately, adults are sometimes fearful of touch and withhold this expression of love and affirmation.

The discerning question about physical touch is the point where physical touching becomes sexually arousing. We must be aware of our responsiveness to touch so we can make good decisions about appropriate touching: what kind, how much and when. The two people involved *must* agree together about the degree of involvement. Here are some guiding principles that may be helpful in making these decisions.

The first principle is that *the degree of sexual intimacy will correspond to the degree of love and commitment present in the relationship.* Where there is no love or commitment in a relationship, a high degree of sexual intimacy is inappropriate because the focus is on the physical dimension rather than the relational dimension. Physical intimacy is meant to enhance the expression of the love and commitment toward the beloved. The committed lover seeks the other because being with that special one is more important than the physical pleasure between them. Covenant love involves a commitment to both the person and the relationship, and this commitment takes precedence over the sexual expression between lovers.

A second helpful principle is the *law of diminishing returns.* As a principle in physics, the law of diminishing returns means that in order for the same stimulus effect to occur over time, a stronger force must be applied. Think of the effect that the very first kiss has on a person. Wow! It is usually an exhilarating experience. However, as time passes and one becomes used to kissing, the effect of the same kind of kiss is diminished in terms of the amount of stimulus it has upon the couple. Over time, people tend to desire more intensity in the physical lovemaking in order to achieve the same stimulus threshold. The goal of increased sexual expression is to ultimately gain a certain sexual response. The closer the couple gets to the point of orgasm, the harder it is to return to a reduced state of arousal. Every couple, then, needs to be aware of this principle so that they can determine appropriate guidelines for their physical involvement. These guidelines need to correspond to their level of commitment and the developmental stage of their relationship (as stated in the first principle).

The third principle is that *each partner must test their personal motive for the physical involvement and activity.* Is the motive for physical involvement an expression of affection or a desire to sexually excite the other and oneself? It does something for the ego of both men and women to know that they can sexually arouse another person. Most people feel a sense of power and control when they can bring another person to the point where they cannot be resisted. Such ego gratification can be the motive behind physical involvement and is more of a self-desire than a desire for the partner. Such motives have a way of separating sex from personhood since the goal does not lead to a deeper personal relationship with the other, but satisfies ego needs.

A fourth principle is that *the two persons involved in the relationship will continually communicate about all areas of the relationship.* A caution should be raised for a couple when the physical dimension of a relationship develops out of proportion to the social, emotional, psychological and spiritual dimensions of the relationship. When the sexual aspect dominates a relationship, the couple is lopsided. The other important dimensions are undernourished, and the relationship is soon weakened. The fullness of a relationship comes through a communication process in which both partners share and get to know each other in all aspects of their lives. Getting to know another person intimately requires that a person appreciate all dimensions of the beloved. The hunger is to be in the presence of the beloved so that one can experience the multifaceted parts of that person. The relationship itself becomes strengthened in the process of such intimate sharing. It is a time of learning to play together, to plan and dream together, to enjoy mutual activities together and to work toward future goals and life meaning together. The spiritual oneness comes as these two persons seek God's presence in seeking God's blessing for the future union.

A fifth principle is that *both members will take responsibility for establishing guidelines and setting physical limits in the relationship.* Christian males must reject the societal norm that endorses the protocol that males should go as far as they can sexually, leaving it up to the female to set the limits. Both partners are responsible together for their sexual involvement in the relationship. The couple needs to discuss the issue of limit setting at a neutral time and place so they can agree on mutual boundaries and guidelines. One partner may be more capable of keeping that limit at any particular time, but since they have both committed to the standard ahead of time, upholding the standard is a way for each to respect the partner and the relationship. There is nothing to be argued in a passionate moment, since the commitment was mutually agreed to ahead of time. Honoring the commitment is honoring their partnership. This agreement eliminates a spontaneous changing of rules in the heat of passion, which both partners will regret later.

Of course, there are times when a couple may want to rethink an already-established boundary, to set either a looser or a more stringent limit. In this case the couple needs to find a place and time where they can honestly look at the pros and cons of such a proposed change in standards.

In this way a mutual agreement is made where both views are respected and considered. It is splendid to practice mutual decision making like this, for this will be an ongoing process throughout the life of any couple.

A sixth principle is that *each partner agrees to commit to following the standard of the person with the strongest felt limits.* This is a position of respect and caring that places the person above the desire for a certain sexual activity. In an authentic relationship, neither person will try to intimidate the other by judging their standards as prudish. It takes an understanding person to want to find out what that particular limit means to their partner. It also takes courage to honestly express one's ideas about a personal value system and what it means. In the end, honoring the limitation of the other indicates that the person is valued and cherished. This brings about a deepening of trust. Also important is that the person who has more freedom in a particular standard not be judged for this. The essential thing is that each partner listens, understands and tries to be understood. Partners open up to each other when they recognize differences without making judgments and accept and respect these personal value systems.

The seventh principle provides an overview of these guidelines: *use Scripture as your guide and recognize your freedom in Christ.* In 1 Corinthians 6:12-13 Paul says, "I can do anything I want to if Christ has not said no, but some of these things aren't good for me. Even if I am allowed to do them, I'll refuse to if I think they might get such a grip on me that I can't easily stop when I want to. For instance, take the matter of eating. God has given us an appetite for food and stomachs to digest it. . . . But sexual sin is never right: our bodies were not made for that, but for the Lord" (LB).

We must refrain from exaggerating or minimizing sexual sin. When Paul talks about immorality, he lists many different kinds of problems that keep us from God's way. When we magnify sexual sin out of proportion to other wrongs in our lives, we can become frozen in our tracks and stuck in our hopelessness to change. When we minimize sexual sin and yield to the temptations that pull us in the direction away from God, we start down another path that leads to destructive sexual behaviors.

The idea is to establish realistic rather than unreasonable rules to govern premarital sexual involvement, in which one makes responsible decisions in accordance with God's Word. Not everything is good or beneficial for every person or couple. You must be honest with yourself and your partner about problematic sexual behaviors that may have a grip on you. This is preventive medicine. When we strive for authenticity, we are seeking to be congruent with ourselves before God. Letting our partner know where we are vulnerable allows the partner to understand us more deeply, to help us in personal temptations, and to keep us on the path toward God's way. Discovering more about how we work to empower each other in our sexual journey is what helps us make decisions that are in the best interest of ourself, our partner and the relationship.

CLAIMING VICTORY IN CHRIST

While one can never erase the past, single persons can always reaffirm their virginity and recommit themselves to celibacy again. We make this suggestion based on our understanding of the encounter Jesus had with the adulterous woman (Jn 8:3-11). The Pharisees quoted Mosaic law as commanding that such women should be stoned. Jesus, however, did not condemn her but told her to go and sin no more.

Showing compassion does not mean compromising standards. We must ardently uphold the standards we think are right, articulate the biblical principles behind them, and move toward God's way with God's help. We need to support one another in our common humanity and our common hope as we strive toward authentic sexuality.

Walter Trobisch gave readers three important reasons to keep sexual intercourse for the covenant of marriage: *the richness of love, the richness of sex* and *the richness of marriage* (Trobisch 1968).

The *richness of love* has to do with keeping focus on the person (beloved partner) and priority on the committed relationship. C. S. Lewis describes eros beautifully in *The Four Loves:*

> Very often what comes first is a delighted pre-occupation with the Be-loved—a general unspecified pre-occupation with her [him] in totality. There is no leisure time to think of sex. He [she] is too busy thinking of a person. . . . One is full of desire, but the desire may not be sexually toned. If you asked him what he wanted, the true reply would often be, "to go on thinking of her. (1963:86-87)

> Eros, though the king of pleasures, always (at its height) has the air of re-garding pleasure as a by-product. . . . Desiring a human being is distinct from desiring the pleasure that person can bring. . . . Love makes one want not a

person, but one particular person. . . . Eros wants the beloved! (1963:88-89)

Romantic attraction certainly leads us to want a particular person. This is evidenced in the Song of Songs, where the two lovers boldly declare, "I am my beloved's and my beloved is mine. . . . His [her] desire is for *me*" (Song 6:3; 7:10 NRSV). These lovers are full of love for each other and take great delight in the other. Their eyes are for each other, and their desire is to give and receive of themselves in person-centered intimacy.

One of the richest aspects of love is the intimacy that comes out of sharing without fear one's thoughts, feelings, dreams, fears, secrets and yearning. Commitment to the person safeguards the highest and deepest qualities of love. The couple desires to know each other in the deepest ways possible. One of the misconceptions about falling in love is that it just happens. We think that when we are mesmerized by the other or smitten with love, we are not volitional in our pursuit. However, just the opposite is true. It is precisely in that falling-in-love stage that two persons intentionally pursue each other. They cannot get enough of each other and spend hours talking in order to get to know the other person more fully. Such attraction involves conscious decisions and purposeful action.

Bonding with each other in the richness of love makes the couple eager to want to seal it forever. The *richness of sex* is intricately related to the richness of love. Good sex has to do with person-centered love. Expressing sexual love to that beloved partner brings delight to one's soul. In the movie *Phenomenon* (1996) the sensual response between the lead characters as she gently shaves his face and cuts his hair is obvious. Yet the attraction is so clearly about the person. Even when sexual desire is an obvious part of allure, it does not overtake them in this intimate exchange. There is no push for sexual involvement, even though he readily acknowledges his sexual interest in her, because it is much more important that she respond to him from the core of her being. It is because sex is so rich that sexual passion is rightly anticipated as the reward of a permanent relationship.

When two lovers give themselves to each other in this manner, it truly is a mystical union of bodies, minds and souls that goes far beyond sexual pleasure. It is more than one body entwined in the other; it is a union of heart and soul. Though the couple will gladly acknowledge that they enjoy the sexual interaction, they will be quick to add that it is because they adore each other.

Granted, not everyone who engages in sexual intercourse experiences such a full, life-giving relationship. Many find it difficult to understand that it takes time to get to know and understand another person at an intimate level. The pleasure of making the most of the encounter comes out of a mutual passion that is well worth waiting for. Listen to these phrases from the Song of Songs to grasp this more completely: "I found . . . him and would not let him go. . . . You have stolen my heart. . . . I opened for my lover. . . . Your love is more delightful than wine. . . . How beautiful you are and how pleasing. . . . This is my lover, this is my friend" (Song 3:4; 4:9; 5:6; 4:10; 7:6; 5:16, cf. NIV/NRSV). We listen to the erotic language and can visualize the passion expressed between these lovers. It seems to come out of pure joy for the other, which brings their bodies and souls into a harmonious rhythm. Sexual fulfillment can be like this! Person-focused passion is an interaction that involves all levels of responsiveness between the lovers.

C. S. Lewis makes the observation that sexual desire is a fact about ourselves like every other desire about us, but when sexual desire is about the beloved, it "has the air of regarding pleasure as the by-product" (1963:89). It takes little effort to simply have a genital experience with someone, but making love to a multidimensional person requires attention, responsive interaction, sensitivity, time and commitment.

The *richness of marriage* is the final reason to keep sex a sacred part of the marriage bond. God ordained marriage as a covenant relationship between two people who will live out their lives in the context of a supportive community. Marriage is not just an event between two individuals: it is a joining of two families, two sets of friends and the community who stands with them in their commitment to each other. It is a private and yet public affair. In the Old Testament a marriage was consummated when the couple began to reside together and had their first sexual union. Whether it was an agreement between the parents with the customary exchange of gifts or a wedding feast in which joining hands in the presence of witnesses made the union public, the community pledged to support the couple in their vows of commitment.

It is quite a remarkable thing that two people exchange vows and promise to love each other unconditionally for the rest of their lives. Agape love calls for the extraordinary self-sacrifice that puts the best interests of the other as priority. Some argue that only God is capable of such a covenant, but with God's help, along with the support of a committed community, agape love truly keeps the couple working toward this goal. It is what keeps a couple going through the thick and thin of marital disappointments and struggles. It is what brings hope during days of discouragement.

Covenant love is the highest response we can give to another. We vow that we will be faithful to our promises and agreements, we will be invested in our partner's well-being, we will be involved in mutual interdependency.

Love demands security if it is to flourish. Lifelong commitment is the anchor in the midst of the unknowns of life. It is a place to make mistakes, to change, to develop, to take risks, to go on when we fail. Marriage offers a place of ongoing respect, devotion, trustworthiness and gracing ways. Covenant marriage gives the context where the highest possibilities of love are possible. It is the *more excellent way!*

FOR FURTHER READING

Balswick, J. K., and J. O. Balswick. 1994. *Raging hormones: What to do when you suspect your teen may be sexually active.* Grand Rapids: Zondervan.

Grenz, S. 1997. *Sexual ethics: An evangelical perspective.* Louisville, Ky.: Westminster John Knox. See chaps. 9-10.

Jones, S. L., and B. B. Jones. 1993. *How and when to tell your kids about sex.* Colorado Springs: NavPress.

Thatcher, A., and E. Stuart. 1996. *Christian perspectives on sexuality and gender.* Grand Rapids: Eerdmans. See sec. 10, "Sexuality and singleness," pp. 411-37.

Winner, L. 2005. *Real sex: The naked truth about chastity.* Grand Rapids: Brazos.

8

Premarital Cohabitation

Cautions and Concerns

F̲ew developments have been as dramatic as the rise of premarital cohabitation—couples not married to each other but living together as sexual partners who share a household. According to recent surveys, the number of unmarried cohabiting couples has increased more than twelvefold between 1960 and 2006 (Poponoe and Whitehead 2007:19). In 2000, Simmons and O'Connell reported that four out ten unmarried-couple households included one or more children under age 18 (Poponoe and Whitehead 2002). It appears that today a majority of young adults cohabit before marriage, and nearly half of all out-of-wedlock births are born to cohabiting mothers (Heuveline and Timberlake 2004:1215; Bumpass and Lu 2000).

In addition to the fact that nearly half of all marriages end in divorce, a majority of couples who cohabit split up before marriage. As might be expected, people who cohabited before their first marriage have a greater propensity to cohabit with another person after they divorce (Wu 1995). Those who lived together before marriage had a 50 percent higher hazard rate of divorcing after marriage than couples who had not cohabited.

Our goal in this chapter is to develop a Christian perspective on the topic. We draw on existing research, mainly self-reported responses to survey research questionnaires or interviews, to address the question "Why do people choose to cohabit?" We then examine the effect of this trend and give a response to cohabitation that is informed by both biblical and social-scientific literature.

WHY COHABITATION?

The best way to address this question is to ask, Is cohabiting an *alternative to being single* or an *alternative to being married?* Premarital cohabitation is actually not a new idea. As early as 1966 anthropologist Margaret Mead tried to address the situation by proposing a two-step plan for single adults. The first step would be a "trial marriage," in which the couple would determine whether they were compatible. The second step would be taken by couples who wanted to legalize the union when they had children. Taking it a step further, Scriven (1968) proposed a three-stage plan whereby a relationship progressed from sexual satisfaction, to social security, to sensible spawning. Cadwallader (1966) believed that cohabiting would free couples from feeling "trapped for life." He liked the idea that couples could establish contracts for stated periods of time and periodically renew them as they saw fit.

These views stretched trial marriage about as far as it could go, eventually leading to the concept of premarital cohabitation. It has only been within the past forty years that cohabitation has become popular among the middle classes, having originated among lower-class and disadvantaged youth.

By examining cohabitation in sixteen industrial societies, Heuveline and Timberlake (2004) identify several conceptually distinct statuses given to cohabitation with respect to family formation. In some societies, cohabitation is *marginal* since it is culturally rejected or even penalized. In more accepting cultures it can be viewed as a *prelude to marriage* status, where legal marriage is expected before childbearing. A similar status is referred to as a *stage in the marriage process*. McRae (1997) suggests that cohabitation serves as a type of marriage preparation, as the stage that occurs between courtship (mate selection) and marriage. In this case, cohabiting gives the couple a chance to test the degree of compatibility in the relationship. If the partners conclude that their personalities "fit," they proceed to marriage.

Cohabitation is usully viewed as an alternative for persons who want a sexual and compansionship living arrangement, but are not ready to form a family. In more accepting cultures, cohabitation is distinquished from marriage as an *alternative to marriage*. Last, in cultures with high acceptance, cohabitation is *indistinguishable from marriage*. For instance, in places like Northern European countries and New Zealand, cohabitation is viewed as if the couple is married (Heuveline and Timberlake 2004).

The above types of cohabitiation can be depicted as ranging on a continuum from the least to the most acceptable status in a modern societies. Given the state of cohabitation in North America, cohabitation is viewed by some as an alternative to single life and for others an alternative to being married.

Based on a study of 1,293 Canadian adolescents, Manning, Longmore and Giordano (2007) report that for most, cohabitation has become part of the pathway toward marriage. As such, most youth "are not replacing marriage with cohabitation, but instead cohabit and then marry" (p. 559). Based on their study of cohabitation in the United States, King and Scott (2005:271) suggest that "older cohabitors are more likely to view their relationship as an alternative to marriage, whereas younger cohabitors tend to view their relationship as a prelude to it." In general, the more accepting a society's attitude toward cohabitation, the more cohabitation is defined as an alternative to marriage.

Many couples admittedly decide to cohabit for the convenience and companionship of being in an exclusive sexual relationship with a chosen partner, whether there is or is not an intention to marry. By its very nature, a cohabiting relationship is one in which commitment is ambiguous. Smock (2000) finds that cohabiting men and women differ in the way they conceptualize commitment. She finds that women perceive cohabitation as a step prior to marriage, whereas men are inclined to view cohabitation as a step prior to making a commitment.

Marriage researcher and Christian therapist Scott Stanley (2005) describes cohabiting as "relationship inertia," in which cohabitors are "sliding" rather than "deciding" on a marital partner. He found that men who live with women they eventually marry are not as committed to the union as those who did not live with their mates before marriage.

The partner's and/or couple's view and understanding of their unique cohabitation agreement is certainly an important factor in the eventual outcome of marriage or no marriage. Given the present state of knowledge, it is probably wise to recognize that for some couples, cohabitation is an *alternative* to marriage, and for other couples it is a *stage* in a relationship that leads to marriage. Each interpretation might be true of different individuals, and both might be true of the same individuals at different times in their life.

What does love have to do with it? This rather detached analysis of the function of cohabitation causes us to ask, "What does love have to do with it?" What distinguishes modern forms of mate selection from the past is the greater freedom young adults have to pursue sexual/romantic relationships without parental involvement. No longer is marriage an economic arrangement, controlled and arranged by parents, but a participant-run system in which the concept of love drives the relationship.

Romantic love had its beginnings in European societies during the eleventh century. At that time, "courtly love" became well known among the privileged class. Courtly love usually involved a romantic relationship between a married aristocratic lady and an unmarried knight or troubadour. As portrayed in literature, the stereotypical courtly love involved a dramatic story in which the knight goes forth into battle motivated by the love of his lady, or a mandolin-playing troubadour sings love songs to a young lady in a balcony on a moonlit night. In this early version of romantic love, it was believed that true love is free of the restrictions of sex or marriage.

The development of courtly love relationships served to introduce tenderness and affection into male-female relationships. "Being in love" began to carry a variety of meanings such as mutual attraction, strong sexual feelings, commitment and enjoying each other's company. This was an uncommon experience for most married persons, who were usually united in marriage for economic reasons.

From the eleventh to the sixteenth century, the nature of these love relationships changed to include sexual involvement between the lady of nobility and her "true" love. During the sixteenth and seventeenth centuries, the middle classes of European society came to value romantic love but still held to faithfulness in marriage. This dilemma was solved when the love object of the single male changed from the married woman to the single woman. For a period of time during the seventeenth and eighteenth centuries, parental-arranged marriage and romantic love existed side by side. As Western societies moved into the twentieth century, the custom of a man asking the father for his daughter's hand became a formality.

During the first half of the twentieth century, the irrational "head-over-heels" concept of romantic love reached its zenith. Confusion over the exact meaning of romantic love made it difficult for persons to really know if true love was present in their relationship.

Psychiatrist Erich Fromm recognized this fact when he wrote *The Art of Loving* (1956). Fromm observed that most people see love primarily as that of being loved, rather than loving the other. He argued that modern persons need to *learn* how to love in the same way they learn how to play a musical instrument. Fromm contended that love is an art to be practiced, and it requires discipline, concentration, patience and supreme concern. When people start "working at love," the noticeable active elements will include behaviors like giving, caring, responsibility, respect and knowledge.

During the 1950s the mate-selection process in Western societies moved to a new stage, referred to as rational/romantic love. This type of love included a strong dose of the participants' rational consideration of their compatibility with their true love. Although few people would marry someone they did not love, it is now true that few people will marry *only* on the basis of love. Rational/romantic love is especially common among college-educated persons who decide to marry after their education is completed. Today marriage is as much a rational decision as it is a head-over-heels response to the partner.

When you link romantic love to erotic love, Henry Grunebaum (1997:296) proposes three identifiable features: First, there is the longing for and desire to be sexually and psychologically intimate with a particular person. Second, the person is not only idealized but also regarded as necessary for one's happiness. Finally, being preoccupied with the person often results in an overestimation of that person.

Dramatic changes in each partner can be observed during the romantic period of courtship. Current research concludes that an area of the brain known as the caudate is associated with romantic passion. Brain scan images during the fevered activity during courtship reveals the "lighting up" of certain areas of the brain. Fisher (2004) believes that romantic love develops over three sequential stages: *lust* (sexual drive), *attraction* and *emotional attachment*. For instance, "falling in love" is a time of attachment that is different from normal relationships with family or friends. During the intense romantic love, disparate emotions may quickly go from euphoria to anger to anxiety, especially if the partner withdraws. However, as a relationship deepens, the neural activity associated with romantic love alters to long-term attachment. The production of hormones and chemical substances known as peptides, vasopressin and oxytocin are activated (Fisher 2004), which contributes to an ongoing, stable love that maintains relationships.

It behooves persons in the romantic stage of love to be cautious since committed love is about faithfulness and loyalty rather than the mushy feelings one becomes caught up with during the "in love" stage.

Developing a relationship beyond initial attraction, however wonderful that feels, demands so much more than being focused on each other. Commitment now includes the hard work of relationship building and making plans for a future life together.

Three kinds of love. Roger Sternberg, back in 1987, tried to sort out the complexity of romantic love. Based on research, he noted three dimensions of love: *commitment,* the cognitive component of love; *intimacy,* the friendship factor and emotional component of love; and *passion,* the motivational component of love. We find these three ingredients of love to be quite similar to the three types of love known from Greek culture: *agapē, philia* and *eros* (J. K. Balswick and J. O. Balswick 2007). C. S. Lewis (1963) has written eloquently about this in his wonderful little book *The Four Loves.* The self-giving *agapē* corresponds to commitment; *philia,* the brotherly/friendship love, corresponds to intimacy; *eros,* the love one feels for the beloved, corresponds to passion; and *storge* corresponds to affection.

The correspondence between these descriptions of love provides a basis from which to discuss the place of cohabitation in a mate-selection system. From a biblical perspective, we believe a *complete love* embraces all three loves; commitment/*agapē,* intimacy/*philia,* and passion/*eros.* However, this is not always the case since any one of these types of love can dominate a relationship.

If only one type is to be dominant, it seems that it should be the self-giving, commitment/agape love. The vow to be faithful in marriage is the desired prerequisite in most societies, and commitment is considered a critical factor in arranged marriages. Observe that a lower proportion of arranged marriages end in divorce than those that are based on romantic love. However, this should not imply that parent-arranged marriages are more likely than love-based marriages to achieve a Christian ideal. The strength of the courtship and premarital relationship involves a commitment that can bring together friendship, emotional intimacy and passion that grow into maturity in marriage.

While there may be a potential for intimacy and passion in arranged marriages, the familial structure may actually hinder the formation of these relationship qualities. The commitment that keeps these marriages together may be less a self-giving commitment to one's spouse than it is a commitment to the extended family and community.

The emergence of cohabitation may be symptomatic of a problem in Western-style mate-selection systems in which commitment is not given a primary place in defining love. In chapter four we asserted that unconditional commitment is the foundation of a biblical understanding of love. Most typically in Western courtship systems, passion is likely to dominate at the beginning of a relationship, followed by emotional intimacy and finally commitment.

The least stable of all cohabiting relationships are likely those based on passion/eros. Most relationships get off to a passionate start out of physical attraction and sexual vibes. Such passionate impulses may override the emotional core and commitment stability needed to sustain a relationship. Since *passion* by itself cannot usually carry a relationship over time, the passionate relationship often burns out before a commitment occurs.

Other cohabiting relationships are based largely on friendship *intimacy*. Although few relationships move into marriage on the basis of friendship alone, it has been found to be an essential factor in marital satisfaction. Persons often describe their spouse as their "best friend," connoting a "soul-mate" connection and emotional companionship that they value.

Although cohabiting couples represent combinations of all types of love relationships, by its very nature premarital cohabitation is a relationship in which intimacy and passion rather than commitment are the strongest elements. Cohabitation conveniently allows for the fulfillment of passion and intimacy, but commitment is often a low priority. This is verified by the fact that the majority of cohabiting relationships (70 percent) fail to culminate in marriage and end in a little over a year.

DOES PREMARITAL COHABITATION LEAD TO BETTER MARITAL ADJUSTMENT?

When premarital cohabitation became fairly widespread in the mid-1970s, social scientists predicted that premarital cohabitation would strengthen rather than weaken marriage (Trost 1975). Danzinger (1976) suggested that premarital cohabitation would serve as a screening device that would ensure the compatibility of prospective spouses. Along this same line of thinking, Peterman (1975) believed that cohabitants would gain experience in intimacy and therefore develop a greater degree of relational competence necessary for an enduring and fulfilling marriage.

However, a number of research studies conducted over the last thirty years have revealed a less optimistic picture of the effect of cohabitation on later marital adjustment. Among other things, it has been reported that married persons who had previously cohabited were more disagreeable about issues such as money, household duties and recreation; had a lower quality of communication; viewed marriage as less intrinsic to their lives and were less dependent upon each other; had lower marital satisfaction; and were more likely to divorce.

Booth and Johnson's (1988) national random sample of over 2,000 married persons who had cohabited, when compared to noncohabiting couples, had a lower level of marital success in the following four ways. First, they had less *marital interaction*, determined by spending time together eating meals, shopping, visiting friends, working on projects or going out on leisurely or recreational activities. Second, they had more frequent and more serious *marital disagreements*, including behaviors like slapping, hitting, punching, kicking or throwing things at each other. Third, they were more prone to *marital instability*, shown through actions such as thinking the marriage was in trouble or considering the idea of getting a divorce; taking divorce action such as talking to friends or their spouse about the possibility of divorce, or consulting with clergy, counselor or attorney; or actually separating from the spouse or filing a petition for divorce. Fourth, these couples reported a higher incidence of *divorce* (Booth and Johnson 1988).

Research done in the 1990s continued to find that those who cohabited before marriage were more dissatisfied with the quality of their later marriages when compared to couples who had not cohabited. However, Thomson and Colella (1992) interpreted the dissatisfaction in these marriages as having more to do with the unconventional attitudes and life-styles of these couples than the fact that they decided to cohabit. He concluded that their more liberal tendencies gave them the freedom to express dissatisfaction and split when things did not go well.

A comprehensive study done by DeMaris and MacDonald (1993) disagreed with this conclusion saying that "controlling for unconventionality had only a minimal impact on the cohabitation effect" (p. 406). These researchers made the point that "although family attitudes and beliefs tend to predict the attractiveness of a cohabiting lifestyle, they do not account for differences between cohabiters and non-cohabiters in instability" (p. 399).

Nock (1994) found that cohabiters expressed lower levels of commitment to and happiness with their relationships and had poorer relationships with parents than did comparable married individuals.

In their analysis of over 12,000 responses to a national survey, Clarkberg, Stolzenberg and Waite concluded, "The choice between cohabitation and marriage is affected by attitudes and values toward work, family, use of leisure time, money, and sex roles, as well as toward marriage itself" (1995:609).

In summary, research in the 1990s found that having cohabited with someone other than one's spouse is predictive of lower marital adjustment. In a study of over 9,000 responses to a national survey, Stets concluded: "After controlling for other factors, results indicate that prior cohabiting relationships negatively influence current married and cohabiting relationships" (1993:236). Stets speculated that those who had cohabited with someone other than the intended spouse are predisposed to problems in relationships that carry over to future relationships.

This was confirmed by a study indicating that cohabiting couples are more likely to experience infidelity (Treas 2000) and another study that found the cohabiting couples were more likely to separate and less likely to reconcile after a separation when compared to married couples (Binstock and Arland 2003).

On the other hand, a study based on a nationally representative sample of women by Teachman (2003) found that premarital sex and premarital cohabitation are predictive of marital dissolution, but *only* for those who had sex or cohabited with men other than their future husband. DeMaris and MacDonald in 1993 reported that especially among serial cohabiters, there is greater instability among first-married couples. Contributing factors like these must be taken into account when making predictions and/ or generalizations about the future of cohabiters who marry.

A study based on over 6,000 respondents in Germany concluded that the same "factors that increase divorce rates also increase premarital cohabitation rates" (Bruderl, Dickmann and Englehardt 1997:205). In surveying over 5,000 Canadian women, Hall concluded that the relationship between premarital cohabitation and divorce could be explained by the tendency for cohabitors to idealize a pure relationship in which one is self-actualized, which eventually "contaminates" marriage reality (1996:1).

Drawing a conclusion. Taking current findings into account, we can conclude that contrary to predictions made in the 1970s, one's participation in premarital cohabitation does not lead to better adjustment in marriage. In fact, evidence points to the contrary of this initial optimistic prediction. In McRae's (1997) review of the relevant literature, she concludes: "The results of research suggest that a strong negative association exists between premarital cohabitation and marital stability." She finds that the link between premarital cohabitation and marriage dissolution is weaker among the younger generation, suggesting that "as cohabitation becomes the majority pattern before marriage, this link will become progressively weaker" (p. 159).

Is there a selective factor? While research continues to find that premarital cohabitation is generally predictive of lower marital adjustment after marriage, part of this might well be explained in terms of a *selective factor*. It is thought that certain characteristics in individuals (less traditional, more independent, less culturally constrained, and so forth) contribute to their decision to cohabit before marriage and put them at a higher risk for a divorce as well.

Indirect support for a self-selection explanation is given by Clarkberg, Stolzenberg and Waite in their analysis of over 12,000 responses to a national survey. They concluded that "the choice between cohabitation and marriage is affected by attitudes and values toward work, family, use of leisure time, money, and sex roles, as well as toward marriage itself" (1995:609).

Thus, the relationship between cohabiting and divorce is real, but one cannot say that cohabitation *alone* contributes to divorce. There are certainly cohabiting couples who have been successful in forming quality marriages. Brown, Sanchez, Nock and Wright (2006:454) conclude that "selection factors largely account for the deleterious effects of premarital cohabitation on marital success."

While selection factors certainly have some influence on the high correlation between premarital cohabitation and lower marital adjustment, the relationship between cohabitation and future marital quality is clearly a complex question.

For instance, research by Rhoades, Stanley and Markman indicates that "men who cohabited with their spouse before engagement were less dedicated than men who cohabited only after engagement or not at all before marriage." In addition, it seems these husbands were "less dedicated to their wives than their wives were to them" (2006:553). These researchers reason that couples who otherwise would not have married end up married due to what they refer to as *the inertia of cohabitation*. In other words, the couple simply remains in a relationship regardless of quality or fit. The obvious implication is that persons do not make their expectations about marriage explicit before cohabiting, and that becomes a problem after they marry.

Phillips and Sweeney (2005) found that premarital cohabitation was positively associated with subsequent marital disruption among non-Hispanic white populations, but not among non-Hispanic black or Mexican Americans. In a similar vein, King and Scott (2005:271) discovered that "older cohabitors report significantly higher levels of relationship quality and stability than younger cohabitors, although they are less likely to have plans to marry their partners."

Research on postdivorce cohabitation reveals that postdivorce in general, and cohabitiation with multiple partners in particular, delays remarriage (Xu, Hudspeth and Bartkowski 2006). These researchers found that postdivorce cohabitation with a spouse is associated with lower levels of remarital happiness and higher levels of remarital instability.

IS COHABITATION GOOD FOR INDIVIDUALS AND SOCIETY?

Sociologists David Popenoe and Barbara Whitehead (2002) at Rutgers University have completed a comprehensive review of research on cohabitation before marriage. They caution young adults to think twice about cohabiting before marriage, offering four principles: First, *consider not living together at all before marriage, since there is no evidence to support the view that cohabiting will result in a stronger marriage.* The evidence, they suggests, shows that living together before marriage increases the chance of divorcing after marriage. The exception may be for those couples who are committed to marriage, have formally announced their engagement, and have chosen a wedding date.

The second principle is *not to make a habit of cohabiting.* They see the evidence as refuting the popular myth that persons learn to develop better relationships from a number of failed cohabiting relationships. Rather, multiple cohabitation is repeatedly found to be a strong predictor of the failure of future relationships.

The third principle is to *limit cohabitation to the shortest possible period of time.* While the Christian community might question the wisdom of this third principle, we should at least understand the intent and spirit with which it is given. It is based on Poponoe and Whitehead's (2002) conclusion that the longer one lives together with a partner, the more likely it is that the low-commitment ethic of cohabitation will take hold. This obviously is the very opposite of what is required for a successful marriage. Participation in a cohabiting relationship can have an eroding effect not only on the participants' view of the importance of commitment but also on societal ethics, which value unconditional commitment as a basis for marriage. From a purely functional standpoint, Popenoe and Whitehead realize that a high-commitment ethic is necessary for marital stability.

The fourth principle is *Don't cohabit when children are involved.* The spirit of this principle is based on the value that children need and should have parents who are committed to staying together for them.

In their summary of research on cohabiting, Heuveline and Timberlake (2004) cite studies estimating that between between 25 and 40 percent of all children spend some time with a parent in a cohabiting arrangement. Brown, Sanchez, Nock and Wright (2006) reports that when compared to children growing up with married couples, children growing up with cohabiting couples tend to have worse life outcomes. Since cohabiting parents break up at a much higher rate than married parents, the effect of cohabiting on children can be devastating.

Aronson and Huston (2004) report that among mothers with infants, those in cohabiting relationships tend to fare worse economically than married mothers. Popenoe and Whitehead (2002) point to evidence of higher risk of sexual abuse and physical violence among children in cohabiting unions. DeLeire and Kalil (2005:286) report the rather sobering finding that "cohabiting-parent families, compared to married-parent families, spend a greater amount on 2 adult goods (alcohol and tobacco) and a smaller amount on education." An interpretation of this finding might be that cohabiting parents invest less in the welfare of their children than married parents.

Although Popenoe and Whitehead write as social scientists, not as advocates for a Christian view of marriage, their advice certainly comports well with the biblical wisdom that marriage is to be based on lifelong covenant commitments. Those who make a marital covenant with their partner will have a better chance for marital stability and happiness than those who merely slide into marriage through default.

A Christian Response

A Christian response to cohabitation needs to be formulated at several different levels. We will organize our response around four questions: (1) What is the nature of commitment in cohabiting relationships? (2) When are two people married in the sight of God? (3) Does cohabitation pose a threat to the institution of marriage? and (4) How should the church respond to cohabiting couples?

Commitment in cohabiting relationships. The prominent reasons people enter cohabiting relationships include love, companionship, sexual exclusivity, economics, ambivalence toward marriage, loneliness and peer pressure. Though many of these are understandable reasons for living with a companion, the noticeable missing piece is covenant commitment. There is no understanding that two persons make a vow before God to commit themselves to each other throughout a lifetime. The biblical concept of a "mysterious one-flesh union" that is blessed by God is the essential missing piece in a cohabiting arrangement. Although an exclusive sexual union is an important aspect of cohabitation, just as it is in marriage, the mutual covenant provides an enduring, ongoing, faithful commitment through all aspects of marriage. It is *hesed* (the Hebrew root for "covenant") love that promises a faithful giving of oneself to the other and keeping that best interest of the partner in mind "for better or worse, richer or poorer, in sickness and health, till death do us part." Although humans cannot love unconditionally as God does, the model of unconditional commitment is a scriptural ideal for marriage.

The cohabiting couple may have a difficult time grasping the value of covenant love. The desired independence that keeps one free from such a commitment places a limit on the deepening maturity of the relationship. When partners are uncertain about permanent commitment, they will be prone to keep a distance and protect themselves from the uncertainty of the future. A relationship of reluctance, a fear of becoming too involved or interdependent, keeps emotional barriers up rather than breaking them down. Thus one of the biggest problems with cohabitation is that it can inhibit deeper levels of personal sharing and knowing. Holding oneself back limits growth in the relationship and keeps partners from developing the deepest capacity for intimacy and loving.

It takes courage to know oneself and then reveal that self to a partner. A clarified sense of self allows a partner to surrender in self-giving ways. The "forever" covenant commitment gives a capacity to share without fear. Differentiation gives partners freedom to express personal longings and fears as well as to respond to the partner's thoughts, feelings, needs and desires.

Communicating covenant love through thought and action, regardless of obvious flaws and failures, means partners are able to be "naked and not ashamed." There is no need to protect oneself from a deeper attachment. Grace-filled love gives partners the courage to risk letting themselves be known. Coveant, grace, empowerment and intimacy are the essential ingredients.

When are two people married before God? The covenantal basis for Christian marriage is modeled after the covenant that God made with Israel. God is pictured as trustworthy and forever faithful in expressing unconditional love to the people of God. The very foundation of covenant love is permanence, upon which sexual and emotional intimacy are built. Trustworthiness and faithfulness are the fruit of a forever love that establishes a solid foundation for secure connection. The deepening of love throughout the years expands into an even fuller and more complete covenant.

James Olthuis (1975) argues that Scripture calls for two main conditions to be present between two persons who want to join their lives together: (1) The relationship is based upon a mutually shared covenantal commitment. (2) It is consummated through sexual intercourse. This places the decision to marry squarely upon the two participants involved. If Olthuis's understanding of Scripture is correct, there might be a variety of ways a couple can cement their covenant commitment without fulfilling all of the societal expectations for marriage. This leads to several important questions.

First, does the couple need consent from parents or family before they can be considered married before God? While familial consent was part of Jewish marriage during biblical times, this was a cultural practice based on the mate-selection process. Though parental consent is certainly desirable, it would be difficult to find scriptural evidence requiring that for marriage.

Second, does a couple need to make their commitment before a community of believers before they are married in God's sight? One could argue that though it is wise to have support from a faith community, it is not a scriptural directive. Reay Tannahill (1980) points out that ecclesiastical consent to marry actually began in the twelfth century, when the Roman Catholic Church decreed that marriage could commence only by consent of the church.

Third, is the consent of civil authorities needed? Those who believe that persons should have the consent of the civil authorities point to health concerns, such as blood tests for the Rh-negative factor or sexually transmitted diseases, which have ramifications for each partner and their future children. Also, this gives the spouse certain legal, financial and property rights. Though there are excellent reasons to seek the consent of civil authorities, it would be difficult to support this as a scriptural mandate.

Following a letter-of-the-law interpretation of Scripture, one could argue that none of the above conditions are required to be married in God's sight. At the same time, we think it is important to understand the spirit of the law, which recognizes family, community and civil structures that support marriage. Cohabiting couples who say they are married "before God" because they have a mutual covenant commitment, yet fail to make it public, miss out on a vital source of collective encouragement. The strength of a commitment is multiplied when it is made before a witness of believers who offer resources as well as a place of accountability. The wisdom of making commitments within a believing community is especially noticeable during times of trouble. A couple depends on others to keep them resilient when life stresses come their way.

Partners who fail to legalize their "marriage" must often lose out on the government's obligation to look out for the welfare of each partner, the couple and their children. This especially has ramifications for spouses and their children in regard to financial and property rights, benefits that occur when a relationship has the legal support of society. There is a sense in which a personal commitment is maintained through a supportive community and society.

Some endorse a mutual covenant commitment made between an unmarried man and woman before God and sealed through sexual intercourse as the minimal biblical standard; others believe there is a need for the commitment to be made in the presence of the Christian community and/or within the accepted formal structure of civil society. The ceremony and the license are aspects that serve to integrate a couple into society. Evidence points to the fact that the individualistic ethic in our society keeps people from fully realizing the importance of personal commitments embedded in a community context.

Is cohabitation a threat to the institution of marriage? The church must make a distinction between how it responds to individuals who are in cohabiting relationships and how it responds to cohabitation as a practice. We advocate that Christians should offer grace over law. At the societal level we do believe that cohabitation poses a threat to marriage and family stability. In response, the church can offer an informed voice to support a societal practice that undergirds marriage and family life. At present, marriage is institutionalized and cohabitation is not. This means that marriage in the United States is the accepted way of recognizing a social and legally binding relationship between a man and a woman. Attempts to deinstitutionalize marriage and institutionalize cohabitation undermine the institution of marriage and therefore pose a threat to marriage.

At stake is the unique institutionalized status granted to marriage by the founders of our country. Rather than being a passive agent, the church can be an active participant in the legal/political system. The move to give the same legal sanction to cohabitation as marriage is not an acceptable solution since research indicates that cohabitation weakens rather than strengthens the marital bond. In Sweden, for example, 30 percent of all couples sharing a household are unmarried (Tomasson 1998). Since cohabitation there carries similar legal rights as marriage in regard to parenting and economic rights and responsibility, it becomes a disincentive to marry. The legitimate concern is the further erosion of marriage as an institution in society due to shorter unions, a higher rate of breakups and an increase in the number of children growing up in single-parent homes.

The negative effect of cohabitation on children should be of especially grave concern to the church. Children born to cohabiting couples are less likely to spend their childhood in a two-parent home than were children born to married couples. And since there is ample evidence that the economic and emotional stresses of divorce have deleterious effects on children, we are concerned about the impact it has on the parent/child relationship.

How should the church respond to cohabiting couples? There are a variety of cohabiting situations, based upon a number of differing criteria for cohabitation: degree of commitment, age of cohabiters, premarital versus postmarital cohabitation, the absence or presence of children, and the intent to have children or not. A detailed discussion of how the Christian community can wisely respond to each of these cohabiting situations is beyond the limits of this paper. We do offer some general guidelines, however, about how the Christian community might best respond to these different situations:

1. The Christian community should uphold the biblical standard that sexual intercourse is meant to be part of a permanent covenant commitment between two people before God and present that standard to couples in a compelling way.

2. When a couple engages in sexual intercourse without sharing a mutual covenant commitment, the church should lovingly help them understand how the biblical concept of covenant commitment can enhance and bring depth and stability to their relationship.

3. When a cohabiting couple is pregnant, the Christian community should be compassionate and offer a church home to them, thereby giving them a glimpse of the faithful presence of love and support of God's people. By experiencing this love, the couple will be more compelled to consider the value of making a mutual covenant to each other and their children.

4. When a cohabiting couple makes a covenant commitment to each other, the church should offer a public ceremony within the community of faith to celebrate the covenant union. There should be no stigma placed on a couple who is pregnant or already have children.

5. When a couple shares a mutual covenant commitment but still chooses a cohabiting arrangement, the Christian community should con-

tinue to show love and grace. Unconditional love expressed through the faith community offers the best model of God as the Christ who accepts people as they are.

The Christian community can win trust by welcoming cohabiting couples into churches. The tragedy is that cohabiting couples who attend church usually stop coming because they feel condemned or unacceptable to the congregation. They turn away from the very body of believers who could surround them with loving support.

Cohabiting couples who have a mutual covenant commitment but fail to make it a public event miss out on the community celebration. Perhaps our society makes it more difficult for a couple to have a ceremony because of the elaborate and expensive weddings in our churches today. In the past, the wedding was a simple ceremony, with local congregation and family members gathered to witness the couple taking covenant vows.

Judy's mother wore a simple gold dress for her wedding ceremony after the Sunday night church service. Her aunt and uncle stood with them, and the church provided cake and coffee for a small reception afterward. Jack's parents had a similar ceremony after the Sunday morning church service. They invited the family and a few special friends over to the house for a light Sunday brunch reception. A wedding was an occasion to support the couple's covenant commitment without all the fuss and flair of an expensive, elaborate wedding. Both pairs of our parents were married more than sixty years, a covenant commitment that lasted over their long lives.

The challenge to the Christian community is to be big enough to hold the tension of all seekers who come to church to consider the claims of Christ. The church needs to hold forth biblically based marriage and family norms, but at the same time show compassion and acceptance of persons who may not be living by these values. The discouraging truth is that living outside of biblically based norms can negatively affect one's attitudes toward those norms. Axinn and Barber found that "the more months of exposure to cohabitation that young people experienced, the less enthusiastic they were toward marriage and childbearing" and the more accepting of divorce (1997:608). Rather than reacting with anger or fear, the church should keep its doors wide open, welcoming all to come. We hope these couples will be drawn to such an embrace of grace.

In its stance toward the practice of cohabitation, we believe that the church can err in two ways: either by compromising the truth of Scripture and failing to uphold the sacred purpose of marriage, or by condemning and shutting the doors to those who cohabit. In upholding marriage as God's way with one hand, we should extend God's grace with the other. Our gospel must be full of *truth* and *grace*. The church needs to be the very place that reaches out to seekers, both those living outside biblical norms and those for whom biblical behavior has not yet become part of their lives. The church will have a minimal influence on the lives of those who are cohabiting until it clearly offers the hands of both truth and grace.

A couple may be on Christ's way without even knowing it. When a cohabiting couple establishes a covenant commitment, they have understood something essential about God's way. The Christian community can nurture a couple's natural inclination to continue to move in God's way through patience, respect and love that point them in that direction. Being compassionate rather than judgmental comes out of the assurance that God, who is the final judge, is the one who loves most fully. "Christ's love sees us with terrible clarity and sees us whole. Christ's love so wishes our joy that it is ruthless against everything in us that diminishes our joy" (Buechner 1992:58). The longing to help cohabiting couples find the joy of covenant love is a great privilege. So, let the Christian community show forth God's love in faithful, engaging ways that will draw those who cohabit closer to the way, the truth and the more abundant life.

FOR FURTHER READING

Popenoe, D., and B. Whitehead. 2002. *Should we live together? What young adults need to know about cohabitation before marriage.* 2nd ed. New Brunswick, N.J.: The Natioanal Marriage Project, Rutgers University. http://marriage.rutgers.edu/Publications/SWLT2%20TEXT.htm.

Lewis, C. S. 1963. *The Four loves.* London: Collins/Fontana.

Stanley, S., and G. Smalley. 2005. *The power of commitment: A guide to active, lifelong love.* San Francisco: Jossey-Bass.

9

Marital Sexuality

Maximizing Sexual Fulfillment

Two are better than one, because they have a good reward for their toil. For if they fall, one will lift up the other; but woe to one who is alone and falls and does not have another to help. Again, if two lie together, they keep each other warm; but how can one keep warm alone? And though one might prevail against another, two will withstand one. A threefold cord is not quickly broken.

(ECCLES 4:9-12 NRSV)

Marriage is a holy place in which profound personal, spiritual, emotional and sexual growth is possible. The partnership formed by husband and wife is an entity that goes far beyond what each one can accomplish alone. As two unique persons support and commit themselves to each other throughout life's journey, they reap rewards of differentiation, connection and united strength. And with God at the center weaving these two lives together into a threefold cord that is not easily broken, the potential for a vital and fulfilling union is at its height.

Transforming oneself in relation to one's spouse is the ultimate grindstone (differentiation process) upon which marriage is sharpened. Each spouse is challenged to round off the rough edges and fill out the flat sides in order to make a more complete whole.

Marriage is full of wondrous possibilities, but it can be a grueling process as well. Heartache and disappointment will be part of the refining process of living and loving in relationship. Hesitation about keeping covenant and fears about establishing closeness can hinder each spouse and the couple from reaching the possibilities described in the first paragraph.

It takes courage to proceed in the direction of "two becoming one," for it takes determination to keep the best interest of one's spouse and the relationship in the forefront. The human tendency is to protect oneself from the vulnerability it takes to become emotionally and sexually interdependent. In fact, it is easy to become discouraged and hopeless about the marital relationship.

In chapter four we presented a biblical basis for understanding how one is to be a sexual being in relationship. In this chapter we build upon the theological foundation presented there, suggesting that the relationality found in the Holy Trinity is meant to be mirrored in marriage.

Ray Anderson (2004) has suggested that in Adam and Eve's human encounter as man *and* women, as well as in their distinctive task of being a man *or* a woman of God, they affirm the divine image. A similar suggestion is given by Stanley Grenz (1990:47) when he states that "the creation narratives in Genesis 1 and 2 provide a hint that the plurality of humanity as male and female is to be viewed as an expression of a foundational plurality within the unity of the divine reality."

Colin Gunton observes that "Adam can find no true fellow creature among the animals, none that will enable him truly to be himself. It is only when he can rejoice in the fellowship with one who is a true other-in-relation that he is able to transcend the merely *individual* state that is a denial of human fullness" (1993:216).

For a couple to reflect the image of God means to become part of a relationship unity, without giving up unique identity. Unity does not mean one spouse is absorbed by the other. Marriage is a sanctifying process where each spouse strives for unity in the presence of the unique differences of each. The ideal for each marriage relationship is that it joins together two persons as one, yet respects the uniqueness of each person as a separate being.

The trinitarian model for marriage comports well with David Schnarch's description of martial sexuality in his book *The Passionate Marriage* (1997). Schnarch believes that a deep sexual encounter is possible only between two fully differentiated mature persons. Sex is not for the young, he asserts, because youth rarely possess a mature differentiated sense of who they are. Without a solid differentiated self, a person has difficulty engaging with a partner without either trying to engulf the other or staying distant out of a fear of being engulfed by the other. Thus, he reasons, most people settle for much less in their sexual relationships.

The *less* that most people settle for is *body-centered* sex rather than *person-centered* sex. In person-centered sex, one is intimately and emotionally engaged with the other in a way that creates a deep connection and interdependence. In contrast to this, body-centered sex involves being engaged with the other for the mere pleasure one gains from the encounter. Though passion and pleasure are important aspects of a sexual engagement, vital sex is so much more than a bodily release expressed through an orgasm.

Schnarch (1997) asks challenging questions: Do persons really see each other during the sexual encounter? Or are they simply going through the motions that bring bodily pleasure? Person-centered sex is the ability to *see and respond* to the other person in mutually engaging ways. It is an encounter *"eye to eye,"* and *"I" to "I,"* and "I-Thou." Unfortunately, according to Schnarch, most people lack the mature differentiation to engage in this meaningful personal-centered sex.

In the giving and receiving of two whole selves, spouses reach the deepest levels of knowing and being known. They are vulnerable as they open themselves up to each other during the sexual engagement. Differentiated persons have the capacity to lose themselves in each other's embrace—without fear of being absorbed by the other. Here they find a mysterious one-flesh unity of body, spirit and soul.

NO MORE LUSTER IN OUR LOVE LIFE

Not long ago a married couple in their forties came to talk to us at the close of a marital sexuality workshop. They were rather hesitant at first, but then the wife blurted out their frustration: "Sex for us is like drinking day-old soda with the fizz gone out of it. Can you help us get the passion back into our marriage that we once had?" Unfortunately, this is a common complaint about the sex life of more than a few married couples. Ironically, when you ask married couples about their courting days, you often hear about the struggles they went through trying to control the fiery passion they felt for each other. But ten, twenty or thirty years later, the fire seems to have fizzled away.

One of the comical scenes in the 1992 film *Fried Green Tomatoes* centered on the attempts of a bored, sexually frustrated housewife trying to rekindle passion in her marriage. After fixing a scrumptious meal, she sets a beautiful table with scented candles, their best china and crystal. She turns down the lights, anticipating her husband's delight with this romantic atmosphere after a long day at the office. As a final touch, she dresses herself in Saran Wrap to meet him at the door. When she opens the door to greet him, he takes one look at her, gasps in disbelief and screams, "For crying out loud, Kathy, have you gone mad? Get out of that silly outfit and let's eat." Her bubble is burst; she feels his rejection and wearily goes back to the complacency of the way things were.

Fortunately, marital sex doesn't have to be this way! We believe that it is not only possible for a couple to rediscover sexual passion but also to increase the capacity for deeper levels of emotional and sexual fulfillment. The trouble is that many couples have accepted a comfortable blandness in their sex lives, thinking that this is the way married sex is supposed to be. When they notice the sexual energy proudly displayed by young couples in public, they think to themselves, *Just wait a few years; it won't last.* Or when they hear an older couple speak about sexual passion in their marriage, they roll their eyes in disbelief, doubting that it is possible.

God created humans with the capacity for intimate, passionate sex throughout their married life. However, only a "blessed few" reach a mature sexual experience, says David Schnarch in *The Passionate Marriage* (1997). Can one maintain passionate sex? The answer lies in recapturing, or perhaps capturing for the first time, the essence of a profoundly meaningful sexual relationship as God fully intended it to be.

The recent survey conducted by researchers from the University of Chicago (Laumann et al. 1994) found that those in monogamous marriages not only had sex more often but enjoyed it more than any other group in their study. Though a third of the married couples reported having sex two to three times a month, nearly 40 percent of the married couples had sex two to three times a week, with the great majority saying they enjoyed orgasm as a part of their lovemaking experience. Marital commitment proved to be extremely important to these couples, and the vast majority had been faithful to their partner. This should not surprise us!

Authentic sexual expression based on covenant, gracing and empowering principles is most likely to occur in a long-term committed relationship. Based on our model of sexual relationship presented in chapter four (covenant, grace, empowerment, intimacy), we look at the factors important in achieving a high level of marital sexual fulfillment.

Marital sexual fulfillment will be high when there is

- a high level of covenant commitment between spouses,
- a low level of conditional relating between spouses,
- a high level of mutual acceptance between spouses,
- a low level of shaming and blaming between spouses,
- a high level of differentiation between spouses,
- a low level of spousal fusion and overdependency,
- a high level of emotional intimacy between spouses, and
- a low level of emotional distance between spouses.

COVENANT ESTABLISHES TRUST

The permanence of lifelong covenant commitment establishes a solid foundation for a relationship as demanding as marriage. Each spouse brings unique strengths as well as human frailties as they pledge to put the priority on the relationship. In this holy marital covenant, spouses have the profound opportunity to know themselves more fully (identity) so they can share themselves more deeply (intimacy). In the vulnerability of the sexual relationship, spouses are learning to be in tune with themselves, their partner and the relationship unity. The role of marital sexuality is to energize the marital bond of respect, trust and intimacy.

A sexual principle based on covenant is that the more secure a couple is in the relationship, the more complete and satisfying is the sexual response. Shere Hite (2006) reports that women consistently say that they are most able to invest themselves sexually in a lifelong, monogamous relationship. When security is lacking, emotional restriction hampers their sexual responsiveness. Women who find their husband untrustworthy or fear being rejected or abandoned by him are less willing to give themselves sexually. This same survey also found that men benefit from a covenant commitment. They report feeling warm, secure and affirmed in their masculinity during sex with their spouse. These relationship themes of security and trust bring authenticity to the sexual act.

An Old Testament view of person-centered passion comes from the Song of Songs. The focus of the love is mutual: "I am my beloved's and my beloved is mine" (Song 6:3 NRSV). This unreserved expression of love bursts forth out of confidence in the person and the relationship. The pleasuring principle in marital sex involves a mutual giving and receiving that takes place between two lovers. The greater the sensory pleasuring in a relationship, the greater the sexual adequacy. Person-centered sexual passion opens the lovers up to each other emotionally as well as bodily through expressions of touch and talk during the lovemaking. The lyrics of a popular country and Western song express this principle in the vernacular: "I want a man with a slow hand, I want a lover with an easy touch." Authentic sexual expression is about the tender touching that communicates affection, desire, warmth and excitement. As evident in the great love scenes throughout the Song of Songs, the couple delights in the erotic passion they have for one another. Sexual exclusivity, according to Waite and Joyner (2001), is related to emotional satisfaction in marriage for both women and men.

GRACE ESTABLISHES ACCEPTANCE

While covenant provides security, grace establishes an atmosphere in which spouses can reach their full potential. Accepting a spouse just as he or she is means accepting his or her sexual value system. The personal value system determines the spouse's unique way of being a sexual person. Having deep regard and respect for a spouse's sexual value system is to have deep regard and respect for the spouse. A desire to know the spouse deeply includes a willingness to know about that person's hurts, failures and pains as well as successes, rewards and victories. Personal preferences about the sexual relationship must be understood in light of the beliefs, values and emotions that underlie them.

Sexual attitudes and values are developed through early childhood experiences and learned from the family, church and society. An important aspect of marital growth has to do with a couple's ability to attend to and grapple with differences. For instance, if either spouse is uncomfortable with some aspect of their sexual relationship, it is imperative that they can speak about their differences without being judged or feeling ashamed. Labels like "prudish" or "overly sexed" have no place in this discussion, for such responses only serve to undermine and condemn.

Acceptance allows the couple to determine what is right for each spouse as well as what is right for the relationship at any particular stage in the marriage. For example, after partners listen carefully to each other and honor their different value systems, sometimes a spouse will relinquish a sexual request for the sake of the other, while at other times a spouse will reevaluate and stretch beyond a comfort zone for the other's sake. The key is that both spouses are working for the good of the relationship toward a loving resolution. The gracing attitude helps the spouses see their differences as an opportunity for growth. Putting the priority on grace, differences become paths of deeper understanding that enhance sexual connections.

Another aspect of grace is forgiveness. Rather than trying to persuade a spouse or hold grudges, mercy softens the sharp edges of differences. Misunderstandings and blunders that are part of every human relationship need to be forgiven so the couple can move on to better places. Undoubtedly, spouses will fail each other in a number of ways in the marriage, for no relationship is ever perfect! Each spouse will disappoint, offend and make mistakes in the sexual arena, which will be hurtful. One spouse, for example, may feel rejected when the other fails to respond to a sexual invitation. Circumstances like busy schedules, young children, hormonal changes, illness and work will sometimes inhibit or alter sexual interest.

Grace is needed on a daily basis to bring restoration after disappointments occur. Those who have experienced traumatic sexual events in their past may struggle in various ways with the sexual relationship. Such situations require extraordinary understanding because of the seriousness of the violation. It takes time for sexual wholeness to be restored in such circumstances. Grace is the environment that helps heal those painful wounds.

EMPOWERING ESTABLISHES POTENTIAL

The model of two becoming one flesh does not eradicate the individual. An individual spouse actually becomes even more defined through self-discovery in the context of the sexual relationship. Behind the "Two are better than one" model is the idea that two independent persons have unique strengths to offer the relationship, which gives a potential that is not possible in isolation. A sufficient self gives each spouse an increased capacity to express and clarify sexual desires or values in a way that enhances the marriage. Without two separate identities, mutual interdependence is impossible. Some hold to the false notion that fusion is the ideal, as in saying, "I can't do it without you, and I must lean on you to be strong." Two spouses who are hanging on to each other for dear life have no solid ground on which to stand. Strength is multiplied by two when each spouse stands on their own feet as they empower each other by working in tandem.

An empowering principle of marital sex is mutuality. This idea is conveyed in 1 Corinthians 7:4-5: "For the wife does not have authority over her own body, but the husband does; likewise the husband does not have authority over his own body, but the wife does. Do not deprive one another except perhaps by agreement for a set time, to devote yourselves to prayer; and then come together again, so that Satan may not tempt you because of your lack of self-control" (NRSV).

This passage acknowledges that each spouse has a separate body with separate sexual desires, and therefore they must be able to work out a mutually satisfying sexual relationship. Paul holds up full mutuality as the highest ideal in marital sexuality. Each spouse is encouraged to express personal preferences as well as acknowledge the desires of their spouse. It's not a matter of either spouse acting only out of their needs, but of finding ways to incorporate the needs of their spouse as well. One does not act simply out of personal needs and must recognize the need to find mutual resolve. The words "by agreement" are translated from the Greek word *symphōnon*, using the same root from which symphony is derived. The idea is to be of "one voice," "out of reverence for Christ" (Eph 5:21).

Authentic marital sexuality is best achieved when spouses engage each other out of mutual desire. There is no place for the misguided idea that the husband initiates while the wife acquiesces. Marital sexuality is to be characterized by mutual regard for the other, for oneself and for the relationship. Just as the orchestra makes harmonious music when each instrument contributes its own unique part, so the married couple reaches sexual harmony through personal expression of sexual interest and mutual consumation.

Some couples succumb to a give-to-get sexual exchange, striving to maximize personal gain. Each gives with the underlying expectation of gaining a return on what has been given. We believe this idea is contrary to a biblical view of marital empowerment. A give-to-get model focuses on power issues in a relationship. Spouses with less interest in sex can easily control the sexual relationship by withholding sex, just as the spouses with more interest in sex can be coercive in trying to get what they believe they deserve.

Control and sexual fulfillment are at basic odds with each other. Sexual fulfillment comes out of desiring and being desired. When one spouse freely expresses desire as an invitation rather than a demand, there is great joy when the partner responds. It is completely unacceptable for a spouse to respond out of obligation or duty, because this leaves the initiator emotionally bankrupt. There is little satisfaction if a spouse responds only because he or she cannot say no. The pleasure and emotional satisfaction comes when one knows the response is out of choice, true desire and love. Here, spouses make room in themselves for the partner and join freely into a union of mutual exchange. Empowering love comes out of vulnerability and strength, rather than out of control and weakness. The empowering principle seeks the full potential of each spouse through a synchronous rhythm of interaction and interdependence.

INTIMACY ESTABLISHES CONNECTION

Finally, sexual intimacy deepens connection and understanding of one's personal sexuality. Sexual disclosure and vulnerability open spouses up to deeper self-knowledge. The ability to know and be known as spouses requires an emotional and sexual exposure in which intimacy flourishes.

"Men want sex! Women want intimacy!" The common notion is debatable that men experience intimacy through sex, while women experience intimacy through emotional closeness. Certainly, many men enjoy emotional intimacy and many women enjoy sexual intimacy. However, though this may not be the whole truth, there seems to be a tendency in this direction. We believe that every couple must find a balance between these two dimensions of intimacy in order to blend them in mutually satisfying ways. Women may need to stretch themselves in sexual areas; men need to challenge themselves in the emotional dimension.

When emotional security is lacking, the sexual appetite usually deteriorates; and when the sexual relationship is lacking, the emotional connection diminishes. A paper by Duncombe and Marsden (1994) investigated attempts that partners make to sustain their sexual relationship. They recognized that today's women refuse to fake orgasms to make their spouses feel good, which means it is more difficult to keep up the illusion that the marriage is fulfilling when it is not. The authors suggest that taking intentional steps to keep sexual and emotional intimacy alive in marriage increases the likelihood of mutual satisfaction. A couple can have the best of both worlds by attending to both aspects of intimacy. The erotic energy moves spouses toward deep emotional connection, which enhances erotic expression. When women take greater responsibility for their sexual satisfaction and men make a stronger link between sexual and emotional intimacy, they say yes to couple intimacy.

Sexuality and spirituality are closely linked to couple intimacy. According to Paul Ricoeur, eros expressed with tenderness and fidelity leads to spiritual fulfillment (1994:73). Eros has creative power for harmony in marriage, for it brings understanding and lessens the effect of differences. Ricoeur believes that many people fear the "yes" to their deepest sexual and emotional cravings. Yet, these cravings call people to accountability to bring their life into accordance with their desires. In acknowledging the cravings, a person is able to choose mutual gratification and enjoyment (1994:80-84).

In the last thirty years the market has been flooded with material on how to enhance the sexual relationship. Perusing the many books on marital sexuality at any well-stocked bookstore will reveal the extent to which couples are interested in improving their sex lives. Though the information for the most part is helpful, we have a nagging suspicion that most approaches focus far too much on the mechanics of sex. Pick up any one of these books, and you will find an emphasis on technique. Based on our technologically oriented society, these books presume that the correct technique is the answer to most problems. To make an analogy, while we would all agree that the secret of maintaining a high-performance automobile is to keep it tuned up in accordance with the automobile manual, human beings are certainly much more complex than a machine.

Good marital sex, we believe, is much more an art than a science. We compare it to playing music or painting a work of art. The ability to complete a paint-by-number picture by matching the numbered paint colors with the numbered areas on the canvas may produce a multicolored landscape, but most of us would find it less than aesthetically pleasing. Unfortunately, instructing couples on strategies to improve the sexual relationship is often given with a sex-by-number mentality.

Some sex manuals present page after page of illustrations depicting different positions that are supposed to enhance sexual pleasure. Reducing sex to body maneuvers often leaves a couple puzzled about just how to get their bodies into those complex contortions. In addition, when disillusioned or dissatisfied with how things are going in the sexual relationship, it is now possible to blame a spouse for not getting the technique right. Imagine, if you will, a couple in one of those incredibly challenging sexual positions. With sex manual in hand, the husband gazes intently at the illustration they are trying to manage. At the most inopportune time, his wife makes an unnerving comment, "You'd better turn back a page, Sam. You must have missed something because this isn't doing a thing for me!"

Person-centered sex is so much more than technique! It involves the *meaning* of the sexual connection for the two individuals who are giving themselves to each other. Their sexual expression tells a story of their love for each other. It is about the mystery of these two unique persons who invited each other to participate in a mutually responsive union. This bold action of giving oneself and receiving the other is an exciting interaction that maximizes emotional and sexual intimacy.

COMMON SEXUAL STRUGGLES

A national sample of 6,029 married persons revealed that 16 percent of the married couples surveyed had been sexually inactive during the month before the interview. Factors that predicted the sexual inactivity in these couples were unhappiness with the marital relationship, lack of shared activity, increased age and poor health. The researcher concluded that the lack of sexual activity is often a danger signal for married couples (Donnelly 1993). The University of Chicago research team (Laumann, Gagnon, Michael and Michaels 1994) found that while 75 percent of the married women said they usually reached and enjoyed orgasm during sex, there were significant variations in spouses when it came to sexual frequency and preferences regarding sexual activities. Every couple has to work out conflicts in their marital relationship, and sexual disagreements are part of that struggle. Resolving differences in the following common struggles in the sexual relationship will make a difference in the marriage.

Keeping the sexual relationship vital. If evidence from advice columns is to be trusted, then many married couples struggle to keep sex vital in their marriage. Ann Lander's asked, "Has your sex life gone downhill after marriage? If so, why?" In response she received over 140,000 replies, with 80 percent indicating that sex after marriage was less exciting. The adjectives most used to describe marital sex were *boring, dull, monotonous* and *rou-*

tine (as reported by Cox 2002:245). Sex therapists Cliff and Joyce Penner (2003) advise couples to keep sex alive and exciting through creativity, inventiveness, fun-loving activities, and openness to new experiences. The question of keeping vitality in the sexual relationship sometimes centers on the question of who initiates sex. This is a crucial point, not just about wanting to satisfy sexual desire but about having feelings about being desired as a person. Some have said that the most important sex organ is the brain, since the mind has more to do with sexual response than the body. To become sexually aroused, the spouse must be in tune with and able to receive the signals that come into the brain so the body will respond. If the mind is saturated with worries, commitments and responsibilities, it easily can prohibit sexual thoughts from entering in.

Sexual desire is not an automatic response, but one that takes purposeful action. While all couples have periodic difficulty with sexual arousal due to external pressures, regular sexual activity is generally conducive to keeping this aspect of married life alive. Each spouse must be intentional in finding ways to get in touch with the sexual side and stay tuned into the sexual aspect of the marriage. Taking time out from a busy schedule to relax, having some moments of quiet conversation together as a couple, or spending some time in each other's arms while listening to music or watching a movie—this is often enough to put the spouses in a responsive, receptive mood. Each spouse, as well as the couple together, is responsible for putting a priority on the emotional and physical connection, which enhances sexual readiness.

Unresolved conflicts. Some spouses have difficulty being sexually intimate because of significant unresolved conflicts in the marriage. In a study of couples in their first years of marriage, it was found that tension had a negative impact on sexual satisfaction (Henderson-King and Veroff 1994). Sex can become a power struggle in which one spouse refuses the other sexually or manipulates in order to gain an advantage over the other. For example, a wife who wants to have a baby may seduce her husband into having sex without using birth control. Or the husband may withhold sexual intercourse because he does not want to risk a pregnancy. Whatever the conflicts, they can become a battleground on the sex field. When sex is used as a bargaining tool or weapon to punish, express anger or gain power, intimacy is sabotaged. The point is, conflict and misuse of power are major barriers to intimate sex. In well-functioning marriages, spouses are able to work out conflicts without carrying them into the marriage bed.

Sexual ebb and flow. The mutual active enjoyment of being erotically attracted to and stimulated by a spouse is ego gratifying and empowering. There certainly will be natural times of ebb and flow in sexual arousal and desire in any marriage. Jobs, combined with child-caring responsibilities, household tasks, hormonal fluxuation, and health problems, tend to diminish sexual responsiveness. The wife who works at an office all day, fixes the evening meal and cares for the children until bedtime is not likely to have much sexual energy when she flops into bed dead tired. The husband who works long hours on a demanding job and spends the evening helping his son with homework and getting the laundry done while worrying about a report that is due the next day will also be depleted and may lack sexual energy.

Dry spells require patience, restraint and support. Good sexual functioning takes time, energy and commitment. Couples who recognize these dry spells and adapt to the particular life circumstances will be better able to maintain their relationship through the ebb and flow. Then, when they have weathered the dry spell, they will avail themselves of the lush and fruitful season.

Diminished sexual desire. A problem far more acute for married couples than regulating ebb and flow is low desire for sex, sometimes referred to as *diminished sexual desire*. This common problem reported by married couples is complex but undoubtedly has a profound impact on the couple. Whether the lack of interest has to do with hormonal factors, physical or mental illness, use of medication, psychological stressors or problems, the formerly positive aspect of coming together sexually now becomes a negative in their life.

Perhaps it would be good to acknowledge some common desire differences between men and women. Baumeister (2000) found women's sexuality to be more flexible, variable and responsive to social norms and settings than men's. The typical male model of desire-arousal-orgasm is inadequate for most women. Women's desire is more connected with believing their partner desires them as a person, not just as a means of sexual release. So, when a woman gives herself out of commitment rather than personal desire, something is lacking for both spouses. Though it may certainly be an appropriate response from time to time, it is certainly less gratifying for the couple overall. Indeed, the encounter becomes less person-centered and more a relationship commitment response.

Differentiation promises to help spouses give and receive in person-centered ways that enhance unity. Mutually desiring and being desired is what drives the relationship dynamic of person-centered sex. Even when there are physical reasons for diminished desire, the desire for touch connnection and engagement is the more important aspect of the love-making. When the couple keeps a quality sex life, it is less about frequency than about enjoying intimate connection. McCarthy, Ginsberg and Fucito (2006:59) encourage couples to establish resilent sexual desire by emphasizing the importance of a person-centered sexuality that includes a vast array of activities, such as expressions of intimacy, pleasure, satisfaction and realistic sexual experiences.

Good sex makes a positive contribution to marriage, and conversely bad sex has a detrimental impact. McCarthy (1999:1) reports that "when sexuality functions well in a marriage, it's a positive, integral component, contributing 15-20% to the marital bond. However, when sexuality is dysfunctional or non-existent it plays an inordinately powerful role, 50-75%, robbing the marriage of intimacy and vitality."

Anxiety about lack of sexual interest in both men and women leads to self-consciousness, guilt, shame, low self-esteem and fear. Unfortunately, most spouses fail to deal directly with this problem, keeping silent about their feelings and avoiding sexual overtones at all costs. Fear about repeated physcial failure and desire keeps the anxiety cycle going.

A person-centered honest discussion about feelings, fears and the impact on the relationship is what is needed. When spouses are vulnerable with each other, expressing their fears and struggles, then there is potential for understanding, change and relationship action.

Feeling neglected as a spouse. In a study of couples in their first years of marriage, researchers found that affirmation was associated with sexual satisfaction (Henderson-King and Veroff 1994). A study of Korean American couples found that higher levels of self-esteem, positive regard, communication and cohesion were all associated with sexual satisfaction (Song, Bergen and Schumm 1995).

Both men and women need affirmation from their partner and complain when they feel neglected. In the busyness of life it is often the couple's relationship that becomes neglected. Keeping alert to a spouse's needs, moods, emotions, thoughts and desires in nonsexual ways can combat some of this feeling of neglect.

Planning creative ways to enhance the relationship through weekly dates, spontaneous lunch meetings or weekends at the beach or mountains will go a long way in helping a couple reconnect. Writing down small requests or desires that the partner can respond to each day will help spouses feel appreciated. These actions of care keep spouses in tune with each other's wishes. Taking time to communicate verbally and nonverbally through expressions of affection and understanding will go a long way in showing the person that he or she is valued. Covenant vows include reaching out and staying in touch with the one you love.

Infertility. Approximately one out of five married couples have infertility problems at some point in their relationship. Infertility can negatively affect a couple's sex life due to the invasiveness of the medical professional, scheduled intercourse times, and sex becoming a means to an end, all being constant reminders of the couple's infertility (Magnacca 2004). These are painful issues for the couple to overcome. Support groups have been especially helpful to couples in this situation. Sharing these circumstances with others who are going through a similar struggle forms a caring community of compassion and hope.

Boredom. Sexual routines quickly become ruts of dissatisfaction. Boredom with sex is a complaint that cannot be addressed unless a couple is willing to talk about the problem and make the needed changes. Talking about sexual dissatisfaction is one of the more difficult areas of communication, yet it is crucial that couples periodically talk together about these feelings. Being open and honest is the pathway to discovering positive steps that will increase couple satisfaction. Working together to keep the sexual relationship fresh and alive is well worth the time.

Sexuality is often enhanced by an element of playfulness. The sexual relationship benefits from enjoyable, uninhibited interaction. The ability to be spontaneous indicates a certain comfort with sexual passion just as self-consciousness inhibits free expression. Ritualized structure can stifle the person-centered process of lovers engaging each other through the sexual interaction. Being authentically differentiated means spouses need not put on pretenses or make a production out of sex, but can respond to the partner's invitation to try new things.

Communication. Intimacy is communicated in a number of ways:

through body language, overt physical behavior, symbolic gestures, and oral and written language. Spouses can also communicate a lack of interest by refusing to participate in an activity, turning silent or neglecting an important event. Love can be expressed through a letter, poem or song. Judy cherishes the love poems Jack has written to her throughout their marriage, although they are disastrous as poetic art forms. Our eyes, lips, face, posture and general body movement do a great deal to express our sexual and emotional feelings. Some find it easy to use words, while others express their feelings through actions. A partner's body language can also give ambiguous messages that result in misinterpretation and misunderstanding.

A couple communicates sexual feelings and desires both verbally and nonverbally. The question is whether the partner picks up on it. It is important to let the spouse know what one desires sexually. There is no room for a guessing game. If a particular kind of touch inhibits rather than stimulates pleasure, it is crucial to let the spouse know. Although sexual desire can be communicated in nonverbal ways, verbal communication ensures that partners do their best to attend to the sexual requests. Guiding each other through touch and short words of encouragement during lovemaking is a good way to care for the sexual relationship.

Spectatoring. A common problem for couples is taking on the role of "spectator" in the sexual event. This occurs when either partner removes themselves mentally during coitus in order to observe what is happening from the outside. Like being a spectator rather than a participant in a sports event, the spouse gets lost in their head rather than being part of it. Unfortunately, when the partner loses the lover, the love gets lost as well.

Spectatoring sometimes occurs because a spouse is overly concerned about her or his performance as a lover. Being self-conscious about how one is doing as a lover often places more anxiety on that person. Invariably it becomes a self-defeating activity because it reduces the interactional aspect to a minimum.

In authentic sexual encounters the couple allows natural feelings, inclinations and actions to be part of the creative process between them. Seeing and sensing the partner gives important cues about how to move in harmony with one's partner. When spouses are passionately involved with each other in the act of coitus, there is no time to evaluate how they are doing because they are totally invested in the moment. In the presence of each other, the erotic dance of love happens between two people who are both acutely aware of and lost to each other in the mutual passion of giving and receiving. It is a fantastic and sacred adventure.

SUMMARY

Monogamous, lifelong marriage has always been the ideal context for authentic sexuality. When covenant love permeates every aspect of life, it permeates marital sexuality as well. When grace offers acceptance and forgiveness, we can freely accept ourselves and each other sexually. When mutual empowerment leads to mature differentiation, our relationship interdependence and sexual unity becomes a reality. When we are vulerable and open to each other, our sexual intimacy deepens. As Christians, our relationship purpose is deeply embedded in our marital and sexual relationship. Our lifelong goal is to reflect the meaning and richness of our God-given sexuality.

In a lovely article titled "Sleeping Like Spoons," John Milhaven explains how the familiar gesture of curling up next to his wife moves him: "The resistance goes out of me. The bed has my full weight on it. The nothingness of sleep has my full weight on it. All of me falls. Nothing holds back. . . . It is a blissful giving way by bodily self to itself. A sweetness of complete relaxing, of luxurious letting go of muscles, skins, nerves, and all. An effortless, sensuous shedding of all concerns, worries, even thoughts. . . . As I slope down with Julie to sleep, thoughts float off. I don't think, I enjoy" (Nelson and Longfellow 1994:88).

Why is falling to sleep in the arms of a spouse such an appealing picture? It's the comfort of being known, accepted and loved by one who is committed to you. And when two lie together, they keep each other warm, for two is better than one. In this place one can be in touch with the hidden parts of oneself. This safe haven is a place where fears do not penetrate. Two wrapped together in bodily trust is what intimacy is all about. The marital relationship is not just a refining crucible of growth but also a comforting container of trust. Sleeping like spoons is what marital emotional and sexual intimacy is all about. Being part of a mysterious one-flesh union leaves a sense of well-being in one's soul.

FOR FURTHER READING

Penner, C., and J. Penner. 2003. *The gift of sex: A guide to sexual fullfill-*

ment. Nashville: W Publishing Group.

Rousenau, D. 2005. *A celebration of sex for newlyweds.* Nashville: Thomas Nelson.

Schnarch, D., and J. Maddock. 2002. *Resurrecting sex: Resolving sexual problems and rejuvenating your relationship.* San Fransico: HarperCollins.

10

Extramarital Sex

Causes and Consequences

The Garden of Eden depicts the image of perfect intimacy between Adam and Eve. There was equality, similarity, diversity and union that God claimed was "very good" (Gen 1:31). Adam's cry "bone of my bones and flesh of my flesh" (Gen 2:23) indicates a deep longing to be with the one who was a suitable partner for deep communion and connection. But not all went well in paradise. This ideal union fell apart when Adam and Eve fell away from God. From this day on, intimacy would be hard to achieve. The propensity to follow their own way rather than God's way would wreak havoc on their one-flesh relationship.

The commandment "You shall not commit adultery" (Ex 20:14) urges couples to work out their struggles in the context of their marriage. In fact, three of the ten commandments warn about veering outside the marriage covenant: "Do not commit adultery," "Do not covet your neighbor's spouse," and "Do not lie" (cf. Ex 20:14, 17, 16 LB). These commands elevate the marital bond as sacred and not to be broken. In other words, married persons should neither *seek* nor *have intercourse* with anyone other than their spouse. Although these Old Testament laws were expressed in a patriarchal, polygamous culture where husbands had the right to take and divorce as many wives as they wished, these sexual options were to be within a legal marriage contract. These commandments protected women because they afforded them rights and privileges.

The warning against adultery sets the marriage bond up as a priority that must be guarded at all costs. The affirmative aspect of these commandments encourages married persons to work together toward an emotional and sexual union that keeps their relationship vital. Each spouse is responsible to God to keep the marriage covenant.

The ninth commandment, "Thou shalt not lie," has implications for extramarital sex too. Lies and falsehoods are an inevitable part of an affair. Secrets come between the marital couple, for one cannot avoid the impact of deceit that impinges on vows of fidelity.

Novelist Frederick Buechner declares, "I AM MY SECRETS!" Secrets indeed tell a story about who we are. The falsehoods told or lived out become part of and reveal truth about that person. When spouses discover that they have been deceived, their tremendous rage has to do with betrayal. When the covenant vow is broken, it pierces to the core of that promise. It is not only the adultery that is hurtful, but also the secret that undermines the integrity of the relationship. The lie keeps the betrayed in the dark (and in a one-down position), giving them no choice in the matter. Lying compounds the destructive effect of adultery upon the marriage relationship. Truthfulness about the affair at least gives betrayed spouses an equal chance to protest, express opinions and feelings, and decide what to do about the particular situation. To rob them of choice leaves them at a profound disadvantage. Our bias for disclosure versus cover-up, must be given with caution. Confessing about an affair must be out of a desire for reconciliation and healing. The confessor must weigh the potential hurt or harm that could come to the resolute spouse. It is wise to have a pastor or therapist help with these questions, the timing and the method of disclosure.

The Ten Commandments remind us that we are fallen creatures and living in a fallen world. Although spouses may not always escape the temptation of wrongful desire, they can ask for forgiveness and seek the help of their spouse and God to keep the promises of the marital vows.

The New Testament teaching builds on the Old Testament views on adultery, but it broadens the focus to include attitudes as well as behavior. In his book *Sexuality and the Jesus Tradition*, William Loader (2005:234) states that "the change of focus from act to attitude in Jesus' teaching (on adultery, as on murder) creates an important ethical perspective. It leads us to consider the attitudes which inform behaviors and to see behaviors as the result of such sin" (Mt 5:22, 28).

By broadening the definition of infidelity to include *emotional* as well as sexual involvement, recent reseach also takes into account the subjective aspects of adultery found in Jesus' teaching on the subject.

Based on their extensive review of the literature, Blow and Hartnett (2005:220) conclude: "Research that limits the defintion of infidelity to sexual intercourse minimizes the devastating effects that other types of sexual involvement and emotional connection can have on relationships."

In summarizing how men and women differ in their experience of infidelity, Blow and Hartnett (2005) report that women experience infidelity more in terms of emotional connection, whereas it is more of a sexual experience for men. While men justify infidelity more in terms of the sexual dimension, women tend to resort to emotion-based justifications (Glass and Wright 1997; Allen and Baucom 2004).

The seriousness of adultery is addressed in New Testament passages such as 1 Corinthians 6:18: "Every sin that a person commits is outside the body; but the fornicator sins against the body itself" (NRSV). Sexual intercourse is regarded not only as an external act but also as an internal offense that impacts self and spouse. One-flesh union symbolically joins a man and woman through memories, expectations, fantasies and secrets, so that even a casual affair has implication for the adulterer, adulteress, the spouse and all three relationships.

It is difficult to estimate the proportion of married persons who actually engage in extramarital sex due to secrecy and differences in defining EMI (extramarital intimacy). One also considers motivational factors and causes for sexual involvement.

Initially, survey reports by Kinsey, Pomeroy and Martin (1948, 1953), *Cosmopolitan* (Wolfe 1981) and *Playboy* (Petersen et al. 1983) indicated the rate of extramarital sex to be over 50 percent for women and over 75 percent for men. However, due to biased sampling, these rates are undoubtedly inflated.

The most recent research, based upon a probability sample of over 3,000 adults, finds that 25 percent of men and 15 percent of women report having had sex with someone other than their spouse while married (Laumann et al. 1994). This is consistent with what we find about people's attitudes toward extramarital sex, since roughly 75 percent of adults believe that extramarital sex is "always wrong," and another 15 percent believe it is "almost always wrong" (Laumann et al. 1994:22). But given the sensitive nature of the question, the authors caution that subjects may underreport incidents of extramarital sexual involvement. Regardless of what persons morally believe about adultery, their behavior may not be congruent with those beliefs. The actual rate for extramarital sex is undoubtedly higher today than it has been in the past generation.

Based on their extensive review of the literature on infidelity, Blow and Hartnett (2005:220) conclude that "over the course of married, heterosexual relationships in the United States, EMI sex occurs in less than 25% of committed relationships, and more men than women appear to be engaging in infidelity."

THE DECISION TO HAVE AN AFFAIR

Although there is no single cause of infidelity, there are a number of factors that have been found to be correlated with it. These factors include premarital sexual involvement, marital dissatisfaction, sexual dissatisfaction, low religiosity, high interest in sex, parental divorce, insecure attachment styles, and attitudes of gender inequality and inequality in marital power and control (Blow and Hartnett 2005; Reiss, Anderson and Sponaugle 1980).

Although the spouse who had more power and control in the marriage was more likely to engage in extramarital sex, Prins, Buunk and Van Yperen (1993) found that females who felt a lack of equality in their marital relationship were more likely to desire and actually engage in extramarital sexual behavior.

These findings are consistent with equity theory, which predicts higher rates of extramarital sex in marriages where there is *unequal* power. The basic idea of this theory is that people need to feel they are getting as much out of the relationship as they are putting into it. Most people keep mental tabulations to figure out whether the benefits outweigh the sacrifices they put forth. Underbenefited partners engage in extramarital sex earlier in their marriage and with more partners than those who feel equitably treated. Women who felt they were not getting all that they deserved in their marriage were more likely to consider extramarital sexual involvement as an acceptable behavior.

Beyond these correlates, infidelity seems to be related to *situation* factors such as an opportunity for infidelity. Such things as daily contact with coworkers and/or frequent traveling away home are examples of this. Another situational factor is age, since younger persons appear to be more vulnerable to infidelity in the relationship (Amoto and Rogers 1997; Atkins, Baucom and Jacobson 2001).

Wiederman and Allgeier (1996) found that young married couples presumed that the major source of extramarital sex is marital dissatisfaction. Although there may be as many reasons for adultery as there are adulterous affairs, affairs are known to follow certain patterns. We shall discuss these patterns in light of different types of affairs, then look at sociological and psychological explanations for why persons have affairs, and finally offer a moral explanation.

Atkins (2003) found that individuals with a tendency toward a narcissistic personality were significantly correlated with higher rates of EMI. Glass (2003) found that employment is a primary context for EMI, where coworkers are emotionally connected and approached as alternative partners to their spouse.

Based on hundreds of clinical cases of infidelity, psychologist Frank Pittman (1989) suggests four types of infidelity in his book *Private Lies: Infidelity and the Betrayal of Intimacy.* In the *accidental affair* there is no advanced planning; the affair "just happens." *Philandering* is the practice of seeking many partners for the precise purpose of engaging in affairs as if it were a sport. *Romantic affairs* are usually the culmination of a developing relationship between two people who feel they love each other. *Marital arrangements* constitute a type of affair in which a couple agrees to stay married (sometimes without living together) but allows for long-term sexual relationships with persons outside of the marriage. Each of these types of affairs involves different reasons for adultery. There is a mixture of sociological, psychological, relational and moral reasons behind the choice to indulge in extramarital sex.

Marital therapists point to both individual and interactional needs and how they are met or fail to be met in the marriage relationship as an important dimension in understanding what leads to an extramarital affair. Based on clinical research David Schnarch (1991, 1997) has developed an explanation of extramarital sexual involvement based on one's level of differentiation. He suggests that spouses with low levels of differentiation tend to be fused (overly dependent) at one extreme or emotionally cut off (overly distant) at the other.

Earlier in this book we defined differentiation as a balanced integratration of one's need for connection and separateness. Key aspects of differentiation in the marital context are (1) the ability to maintain a clear sense of self in close proximity to one's spouse, (2) the ability to soothe personal fears and anxieties (self-regulate) from within the self, (3) the ability to be nonreactive to the anxiety of the spouse, and (4) the ability to tolerate the natural struggle and discomfort of marital discord in order to grow toward a healthy interdependence.

According to Schnarch, " The struggle in marriage is to find out who you are while maintaining your boundaries with a partner who is all too eager and ready to tell you who you are" (1993:1). Herein lies the "marriage crucible," a refining place where spouses must grapple with their unique differences in the context of forming a bond as a couple. It can be described as developing a "self-in-relation." Each spouse holds on to a fully differentiated self, resisting the partner's attempt to define him or her, and in the process is rewarded by a deeply rewarding interdependency.

One becomes more highly differentiated in the context of the relationship by taking risks (expressing wants, needs, desires, passion) and being vulnerable (expressing hurts, pains, weakness, hopes, fears) with one's spouse. Intimacy occurs because spouses let themselves be known and seek to know and be responsive (not reactive) to their spouse. Through open communication and relationship struggle, highly differentiated spouses have an increased ability to put the best interests of the spouse and the relationship as a priority.

People who lack a healthy degree of differentiation are ripe for extramarital affairs, according to Schnarch (1993). There is a tendency to confuse fusion with emotional closeness. In marriage, therefore, undifferentiated spouses tend to be overly dependent on each other for validation and self-definition. In many ways this places an incredible power in the hands of the spouses. It is extremely disconcerting not to be validated (one has failed to be validated internally), and therefore an extramarital affair becomes attractive.

The affair gives undifferentiated spouses the impression that they are desireable, sexy, admired, and they thrive on this idea. Feeling inadequate to meet the spouse's needs, the affair gives a new focus and becomes an escape route to personal growth and real differentiation. Idealization of the new relationship (affair) flames a fantasy about oneself. The thinking goes something like this: *I must be really attractive for this person to take such an interest in me. Therefore I'm perfectly adequate and don't need to change anything.*

Living in the real world of marriage, spouses must face various struggles, disappointments, desires and failures together in a way that brings mutual respect and relational interdependence. The two spouses are in it together and accountable to each other, so there are no illusions about self or the other. Honest communication, self-awareness, vulnerable reflection and open sharing lead them to deeper levels of intimacy, increasing differentiation that deepens connection.

Highly differentiated spouses do not fear losing themselves in the emotional closeness of the marriage, because their solid sense of self frees them to love in more expressive and more vulnerable ways. The bottom line, according to Schnarch (1993), is that affairs occur more frequently among those who fear intimacy rather than those who desire to become more intimate with one's spouse.

Booth and Dabbs (1993) considered biological evidence that may affect one's tendency to have affairs. They found that men who produce high levels of testosterone were less likely to marry, and when they did marry were more likely to show violence toward a spouse and have troubled marital relations, extramarital sex violations, and a lower quality of marital interaction.

Though one must consider the complex social, psychological, relational or even hormonal factors that influence the decision to have an extramarital affair, we must not forget that the person makes a moral choice. Although some may follow a spur-of-the-moment impulse, the extramarital affair is more often a premeditated act. Based on her early research, Lynn Atwater (1982) found extramarital affairs usually move through five stages:

1. A tolerant attitude toward the possibility of the affair
2. The opportunity for the affair
3. The presence of extramarital models (in novels, movies, television dramas)
4. A time of mental rehearsing about how the affair will take place
5. The consummation of the affair

The progression from thought to action suggested in these stages is consistent with the social-psychological literature that indicates how human attitudes and behaviors are related. Just as behavior can affect our attitudes, so can our thoughts affect our behavior if we allow them to germinate in the desires of our mind.

This understanding of why affairs occur is consistent with the biblical view of sin, holiness and temptation. Sin is not only a matter of the external: our behavior. It is also a matter of the heart: our attitudes and desires. Jesus spoke of adultery of the heart in Matthew 5:28. The thrust of this teaching is that adulterous thoughts can be the beginning of adulterous affairs. Jesus shows how hidden thoughts, as well as actions, keep a person from reaching the deepest possible communion with their spouse.

Coveting or lusting after someone outside the marriage harms those involved. The one who commits adultery shapes his or her character through the deceitful and unfaithful action. The abandoned spouse feels betrayed, angry, neglected and confused about what's happening. The children are insecure as they sense the distance and disruption between their parents. And the other person involved in the affair remains uncertain about his or her place and future in the adulterer's life.

Thoughts and action go together, says Jesus; adultery (even of the heart) is against God's way. We must not merely do the right things; we must also desire the right things. When desire goes astray in thought, action is soon to follow. To live responsible lives in contemporary society means we must cope with temptations in a culture saturated with sexual messages. We must keep our conscience clear, drawing appropriate boundaries so we will make responsible choices about what we desire and toward whom our desire is directed. When we read Atwater's findings in the light of Scripture, we realize that movement from each stage to the next involves a conscious choice. And everyone is responsible for their choices and the consequences of their action.

CONSEQUENCES OF BROKEN COVENANT

Affairs can have very serious consequences on marriage. In writing about the crises of infidelity, Pittman and Wagers (1995) contrast seven myths with seven truths about infidelity. The *first* myth is that since everybody is unfaithful, affairs are to be expected as a normal part of marriage. In truth, infidelity is not normal behavior but a symptom of some problem, usually having to do with the person or the marriage relationship. The *second* myth is that affairs are good for a marriage. In truth, while affairs can bring about a crisis in which an enduring marital problem can be solved, affairs are dangerous and often inadvertently end marriages. Though the *third* myth states that affairs prove that spouses no longer love each other, the truth is that before the affair the marriage may be seen as quite good, and many spouses still claim to love each other. The *fourth* myth asserts that the unfaithful partners are the sexier spouses since they are seeking more sex than what is available in the marriage. The truth is that, although affairs involve sex, sex is usually not the primary reason to have an affair. The motivation is usually to bolster a lack of ego or sexual confidence. Myth number *five* is that the affair is the fault of the resolute (faithful) spouse. The truth is that no one can drive someone else to have an affair. Although the *sixth* myth states that there is protection through ignorance of a spouse's affair, the truth is that affairs are fueled by secrecy and threatened by exposure. Finally, the *seventh* myth is that after an affair, divorce is inevitable. The truth is that marriages can, with effort, survive affairs if the affairs are exposed and relational trust is rebuilt. Based on their clinical experience, Pittman and Wagers (1995) believe that this last truth is a crucial point. Couples need to know that it is important to rebuild trust by dealing openly with the two key factors—dishonesty and jealousy—if the marriage is to survive.

Balance of power. Another consequence of an affair is that it affects the balance of power in the marriage. For example, the resolute (faithful) spouse may take a morally superior attitude and blame or shame the unfaithful spouse. The offended spouse may hold the affair over the other by pointing out the moral weakness in the other. This shift in power can be especially noticeable when marriage partners hold to faithfulness in marriage as a standard.

Although we might assume that the resolute spouse has the upper hand and gains the power in the marriage, the reverse can also be true. Resolute spouses can be peppered with questions of self-doubt and inadequacy, asking themselves, *What's wrong with me?* and wondering whether they are attractive or adequate as a sex partner. The emotional fusion common in many couples leaves them with the unspoken belief that the affair is a negative reflection on their competence. Even language that is used, such as "dumpee" and "dumper," puts the power in the hands of the one who has had the affair.

In a strange way, the spouse who strays is somehow validated because he or she has found acceptance by somebody else. Now it is two against one, and the offending spouse may actually have more status than the resolute spouse. In a certain sense, spouses who are having the affairs are powerful because they have been able to diminish or betray the resolute spouse through their actions. Especially if the resolute spouse is overly dependent, it is easy for the offending spouse to insinuate that the resolute spouse is blameworthy or inadequate. In this case, they use the affair to their advantage and can be defiant and seemingly gratified by depriving, hurting or being "one up" on the resolute spouse.

In cases where there is unequal power, the resolute spouses often succumb to the defeating self-doubts and spousal-inflicted doubts, failing to rightly protest the broken covenant. This lets the offending spouses off the hook, fails to keep them accountable, and continues to let them escape with little consequence. The lack of confrontation not only avoids the issue of the affair, but also fails to deal directly with important differentiation issues in the marital relationship. Therefore the inability to deal effectively with the affair leaves the problem unresolved, maintains the emotional fusion (dependency) in the couple, continues the lack of self-determination in each spouse, keeps the power hierarchy one-sided, and allows a lack of intimacy to continue permeating the marriage. In other words, things stay the same rather than partners letting this situation become an impetus for growth and change.

Emotional versus sexual infidelity. Though we generally think of affairs as being sexual, there can also be such a thing as emotional infidelity or affairs of the heart. Research indicates that "women tend to feel more threatened if their mate develops a close, emotionaly intimate relation with another women, [while] . . . men appear to feel more threatened when their partners are sexually unfaithful" (R. Firestone, L. Firestone and Catlett 2006:206). One explanation for this is that "men derive relatively more self-esteem from their sex lives, whereas women's self-esteem is more contingent on romantic commitment" (Goldenberg et al. 2003:1585).

In a study of Dutch couples, it was found that though jealousy evoked by emotional infidelity was primarily characterized by feelings of threat, jealousy evoked by sexual infidelity was primarily characterized by feelings of betrayal and anger (Buunk and Dijkstra 2004:395). When the authors looked at differences by sex, they found that "following emotional infidelity, in men, a rival's dominance, and in women, a rival's physical attractiveness, evoked feelings of threat but not feelings of anger-betrayal. In contrast, after sexual infidelity, in men, but not in women, a rival's physical attractiveness evoked feelings of betrayal-anger but not anxiety or suspicion" (p. 395).

Whatever the response, threat, anger, betrayal, fear, depression or even apathy, the affair takes a serious toll on the relationship itself. Emotional and physical affairs have broken the covenant trust, and that must be repaired if the marriage is to survive and thrive.

IS HEALING POSSIBLE?

Infidelity can have such a devastating effect upon a marriage that it does not survive. However, an affair can be a wake-up call in which spouses make incredible strides in working through the pain and efforts to renew their marriage in the process. One study found that infidelity had unintended positive outcomes such as developing a closer marital relationship, realizing the importance of good marital communication, increasing assertiveness, placing higher value on family, and taking better care of oneself (Olson et al. 2002).

Atkins and others (2005) report that couples who were in therapy and openly dealing with the infidelity made as much or better progress as other distressed couples. The manner in which disclosure of the infidelity takes place is an extremely imporant factor in the healing process. Progress is greatest among couples for whom an infidelity is shared rather than kept a secret (Atkins et al. 2005). In addition, while disclosure is a process, it is best for the offending partner to fess up rather than give information a little at a time. Also, the most effective therapy focuses on the whole of a couple's relationship and not just the infidelity, according to J. Schneider, Irons and Corley (1999).

Based on their qualitative research, Olson and others (2002) describe a three-stage process following the disclosure of infidelity. The beginning *roller-coaster* stage is chacterized by a range of strong feelings (anger, ambiguity, self-blame, panic) that causes spouses to alternate between giving up on the relationship and determining to make it work. In the *moratorium stage* there is less emotional reactivity, with only occasional emotional flare-ups. Finally, couples who make it through the second stage enter the *trust-building* stage. This third stage is characterized by increased communication, forgiveness and recommitment. It is important for a couple in this stage to be willing to focus on problems leading up to the infidelity.

We know that it is possible for a couple not only to survive an affair, but also to experience healing of the broken trust and to transform their relationship by facing the affair head-on. It is important to have family members, friends, counselors and ministers who support and wisely come alongside the couple to bring hope.

A ministerial response to an affair is to walk with the couple at a slow enough pace so they can deal with what has happened rather than rush into a quick solution. Staying with the anxiety and tension is essential so that the wronged spouse can express the myriad feelings, thoughts and reactions about what has happened. Whether this is done alone or as a couple takes discernment.

Once the secret has been disclosed, it is important that there is an acknowledgment of one's disobedience to God and awareness of the consequences of sin. Personal confession to the spouse quite likely will be an ongoing process throughout the course of healing. Asking forgiveness, showing repentance, and making amends is an essential part of expressing one's brokenness, humility and serious intention to recommit to the spouse and the marriage vows.

Relationship recovery continues on a path of healing. From a psychological point of view, it is important to help spouses grapple with their internal as well as external responses. There is a likelihood that unequal power or dependency are common themes. The affair may bring up important issues about fusion and fear of intimacy in a relationship, as discussed in the section on differentiation.

As the couple is able to tolerate the tough examination of themselves and their marriage, they will need to find the strength to eventually relinquish their pain and the desire to punish. Hope for recovery has to do with focusing on the future. They begin to ask questions like "What do I want to do?" "What would God have me do?" "What kind of relationship do we want to create?" During this period of redefinition, a couple usually is able to grow as they humbly stand before God to ask a blessing on their renewed covenant.

If the spouses happen to be particularly young in their faith or lack maturity in the Lord, we can gently offer Christ as the solid place to stand.

It is God who ultimately validates, forgives, empowers and renews. While is it certainly good to be validated by others, and our spouse in particular, our true validation is in Christ Jesus. Understanding the concept of being "differentiated in Christ" gives freedom to make choices out of spiritual strength.

The nature of marriage changes when people raise their level of differentiation in Christ. It means that a spouse chooses to be faithful out of a personal, moral conviction, not because it is demanded by spouse or society. Actions are *not* out of desire to control or hurt a partner or because one is afraid to challenge a spouse. The decision to be monogamous comes out of a clear conviction that this is God's best plan. A covenant is not a social exchange that says faithfulness begets faithfulness, but one of personal conviction and obedience to God's law. Thus we seek Christ's validation, and no one else can take our identity in Christ away from us. This spiritual perspective means the resolute spouse does not have to spend an inordinate amount of time focusing on the wrong that has been done. Demanding penance and placing guilt on the unfaithful spouse may make the resolute spouse feel powerful, but the obsessive thoughts and angry desire to punish actually are attempts to control the spouse. True repentance and accountable action through the power of God's Spirit ultimately move the couple forward.

The move toward reconciliation does not excuse or make light of the seriousness of the wrongdoing or the breaking of God's command. Neither does it minimize the grievous consequences of broken trust. Both spouses are encouraged to find their true place of belonging in Christ as they respond to what has happened between them. Dealing honestly with hurt, pain and betrayal is part of the personal healing process that eventually clarifies one's identity and self-worth in relationship to God. Indeed, genuine repentance and forgiveness lead to the needed restoration.

The resolute spouse can draw strength from the book of Hosea, considering the anguish and anger that God expressed to Israel, who had gone "whoring" after other gods. Israel's choice was a reflection on them, not on God. Yet their unfaithfulness broke God's heart, so he reminds them how much he loved them from the beginning, how he held them close to his heart and guided them by the hand of loving-kindness. Rejection is especially heartbreaking when one has experienced such deep connection.

The unfaithful spouse can also be encouraged by the parable of the

Prodigal Son (Lk 15:11-32) and know that even when one strays away from the Father, God is waiting with open arms to offer grace and forgiveness. God's loving arms are wide open, ready for the one who has strayed to turn around and come back home to the Father—a beautiful picture of restoration. When the unfaithful spouse repents and changes through action and attitude, recovery is well on its way.

THE HEALING HAND OF GOD

Frederick Buechner (1992) offers the following reflection about the ramifications of keeping secrets in a covenant relationship and how healing is necessary to restore that breach of trust. He opens the scene with God strolling through the Garden of Eden the day after Adam and Eve have eaten the forbidden fruit. They did what was forbidden and in the process broke their covenant with their Creator. God quickly lays bare the present situation by asking them, "Where are you?" They must admit that they are hiding themselves from God. Buechner wonders, "What is it they want to hide? From whom do they want to hide it?" and "What does it cost them to hide it?"

Then to lay bare the past, God asks them what they have done. Once again, Buechner ponders, "What did they hope would happen by doing it? What did they fear would happen? What was it that made them so ashamed?" They must face the consequences of what they have done. These questions offer them a way to reveal the truth so they then have the opportunity to heal what has been broken between them.

But this is not all! The most moving part of the story comes next, as God makes garments of skins and clothes them with his own hands. Buechner writes, "They can't go back, but they can go forward clothed in a new way—clothed, that is, not in the sense of having their old defenses again behind which to hide who they are and what they have done but in the sense of having a new understanding of who they are and a new strength to draw on for what lies before them to do now" (p. 70). Healing and blessing are possible as the couple reestablishes their covenant commitment.

AFFAIR PREVENTION: THREE TYPES OF FRIENDSHIP INTIMACY

Sexuality is an integral part of ourselves as we interact with opposite-gender persons outside the marriage. Sharing different sides of ourselves with others in close friendship is a wonderful part of being created in relationship. In modern society, men and women work and socialize together in close proximity, have meaningful friendships, and develop significant relationships with others. We have much to gain from these interactions, but we have much to lose if we do not learn how to integrate them into our lives as married persons.

One answer to preventing extramarital affairs is to avoid close contact with those of the opposite sex. But such an extreme reaction contradicts the biblical ideal of living in community and being members of the body of Christ. It also assumes that we are incapable of being morally responsible in our relationships. Also, the idea that a spouse must meet all our needs gives an unrealistic picture of marriage. God brings people into our lives to deepen our experiences and help us become what God wants us to be. The key is not to pull away from others, but to establish guidelines about the relationships we have outside the marriage. We might ask ourselves, "Does the friendship enhance or threaten our marriage?" Following are descriptions of three types of friendship intimacy and discussions of the implications of each in terms of marital fidelity.

Similar interest and intellectual intimacy. Common interests and similar intellectual pursuits bring people together in engaging interactions. Colleagues in any field of interest love to debate and dialogue with one another about their specialties. Just go to any party and notice how people gravitate to each other according to their interests. The discussions are often invigorating, whether it be the latest theory about something or a classical debate about an issue. Discussions like this are stimulating; they help us define our ideas, beliefs and values. Dialogue with others brings us fresh ways of thinking and expands our horizons.

Intellectual intimacy is seldom threatening to a spouse, so there is usually no need to restrict connections on this plane. It often even relieves a spouse from feeling obligated to be interested in everything one's partner is invested in. One example is those who love talking sports as opposed to those who have no interest whatever in that topic. There certainly are times, however, when for one reason or another a spouse may be threatened by such a relationship; these situations must be discussed and attended to with care.

Emotional intimacy. Sharing with friends about our life's journey is a special way of coming to know them at a personal level. In particular, having someone share disappointments, joys, feelings, doubts, hopes and dreams can bring about a level of emotional connection. This may include talking to each other about the friendship itself, disclosing how we feel about events going on in our lives, or opening up in other vulnerable ways that let this person know us better. We often look for someone to talk to about our problems when we are down or facing particular struggles in our lives. Being listened to, cared for and understood deepens our emotional connection with this special person in our life.

You may rightly suspect that this kind of intimacy has more potential for misunderstanding. Your spouse may understandably be uncomfortable with the depth of emotional sharing and personal disclosure between you and another person. Perhaps the spouse is jealous of the closeness and tenderness shared between you and another person. Other spouses are quite relieved that their partner has someone else to share with, because they may feel overly responsible or have difficulty relating on an emotional level.

In most cases, emotional sharing with a same-gender friend is no threat to a spouse. However, inattentive spouses can lose out on these deeper levels of personal disclosure. When spouses abdicate this position to others, spousal intimacy is limited, increasing distance between spouses.

Emotional sharing with someone of the opposite gender is more likely to lead to jealousy and anger. Such spousal concerns, when openly discussed and negotiated, can lead to clear and reasonable boundaries and appropriate guidelines in opposite-gender emotional sharing. One obvious guideline is to take time and effort for spousal communication. A couple must make concerted efforts to share what is going on in their lives. Though some spouses are better at sharing than others, interacting about personal things needs to be practiced throughout the marriage. When emotional sharing needs go unmet, the desire for emotional connection with someone outside the marriage increases the potential for an affair.

Physical intimacy. All people need to be touched in caring ways by caring friends. Some people are skin hungry because they have received so little physical affirmation in childhood and have an enormous need for concrete evidence of love expressed through touch. We call some friends "teddy bears" because they give such wonderful, warm hugs to let us know that we are loved. Some people are great at giving us that pat on the back, a shoulder to cry on or a comforting touch when we need encouragement.

This is physical touch without sexual connotation. It is genuine friendship freely given, no matter who is around to see. Even when such touch is offered in private, it is free of sexual overtones.

However, although physical touch can bring warmth, comfort and closeness, it can also be misunderstood. Sometimes even a comforting touch can unknowingly bring out a sexual response. One person may feel it and the other be totally unaware or deny anything sexual. Sometimes both persons sense the sexual vibes and pull away in order to keep appropriate boundaries. However, it may happen that one or both will not only sense the sexual feelings but also choose to follow through on them.

How does one deal with physical intimacy? How is the touch you give received by the other person? Are boundaries unclear or being violated in any way? Is there ever discomfort or confusion about the touch? What about kisses—are they okay? What kind, how long, and in what context? What is the meaning of the kiss? Is it simply a greeting of fond expression, or is there a romantic or sexual connotation? For instance, in our couples' group, we greet one another with a "holy kiss." It is an agreed-on way we show our affection for one another.

Once again, in the area of physical expression, spouses need to discuss together how they feel about the giving and receiving of touch in relationships outside the marriage. Perhaps one simple guideline is to always touch in a public setting. Some spouses are quite comfortable making personal choices in this matter, based on trust and disclosure. Yet it behooves spouses to openly share experiences they have with others outside the marriage. Couple integrity is increased by discussing implications of these relationships and faithfully following through on mutual decisions about touch.

AFFAIR PREVENTION: GUIDELINES FOR COUPLE INTEGRITY

Affair prevention begins with an awareness of the type of relational needs discussed above. Beyond this, we must realize that we will have attractions for others, and we need to recognize our vulnerability and have a plan in mind about our behavior. We offer the following guidelines for couples.

Be aware of feelings. A first principle is to be alert and aware of thoughts and feelings you have about your friendships. This is best accomplished by openly communicating with your spouse about your interactions with same- and opposite-sex friends. Denial and defensiveness are the first signs that indicate a questionable intention or motive. Deceit is tempting when you want something bad enough, writes Lewis Smedes in *Sex for Christians* (1994). It is not lust that gets most people into trouble but their lack of awareness of, or denial of, attractions and temptations, and their tendency to make exceptions for themselves. Honesty with self and partner is the only policy.

We believe it is important to talk openly with your spouse about anything that comes up for you in any particular friendship. Discuss the extent of the intellectual, emotional and physical interaction. Mutually set limitations in terms of the kinds of activities or amount of time you spend with friends. Establish appropriate boundaries in each unique situation. For the best interest of your marriage, come to a united decision about any matter of concern and mutually commit to it.

No secrets, please. Keeping secrets about a friendship is an automatic red flag that must be addressed immediately. If there are sexual feelings, you must admit this to your spouse so the two of you can decide how to appropriately proceed with that situation. If as a spouse you are uncomfortable for any reason, you are obliged to bring this up for discussion. The integrity of the marriage is of foremost importance. Bringing out all feelings and questions is absolutely the right thing to do. Sometimes a spouse is the better judge of things you may not notice in a social interaction. For example, listen when a spouse says, "I notice you being especially flirtatious around so-and-so. Are you aware of how much she/he seems to seek you out?" Your willingness to hear what your spouse says is a sign that you are completely open in these areas. In an attitude of love, keeping a spouse's best interest and the integrity of the marriage as the top priorities will safeguard your relationship.

The current state of the marriage. When a marriage is at its peak strength, there are more possibilities for a spouse to be close to others at all levels of friendship. When a marriage is at its weakest, there is greater vulnerability, and special caution must be taken to keep the integrity of the marriage as the priority. Questions to ask yourself and your spouse center on how each spouse's personal needs are being met in the marriage and what might be lacking at this particular time in married life. Until you address your marital issues, friendship intimacy may have to be put on hold because it takes away from working on your own relationship. When the marriage is at a vulnerable place, this is exactly when the spouse is most tempted to look for attention outside the marriage. The new relationship becomes a distraction or substitute for what is missing in the marriage, and the marital troubles are sidetracked or avoided altogether.

Marriage always has priority. Couples who are newly married have strong expectations that they will be faithful to each other. Marriage is your primary commitment, and friendship is always secondary. When your intimate friendships support and strengthen the marital dyad, you will feel safe and content with those intimate connections. But when such a friendship takes away or undermines the marriage in any way, it jeopardizes your marriage covenant.

Unfaithfulness is a serious offense because it breaks the marital vows made to each other in the presence of God. However, lest we be smug, we must remember that one can commit adultery of the heart, as Jesus reminded us. This is a sin that easily besets us. Every spouse must take an honest look at their positive contributions to the marriage rather than acting pious because they have never technically committed adultery. Lewis Smedes helps us take an honest look at ourselves by asking how we have failed to keep our marriage covenant:

> A man or woman can be just too busy, too tired, too timid, too prudent, or too hemmed in with fear to be seriously tempted by an adulterous affair. But this same person can be a bore at home, callous to the delicate needs of the partner. He or she may be too prudish to be an adventuresome lover, and too cowardly to be in honest communication and too busy to put oneself out for anything more than a routine ritual of personal commitment. One may be able to claim to have never cheated . . . but may never have tried to grow along with their partner into a deep personal relationship of respect and regard within marriage. Their brand of negative fidelity may be an excuse for letting the marriage fall by neglect into dreary conformity to habit and, with that, into a dull routine of depersonalized sex. I am not minimizing the importance of sexual fidelity, but anyone who thinks that morality in marriage is fulfilled by avoiding an affair has short-circuited the personal dynamics of fidelity. (1994:168-69)

William Loader (2005:134-35) affirms and broadens Smede's insights by stating that "the healthy marriage is not only the one free from adultery or even adulterous attitudes in either partner, but one in which other values we have learned in the Jesus tradition become central, such as respecting the dignity and worth of all people and engaging in love for one's neighbor as for oneself. Many marriages totally free from adultery or adulterous attitudes have been highly destructive for one or both parties when these other values have been missing."

FOR FURTHER READING

Harley, W., Jr., and J. H. Chalmers. 1998. *Surviving an affair.* Grand Rapids: Revell.

Glass, S. 2003. *Not "just friends": Protect your relationship from infidelity and heal the trauma of betrayal.* New York: Free Press.

PART THREE

Inauthentic Sexuality

11

Sexual Harassment

The Uninvited Eroticizing of a Relationship

Though sexual harassment is technically not a sexual offense, it is a sin in that it is a trangression of biblical norms of relational morality, in addition to being a liability to victims, employers, coworkers and the humanity of sexual harassers themselves. Sexual harassment is any form of unsolicited language or touching containing sexual overtones. It includes sexual jokes, suggestive talk and unsolicited physical advances. Other forms of sexual harassment include giving compliments that are uncomfortable for the receiver and denying a person the choice to avoid listening to sexual conversations or sexually oriented jokes. Whether implicit or explicit, such conversation or behavior should not continue.

In their book *Evaluating Sexual Harassment*, Foote and Goodman-Delahunty (2005) review the research on sexual harassment and acknowledge their difficulty in drawing conclusions due to the lack of precision and consistency in defining sexual harassment. Carol Jones, for example, discusses the differences between sexual harassment and workplace bullying. Although some bullying may not be sexual harassment, there certainly can be areas of commonality between gendered bullying and sexual harassment (2006:147).

Since allegations of sexual harassment occur primarily within the context of the workplace, a workplace definition is helpful. The Equal Employment Opportunity Commission (EEOC) defines sexual harassment as "unwelcome sexual advances, requests for sexual favors, and other verbal or physical conduct of a sexual nature." The EEOC suggests three defining features regarding sexual harassment: (1) submission to sexual misconduct is either explicitly or implicitly a term or condition of employment; (2) submission to or rejection of such conduct by the employee is used as the basis for employment decisions regarding the employee; and (3) sexual misconduct unreasonably interferes with an employee's work performance due to an intimidating, hostile or offensive work environment (2007).

In their edited handbook *Academic and Workplace Sexual Harassment*, M. Paludi and C. Paludi Jr. (2003) give evidence of the controversy and complexity surrounding the topic of sexual harassment. A study of workplace harassment showed evidence of *double jeopardy for minority women*. Berdahl and Moore (2006) report that "women experiencd more sexual harassment than men, minorities experienced more ethnic harassment than Whites, and minority women experienced more harassment overall than majority men, minority men and majority women." A Canadian study reports evidence of a *triple* sexual harassment jeopardy among women who are of color and are not Canadian citizens (Welsh et al. 2006).

The negative effect of sexual harassment is not confined to the work situations: its damaging effects are also found among women in such "enlightened" institutions as colleges. A study of over 1,455 college women suggests that "sexual harassment experiences are associated with increased psychological distress, which then relates to lower academic satisfaction, greater physical illness, and greater disordered eating" (Huerta et al. 2006). A study of high school students found that sexual harassment was predictive of decline in psychological health, decreased work productivity, and increased absenteeism at school (Chesire 2006).

Although it may be tempting to limit concerns about sexual harassment to the workplace, a Christian perspective must go beyond that to widen the awareness of all forms of sexual harassment as equally wrong, no matter what the circumstances or where it happens.

EXPLANATORY MODELS

After summarizing the research on sexual harassment in 1982, Tangri,

Burt and Johnson offered three explanatory models about harassment: the organizational, sociocultural and biological. Fitzgerald and Shullman (1993) organized the research findings in terms of the incidence, context and consequences of sexual harassment.

Tangri and Hayes (1997) use the onion as a metaphor for explaning harassment. Using a sociobiological-evolutionary process model, they begin with the "deep structure," or innermost layer, of their theoretical onion in identifying *natural/biological* explanations of harassment. For example, *hormonal* factors intrinsic to the genetic male system contribute to the tendency for men to be promiscuous in their pursuit of women. Another influence is the *evolutionary adaptation process*, which explains sexual harassment in terms of adaptation to reproductive cost-benefit ratios. As discussed earlier in the book, the idea is that reproduction entails different costs and benefits for men and women. Since women have only a few eggs, their investment in the reproductive process is great; but men have a need to diversify their "investment" by passing down their genes. At this point, Tangri and Hayes agree that the *natural/biological model* is insufficient as a complete explanation, but it is a good place to start (1997:114-16).

The next layers of the onion comprise *organizational models* that focus on structural arrangements making it more likely for sexual harassment to occur in the workplace. One example is *sex-role spillover theory*, which sees sexual harassment as a carryover of normal, day-to-day gender-based societal attitudes and behaviors brought into the workplace. Although flirtation would be viewed as legitimate in a certain social situation, this kind of behavior could qualify as sexual harassment in a work situation. A limitation of this theory is that it does not explain why there is a disproportionate number of men who engage in sexual harassment. Ultimately this theory also relies on sociocultural explanations of sexual harassment.

Organizational power theory is another model that identifies social structures maintaining power differentials that perpetuate sexual harassment by enabling the more powerful to manipulate the less powerful. As a result, sexual harassment is more likely to occur in hierarchical organizations that promote and perpetuate power differentials. J. K. Rogers and Henson (1997) show how asymmetrical power relationships explain the high incidence of sexual harassment with temporary workers.

A study investigating the prevalence of sexual harassment among 916 female family practice (medical) residents indicates that 32 percent reported unwanted sexual advances, 48 percent encountered sexist teaching material, 66 percent experienced favoritism based on gender, 36 percent were given a poor evaluation based on gender, 37 percent were targets of malicious gossip, 5.3 percent were punished punitively based on gender, and 2.2 percent were sexually assaulted during residency (Vukovich 1996). As a result almost one-third of these female residents experienced low self-esteem and depression. In some cases the effects were so severe that the residents required therapy or requested a program transfer. Power differential in the workplace sets up potential sexual harassment that can lead to serious emotional trauma and professional liability.

Sexual harassment of males is also reported in the context of power differentials. Men report being most threatened by coercive behavior that challenges their male dominance (Berdahl, Magley and Waldo 1996). It may be that because males tend to organize relationships around hierarchy, a distorted sexualizing of power and control is especially intimidating by men who are in one-down positions.

The next layers of the onion are the *sociocultural models*, which consider sexual harassment to be part of the larger cultural system. Sexual harassment is viewed as a fulfillment of culturally prescribed behavior rooted in sociocultural norms, values and institutions.

When this is the case, it might be appropriate to speak of a *culture of sexual harassment* since sociocultural structures are at the root of harassment. Thus, when a social structure includes both a power differential and exploitative cultural attitudes toward females, sexual harassment is more pronounced. Examples of this are restaurants that require waitresses to wear skimpy, tantalizing outfits with sexually suggestive slogans on the back. In studying the relational dynamics between the waitresses, the customers and management, Loe (1996) concludes that female employees "commodify" their sexuality as a means of earning a living. Unfortunately, the active participation of female employees in an exploitative workplace minimizes the offense in the minds of many. In this case the frequent occurrence of sexual harassment fueled by these two factors leads to a normalization of commodification in the workplace, and a cyclical reinforcement that sexual harassment is to be expected.

Although sociocultural models provide an explanation of why sexual harassment happens, they nevertheless fail to answer the questions of why all men or all of the powerful people do not harass, and why the same behaviors are perceived and experienced differently by men and women. For an answer to this, we must turn to the outer layer of the onion: *individual differences.*

Questions about individual differences center on how those who sexually harass are different from those who do not, and how those who are harassed differ from those who are not harassed. Among other things, when compared to nonharassers, male sexual harassers have difficulty taking the perspective of another, are more authoritarian, have negative feelings about sexuality, and have a low view of their masculine self. In comparison to nonvictims, victims of sexual harassment depart more from conventional sex-role scripts and are less traditional in sex-role attitudes (Tangri and Hayes 1997).

In conclusion, Tangri and Hayes see a consensus emerging across all of the theories of sexual harassment. "When it comes to heterosexual interactions, women experience a narrower range of male behavior that is acceptably sexual. . . . The *system* of heterosexual relations is adversarial and coercive" (p. 125). Though Tangri and Hayes give a helpful explanatory model of sexual harassment, there is a need to move beyond the value-free stance they take.

As applied to an understanding of sexual harassment, *critical theory* would not only focus on the power differentials between sexual harassers and those who are harassed, but also challenge the legitimacy of organizations and systems in which it is perpetuated. Critical theory also assumes that persons who are harassed, regardless of their circumstance, are not stripped of the abilities to think critically and to act as agents of change and transformation of systems tolerant of sexual harassment.

In the next section our strategy is to utilize a critical-theory approach anchored in the biblical text as a basis for understanding sexual harassment and determining what can and should be done about it on individual and structural levels.

A BIBLICALLY BASED INTEGRATIVE PROCESS MODEL

Based on the above social-scientific explanation of sexual harassment, we are ready to offer a biblically based process model of sexual harassment and an appropriate grievance process in response to this behavior. We begin by suggesting that sexual harassment can best be understood as a complex process of interaction involving individual behavior within the context of power-based sociocultural systems. To this we add a biblically based understanding of sexual harassment that includes three elements: (1) a definition of sexual harassment that considers both the motive of the initiator (harasser) and the experience of the one offended (harassed); (2) a distinction between affirmation and harassment; and (3) a comprehensive grievance process.

Our decision to include the subjective dimensions of motive, experience and perception has been verified by a recent study revealing that sexual harassment is a complex phenomenon that involves the individual factors of age, gender, gender role, past experiences, as well as the organizational factors of gender ratio and workers' perception of management's tolerance of it (McCabe and Hardman 2005).

Readers need to recognize that although sexual harassment applies to both men and women, for the sake of simplification and because it represents the most common pattern, most of our illustrations will portray the male as the harasser.

DEFINING SEXUAL HARASSMENT: BALANCING MOTIVE AND ACT

Attempts to objectively define sexual harassment are based typically on a narrow individualistic view, which fails to take into account the motive of the initiator and the experience of the offended. Sexual harassment has both an objective (the act of harassment) and subjective (the perception of harassment) dimension. In considering any alleged offense, the Bible points to the importance of considering both the motive of the accused and the effect of the act upon the accuser. This is perhaps most clearly stated in Exodus 21:12-14, "Anyone who strikes a man and kills him shall surely be put to death. However, if he does not do it intentionally, but God lets it happen, he is to flee to a place [God] will designate. But if a man schemes and kills another man deliberately, take him away from my altar and put him to death." A right understanding of the Ten Commandments also involves God's intent for a moral law that takes into account both the act and intent. Even though the first nine commandments refer to acts, the intent is implied within each (Kaiser 1983). That the act includes the intent is most explicitly seen in the Tenth Commandment: Do not *covet* your neighbor's house or your neighbor's wife (cf. Ex 20:17).

Determining the appropriate response to a charge of sexual harassment requires a consideration of both the act and the intent. For example, one man might embrace a woman while she receives it as a genuine expression of emotional support. Another man might embrace the same woman while she feels a sexual overtone. The two acts of embracing are not the same, because of differences in how they were intended or how they were received. The intent of the man and the woman's interpretation of the act determine whether it is sexual harassment, and both must be taken into account in the grievance process.

If a woman responds to the first hug with discomfort, the man acting from pure intent is still accountable for his behavior. At the very least, he may be guilty of a lack of good judgment in how he expressed support. Upon sensing her reaction, he should respond accordingly—by acknowledging her discomfort and apologizing, if necessary. Generally, it is best to ask before embracing.

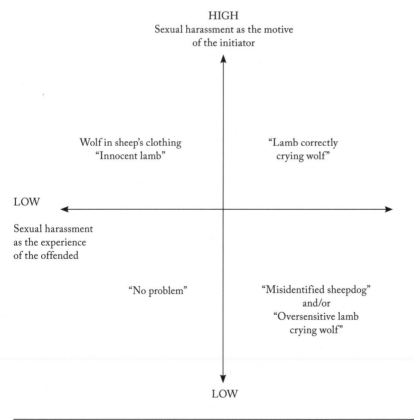

Figure 11.1. Defining sexual harassment: Balancing the motive of the initiator and the experience of the offended

At the personal level, individuals will vary greatly in what they report to be incidences of sexual harassment. Much of the variation reflects differing social background and life experiences. For example, factors such as having an overly protective mother, observing fewer positive behaviors between parents, and experiencing unwanted sexual contact during childhood—these are all associated with experiencing a greater number of objective incidents of sexual harassment (Houston and Hwang 1996). Beneath the experience of sexual harassment is the woman's perception of the event. However, there is evidence that some background factors can desensitize one to sexual harassment. Strouse, Goodwin and Roscoe (1994) found that exposure to high levels of pop music videos as well as dysfunctional family dynamics increase tolerance of sexual harassment among adolescent girls.

Figure 11.1 depicts an attempt to balance the motive of the initiator with the experience of the offended.

Sexual harassment as the motive of the initiator is represented on a continuum ranging from *High* at the top to *Low* at the bottom. Sexual harassment as the experience of the offended is represented on a continuum ranging from *Low* at the left to *High* at the right of the table. A given social encounter may be anywhere within the bounds of the figure. At the lower left corner is a social encounter that is clearly not sexual harassment. There is no motive to harass on the part of the initiator, nor is harassment experienced by the recipient. At the upper right corner we have the exact opposite. Here the initiator is the sexual aggressor, and the encounter is clearly perceived as harassment by the recipient. This is clearly an offense; the "wolf" has been identified, and both parties know it.

The difficulty in identifying sexual harassment occurs when there is a lack of congruency between the motive of the initiator and the experience of the offended. The upper left corner of the figure represents an encounter in which the initiator is sexually harassing the person, but that person does not perceive it as harassment. This might be a case of a "wolf appearing in sheep's clothing," or a woman being so used to this treatment that she rationalizes that "men will be men" and does not even judge this behavior as harassment. In the lower right corner we represent an incident in which the initiator does not intend sexual harassment, but the action is perceived as sexual harassment by the receiver.

The incongruence can stem from two types of situations. First, this might be a case of the overfriendly protector who is misidentified as an aggressor. Without meaning to convey sexual innuendoes, some men (and women) might relate in a way that is perceived by the other as sexual harassment. For example, a man who offers a woman a ride home out of genuine concern for her safety might be guilty of bad judgment but not of sexual harassment. Second, some women may be overly sensitive to a male's initiation in a social exchange. The innocent question or statement offered is perceived by the woman as having connotations that the man did not intend. She may have misread this situation because of previous experiences of sexual harassment or exploitation.

O'Donohue and Bowers (2006) suggest fourteen possible pathways to false allegations of sexual harassment: lying, boderline personality disorder, histrionic personality disorder, psychosis, gender prejudice, substance abuse, dementia, false memories, false interpretations, biased interviews, sociopathy, personality disorders not otherwise specified, investigative mistakes, and mistakes in determination of the degree of harassment. The worthy goal of identifying sexual harassment needs to include the protection of the accused from possible false allegations.

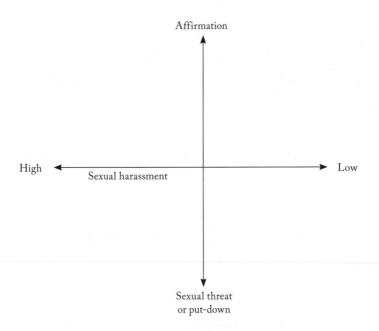

Figure 11.2. The relationship between sexual harrassment and affirmation

We have given some examples to illustrate the four extremes, but in reality, sexual harassment comes in different degrees and shades. Thus, at the very center of the chart are incidences in which compliments are given where the intent of the initiator and the experience of the receiver vary greatly depending on a variety of social contexts, such as differences in age, status and power; the degree that two people know each other; and the social situation. The "dance" between men and women is fraught with multiple layers of possible mixed motives and multiple interpretations.

DISTINGUISHING BETWEEN HARASSMENT AND AFFIRMATION

This leads us to a related issue: a statement that might be given and taken as affirmation in one social context may come across as sexual innuendo, a put-down, or even a sexual threat in another. Spoken words or behaviors might be considered affirmation or sexual harassment depending upon the intent of the initiator and how it is experienced by the receiver. For instance, upon meeting for the first time, a man may say to a woman, "Your red hair is astonishing!" Is this affirmation or sexual harassment?

Figure 11.2 illustrates the relationship between sexual harassment and affirmation during a social encounter. The vertical continuum represents the verbal content, from a statement of affirmation at the top to a sexual threat or put-down at the bottom. The horizontal continuum represents the degree of sexual harassment from *High* at the left to *Low* at the right.

As a way of gaining a functional understanding of the issue, examine the following statements and try to place each comment within the figure: (1) "I admire your creativity and style." (2) "You have an illogical mind." (3) "I could open up a sexually uptight person like you." (4) "You have a beautiful body." (5) "Your work reflects a feminine [or masculine] sensitivity." We suggest that the first statement most clearly fits in the upper right quadrant, the second statement in the lower right quadrant, the third statement in the lower left quadrant, and the fourth statement in the upper left quadrant. The last statement might be the most problematic, for some might argue that behavior cannot be both affirming *and* involve sexual harassment. However, the recipient of such a comment can at one level feel affirmed, but at another harassed.

Our point is that we must think in both dimensions when assessing a given behavior. Sexual harassment applies to both men and women. Although it is less common, women do sexually harass men, and certainly sexual harassment within the same gender occurs as well. Most people perceive behavior differently based on the gender of the initiator. Reversing the gender of the initiator and victim can affect the way sexual harassment is interpreted: often the traditional view of men as the sexual aggressor shades our interpretation of his behavior.

A meta-analysis of sixty-two studies of gender differences in the perception of sexual harassment reveals that "women perceived a broader range of social-sexual behavior as harassment" (Rotundo, Nquyen and Sackett 2001:914). Difference in perception might explain some, but not all of the differences between males and females in experiencing sexual harassment. The greater experience of sexual harassment by females than males is true at virtually all ages and circumstances. Thus girls in secondary school experience nearly twice as much sexual harassment as boys, girls in secondary school receive unwanted sexual attention more than boys, and women in a variety of workplace settings report experiencing more sexual harassment than men. Sexual harassment of males is almost always in the context of power differentials. Men are most threatened by coercive behavior challenging their male dominance. Possibly males tend to organize relationships around hierarchy, resulting in a distorted sexualization of power and control, which is especially felt by men in power-down positions.

Cultural context is another factor important in determining sexual harassment. Objective definitions and subjective experiences of sexual harassment are embedded in a wider cultural context. Persons from different cultural backgrounds differ in their interpretations of what constitutes sexual harassment. Studies of sexual harassment in formerly all-male institutions, such as the armed services, illustrates how subcultural contexts are important. Laura Miller (1997) found that men who believe and resent that women in the military have unfair advantages (for example, exemption from combat roles and less stringent requirements) and admit to harassing their female counterparts. The study suggests that harassment may be strongest from men who feel passed over or stuck in the Army's system of rank. Other studies support the influence of resentment as a motivation for sexual harassment. For example, interviews of twenty-two African American female firefighters report a climate of resentment among male firefighters that was expressed in passive-aggressive ways (Yoder and Aniakudo 1996). The study found that a climate of initiation rites and pranks among male firefighters fueled resentment by excluding female firefighters.

Although the sociocultural context of sexual harassment is vast, these studies illustrate the complex factors involved in sexual harassment. A comprehensive understanding of sexual harassment includes individual, social and cultural factors that shade our response to sexual harassment on individual and structural levels.

GRIEVANCE PROCESS

Grievance is the process of addressing the wrong of sexual harassment. Recent notorious legal cases are responsible for the increased public attention surrounding sexual harassment. Virtually all moderate- to large-size organizations use a grievance process for handing sexual harassment charges.

Although there are many sexual harassment grievance programs, we believe the best approach includes an emphasis on *relapse prevention* (see Brunswig and O'Donohue's book *Relapse Prevention for Sexual Harassers* (2002) or Lenhard's *Clinical Aspects of Sexual Harassment and Gender Discrimination: Psychological Consequences and Treatment Interventions* (2004).

A Christian perspective on sexual harassment must develop a grievance process that is based on the biblical themes of justice, mercy, retribution, restoration and reconciliation. Figure 11.3 illustrates a biblically based model for handling sexual harassment.

Justice versus mercy. Besides the tension between act and motive discussed in a previous section, Scripture holds justice and mercy in balance. A biblical perspective of grievance encompasses concern for the victim and the community (justice) and concern for the offender (mercy). In figure 11.3 an emphasis on justice is represented horizontally from *Low* at the left to *High* at the right. An emphasis on mercy and correcting the offender is represented vertically from *Low* at the bottom to *High* at the top. This dual concern is part of the larger biblical teaching about law and grace.

Our understanding of the relationship between law and grace is clearly addressed by Paul: "Christ is the end of the law so that there may be righteousness for everyone who believes" (Rom 10:4). As Paul elaborates on this text, we learn that there is nothing wrong with the law itself, for it points the way to live according to God's intention. The problem with the law is that because no one is perfect, the law cannot be fulfilled. In his excellent book on New Testament ethics, Richard Hays proclaims, "Christ is the *telos* of the Law" (1996:414). Thus, Christ is the "end of the law" in the sense that he is the perfect fulfillment of the law. Because of Christ's perfection and righteousness, our righteousness is not dependent upon our keeping the law, but upon our faith in Christ.

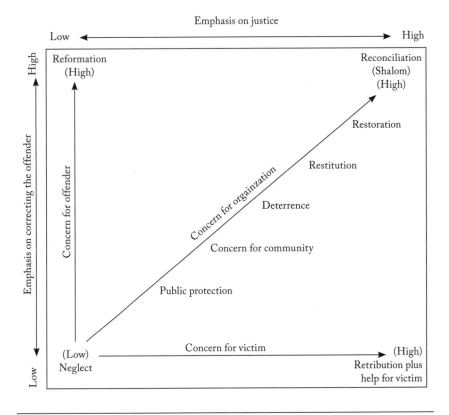

Figure 11.3. A biblically based model for handling sexual harassment

Understanding our relationship between law and faith in Christ gives clarity to the relationship between justice and mercy. God's holiness demands his justice, but Christ's incarnation and resurrection provide mercy. The following is an example of how both principles need to be part of a grievance process.

In a general sense, *justice* involves *concern for the victim* (represented by the horizontal arrow at the bottom of figure 11.3), while *mercy* shows *concern for the offender* (represented by the vertical arrow at the left of the figure). The Old Testament emphasizes concern for the victim above the offender. However, a rationale of grievance based on Old Testament teachings alone is one-sided, showing little concern for the offender. The life and teaching of Christ temper justice with mercy toward the offender.

Under God's justice, we are accused and found guilty. But God shows mercy to us through Christ. Jesus illustrates the balance of justice and mercy in Matthew 5:38-39: "You have heard that it was said, 'Eye for eye, and tooth for tooth.' But I tell you, Do not resist an evil person. If someone strikes you on the right cheek, turn to him the other also."

When the Pharisees brought a woman caught in the act of adultery to Jesus, they were right in asking whether she should be stoned according to the law of Moses. (Actually, according to the letter of the law, *both* she and the man with whom she committed adultery were to be stoned [Deut 22:22-24].) Jesus, however, showed mercy when he challenged, "If any one of you is without sin, let him be the first to throw a stone at her." After her accusers had left, Jesus turned to the woman and said, "Then neither do I condemn you. . . . Go now and leave your life of sin" (Jn 8:7, 11). Mercy is not simply letting the offender off without consequences, but rather mercy demands repentance and rehabilitation. The mercy Jesus teaches is a call for change. Jesus' call for mercy is contingent upon balancing two elements: the act of the offense and the intent of the offender. As recognized in a previous section, the Bible teaches that redress for an offense must take into account both the act and the motive.

Grievance within the Christian community. A biblical model for handling grievance equips us to address the question of sexual harassment in a church or Christian organization. First, Christian organizations handling cases of sexual harassment incorporate a respectful balance of concern for the victim, for the offender and for the organization. By working toward healing and restoration, persons demonstrate accountability for their actions.

Figure 11.3 represents a balance between concern for the victim, the offender and the organization. Unfortunately, denial is a common response within the Christian community regarding the existence of sexual harassment. Neglect is represented in the lower left corner. Failure to implement a grievance process in the face of a sexual harassment charge is neglect of the victim, the offender and the organization.

However, there may be good reasons why a victim fails to pursue a grievance. Serious matters that need to be taken into account include feelings of powerlessness, shame, fear of job loss or other retaliation, and need for taking time to process the offense before making it public.

The victimized individual is the first concern in any sexual harassment grievance process. A primary concern for the victim is thematic in the Old Testament and in Jesus' teachings. In the parable of the Sheep and the Goats, Jesus taught, "Whatever you did for one of the least of these brothers of mine, you did for me. . . . Whatever you did not do for one of the least of these, you did not do for me" (Mt 25:40, 45). However, a church or religious organization that shows high concern for the victim, but none for the health of the offender or the organization in which the offense took place, narrowly limits its response to a *retribution* model.

The purpose of retribution is revenge for the victim by having the offender "pay" for the offense. The law of revenge was enforced by the ancient Hebrews, often providing a punishment similar in nature to the offense, but specifying the maximum limit the punishment could take (Ex 21:23-36). Retribution not only attempts to equal the score between the offender and the victim, but it hopefully also serves to have a unifying effect upon society. When a societal norm has been violated, retribution draws attention to the legitimacy and need of the norm for the preservation of society. The practice of secrecy within the church and parachurch organizations regarding sexual offenses sabotages healing at the community level.

The opposite view emphasizes the belief that *rehabilitation* is the only consideration for deciding appropriate punishment. Such thinking promotes a victim society, excusing offenders as victims of dysfunctional families or hostile, uncaring communities. According to this view, punishment is replaced by treatment. This view is problematic in that it fails to show concern for the victim and fails to treat the offender as a responsible human being. Failure to hold people responsible for their behavior minimizes their humanity as creatures of God who are divinely given self-will.

Concern for the community is another reason given for advocating punishment of the offender. Punishing offenders for the good of the community is usually referred to as *deterrence.* The theory of deterrence proposes that punishing by example will discourage others from committing the same offense. Obversely, lack of accountablility for the offense will diminish the community's resistance to the same offense. Theoretically, concern for the community might be thought to correspond to the use of deterrence. When there is low concern for the community (represented in the lower left corner of fig. 11.3), the motivational force of deterrence is low. As concern for the community increases (represented in the figure as a movement diagonally toward the upper right corner), there is an increase in deterrence. However, concern for the good of the community can be motivationally expressed at several different levels.

At a basic level, community protection from sexual harassment stems from a motivation for community safety. Merely removing the harasser protects the community; however, this does not deal with the offense within the context of the community, as deterrence does—holding the offender up as an example. For this reason, public protection (such as removal of the offender) is lower than deterrence on the "concern for community" continuum. Although the Bible advocates deterrence as a response to an offense in social relationships, it has more to say about *restitution* and *restoration*.

Restitution uses punishment to compensate for the harm done to the victim. Exodus 21 contains a number of examples of punishment as restitution:

> If men quarrel and one hits the other with a stone or with his fist, . . . he must pay the injured man for the loss of his time and see that he is completely healed. (Ex 21:18–19)
>
> If a man hits a manservant or maidservant in the eye and destroys it, he must let the servant go free to compensate for the eye. (Ex 21:26)
>
> If a man uncovers a pit or digs one and fails to cover it and an ox or a donkey falls into it, the owner of the pit must pay for the loss; he must pay its owner, and the dead animal will be his. (Ex 21:33-34)

Exodus 22:1 teaches that restitution needs to be more than the loss inflicted on another: "If a man steals an ox or a sheep and slaughters it or sells it, he must pay back five head of cattle for the ox and four sheep for the sheep." So strong was the Old Testament emphasis upon restitution that inability to pay back a loss to the victim could result in the offender being "sold to pay for his theft" (Ex 22:3). The rest of Exodus 22 continues to detail the types of punishment to be carried out, based on the principle of restitution.

The absence of restitution in society today may reflect the hyper-individualistic emphasis that pervades contemporary society. The exception to this, or perhaps its consequence, is the increasing number of exorbitant civil suits, including those for sexual harassment. The legal system seeks punishments that are equivalent to the harm done to the victim. However, rarely does the offender make recompense to the victim directly. Only restitution offers the victim the hope of compensation for the real loss incurred at the hands of the offender.

The absence of restitution may be one of the reasons why victims in our society cry out so harshly for revenge. Our grievance systems rarely provide for any other way in which the victim can feel that his or her loss is being "paid for." Restitution is especially appropriate when society at large is victimized. An example of this took place a few years ago when a highway contracting company in Nebraska pleaded guilty to bribery. Instead of sending the guilty to prison, the judge ordered them to endow a $1,475,000 chair of ethics at the University of Nebraska. A similar approach in cases of sexual harassment might order the offender to distribute literature and educate others on the issue of sexual harassment. Restitution may also prove more effective in rehabilitating the offender.

The upper right corner of figure 11.3 represents an ideal concern for the victim, the offender and the community. The practice of these three motivations by the community (public protection, deterrence and restitution) constitutes *restoration*. At the interpersonal level the process of restoration repairs or reestablishes unity. Restitution begins the process of restoration at the interpersonal level. Restitution reestablishes equity in the relationship between the harasser and the victim. Some interpersonal changes are necessary to foster restoration. The harasser must go through a process of sorrow, confession, true repentance and asking forgiveness for the wrong committed. In response to true repentance, the victims must be able to deal with feelings of anger, rage and hurt, with the hope they can ultimately forgive.

The Christian basis for interpersonal restoration is the biblical model of reconciliation. In the Old Testament, reconciliation was made possible when a sacrificial atonement (the Hebrew verb *kāpar* means "to cover") was offered for sin (Lev 6:30; 16:20-22). Jesus elaborated the meaning of reconciliation by tying it to reconciliation from an offending brother: "So when you are offering your gift at the altar, if you remember that your brother or sister has something against you, leave your gift there before the altar and go; first be reconciled to your brother or sister, and then come and offer your gift" (Mt 5:23-24). The Greek word for being reconciled is *diallassomai*, which means "to be changed entirely." Reconciliation or interpersonal restoration is for the benefit of the offended as well as the offender. God desires that all broken relationships be restored.

Jesus taught his followers to take the initiative in seeking reconciliation. The basis of this teaching on reconciliation is powerfully illustrated by Christ's atoning death: "Be reconciled to God. God made him who had no sin to be sin for us, so that in him we might become the righteousness of God" (2 Cor 5:20-21). The theology of the cross provides a basis for Christians to pursue and achieve reconciliation with an offending person.

Reconciliation or the attempt at restoration in the harasser-harassed relationship must not be prematurely rushed, however. Individuals must be given time to admit to and experience deep feelings of betrayal, grieving, anger, rage and desire for revenge. Each individual process in moving toward reconciliation is unique and different. The last thing victims need is pressure to forgive the harasser. Only after the offended have been able to let go and disarm the emotional power that the offense has in their life—only then is forgiveness possible. However, forgiveness never means condoning or excusing the offense. It is the conscious choice of the one offended to let go and extend forgiveness by the empowering of God's grace. True reconciliation requires penitence of the harassers for their offense. When there is true repentance from the harasser and forgiveness from the harassed, restoration transforms into interpersonal reconciliation. Jesus illustrates the process of interpersonal restoration in the parable of the good neighbor, in which two enemies become as neighbors to one another (Lk 10:29-37).

SEXUAL HARASSMENT AS A SOCIAL JUSTICE ISSUE

A biblical view of reconciliation also calls for restoration at the *social structural* level. Communities have the potential to create environments in which sexual harassment is likely to be the accepted norm, most notably in all-male institutions. An example of this situation is the Tailhook scandal, which arose at the 35th Annual Symposium (Convention) of the Tailhook Association (Tailhook 91), held on the third floor of the Las Vegas Hilton Hotel from September 5 to 7, 1991. Naval officers had a tradition of celebrating their graduation at this symposium. In former times, when no female officers were part of the festivities, sexist jokes and skits were an acceptable part of the rite of passage. However, the addition of female naval officers added a new dimension to this sexist subculture. The situation got out of control as the male officers began grabbing, fondling and trying to disrobe female officers. After an initial denial, the Navy commander minimized the situation by suggesting, "Boys will be boys." Marginalized and insulted, a number of the female officers filed official complaints of sexual harassment. This not only ended in the forced resignation of the commanding officer but also in a self-examination and restructuring within the Navy.

There is a logical relationship between sexual harassment and sexual discrimination. Communities practicing sexual discrimination, including churches and parachurch organizations, by their very nature provide a social environment conducive to sexual harassment. Furthermore, it is unlikely that a community promoting sexual harassment will be challenged by anyone within the community, and so it is likely that the community will continue the practice. In a community allowing racial discrimination, certain members deny equal rights to others because of their race. When a conflict develops between a member of the majority group and the minority group, an opportunity is created for the system to be challenged. Any minority member refusing to accept a place of subordination will encounter organizationally sanctioned harassment. One need only to examine the response of racially discriminatory social orders for more insight into this type of social structure. Thus inappropriate sexual behavior is often not defined as "harassment" but rather as "just rewards" to persons who do not know their place.

Sexual discrimination, like racial or any other form of discrimination, needs to be thought of as a social justice issue. An excellent model on how justice in biblical perspective might be applied to gender relationships is given in *After Eden: Facing the Challenge of Gender Reconciliation* (Van Leeuwen et al. 1993). These authors find that "nowhere in the Bible is there any suggestion that 'justice' is limited to the marketplace and other 'public' arenas of activity. . . . Those who would be members of God's kingdom, *whatever* their race, nationality, class, or gender, are called to weave a seamless web of justice *and* righteousness *and* peace throughout all areas of their personal and corporate lives" (pp. 426-27).

Christians need to regard social structures that are prone to sexual harassment as a social justice issue. Biblical justice is oriented toward *recreating* communities so that each gender participates fully and equally in society. Mott (1982) states: "The difference between scriptural and classical justice lies in the understanding of what is to be the normal situation of society. The Scriptures do not allow the presupposition of a condition in which groups or individuals are denied the ability to participate fully and equally in the life of the society. For this reason, justice is primarily spoken of by the biblical writers as activity on behalf of the disadvantaged" (p. 65).

When women are not free to live in their full femininity because they fear being sexually harassed, there is no *shalom* (see upper right corner of fig. 11.3). Shalom is "the human being dwelling at peace in all his or her relationships: with God, with self, with fellows, with nature" (Wolterstorff 1983:69). A characteristic of groups, communities or organizations embodying shalom is *just peace*. If peace and order are present, but sexual harassment is the norm, there is no shalom. Punishing those who are committing sexual harassment without addressing the problem of harassment-friendly social structures falls short of a full view of biblical justice. The principle of *redress* is foundational to biblical justice and stands as an obligation to correct an unjust social structure (Lev 25:25-28; Ps 107:39-41).

Research shows that programs utilized by organizations to sensitize their members to better recognize and prevent sexual harassment can be effective (Antecol 2003). Such planned intervention can be effective not only in changing individual behavior, but also in changing an organizational climate from one that tolerates harassment to one in which the full humanity of each individual, regardless of sex, ethnicity or rank, is respected.

CONCLUSION

In response to the question of which is the greatest commandment, Jesus replied, "Love the Lord your God with all your heart and with all your soul and with all your mind, . . . and . . . love your neighbor as yourself" (Mt 22:37, 39). Sexual harassment violates Christ's commandment to love our neighbor as ourselves. The Bible further teaches that both male and female are made in the image of God (Gen 1:27), in Christ there is neither male nor female (Gal 3:28), and followers of Christ are to be in mutual submission to one another (Eph 5:21) instead of lording it over one another (Mt 20:25-27). Sexual harassment denies the image of God in the other, negates our oneness in Christ, and usually involves an abuse of power; therefore, the Christian community must actively combat it, for when one member suffers, all suffer together (1 Cor 12:26).

We have suggested that a biblical response to sexual harassment will incorporate high concern for the harassed, the harasser, and the community in which the harassment takes place. Failing to be concerned for the harasser not only ignores the humanity of the perpetrator; it will also result in the perpetrator repeating the harassment in the future. The evidence suggests that those who sexually harass are likely to be repeat offenders. Sexual offenders first need to be stopped, but second, need to be helped to develop healthier, more-human ways of relating.

A biblical response to sexual harassment involves redress and restoration at both the interpersonal and community level. A concerned response is incomplete if it focuses *only* on the victim and the offender; it must also seek the restoration of a just peace at all social structural levels. Such a situation is poignantly described in Isaiah 11:6-8: "The wolf shall live with the lamb, the leopard shall lie down with the kid, . . . and a little child shall lead them" (NRSV). Without losing concern for the victim and the offender, a biblical view of restoration following sexual harassment will also encompass the holistic connotation of shalom as community well-being.

FOR FURTHER READING

Foote, W., and J. Goodman-Delahunty. 2005. *Evaluating sexual harassment: Psychological, social, and legal considerations in forensic examinations.* Washington, D.C.: American Psychological Association.

Lenhard, S. 2004. *Clinical aspects of sexual harassment and gender discrimination: Psycholgical consequences and treatment interventions.* New York: Brunner-Routledge.

Paludi, M., and C. Paludi Jr., eds. 2003. *Academic and workplace sexual harassment.* Westport, Conn.: Praeger.

12

Sexual Abuse

A Violation Deep Within the Soul

Sexual abuse leaves a gashing wound deep within the heart and soul of a child. It is a "hushed-up secret that's too big for seventy-times-seven forgiveness," according to one survivor. We must face sexual abuse for what it is: a spiritual violation that has a profound impact on the child, the family and society at large.

Celie, a fourteen-year-old girl, tries to put words to her experience of being sexually abused by her stepfather in *The Color Purple*, by Alice Walker (1982). She writes to God in her private diary since her stepfather has warned her to "never tell nobody" about what he has done. Here are a few excerpts to help us understand her pain.

Dear God,
I am fourteen years old. ~~I am~~ I have always been a good girl. Maybe you can give me a sign letting me know what is happening to me. (p. 11).

Dear God [written after she told her friend Shug about the abuse],
It hurt me, you know, I say. I was fourteen. I never even thought bout men having nothing down there so big. It scare me just to see it. And the way it poke itself and grow. . . . I start to cry. I cry and cry and cry. Seem like it all come back to me, laying there in Shug arms. How it hurt and how much I was surprise. How it stung while I finish trimming his hair. How

the blood drip down my leg and mess up my stocking. How he don't never look at me straight after that. (pp. 108-9)

Celie's world got turned upside down, leaving her in utter disarray about what went wrong. This young girl was not only shattered by the basic trust that was broken between herself and her stepfather, but also by the long-term effects of the incestuous intrusion later in her life. It was a pain too deep for words; yet when she finally shared the unspeakable secret with her trusted friend Shug, it was this woman's accepting love that helped bring healing to Celie's soul.

As we shall document later in this chapter, childhood sexual abuse can have serious lifelong traumatic effects. R. Firestone, L. Firestone and J. Catlett (2006:5) state that the result of such experiences "may lead to a defensive posture and a tendency to depersonalize that often have a profound adverse effect on the willingness to remain vulnerable and close during intimate moments."

DEFINING SEXUAL ABUSE

Sexual abuse is broadly defined as a sexual act imposed on a child or person who lacks emotional, maturational and/or cognitive development. Being in a dominant position (because of age, physical strength, or being in a parental or older sibling role), perpetrators invite, lure or force a child to have sexual contact with them. This may include such behaviors as showing pornographic material, telling explicit sexual stories, disrobing inappropriately, sexual touching, intercourse, oral or anal sex, or penetration of genital or anal openings with an object. Using their more powerful position, perpetrators take advantage of a child's normal curiosity, innocence, and physical and mental vulnerability.

Sexual abusers come from all walks of life and economic and cultural groups. Whether blue collar or professional, rich or poor, male or female, adult or minor, religious or nonreligious, Caucasian or non-Caucasian—perpetrators commit heinous crimes against children. Sex offenders are usually known (relative, friend, professional or family acquaintance) to the child who is abused. It is less common that a child is sexually abused by a complete stranger.

Pedophiles are sex offenders whose preferred or exclusive method of achieving sexual excitement is through engaging in sexual activity with children. These adults have a conscious interest in using prepubescent children for sexual gratification. Pedophiles are high-risk offenders who often begin offending at a young age and have a record of prior offenses and multiple victims.

Incest is more specifically defined as a sexual violation between persons related by blood or marriage, including stepparents, caretakers or live-in partners who assume a parental role. The powerful parental position leaves the child especially vulnerable to their requests or demands. Instead of protecting and providing for children dependent on them, the offender misuses authority to coerce them into sexual compliance. It is a shattering blow of betrayal when the sacred parent-child trust bond is broken. No child is ever prepared for such a twisted reversal of relationships.

The most common type of familial sex offense is sibling incest, usually an older child with a younger child. The two dominant patterns of sibling incest are power-oriented/aggressive acts and enticing/erotic acts. The power position of an older sibling is an important factor in sibling abuse, with the abuse usually being preceded by verbal coercion. Sometimes sibling sexual abuse is motivated by anger or jealousy toward a sibling who is perceived to be favored by the parents. In other cases siblings who cling together for comfort in physically abusive or neglectful homes may find that the overly close relationship becomes sexual.

Many families minimize sibling sexual abuse because they define sexual contact between siblings as normal sexual curiosity. Maddock and Larson (1995) point out how attitudes about normal sex play between siblings vary across cultures and even within cultural groups. Some groups are very casual about sibling sexual contact while others impose strict sanctions. In most cases, however, concern is rightly expressed when sexual activity takes place under any kind of coercion or force. Age differences between the siblings, duration of contact, and motivation of participants are other factors to take into account when assessing sexual sibling abuse. It certainly is always a serious offense when specific acts like vaginal or anal penetration, oral-genital contact, or intercourse occur. The family must never close their eyes but remain appropriately alert to any sexual activity that occurs between siblings.

Family involvement in the treatment of sibling abuse plays a significant role because it shores up the leadership role of parents in terms of providing proper supervision and guidance. Family therapy can be a resource in helping family members learn appropriate ways of caring, connecting and upholding the sacred bonds of family trust.

In his recent book *Sexuality and the Jesus Tradition*, William Loader (2005) builds a strong case for understanding the "causing a child to stumble" passage (Mk 9:42-48) as probably pointing toward the sexual abuse of children, which was widespead at that time in the world. Mark 9:42 states, "If anyone causes one of these little ones—those who believe in me—to stumble, it would be better for them if a large millstone were hung around their neck and they were thrown into the sea" (via Loader). Loader states that "the saying would most likely evoke in Mark's hearers what was a common danger and one which every Christian community would need to address: sexual abuse of children" (p. 236). Loader points out that Mark places the warning about pederasty next to the warning about sexual immorality, to highlight the despicable blind spot about child sexual abuse.

PREVALENCE OF SEXUAL ABUSE

It is difficult to obtain reliable statistics on the actual number of sexual abuse cases in any culture due to the shame and stigma felt by victims, offenders and their families. Reports of sexual abuse from studies of women in general populations have ranged from 7 percent to 50 percent (Roosa et al. 1997), depending on how abuse is defined.

An encouraging report substantiated by child protective services indicates that child sexual abusers dropped by 40 percent between 1992 and 2000 (Finkelhor and Jones 2004). Hopefully this drop is an indication that increased prevention efforts, incarceration of offenders, and treatment progrms are having an effect. However, it is also possible that part of this decline is a result of welfare agencies narrowing their scope of child welfare responsibilties due to heavy case loads.

The actual number of sexual abuse incidents is most likely to be higher than studies indicate, especially among boys. Males are more reluctant to report sexual abuse experiences with other males, due to stigmas about masculinity and implications of homosexuality. Other factors that contribute to underreporting in both males and females include shame, a feeling of responsibility in some way for the abuse, blocked memories, and confusion about what constitutes sexual abuse.

Of children who are sexually abused, females are at a higher risk (83 percent) than males (17 percent). Preadolescence, a time when sexual development is pronounced, is the time of greatest risk. Social isolation is another factor that places a young person at risk for sexual abuse. It is unclear whether loneliness and isolation from peers come before the abuse, or if the isolation is a way to cope with abuse that has already occurred (Finkelhor 1997).

Living in a home with a nonbiological father also places a child at greater risk for sexual abuse in that home. Trepper and Barrett (1989) found stepfathers to be five times more likely than natural fathers to sexually abuse children, and the abuse is of a more serious nature. The explanation for this finding may be that the strong incest taboo observed throughout most cultures of the world keeps biological fathers from sexually abusing their daughters. Especially when the biological father is sufficiently bonded with his children, he is less likely to treat them as objects of his sexual desires. Some surmise that the presence and participation of a father during the birth of his children increases his emotional attachment, dissuading him from incestuous thoughts and behaviors toward his own children.

THE INCESTUOUS FAMILY

The incestuous family may look normal on the outside, but inside the home, relationships are seriously disrupted. In many of these homes, a closed boundary around the family keeps others out, while rigid roles within the family promote male dominance, female subservience and authoritarian parenting. These dynamics set up a conspiracy of silence. No one dares tell an outsider what goes on inside the family, for this would be considered a profound act of disloyalty. Power and fear are tactics used to undermine weaker family members, who are not allowed to question authority or expose the truth. Family members learn to walk on eggshells, be extremely cautious, and keep their feelings to themselves.

While rigid family dynamics, as mentioned above, can lead to an extremely harsh reaction to sexuality, the chaotic home is also problematic. For example, when there are no clear boundaries or respect for personal space, a child's privacy can be invaded physically, sexually and emotionally in a variety of ways. Whether it is a case of sleeping in a crowded room or in the same bed, or having an open-door policy that gives free access at anytime to any member, a child's personal privacy is being invaded. Practices in the home such as vulgar sex talk, erotic suggestions and sexual innuendos cause discomfort and confusion. Substance abuse is often part of the chaos, breaking down normal inhibitions and opening up unacceptable sexual possibilities that otherwise would be contained. Laxness in boundaries as well as hostile and rigid interactions leave children fearful, vulnerable and unprotected.

A study conducted in Dunedin, New Zealand, found the postabuse adjustment of 138 women to be especially poor when there was a negative relationship with parents. One way these children escaped a difficult home situation was to participate in sports or achieve in academics (Mullen, Martin, Anderson, Romans and Herbison 1996).

Father-daughter breach. A characteristic of incestuous families is emotional disconnection and inability to empathize with others. The father who sexually abuses his children sees them as property. He is emotionally immature and often unable to fulfill his needs in nonsexual ways. He has little capacity to take the feelings or wishes of others into account and resorts to controlling, coercing and seducing children under his control.

In a large sample surveying 775 women survivors of childhood sexual abuse (ages 25 to 44), 80 percent of the subjects also reported emotional and physical intrafamilial abuse (Ussher and Dewberry 1995). Family dynamics included frequent verbal coercion, blaming, making threats, and being exposed to various acts of physical and sexual violence. Onset of puberty at a young age, suffering abuse from one's father or stepfather, repeated sexual intercourse, and prolonged abuse—these are factors that contribute to the extensive negative impact on the victim.

Mother-daughter breach. When a daughter is sexually abused by her father, she often feels angry at her mother for not having prevented the abuse. Whether a mother was in denial, neglectful, self-engrossed or in a powerless position, she nevertheless failed to protect her daughter.

An overly dependent, passive wife may find it easier to pretend that abuse is not occuring than to confront her perpetrator husband or boyfriend. She may choose to keep quiet because she fears the ramifications of exposing what she knows. Sometimes mothers are willing to sacrifice their daughters in order to appease their husbands. A mother may blame her daughter for what happened, calling her a "slut" or "home-wrecker." This mother may be resentful, jealous or hostile toward her daughter after the abuse is revealed. Such reactions drive an enormous wedge between mother and daughter. Sadly, in a small percentage of cases, the mother is an active participant in the abuse, leaving the daughter with a double dose of betrayal.

Intergenerational abuse. The Bible speaks of intergenerational sin in Exodus 20:5 and Deuteronomy 5:9. The fact that sins are passed from generation to generation can be seen through studies that show how sexual abuse tends to repeat itself over generations. Among other things, social science research reveals a higher prevalence of and more severe childhood sexual abuse reported by sexual perpetrators when compared to non-sexual offending criminals. Likewise, women also, as women who have been sexually abused more than those who have not, are likely to sexually abuse others. Based on their review of relevant literature, Serbin and Karp (2004:333) conclude that "a generation of parents may place their offspring at elevated risk for social, behavioral, and health problems."

Sexual abuse victims and their families need special help to cope with the pain of sexual violation. Some withdraw by burying their heads in books, some are compliant by trying to make everything all right in the family, some use distraction to numb the pain, and some act out in self-destructive ways.

Some time ago I (Judy) counseled Jennifer, a young mother, and her eight-year-old daughter, Katey. I noticed how Jennifer distanced herself and was unresponsive to her daughter as she desperately tried to make connection with her mother. Something seemed drastically wrong, but it was not until I learned about the generational abuse history that the pieces of the puzzle came together. During one session, Jennifer revealed the physical and sexual abuse she had endured as a child by her mother, who had been sexually and physically abused as a girl by her father and grandfather. It dawned on me that the mother was keeping distance from her children so she would not repeat abusive behavior; staying disconnected was the best way she knew to protect her children. Her mother's twin sister, Aunt Mae, finally assured her niece that one does not have to continue the generational abuse patterns. Aunt Mae proudly announced, "The buck stops here!" She had never laid a hand on her children, and she promised to spend time in Jennifer's home to show her how to be close to her children without repeating the abusive patterns. That day Jennifer broke through the fear and replaced it with a new picture of family interaction.

Creating a safe environment. Having considered the various ways parents abuse or fail to protect their children from abuse, let us explore what parents can do to create a protective home environment.

Setting and keeping appropriate boundaries is a good place to begin. When personal boundaries are identified and respected, each family member is awarded a sense of personal worth and power. Being alert to discomfort between family members and disruptions in relationships gives the family an opportunity to talk openly about what is happening to cause this reaction. When communication paths are open, children can share their concerns about any sexual indiscretions that occur. So often the reason a son or daughter does not disclose sexual information to parents is out of fear that they will not be believed or that parents will be unable or unwilling to do anything about it. A parent who takes immediate, appropriate action when sexual issues are disclosed gives children assurance that such matters will be effectively dealt with and not tolerated in the home.

Developing connection through careful listening and appropriate response to children's requests for change means parents are alert to their children's concerns. Actions to make needed changes give family members a sense of security that their expressed needs will be met.

PROFOUND DAMAGE

Sexual abuse, whether done by a family member or a stranger, whether a single act or ongoing pattern, cuts to the very core of a child's soul. Survivors of sexual abuse suffer from a wide variety of disorders like major depression, dissociative disorders, eating disorders, anxiety disorders, body pain, addictions, substance abuse, acting out behaviors, posttraumatic stress disorders, bipolar disorders, suicide and self-esteem issues (R. Firestone, L. Firestone and Catlett 2006; Bergen et al. 2003).

The power differential automatically places the child in an out-of-control situation. Robbed of personal power, the child is at the mercy of the abuser. Hays and Stanley (1996) discovered that women who were sexually abused as children, for example, experience extreme stress in keeping dental appointments due to similar feelings of being out of control and in close proximity with the dentist. Peters and Range (1995) found that subjects who had been abused were more likely to be suicidal as adults than those who were not abused.

Mental disorders. Research indicates that prolonged, severe childhood abuse plays a significant role in the development of serious mental illness. "Numerous well-documented studies done since 1987 indicate that

50-60 percent of psychiatric inpatients, 40-60 percent of outpatients and 70 percent of all psychiatric emergency room patients report childhood physical and sexual abuse or both" (Wylie 1993:29). Bessel van der Kolk, a professor at Harvard Medical School, and a team of researchers conducted a comprehensive study of trauma patients, finding that nearly half of the psychiatric patients had experienced extreme distress as a result of childhood sexual abuse. The symptoms included inability to regulate emotions, intense suicidal ideation, somatic disorders, negative self-perception, poor relationships, chronic feelings of isolation, despair and hopelessness (Wylie 1993:70). It is astonishing to think that the prevention of child abuse and neglect could drastically reduce the number of patients needing psychiatric treatment.

The physical and emotional experiences of childhood sexual abuse leave many victims wanting to erase themselves from life. They avoid situations in which intimacy is required and stay away from others (men in particular) in order to protect themselves from further abuse. Like most defenses, such strategies may provide temporary relief, but they also keep a person frozen in the pain and loneliness.

Ava said she just wanted to cuddle up in her afghan, lock all the doors and windows, pull down the shades, and rock herself for hours in her rocking chair every day after work. To be by herself in her controlled world was all that mattered to her. When someone knocked on the door, it sent a streak of fear through her heart that she could not explain. All she knew was that she did not want to open the door and face the person on the other side. She felt safe in her cocoon, worlds away from people she believed could harm her. Although Ava managed to drag herself to work each day, she was always relieved to return to the security of her apartment. In her extreme difficulty in trusting others, she surrounded herself with animals who felt safe to her and brought her comfort.

She hid from the world because interacting with others made her feel extremely fragile. Beneath the external mask she wore in public dwelt a confused, fearful, lonely person. Ava pretended to be cool, calm and collected so no one would discover the truth about her sexual molestation. She was desperate to find ways to soothe the trembling injured child within.

Ava's desire to protect herself is understandable. Basic survival needs supersede any thought of connecting with others. In her own protective cocoon, she could at least prevent another betrayal from ever happening again. The enduring pain of her childhood has robbed her of vitality.

Living with the scars of sexual abuse. A myriad of feelings (rage, horror, terror, regret, anguish) flood a survivor after she is abused. If pregnancy occurs, there are further excruciating decisions about whether to abort the fetus, keep the child, or release the baby for adoption. It seems impossible that a young girl could go back to being a "normal" teenager after going through sexual experiences far beyond her age. Some abuse survivors describe themselves as "damaged goods," recalling how they felt after enduring the sexual abuse. While no one should ever be labeled as damaged goods, it is understandable why she feels this way. Her innocence and virginity have been taken from her against her will, and she has subsequently suffered a significant loss of self.

Survivors of sexual abuse often judge themselves harshly, in addition to feeling condemned by others for what happened. What a sexual abuse survivor needs more than anything is a trustworthy, supportive person to listen to her story. She needs a safe place to let her defenses and pretenses down. She needs a Christlike presence so she can share her deep hurts.

By facing the hurts of the past, it is possible to heal from the crippling effect of the abuse. Although it takes a solemn commitment to confront the painful experiences of sexual abuse, the process of remembering eventually helps a person release the destructive impact of the abuse. Revealing the truth is difficult work, for it brings up primitive, intense emotions, but naming the abuse means that the person is no longer fighting an invisible enemy. Venting bottled-up feelings helps release the rage, which eventually opens up a space to feel and grieve the deeper pain. Now that the enemy has been brought into the open, the sexual abuse is no longer a secret; the victim can place the blame where it belongs and enter into recovery as a survivor.

Survivors of sexual abuse need to define themselves by the whole of who they are, rather than by this one aspect of their life. The suffering is not to be denied or forgotten, and talking about the pain can become an eventual pathway to healing and restoration. When released from the crippling effects of the sexual abuse, a person is then free to construct a new identity. This old story has a new ending because it no longer haunts like a ghost from the past. Victory often comes through the help of a professional therapist, a supportive friend, a small group and a faith community. The following story is an example of this kind of healing.

Cindy was sexually abused as a child and desperately sought love and affection from others. Unfortunately, she became stuck in a continuous pattern of chaotic and destructive relationships. As a result, her self-esteem plummeted to an all-time low, and she believed she would be better off dead. At this point of desperation she entered therapy.

The first thing Cindy asked was, "Will I ever be normal?" She certainly had not lived a normal childhood when compared to her peers, and she began to tell her painful story in bits and pieces to her therapist. Gretchen listened with compassion and acceptance. Little by little, Cindy began to trust and felt hopeful for the first time in years. She could reveal her painful experiences in the context of an unconditional committed therapeutic relationship. After much exploration, self-disclosure and empowerment, she experienced a healing of her heart and soul.

A year later Cindy met a wonderful man named Geoffrey. Over time, she was able to share her story with him. Although they were romantically attracted, it was the solid friendship that brought them into a step-by-step growing intimacy. The sexual aspect of their relationship was "on hold" while Geoff wisely put the priority on Cindy as a person. Time in therapy together gave him a deeper understanding of the dynamics of Cindy's sexual abuse. His patient, gentle approach is what mattered most to her, and it was not surprising that their friendship blossomed into a satisfying, deeply committed love.

Research indicates how important it is to work with the partners of sexual abuse survivors in a conjoint therapy modality (Reid, Wampler and Taylor 1996). An important component of sexual abuse recovery is receiving support from a partner who is educated about the implications of childhood sexual abuse. The partner's needs and issues about the abuse must not be overlooked (Firth 1997). The therapist can pace the therapy in ways that are best for the survivor and the partner, to ensure a successful outcome for the relationship.

THE ISSUE OF REMEMBERING

Some children may block out memories of being sexually abused in order to remove themselves from the terror of the experience. This response is understood as a defense mechanism that allows children to survive what they cannot comprehend at the time it is happening.

The therapeutic community has recently been under scrutiny for taking early childhood memories of sexual abuse as fact. Elizabeth Loftus, a professor of psychology at the University of Washington, is outspoken in her efforts to dispel the myth that human memory is infallible. She believes that memory can be inaccurate, confused and altered, while the subject cannot separate memory from fact. Since current research shows that memory is marginal before age 2, she questions whether a young child has the mental structure to form coherent long-term memories. Along with others, she cautions that people's memory can be particularly unreliable because it is a complex process that involves a selective perception of past events (Wylie 1993). It is important to acknowledge that not all accusations are true and that false accusations (some of them malicious) can have devastating effects on the falsely accused.

Those who have admitted to making false accusations against family members later say their therapist planted the idea in their heads. The False Memory Syndrome Foundation (FMSF) advocates for parents who they believe are innocent victims of a collusion of revenge that occurs between a therapist and their adult clients. They say the therapist encourages clients to make an accusation as a way of cutting the "umbilical cord" so they can differentiate from their family. Psychiatry professor George Ganaway believes that in a "delayed adolescent rebellion," the daughter blames her parents, displacing her dependency needs on the "all-accepting" therapist, who becomes a substitute parent figure (Wylie 1993).

Professional sexual abuse therapists consider this explanation as an unlikely scenario since the primary goal of therapy is to work toward independence, not dependence on the therapist. Though it is certainly possible for some clients to be motivated and persuaded by their therapist, most sexual abuse victims minimize the trauma of what happened. They are actually quite willing to accept blame rather than place blame on those who did the abuse. In addition, memories bring up such deep feelings of shame that survivors do anything to avoid the intense pain that arises when remembering.

It is more likely that therapists find it very difficult to hear the details of the sexual abuse horror and the excruciating memories it stirs up for clients. It is exhausting work for both client and therapist. An ethical therapist listens with an open mind in order to help the client discern the truth and would not try to convince, persuade or draw conclusions for clients.

The main role of the therapist is to create a safe sanctuary in which clients can ultimately tell their story while seeking wisdom and discernment, which brings healing to their soul. The "emotionally focused" theraputic approach developed by Susan Johnson (2002) not only seeks to create a feeling of safety, but also emphasizes the need to give the abuse survivor control over the pace and direction the therapy takes. Only then, Johnson believes, will the therapist be in a position to help survivors manage and contain their stress.

A SPIRITUAL MATTER

Family therapist Cloe Madanes (1995) addresses the impact of sexual abuse on the family system. She sees sexual abuse as a "spiritual pain" in the heart of the child and believes it is necessary to explore the spiritual implications of this offense. She believes the first step for the offender is to recognize that he has inflicted a serious spiritual wound on his victim. Second, he must confess, with sincere and deep remorse, and be able to convincingly explain *why* what he did was wrong. Restoration, she writes, is a total package of making confession, seeking forgiveness, and making amends.

In the case of sibling incest, a brother's rightful role as protector of his sister has been broken and must be restored. The violation of the sibling covenant requires specific steps to bring about a necessary healing to that broken relationship. The offender must recognize the deep distortion of his actions so he can sincerely ask forgiveness and confess that he has caused her great suffering. When he is able to acknowledge the impact of his abusive actions, he can then ask for forgiveness and make reparations. Madanes (1995) works with the entire family to eliminate the destructive patterns of intrusion, domination and violation and replace them with constructive patterns of love, protection and empowerment.

The secret of the abuse must be entirely out in the open so that all family members can recognize what went wrong and how they can join together to make things right. They are challenged to make the home environment a safe place, where abuse will never happen again. One aspect of becoming responsible and caring is for the offender to make concrete restitution for what he has done. In a proper protective role, he needs to give sacrificially out of his care for the victim. For example, he may start a savings account for her future education, to which he contributes money each month. When the perpetrator sees himself in a new light, he gains the self-esteem needed to be in rightful relationships with others. We agree with Madanes that it is critical to reach offenders at an early age if the cycle of abuse is to be broken. Changes in the family environment and relationship patterns offer hope for a new way of living.

FACING THE PAIN OF THE PAST

Telling your story to someone you trust is a courageous first step in the healing process. You need to have a safe place to feel the anger and grieve the pain. Giving yourself permission to express the wrong done during your childhood is a crucial step because it acknowledges the truth of what happened.

Forgiving those who have caused the pain is the most difficult action ever asked of a survivor. It is difficult to even imagine forgiving someone who has caused such extreme harm, especially if the offender is unwilling to admit the wrong committed and shows no remorse. Coming to a place of forgiveness never means you condone the actions of the offender. What was done is never acceptable! Forgiveness does not mean that one forgets or ignores the impact of being wronged, nor does it release that person from accountability for their actions. In fact, forgiveness does not even require extending reconciliation, for this may not always be possible. Forgiveness means you are able to let go of the destructive impact the abuse has had on you so you can be free.

Remember that forgiveness is not a single action, but an ongoing process that continues throughout life. Survivors recover by fully understanding the depth and meaning of what they are forgiving. Every step is a courageous step that moves a person in the direction of internal change. Irreparable damage has been done, and the relationship itself may be irreparable, but a person's inner journey of healing is what brings a peace that passes even human understanding. It is God's way of freeing survivors from the brutal spiritual wounds that have left a bitter stain. Forgiveness releases survivors from the bondage of self-destruction.

God is waiting and eager for survivors to experience the life-changing power of God's Spirit to empower them to put the past in perspective so they can move forward with revewed vigor and purpose.

Please check the section "Ministering to Rape Survivors" in chapter thirteen for a more in-depth coverage of ministering to survivors of sexual abuse.

SUMMARY

In this chapter we have concentrated on restoring authentic sexuality where harmful sexual acts have left serious injury. Once again, referring to the four biblical principles of authentic sexuality, we see how possessive love is the exact opposite of covenant love. Exposing children to shameful sexual acts is the exact opposite of accepting and nourishing them. Sexual control, coercion and manipulation crush rather than build up and are the exact opposite of empowerment. Secrets and denial distort the truth. In contrast, love that protects, graces, empowers and connects promotes hopeful, healthy sexual relating in family environments.

Space does not permit us to give a full treatment of how to handle the abuser. Jesus's words on what needs to be done with anyone who causes a child to stumble (Mk 9:42-48) should certainly help us see the seriousness of the offense.

We must be a faithful presence as a community of prayer and support to abuse survivors, pointing them to the all-knowing, all-loving God, who is capable of restoring wholeness. These verses from Psalm 6 bring comfort, understanding and hope in this journey:

> I flood my bed with tears;
> I drench my couch with my weeping.
> My eyes waste away because of grief;
> they grow weak because of all my foes.
> Depart from me, all you workers of evil,
> for the LORD has heard the sound of my weeping.
> The LORD has heard my supplication;
> the LORD accepts my prayer.
> All my enemies shall be ashamed
> and struck with terror;
> they shall turn back, and in a moment be put to shame. (Ps 6:6-10 NRSV)

FOR FURTHER READING

Duncan, K. 2004. *Healing from the trauma of childhood sexual abuse: The journey for women.* Westport, Conn.: Praeger.

Fortune, M. 2005. *Sexual violence: The sin revisited.* Cleveland: Pilgrim Press.

Heitritter, L., and J. Vought. 2006. *Helping victims of sexual abuse: A sensi-*

tive, biblical guide for counselors, victims and families. Minneapolis: Bethany House.

Langberg, D. 2003. *Counseling survivors of sexual abuse.* Fairfax, Va.: Xulon.

Miles, A., with foreword by M. Fortune. 2002. *Violence in families: What every Christian needs to know.* Minneapolis: Augsburg.

13

Rape and Sexual Violence

Destructive Sexualized Power

Sexual violence of any kind is an extreme form of inauthentic sexuality. Sexual force against the will or without the understanding of another person is a problem that most find difficult to comprehend. The encouraging news is that since 1993 rape and sexual assault has fallen by over 69 percent (RAINN 2006). The discouraging news is that every two and a half minutes a person in America is sexually assaulted, based on the U.S. Department of Justice statistics. According to the 2005 National Crime Victimization Survey, there were 191,670 victims of rape, attempted rape or sexual assault in 2005 (RAINN 2006). About 44 percent of rape victims are under age 18, and 80 percent are under age 30. In reality, many sexual assaults are not included in these statistics since it is one of the crimes least likely to be reported. Males, who make up 10 percent of sexual assault victims, are even less likely than females to report the crime. The most common reasons these crimes are underreported is the shame attached to the sexual nature of the assault and the fear of the assailant's reprisal.

This chapter will focus on individual, familial and sociocultural aspects of rape crimes. We will consider the dynamics surrounding those who commit violent crimes as well as the impact that sexual violence has on victims/survivors, their families and the community. We urge the church to be involved in the recovery process so that substantial healing and transformation can be experienced at all levels. This includes actions like consciousness-raising education about gender inequality and power patterns; promotion of positive, authentic sexuality values; reconstruction of beliefs and attitudes in the broader community; and social-political endeavors that will reduce sexual violence in our world.

THE CULTURAL CONTEXT

By surveying anthropological data on the prevalence of rape in 156 cultures over 4,000 years of human history, Sanday (1981) identified the cultural context of rape. The survey identified 47 percent of these cultures as *rape-free societies*, where rape was either infrequent or did not occur, and 18 percent as *rape-prone societies*, where rape was either culturally allowable or largely overlooked. Rape-prone societies embrace a social ideology of male dominance and are characterized by a high level of interpersonal and intergroup violence.

Rape has too often been tolerated in many cultures, with women having little protection or recourse, and perpetrators being treated leniently. Rape-prone cultures tolerate rationalizations for rape, such as viewing it as an act of punishment (more often as revenge against a particular woman rather than against women in general), or as a demonstration of power and control over women. A closer examination reveals that the reasons for rape are often compensation for an inadequate masculine identity and self-confidence, and as an act of gratifying oneself at the expense of a less powerful person (Jewkes, Peen-Kekana and Rose-Junius 2005).

It is disturbing that the United States ranks as one of the more rape-prone cultures. One in six American women are vicims of sexual assult (RAINN 2006). The high incidence of rape in our culture seems to correlate to three main factors: (1) masculinity that is defined by aggressiveness rather than gentleness; (2) commonly held myths suggesting that women frequently mean yes when they say no, and that men cannot control their sexuality once it is aroused; and (3) dating patterns that sanction privacy and time alone between a man and a women who barely know each other (Holzman 1994).

At one extreme, rape is explained as an act of uncontrolled passion due to a lack of female partners, and at the other, a biological drive that impels men to maximize the number of women with whom they procreate. In an effort to synthesize the extremes, L. Ellis offers a biopsychosocial theory of rape and states: "Rape is sexually motivated, not only by the sex drive, per se, but [also] by the drive to possess and control others to whom one is sexually attracted. . . . Natural selection has favored a stronger sex drive in men than in women" (1991:638). Although Ellis believes that these sexual motivations are innate, he thinks the violence is learned. We believe these explanations are vastly inadequate.

Accumulated clinical evidence seems to indicate that rape is less an expression of sex than it is of violence and represents an extreme expression of male power. Out of this suggestion, a sociocultural theory of rape has developed, which finds that cultural constructions of gender and sexuality serve to shape men's beliefs and attitudes about their masculinity, about women and femininity, and about relational expectations in a sexual encounter. Research supports a correlation between men's beliefs about rape myths and the sexual aggression in their behavior (Malamuth 1996).

Lisak and Ivan (1995) suggest that men lacking the capacity for relational intimacy and empathy are more likely to be sexually aggressive. Rape is viewed as an unnatural, pseudosexual act. It is an irrational, nonsexual desire used to meet unfulfilled power needs. Rapists use sexual behavior to act out their anger, aggression and hostility toward women and rarely mention sexual satisfaction or pleasure as a reason for the assault.

The erroneous belief that any act employing sexual organs must be sexual is what has confused theories of motivation for this crime. Rape is primarily about violence, not sex. It is an act in which sexual organs are the tools of aggression and dominance. On a broader level, rape can be understood as reflecting societal attitudes that people have a right to impose their sexuality on others regardless of the other's wishes. This societal attitude perpetuates the idea that dominant-subordinate relationships between two people are acceptable. When coercive sex is sanctioned, violence is a logical end. When sex is viewed as a mutual choice between equals, intimacy is a logical end.

In part, the myth of manhood is a reflection of our "seductive society." The playboy image defines a real man as one who is successful in seducing women. The playboy is admired for being able to entice, persuade or coerce a woman into what he wants from her: sex. Granted, the ideal playboy is so irresistible that resorting to physical force as a means of obtaining sex is a strike against him. Nevertheless, the playboy models two characteristics common to a cross-section of men who attempt acquaintance rape: First, they reduce a woman to a sexual object rather than a person. Second, they lack respect for women.

PROFILE OF A RAPIST

A little more is known about men who attempt stranger rape than those who try acquaintance rape. The majority of these men come from disturbed family backgrounds in which their parents neglected, deprived or harshly punished them as children. Home life is characterized by low income, marginal employment and inadequate supervision. Many were raised by only one parent or by a relative or foster parents.

On the personal level, rapists have an aggressive attitude toward women. These men are motivated by feelings of hatred, rage and contempt for women. They desire to control and humiliate their victim, which may be related to the link between viewing pornography and rape. Using polygraph tests to assess truthfulness, Walp (2006) validated the relationship between viewing pornography and rape from interviews with rapists serving jail time.

Rapists have very low self-esteem and special insecurities about their manhood. Most feel weak and ineffective in relating to women. The greater their insecurity, the greater the desire to attack, subjugate and subdue the victim. They have little or no capacity to view women as human beings. Far from being oversexed, rapists are usually sexually inadequate. In fact, a majority of married rapists have problems with erection and orgasmic functioning. In addition, many report that they frequently cannot function sexually with their victims (Janssen 1995). Other research shows that rapists have a hostile and distrustful view of women (Milner and Webster 2005), that sexual assult against women is higher when men leave a relationship (DeKeseredy and Joseph 2006), and that fraternity men had significantly more degrading images of women than nonfraternity men (Bleeker and Muren (2005).

Monahan, Marolla and Bromley (2005) describe the rape event in term of five sequential phases: *preexisting life tensions, transformation of motivation into action, perpetrator–victim confrontation, situation management,* and *disengagement.* There are, however, a wide range of differences within these five phases.

In a comprehensive study of eight hundred convicted rapists, R. Prentky and A. Burgess classify rapists into four types (Goleman 1985). Fifty percent are *exploiters,* those who find a victim in a vulnerable situation and decide to rape without premeditation. These men are the least violent and stand the best chance of being rehabilitated. Twenty-five percent are *compensatory* rapists. Feeling themselves to be severely inadequate sexually and totally unattractive to women, they believe that force is necessary and even deserved because women reject them. *Enraged* rapists make up 20 percent of the rapists studied. These men are seldom motivated sexually, but want to humiliate and dominate women. For these men, rape is usually an act of hate. Five percent are *sadistic* rapists, who try to inflict as much pain as they can upon their victims. The bizarre fantasies of these men can result in a fatal injury to the victim.

DIFFERENTIAL VULNERABILITY

Differential vulnerability simply means that some women are more vulnerable to sexual aggression than others. Although we point out this research, we are quick to vehemently state that the perpetrator who commits this crime is *never* to be exempt from responsibilty for what occurs, an assertion that avoids a "blame the victim" criticism.

Risk factors. Buddie and Testa (2005) found that women college students with heavy episodic drinking and a higher number of sex partners have experienced more sexual aggression. They found that college women are no more at risk than non–college students, yet less at risk when living at home. Certain characteristics such as low socioeconomic status, low self-concept and neediness are related to being more at risk for assault. Perhaps these factors have to do with these victims questioning what they did to bring on the attack or even worse, that for some reason they deserved the abuse.

Rape prevention programs teach that assertive women who portray self-confidence and self-assuredness are less likely to be singled out as a victim. Rapists are more inclined to choose a victim they view as weak and defensiveless.

Blame the victim. Gender is a factor in the tendency to blame the victim, since rape victims are generally viewed more sympathetically by females than males (Nagel et al. 2005). Another study investigating "blame the victim" attitudes had subjects read scenarios of a rape incident where the victim was dressed somberly or seductively (Whatley 2005). It was found that males rated the seductively dressed victim more deserving of the attack than females, and those with traditional rather than equalitarian attitudes toward marriage were likely to assign more victim responsibility and deservingness than equalitarians.

DATE RAPE

Until fifty years ago, rape was rarely reported or even openly discussed. It was assumed that all rape happened between strangers. As rape has become an issue of public concern, the increase in reported numbers of acquaintance rapes come as no surprise. Reports by the U.S. Department of Justice consistently indicate that about one-third of all rapes are acquaintance rapes. In a study of 332 female Christian college students, 51 percent reported that they had experienced an unwanted sexual incident in their past, of which 15 percent were described as stranger assault and 11 percent as date rape (Neal and Mangis 1995). Gross and others (2006) reported that 27 percent of college women interviewed stated that they had experienced unwanted sexual contact on a date. It is assumed that date rape is mostly underreported, since many women may define it as unwanted sexual contact rather than rape or simply choose not to report it because they know the victim. In general, the greater the intimacy in a relationship, the less likely one is to resist sexual advances or view them as a threat.

Four major perspectives have been used to explain date rape (Humphrey and Herold 1996; Poulin 2005). *Socialization theory* emphasizes gender socialization processes promoting a culture that supports date rape. Normalization of sexual coercion as an acceptable masculine behavior is the core element of date rape. Truman, Tokar and Fischer (1996) have found more date-rape-supportive attitudes and beliefs among men who endorse rigid traditional gender roles, express negative attitudes toward feminism, and evidence homophobic attitudes. *Feminist theory* points to patriarchy, with its corresponding norms of unequal power distribution between females and males, as the cause of date rape. *Psychopathology theory* tends to treat rapists as psychologically maladjusted individuals who have had unusual childhood experiences. Sexual aggression is understood as developing primarily within the individual rather than explained by external factors. Finally, using the most controversial explanation, evolutional psychology theory (Poulin 2005) suggests that rape is a "mating effort" closely associated with men being hardwired to disperse their sperm as widely as possible.

Building upon research of gender differences in patterns of communication, some have suggested that date rape could be an extreme form of miscommunication (O'Byrne, Rapley and Hansen 2006). The idea here is that women have implicit understanding of the normative interactional structure of refusal, while men have an equally refined ability to "ignore" the subtle nonverbal sexual refusals. Therefore, men interpret a woman's "no" as a "maybe," or failure to say *no* as consent.

For many men the line between friendly sexual persuasion and coercion is often a boundary they have trouble defining for themselves. They act on the myth that woman engage in token resistance, believing that when a woman says no to a sexual advance, she really means yes. She only says no to show she is not a "pushover," or to play a game of resistance when she really wants sex. They tell themselves that she is really inviting the advances through subtle verbal and nonverbal cues, such as the way she dresses. High school seniors, for example, were more likely to view a date rape victim dressed in provocative clothing as more responsible for her assailant's behavior and therefore determine that the rape was justified (Cassidy and Hurrell 1995).

A study of 112 adolescent girls revealed that victims of unwanted sexual activity tend to have more sexually active same-sex friends, poor peer relationships, low emotional status among peers, an earlier age of menarche, and early sexual involvement (Vicary, Klingaman and Harkness 1995). The authors concluded that adolescent females who date at an early age could be more at risk for unwanted sexual advances.

There is evidence indicating that males resort to deception as a means of gaining sexual favors from a date. In reviewing studies on premarital sexual conflict, Long and others conclude: "Males are more likely than females to use strategies that encourage coitus to the point of lying about their motivation for intimacy, whereas females are more likely to use strategies that avoid intercourse" (1996:302). A study of 673 college males found that one in four admitted to having lied to have sex, with most lies centered on the theme of caring for or being committed to the person. This researcher also found that alcohol is commonly used as part of the male strategy for sexual aggression (Fischer 1996).

Studies comparing male and female attitudes about sexually aggressive behavior show that males are more prone to blame the female for aggressive sexual behavior and view sexual aggression as more excusable when alcohol is used, when it is part of a long-term relationship, or when a woman is provocatively dressed. In general, males are more accepting of sexually aggressive behavior and less demanding that an aggressor be punished for such behavior. These studies indicate that males both under-rate the seriousness of this crime and undermine efforts to control it.

RAPE PREVENTION

Undoubtedly the first and primary concern after a sexual assault has been committed is the victim. However, if essential change is to occur, the beliefs, myths and attitudes of the rapist and the rape-prone society must be addressed. All too often a convicted rapist commits another sexual crime soon after he is released from jail. Our immediate response is to lock up sexual offenders and throw away the key. Our motive to protect ourselves and to make society safe from sexual predators is certainly appropriate. However, by itself this response is short-sighted because it fails to address the need for radical, long-term behavioral change in the offender. Also, it fails to include the familial, communal and sociocultural levels.

That there are rape-prone societies is exremely troubling, and therefore we must examine the sociocultural elements in society that account for such a dishonorable status.

The family of origin. At the familial level, sexual offenders usually come from inadequate, neglectful and abusive home environments, which are lacking in nurture and solid guidance. At the community level, the absence of positive models of manhood makes it difficult to develop a secure and adequate person who can engage in satisfying adult relationships. At the societal level, self-interest and lack of regard for others lead to dehumanizing, marginalizing and violating practices. Digging even deeper into the cultural layers of society, power and control are dominant themes of masculinity that are harmful to women.

Rape myth acceptance. One cultural layer that needs to be challeged among men is what has come to be know as *rape myth acceptance:* the belief that rape is a normal part of the encounter between males and females. The following items taken from the Rape Myth Acceptance Scale reveals some of the dimensions of this belief: "Women have a secret desire to be raped." "Only bad girls get raped." "Men can't control their sexual desire." Research has demonstrated that men's rape myth acceptance is associated with rape proclivity (Bohner et al. 2005).

Rape myth acceptance has been found to be highest for athletes lacking a strong sense of self and for men who were supposedly noted for their physical prowess, but in reality had spineless, gullible and servile characteristics (Gildner 2006). Also, persons with traditional rather than equalitarian gender-role attitudes and beliefs accept rape myths and blame the victim more (Anderson and Lyons 2005). Traditionalists also minimize the severity of all rapes more than equalitarians (Ben-David and Schneider 2005).

At the more concrete level, self-defense and assertiveness training have been demonstrated as effective ways of assisting women against sexual aggreession. Women with training, more than those without, were angrier, less afraid, and say that their resistance was effective in stopping the sexual aggression (Brecklin and Ullman 2005). There is also evdience that an assertive stance toward a sexual agresssor is likely to result in *less* personal harm. In reality, most sexually aggressive men are emotionally weak and usually can be foiled by the presentation of strength in the person they seek to prey upon.

Changing offenders. What can be done to change the rapists who commit sexually violent acts? This is a difficult question to answer! Some research has been done on the sexual arousal patterns of sexually violent men in an effort to find solutions. According to Blader and Marshall (1989), rapists and nonrapists have different sexual arousal response patterns. Though rapists have the ability to perform the responses of hostile aggression and sexual arousal at the same time, normal males find these two responses quite incompatible.

Related research focusing on stimulus control discovered that rapists were more aroused by descriptions of forced sex than were nonrapists (Quinsey and Chaplin 1984). In an insightful article, Janssen (1995) described a pattern in which rapists were motivated by hostility (emotions of rage, hatred, contempt) and the desire to humiliate the victim. Through physical dominance and control, the rapists express hatred toward women.

A variety of treatment programs are offered to offenders, although the effectiveness of these programs is inconclusive. Most community programs, like the Sexual Violence Northwest Treatment Center in Seattle, use a combination of treatment intervention strategies. In individual and group therapy, cognitive and behavioral modification approaches are used to help offenders practice impulse control as well as to reformulate internal patterns of sexual desire. Men with less robust cases of sexual violence may make good progress with treatment, but like the alcoholic, may be a few steps away from reoffending unless they stay in treatment or in twelve-step groups that keep them accountable. Success is defined as the ability to control one's behavior by not acting out inappropriate sexual impulses when they occur.

Violent sex offenders are less likely to change. Many have sociopathic tendencies and express little or no empathy for their victims. Some prison treatment programs make use of group sessions in which rape survivors confront rapists as a way of getting them to have empathy for the victims, feel remorseful, and take responsibility for their crime. The success of such programs is mixed, depending on the severity of the offense and the response to the treatment.

Most date-rape offenders do not have the psychological aberrations of stranger rapists. These men are more likely to deny the intent of their behavior and excuse themselves for failing to respond appropriately to the protests of their date. In this case, treatment focuses more on educational interventions. Based on results of college campus consciousness-raising programs about rape, these preventive programs are effective.

One such program targeted the commonly held false beliefs that promote or condone coercive sexual behavior. This cognitive-based intervention treatment was successful in significantly changing the date-rape beliefs of college males. Another model focused on men who had little ability to show empathy toward their victims. This model was also successful in increasing empathy skills and awareness among college men (Schewe and O'Donohue 1996). In another case, a mixed-gender intervention program reported favorable change in attitudes of college males toward date rape (Holcomb et al. 1993).

It is encouraging to learn that consciousness-raising workshops have proved effective in changing attitudes and beliefs about rape. The church can use similar methods to heighten awareness. Christian singles need to be aware of destructive sexual beliefs, attitudes and behaviors. Marie Fortune (1996) has developed a workshop for church youth groups and Sunday school classes titled (in book form) *Sexual Abuse Prevention: A Study for Teenagers*. This workshop addresses the topic of date rape in five sessions: (1) "Rape Is Violence, Not Sex." (2) "The Good, the Bad, and the Confusing." (3) "All in the Family." (4) "Expectations of Ourselves and Others." (5) "Truth in Advertising." Fortune uses a variety of role-play and case situations to help youth recognize red flags when they occur so they will be able to assert and protect themselves from such unwanted encounters. It is a great service to offer educational programs that help singles establish and maintain authenticity in dating relationships.

MINISTERING TO RAPE SURVIVORS

(*Note:* To avoid the negative ramifications of labeling someone a rape "victim," from this point on we will use the term *survivor*. And since most survivors are female, we will use the female pronoun for the rest of this chapter.)

Rape survivors all share an overwhelming experience of having been physically and emotionally violated by the rapist. In addition, they report a number of intense feelings like fear, powerlessness, shame, guilt, anger and hate (Resick 1993). At the appropriate time, the survivor needs a safe place to deal with each of these primal feelings. Discerning how, when and who will come alongside to help her work through the loss, grief, rage, denial, helplessness, depression and fear is of crucial importance. The survivor not only needs a safe place, but also a trusted person and the right pacing for her unique process.

Unfortunately, some women are "doubly victimized," a second time by the social, health, mental health, and legal systems that are suppose to assist them (Berliner 2006). It is important that persons working with rape survivors obtain the needed training that allows them to be sensitive and understanding of the survivor's range of emotions and needs.

Rape survivors are negatively affected in a number of ways: depression, low self-esteem and self-worth, and suicidal feelings (Cecil and Matson, 2005). In addition, males who have been sexual abused experience damage to their sense of sexual and masculine identity (Walker, Archer and Davies 2005).

Coping after the sexual assault varies widely. In general, survivors with less education, with a history of other traumas, those who blame their own character for the assault, and those who used alcohol to cope with the assault—these cope less well (Ullman et al. 2006). Factors positively effecting recovery are emotional support from friends and family, and the presence of social and community support (N. Sarkar and R. Sarkar 2005). Cognive-processing therapy has been found to be more effective than prolonged focusing on the survivors' guilt and depresson (Nishith, Nixon and Resick 2005).

Research on posttraumatic stress disorder has been informative in describing the various emotional phases a survivor is likely to experience. Initially, she is overwhelmed by the shock and disbelief of what has happened. The survivor wonders, *Did this really happen to me?* Later, when awareness is acute, she asks, "How could this happen to me?" There can be extreme feelings of fear and anger, which may be expressed through uncontrolled crying or total withdrawal from others. This is a time when the survivor is acutely preoccupied with the offense, and these responses can last from a few days to a few months, depending on the seriousness of the abuse trauma. Physical reactions such as loss of sleep, eating disturbances, vaginal irritation or bleeding are common complaints. The emotional reactions include mood swings, extreme expression of feelings, and distrust or cautious attitudes toward others.

After the violation has occurred, she is acutely aware of what it means to live in a threatening and dangerous world. She realizes that bad things do happen to good people. Her lifestyle choices are now made in light of what has happened to her. This reorganization phase can last from weeks to even years. Adjustments may involve changing one's routine, such as driving rather than walking to and from work, changing one's job, or even moving to a new location. There might be dreams or nightmares in which the survivor plays back the rape, sometimes imagining different endings, such as being killed by the rapist. The trauma may express itself in a phobic reaction, a hatred or extreme fear of men, especially those who possess characteristics similar to the rapist. Phobias may also be centered on places similar to where the rape took place or certain activities that were part of the rape experience.

Survivors need to be assured that it is normal to experience this vast array of feelings. In addition to pastoral care and personal counseling, many rape survivors benefit from being part of a support group of other rape survivors. Discussions with those who have been through a similar experience can help to normalize the traumatic feelings, ongoing anxiety and unexplained reactions. It helps to see one's progress over time and to be supported by those who can truly understand what a victim is going through.

Counseling for the survivor's family is another area of ministry. Each member is affected by the offense, and each person needs a place to work out the implications of what has happened. The mother of the victim may cry, "How could this happen to my child [or our family]?" Although the crisis belongs to the victim, family members feel a similar helplessness and have strong emotional reactions as well. The father or brother of the victim, for example, may react in a fit of rage and seek revenge.

Though these responses are understandable, more than anything else the survivor needs the family's support. She should not be put in a situation where she has to take care of others at this point. Sometimes the survivor is so concerned with the reactions of family members that she will try to hurry her own process to prove to everyone that she is all right. This keeps her from proceeding in her own time so that a complete process of healing can take place. A false sense of renewed health will not last long if not all the feelings have been addressed. She needs her family to be by her side, responding in supportive, trustworthy ways that affirm her process.

The husband or boyfriend of the survivor will also have a range of feelings and human reactions about what happened. This deeply affects their relationship, and he must be part of the counseling as well. However, these husbands or boyfriends may be reluctant to participate in counseling, as found in a study by Brookings, McEvoy and Reed (1994). They reported that 85 percent of crisis counseling centers surveyed indicated that males did not use the services. These authors believe that the presence of male counselors at these crisis counseling centers would give men the message that counseling is important for them as well.

A wise counselor will honor the differences in how God is uniquely at work in each survivor as well as in the lives of those who love them. Some work through feelings and issues rapidly, while others take more time; some talk a lot, others very little; some find creative ways to express emotions while others need to write things down in a factual manner. The survivor is the only one who can decide about how fast to travel through the path of recovery.

Sexual violence may become a crisis of faith for the survivor. When this happens, the survivor needs to be able to know that such doubts are acceptable. The counselor, friend or family member can encourage the survivor to express feelings and think through doubts because God is big enough to embrace these anguishing questions. Rather than admonish,

"You don't really believe that!" one must give reassurance, "God knows about your profound hurt and loves you deeply."

A spiritual issue may center on the survivor trying to make sense out of her experience. Here it is important to focus on the details of what happened to her. This is a way she regains a sense of control over the situation, a way of coming to grips with the actual event. Simplistic formulas that minimize the experience of the survivor are not helpful.

The offense against the survivor may raise the question, "Why did I have to suffer this heinous crime?" It is important to affirm that this violence is a grave offense to God. In struggling with her involuntary suffering, the survivor may ask, "Is there any meaning in this experience for me?" Here it is vital to be aware of the cultural and religious beliefs that the survivor holds. One study found that in their struggle to bring meaning to the experience of being raped, women were negatively influenced by unhealthy cultural beliefs, myths and stereotypes about women and sexuality. For example, making reference to the survivor being "soiled" or "ruined" as a result of the rape brings up negative and shaming connotations (Lebowitz and Roth 1994). The belief that the violation has ruined one for life has spiritual implications. This might be especially true of the unmarried victim who was saving herself sexually for a life partner in marriage. She may be tempted to think of herself as "tainted goods," similar to a victim of child abuse.

We must assure the survivor that virginity is no more affected by this assault than by a person's first gynecological exam, which may rupture the hymen. A woman's virginity symbolizes her integrated sense of self-worth. The victim must be able to hold on to her sexual worth as a function of her personhood rather than her physical status as a result of the rape.

The survivor can often grasp the idea that God is present in her pain and cares deeply about what she has suffered. Out of the pain and suffering, she can be sustained by a deep connection with her personal Savior. When she is tempted to feel that God has abandoned her, she can cry out with the psalmist, "My God, my God, why have you forsaken me? Why are you so far from saving me, so far from the words of my groaning?" (Ps 22:1-2). Faithful Christians throughout history and Christ himself have felt such abandonment. The fact that she is able to shout out her anguish to God means that she believes God is there to hear her cry. God hears, understands and does not turn away. When we act as God's representatives, our presence and acceptance of her anger can mediate God's faithful presence during recovery.

When anger comes, it must not be judged as bad or good, but as appropriate. Anger on the part of one who has been sexually assaulted is a healthy response. The survivor should be able to vent her anger, for she has been wronged. When anger is turned inward, it can lead to depression, loss of self-esteem and helplessness, and can be expressed through self-destructive behaviors such as substance abuse or suicide. Awareness and expression of the anger energize the survivor to take appropriate action that can restore her sense of power and self-worth. For example, reporting the crime and testifying in court takes courage and strength. Yet taking such action that protects innocent victims is empowering.

The last step is a conscious decision the survivor makes that the rape experience will no longer have a disarming power over her life. This is a vital aspect of healing, for it allows the survivor to move on with her life. It does not mean that the offense is minimized, but the negative effect no longer has the intensity it once did. She is empowered through the resources of faith, family, friends and community who have shown the love of God to her in her time of crisis.

CONCLUSION

A holistic response to sexual violence includes concern for the victim, for the behavior of the offender, and for the community or society in which the offense occurs. In chapter eleven we presented a model detailing an adequate response to sexual harassment that balances these three concerns (see figure 11.3). Although sexual violence is a more serious offense, the responses are applicable. Brokenness caused by sexual violence requires a repair that encompasses every aspect of this crime.

FOR FURTHER READING

Kroeger, C., and N. Nason-Clark. 2001. *No place for abuse: Biblical and practical resources to conteract domestic violence.* Downers Grove, Ill.: InterVarsity Press.

La Fond, J. 2005. *Preventing sexual violence: How society should cope with sex offenders.* The law and public policy: Psychology and the social sciences. Washington, D.C.: American Psychological Association.

14

Pornography and Erotica

The Greek root for pornography is *pornē*, meaning a "female captive" or "prostitute." Under its original meaning, pornography depicts the use of sex for subjugation, aggression, degradation, abuse, coercion, violence, dominance, control, sadism or rape. Today's contemporary use of the term *pornography* has a much broader meaning, including sexually explicit art, literature and film. Pornography's expansion into the arts has led to relativism in determining and defining it. As a result some would argue that pornography is in the eye of the beholder. While we think this is going too far, labeling anything that is sexually stimulating as pornography is also inaccurate. In deciphering the difference, a distinction must be made between pornography and erotica (erotic material).

Both erotic and pornographic material can be sexually stimulating; however, pornography is used to degrade others, while erotica celebrates human sexual experience. Although erotica is sexually arousing material, it is not meant to degrade women, men or children. Pornography, on the other hand, uses subjugation themes for the explicit purpose of sexual arousal. Pornography *always* dehumanizes, and we believe dehumanization is a violation of the value God places on human life and sexuality. Therefore we believe pornography is offensive and unacceptable.

Although traditionally men have been the main consumers of pornography, media and culture now use "fashion 'n' passion" to target women as sexual consumers. "Against a backdrop of a 'pornographication' of mainstream media and the emergence of a more heavily sexualized culture, women are increasingly targeted as sexual consumers" (Attwood 2005:392).

Our Internet search of the term *pornographication* turns up 385 references, most referring to the pornographication of mainstream culture and society. If indeed there is a pornographication of culture and soceity, we may be witnessing an important watershed: what has traditionally been defined as pornography is becoming a standard part of culture. Some question whether it is an erotification rather than a pornographication of culture.

DISTINGUISHING BETWEEN EROTICA AND PORNOGRAPHY

Although it would be helpful to have a sharp distinction between pornographic and erotic sexual materials, this is often more difficult than one thinks. It is important to consider both the objective *content* of sexual material and the subjective *effect* the content has upon any particular person. Recognizing that the impact of sexual material can be as different as the persons consuming it, we focus first on the content dimension.

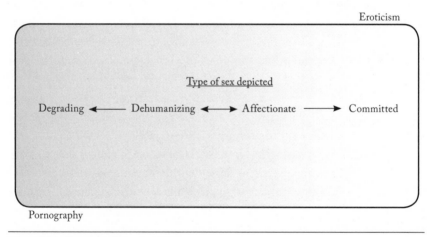

Figure 14.1. Pornography and eroticism

In figure 14.1 we suggest that the portrayal of sexual content ranges along a continuum from *degrading sex* (at far left), to *dehumanizing sex* (just left of center), to *affectionate sex* (just right of center), to *committed sex* (at the far right).

The important criterion in trying to distinguish between pornography

and erotica is the *value* or *meaning* (or lack of it) given to sex, not necessarily the degree of sexual explicitness. For example, a film containing
sexually explicit scenes of tender, passionate lovemaking between married partners may be described as erotic but not pornographic. On the
other hand, a film glorifying degrading or dehumanizing sex but with less
sexually explicit material is still pornographic. The shading from dark to
light in figure 14.1 represents the murky distinction between erotica and
pornography.

Distinguishing whether sexual *content* is pornographic or erotic is even
more problematic when the purpose of the artist or filmmaker may be to
communicate destructive aspects of pornography. Recent films—such as
Pulp Fiction, Leaving Las Vegas, Boogie Nights; or those of screenwriter and
director Paul Schrader, such as *Taxi Driver, American Gigolo, The Pornog-
rapher*—powerfully illustrate the destructiveness of pornography. Some
Christians consider Schrader's films pornographic because of the explicit
sexual material. Actually, these films are among the strongest and most
effective antipornographic messages produced in popular culture. In his
films, Schrader exposes the tragic effects of the dehumanization process,
involving objectification for sexual stimulation. Films depicting a distortion of sexuality may be stimulating, even though the purpose of the work
is not for sexual stimulation or glorification of dehumanization. An educational documentary condemning sexual abuse may contain material that
is sexually stimulating. Many things people see or read can be a source of
sexual stimulation. Therefore it is appropriate to guard our thoughts and
emotions with careful discernment. Recognizing distortions and identifying dehumanizing sexual messages within our society do not eliminate
but certainly can minimize the effects of the material on us.

Exposure to pornographic material can be both educational and tantalizing. It is important to recognize, normalize and monitor the con-
flicting motivations that exposure to pornography can produce. For example, a made-for-television movie on rape can educate the audience about
the extreme emotional and psychological damage of rape to survivors.
However, the same material can also be used to tantalize a large audience
and produce a higher rating.

Schrader is candid about the need for commercial success in the entertainment business. He explains that a screenwriter must find "a rip in the
social fabric and create a film metaphor which deals with the tear. That

is as good a way as any to be commercial. . . . Sex and violence are all-encompassing fantasies that permeate every possible market. Screenwriting appeals to these needs more than the other forms of media because the numbers have to be bigger" (cited in Schultz et al. 1991:97-98). One cannot label all works exposing the dehumanizing effects of inauthentic sex as pornography. However, it is important to question the motives and presentation of these works.

Sexually graphic material can expose sexual depravity in a nonerotic way and also arouse the sexual appetite. There is a place for depicting the harmful, degrading effect of pornography, but the usefulness of graphic, realistic depictions of pornography can become lost in the titillation of the content depicted. When this happens, the content of a work depicting pornography may itself be seen as pornographic. The graphic material depends on its immediate context and on the content of the film as a whole to give the work meaning.

Regardless of the work's motive or the truthfulness of the content, it is difficult to predict the *effect* of explicit material on a particular viewer. What one viewer experiences as erotic, another may experience as disdainful and disgusting. Unquestionably, sexually explicit material, regardless of the context and content, should be restricted to mature viewers, although age is no guarantee of psychological or sexual maturity. To recognize sexual degradation, one needs a certain degree of sexual health and moral discernment. The absence of these two factors increases the likelihood that one will concentrate on the sexual stimulus, missing the deeper meaning of the work.

INTERNET SEX/CYBERSEX

Internet access has radically changed the form of delivery of pornography and its consumption. The consumption of pornography on the Internet is abundant, convenient, private and relatively inexpensive. Griffiths (2003) found that in addition to accessing online pornography in the home, Internet pornography and Internet sex were the two main ways in which the computer is used in illegitimate ways in the workplace.

Fisher and Barak (2001) divide sexual material on the Internet into the three categories of *erotica*, *degrading pornography*, and *violent pornography*. While the viewing of degrading or violent pornography might be an indication of the degree of sexual aberration in the viewer, persons can become addicted to consuming each of these three types of pornography.

While men are six times as likely to view cyberporn as women (Stack, Wasserman and Kern 2004), there is also evidence of gender difference in involvement in Internet pornography. A study of college students revealed that while males were more likely to use visual stimulus for sexual arousal, females were more apt to use chat rooms (Goodson and McCormack 2000). However, a further study found that women are drawn from chat rooms to sites that provide visual imagery (Gardner 2001:45).

In studying male/female differences in consuming Internet pornography, Ferree (2003) found that of the women who use the Internet for sexual means, close to 70 percent engage in interactive aspects such as chat rooms. Women more than men are likely to create interpersonal online relationships based on social support and communication. Women enter chat rooms and discussion groups as a means of experiencing "safe" flirtation in their cybersex activities. Whitty (2003) found that women tend to rate viewing of explicit sexual material on the Internet as infidelity more often than did men.

Although less research has been done on women, one study revealed that women who viewed pornography maintained a highly negative mood, while women who viwed erotica experienced a substantial improvement in mood (Senn and Desmarais 2004).

A strong relationship has been found between the consumption of Internet pornography and loneliness, although it is difficult to know which leads to the other (Yoder, Virden and Amin 2005). Hypothesizing that persons with weaker social bonds were more likely to use Internet pornography, Stack, Wasserman and Kern (2004) found that users of the Internet for pornography were more likely to have weak ties to religion and lack a happy marriage. Chaney and Chang (2005) identified *boredom proneness, social disconnectedness* and *online dissociation* as the characteristics of men addicted to Internet sex.

Birchard reports that pornography can be used addictively to "control painful affect, to avoid feelings of loneliness, and to ward off the dread of non-being" (2004:82). He believes that the use of pornography serves to blunt the effect of narcissistic woundedness that is at the root of addictive behaviors. He suggests that some who are drawn to religion as a coping strategy for their narcissistic damage may also be vulnerable to the use of pornography as a coping strategy (p. 84). One study reported that two-thirds of all Christian men struggle with pornography (as cited in Laaser 2004).

Philaretou, Mahfouz and Allen (2005) classify cybersex use into three categories of increased loss of self-control over the activity: *recreational*, *sexually compulsive*, and *at risk*. At-risk users are found to be of three types: *stress reactive*, those who engage in cybersex during times of high stress; *depressive*, those who engage in cybersex as a way of finding relief from depression; and *fantasy*, those who engage in cybersex because they would like to engage in these activities in real life. The personal effects of Internet sex can be seen in increased depression, anxiety, and intimacy problems with their real-life partners. Compulsive cybersex was described as a quest for the "perfect sexual visualization that will match their 'love map,' only to get disappointed at its fleeting nature" (Philaretou, Mahfouz and Allen 2005).

Out-of-control consumption of pornography can be classified as either compulsion or addiction. Those who prefer the term *compulsion* argue that addiction language unnecessarily pathologizes and medicalizes the problem (Birchard 2004:81). Some find it more helpful to simply use the descriptive term *out-of-control* behavior (Bancroft and Vukadinovic 2004:81). (See chapter 15 for more information on this topic.)

PORNOGRAPHY AND MARRIAGE

In her testimony before a United States Senate subcommittee, Jill Manning (2005) reported on research indicating that "pornography consumption is associated with trends toward increased marital distress, and risk of separation and divorce; decreased martial intimacy and sexual satisfaction; infidelity; increased appetite for more graphic types of pornography and sexual activity associated with abusive, illegal or unsafe practices; devaluation of monogamy, marriage and child rearing; and an increasing number of people struggling with compulsive and addictive sexual behavior." Yet we should point out that *associating* pornography with each of these trends does not necessarily mean that it is the *cause*. Other societal factors—secularization, changing values, and so forth—also contribute to trends of greater pornography consumption. But since a majority of those seeking help for problematic sexual online behavior are married heterosexual males, we need to examine the relationship between Internet pornography use and marriage. A study of 531 Internet users reports that people who stated that they were happily married were 61 percent less likely to report using Internet pornography. The same study also reports that "individuals who have had an extramarital affair are 3.18 times more likely to have used Internet pornogrpahy than individuals who did not have affairs" (Stack, Wasserman and Kern 2004:75).

Information is beginning to emerge on the effect of pornography consumption on marriage. Wives attending co-addicts of sex addicts anonymous groups feel torn between trying too hard to help change their husband's behavior and withdrawing from the relationship. Based on her qualitative study, Cebulko reports that co-addict wives share a psychosexual developmental history that may have hindered them in choosing their mate and in managing their lives after marriage. Although these wives seem to have normal sexual drives and interest, they repeatedly refer to the need to forgive their sexually addictive husbands, which heightens their feelings of hopefulness. Sexually addicted husbands and their wives are described as having corresponding splits in their respective self-structures that serve to reinforce a continuing cycle (Cebulko 2006).

Based on his qualitative analysis of the effect of Internet pornography on marriage, J. Schneider (2003) reports that pornography use results in serious adverse consequences for the spouse. Two-thirds report sexual problems in the marriage resulting from the sexual addiction. Consumption of Internet pornography was found, likewise, to have an indirect adverse effect on children, due to the user spending less time with them.

PORNOGRAPHY AND CHILDREN

Due to easy access, children are targets of Internet pornographers. Although there is a lack of good data on frequency of viewing Internet pornography by children, it is estimated that 90 percent of youth aged 12-18 have access to the Internet. It could certainly be assumed that the viewing of pornography by children dramatically increases in correspondence to their sexual awakening around puberty.

Based on telephone interviews of 1,501 children aged 10-17, it was reported that most seekers of pornography are male and over thirteen years old. Seekers are more likely to report clinical features associated with depression, lower levels of emotional bonding with their caregiver, more delinquent behavior, and more drug use (Ybarra and Michell 2005).

Gender differences in teen viewing of pornography seem to correspond to similar gender differences in adults. While teenage boys are drawn to sexually explicit material, teenage girls are more apt to pursue chat rooms and other interactive ventures. In reporting on the attitudes and behavior of forty youths aged 14-17, K. Cameron and others (2005) found that while all females found sexual explicit websites distasteful, some males did and some did not. Most adolescents do not believe exposure to sexually explicit websites had an influence on them; all agreed that their parents were unaware of what they viewed online.

A serious danger for youth utilizing the Internet is the possibility of online sexual solicitation. Based on interviews with Internet-using youth aged 10-17, Mitchell, Finkelhor and Wolak (2007) reported that youth were at higher risk of online sexual solicitation when they were "female, using chat rooms, using the internet with a cell phone, talking with people met online, sending personal information to people met online, talking about sex online, and experiencing offline physical or sexual abuse" (p. 532).

In her search of the literature, Manning summarizes that a child's direct exposure to pornography can have the following effects: "lasting negative or traumatic emotional responses; earlier onset of first sexual intercourse, thereby increasing the risk of STDs over the lifespan; the belief that superior sexual satisfaction is attainable without having affection for one's partner, thereby reinforcing the commodification of sex and the objectification of humans; the belief that being married or having a family are unattractive prospects; increased risk for developing sexual compulsions and addictive behavior; increased risk of exposure to incorrect information about human sexuality before a minor is able to contextualize this information in ways that an adult brain could; and overestimating the prevalence of less common practices (e.g., group sex, bestiality, or sadomasochistic activity)." In addition, she asserts that "merely living in a home where an adult is consuming pornography can result in the following risks: decreased parental time and attention; increased risk of encountering pornographic material; increased risk of parental separation and divorce; and increased risk of parental job loss and financial strain" (Manning 2005).

THE EFFECTS OF VIEWING PORNOGRAPHY

In 1971 the Commission on Obscenity and Pornography came to the controversial conclusion that there was not enough evidence to support the "antisocial effects" of pornography. The stimulus material in the study did not include rape or coercive behavior.

Some actually believe pornography may serve a positive purpose. Those advocating this view emphasize the cathartic effect of pornography, relieving feelings and desires that can lead to harmful effects if acted out. A parallel view maintains that vicarious viewing of violent behavior releases pent-up violent impulses rather than encouraging violence. The application of this reasoning to pornography normalizes aggressive sexual urges in men, and such thinkers argue that pornography releases aggressive feelings, thus lessening inappropriate sexual behavior toward women. This view assumes an evolutionary process, depicting men as more sexually aggressive than women. Pornography is seen as serving society by reducing sexual aggression in men that may harm women.

Research conducted in the 1980s and 1990s did not support the cathartic effect. Evidence actually pointed in the exactly opposite direction, suggesting that pornography *increases* sexually aggressive urges and attitudes of men toward women. Allen, D'Alessio and Brezgel (1995) analyzed thirty laboratory studies on the effect of exposure to pornography on aggressive behavior. They concluded that sexually aggressive behavior was induced by pictorial nudity, material depicting nonviolent sexual activity, and media depictions of violent sexual activity.

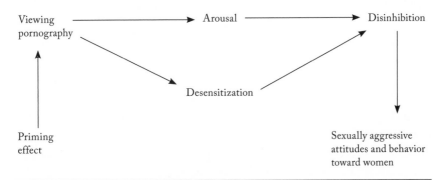

Figure 14.2. The effect of viewing pornography

Figure 14.2 represents our attempt to summarize the effects of pornography on the viewer. Most notably the figure traces the procedural effect of viewing pornography on individuals with sexually aggressive attitudes and behavior.

This summary is based on an experimental research design that tested attitudes and beliefs before and after the viewing of pornographic material. In general the research concludes that after viewing pornographic material subjects have a *more* callous attitude about sexual violence toward women and rape victims. Furthermore, they are more likely to say they would *commit* a sexually violent act if they would not be caught!

Priming effect. The arrow leading from the bottom left side of figure 14.2 to "viewing pornography" represents the priming effect. This priming effect suggests that the impact of communication is greater when the viewers' beliefs are consistent with the information in the communication. Beliefs of viewers who oppose the messages in pornographic material are less likely to be influenced or changed as a result of viewing pornography. However, pornography is more likely to reinforce attitudes of those having beliefs similar to pornographic material, because these individual beliefs are primed to accept the information.

Arousal and desensitization. Figure 14.2 shows two major ways pornography directly affects the viewer. First, pornography influences sexual *arousal.* Those with a healthy psychosexual self find the dehumanizing aspects of pornography unappealing. However, consistent viewing of pornography initiates a conditioning process associating sexual aggression with sexual arousal. Behavior is influenced and acquired by modeling. Watching women become sexually aroused while being raped can become sexually arousing to a viewer. The modeling of sexual aggression therefore influences behavior, in this case, sexual arousal. In its most aberrant form, a constant diet of pornography creates a distorted sense of sexuality. As a result of this distortion, normal eroticism becomes insufficient for sexual arousal. Arousal becomes a function of increasingly dehumanizing and sexually degrading stimuli. Since most of the material cannot be acted out, the viewer must personalize the content in order to achieve arousal. By inserting themselves into the content, viewers take on a psychosexual persona that is both dehumanizing and dehumanized.

Second, pornography *desensitizes* the viewer to attitudes about dehumanizing human psychosexuality. The psychological process of desensitization decreases the emotional effect of a dehumanizing event. For example, the repetition of the Rodney King beating in the media was responsible for *desensitizing* members of the jury to the brutality of the beating. After viewing the tape for the first time, some jurors were horrified. The same jurors also admitted that repeatedly viewing the tape increased desensitization to the material. The application of this process to pornography suggests that repetitive exposure to sexually aggressive material against women leads to a desensitizing effect on the viewer. One study reports that some men began to believe that women enjoy being raped (Malamuth 1984). It is significant that these men had been shown pornography depicting a woman becoming sexually aroused while being raped.

This desensitization process initiates a rationalization process minimizing the protests of women against sexual aggression of men. Such rationalizations create the belief that, despite their protests, women desire sexual aggression (M. Allen, Emmers et al. 1995). This myth is a familiar and consistent message promoted in pornographic material. Ultimately, viewers internalize this message, become less emotionally affected by the content, and objectify the victimized female.

Disinhibition. Disinhibition is a result of the conditioning effects and desensitization of sexual aggression in pornographic material. The disinhibiting effect increases the viewer's sexually aggressive attitudes and behavior toward women. Currently there is little information *directly* linking exposure to pornography with illegal sexual behavior, although research shows compelling correlational evidence that persons who engage in illegal sexual behavior have been high consumers of pornography (H. Schneider 1996). However, there is ample evidence suggesting that aggressive and coercive sexual materials depicting women in submissive roles are salient disinhibitors. It is safe to conclude that viewing pornography may not *cause* sexual aggression toward women, but it is a significant factor in attitudes of sexual aggression and behavior.

In his research on the effects of pornography on college males, Malamuth (1984) reports that 41 percent *might* rape if they were certain of not being caught. Malamuth concludes that the aggressive content of pornography is the major contributor to subsequent aggression toward women. Because subjects showed an increased lack of inhibition after viewing the pornographic material, Malamuth concludes that viewing pornography makes a significant impact in reinforcing a cultural climate that accepts, and in some cases promotes, sexual aggression toward women.

By the end of the 1990s, the reliable asssociations between frequent violent pornography use and sexually aggressive behavior had been established (Malamuth, Addison and Koss 2000; Oddone-Paolucci, Genuis and Violato 2000). A meta-analysis of forty-six published studies of the effect of pornogrpahy on sexual aggression, which included a combined sample size of 12,323 persons, provided evidence "confirming the link between increased risk for negative development when exposed to pornography" (Oddone-Paolucci, Genuis, and Violato 2000:38).

More recent research has focused on understanding the behavior of actual sex offenders. A study of 561 sex offenders revealed that 17 percent had used pornography at the time of the offense, with greater use among child offenders. Of the users, 55 percent showed pornographic material to their victims, and 36 percent viewed pictures, mostly of children (Langevin and Curnoe 2004).

IS EROTICA HARMFUL?

The 1986 Commission on Obscenity and Pornography reversed the decision of the 1971 commission, concluding that evidence *does* link pornography to sexually aggressive attitudes toward women. Like pornography, erotica arouses one's sexual feelings and desires, but unlike pornography, it does not necessarily reinforce sexual aggression or coercion (Pallard 1995). Aggressive content that occurs within an erotic context is the *key* contributor to aggression against women (Pallard 1995). Based on the differential effect of erotic and pornographic film content upon subjects in their study, Saunders and Naus conclude that their results "provide empirical support for the conceptual distinctions between 'erotica' and 'pornography'" (1993:117).

However, the commission's conclusions about sexual aggression do not exonerate eroticism as unharmful. In their review of relevant research, Allen, D'Alessio and Brezgel (1995) concluded that "consumption of material depicting nonviolent sexual activity increases aggressive behavior." Although pornography depicts sexual aggression toward women, erotica can depict *dehumanizing* sex. From a biblical point of view, dehumanizing sexual material is pornographic rather than erotic, promoting self-gratification void of intimacy or intimate affection. Erotica that elevates dehumanizing sex creates a cultural climate that depersonalizes sex. Within this context, sex is merely a primal and mechanistic physiological need, like scratching an itch. Therefore depersonalized sexually explicit material is pornographic because it elevates the sex act above sexuality, dehumanizing both the individual and the relationship.

Depersonalized sex is not central to all erotica, and some erotic material can be a helpful context for developing sexuality. Avoidance of all erotic material would rule out exposure to much of what is accepted as fine artistic expression. There is a significant amount of erotic material in classic novels, plays and films, especially when depicting sex within the context of a caring, loving and even committed relationship. Painting, sculpture, literature, theater and film are powerful media for eliciting erotic responses. In addition, sexually explicit material is not a necessary component of erotica. A glance, a slight touch, or even the unbuttoning of a glove can elicit a strong erotic response. The questions then become, When is exposure to erotica good? When is it harmful? Following are four guidelines.

First, unlike pornography, *erotic material is often subjective.* A significant component in defining erotica is explained in the principle of diminishing returns. This principle suggests that the more familiar something becomes, the less effect it seems to have. What is wildly erotic to one individual may lack any stimulus for another. A gothic romance novel may be erotic to a fourteen-year-old girl but dull and uninteresting to a thirty-four-year-old woman. Since a kiss between a man and a woman is forbidden in some countries, depicting a kiss in a film could be a powerful erotic stimulus in those cultures. Although the principle of diminishing returns applies to all cultures, its application is subjective and depends on the context of the culture.

Second, *it is important to respect our Christian liberties when viewing erotica.* Although we have referred to the apostle Paul's words in 1 Corinthians 6:12 earlier, his instructions are applicable to respecting Christian liberties: "I can do anything I want to if Christ has not said no" (LB). Although this principle may feel uncomfortable, it is important not to judge another's actions where Scripture's teachings are not absolute. In addition, honest discernment is helpful in discriminating between the things that direct us in God's way and those that do not.

Third, *the effects of erotica are dependent on the context of one's situation.* Paul continues in 6:12, "But some of these things aren't good for me. Even if I am allowed to do them, I'll refuse to [do so] if I think they might get such a grip on me that I can't easily stop when I want to" (LB). Paul's use of *but* qualifies freedom in Christ. The qualification addresses the degree of influence and the range of negative effect that something other than

God may have on us. The third principle does not negate the second. Paul is not saying that "these things" are not good, but that they are not good for him.

For the Christian, "these things" may include erotic material. It is a strong possibility that Paul was specifically addressing the issue of erotica. In the following verse, Paul writes, "But it is not true that the body is for *lust*" (1 Cor. 6:13 NEB, emphasis added). According to Paul, certain types of erotica may not be wrong in and of themselves. However, the context of the erotica can determine whether erotic material is healthy or unhealthy. Paul warns that things such as lust "might get such a grip on me that I can't easily stop when I want to." A second issue Paul addresses is control. Scripture clearly teaches that the Christian should only be under the control of the Holy Spirit. When erotica becomes part of a personal compulsion, it has an inappropriate degree of control or influence on us, and it is outside of God's desire for our lives. Paul hints at the addictive danger of eroticism in its strongest sense. An addiction to erotica works in a similar way to a drug addict needing a fix. Like the physiological need for a drug, the psychological need for erotic material controls the viewer or reader.

Fourth, *erotic content can be seared into the memory*. The images of graphic erotica can be difficult to erase from memory. An erotic memory can flash into one's mind at the most inappropriate moments, similar to videotape suddenly playing back in the mind's eye. A recent client of ours, Brad, told us of the toll that past exposure to pornographic films was taking on his sex life with his bride of just two years. He regrets his decision to watch X-rated videos with high school friends. Some of the images from those videos haunt him when he is having sex with his wife. Pornographic images replay in Brad's mind, tarnishing his attempts to engage in a person-centered sexual experience with his wife. He admits that these images are difficult to erase from his mind.

Erotic material seems to be especially tempting and influential to men. Many men empathize with Brad and share his struggle (Hart 1995). Amid a deluge of mass media seeking control of our minds, we are in a constant battle to maintain purity. We need to admit the problem, resist further exposure to dehumanizing material, and try to take captive images that are incongruent with God's design for our sexuality. Confession and accountability are important aspects of change and growth toward purity. We may not be able to keep images from entering our mind, but we can decide how long these thoughts remain and what we do with them. Since we create and reinforce our fantasy life, it is possible for us to choose to eliminate dehumanizing fantasies from our minds. Reminding Brad that he had a choice gave him hope and a renewed vision for loving his wife with his whole heart and mind (cf. 2 Cor 10:5).

It is important to monitor fantasy processes for dehumanizing elements or aspects. Scrutinizing our fantasy life helps us to discern when we are disregarding God's commandment to love purely. We must deny our self-absobed tendencies and be responsible for what we let enter into our minds, heart and soul.

MASTURBATION

Since fantasy and the use of erotic and pornographic material often accompany the act of masturbation, there is much confusion surrounding this form of sexual release. Historically, society has fabricated myths in an attempt to discourage people from masturbating. Folk wisdom has associated masturbation with hair loss, warts, pimples, skin disease, blindness, impotence and mental illness. As a result many who were raised under these myths have attached an intense amount of guilt to masturbation. Laumann and others (1994) found that 54 percent of men and 47 percent of women report feeling guilty after masturbating.

From an early age, boys typically engage in self-stimulation more than girls, possibly because their genitals are external. Unfortunately society often sends a message to girls very early in life that they are not to touch themselves below the waist. Self-discovery through masturbation can help boys and girls learn about their bodies and affirm themselves as sexual beings. Masturbation can allow one to explore the pleasures of the body without guilt or shame.

The most common reasons given for masturbating are, in descending order of frequency, relief of sexual tension, physical pleasure, unavailable partners, relaxation and aid in falling asleep. The best available study, based on a cross-section of over three thousand persons ages 18 to 60, found that 37 percent of men and 58 percent of women report they did not masturbate during the past year (Laumann et al. 1994). These figures differ by individual circumstance; most noticeably, masturbation is less frequent among those in a stable sexual relationship. About 80 percent of men and 60 percent of women report that they usually or always experienced orgasm when masturbating.

Christian perspectives. How are Christians to view masturbation? First, we must realize that children's self-exploration of their body is natural and a necessary process for developing an awareness of their anatomy. They need to form good feelings and attitudes about every part of their body, including the sexual zones. This will help children understand that these parts of their body are good parts of themselves.

Next, we must recognize that the Bible is silent on the topic of masturbation. Therefore any case built either for or against it is based on inferences made from biblical passages that do not directly address it.

There are three major Christian views on masturbation. The *restrictive* view maintains that masturbation, under any circumstance, is sinful. In contrast, the *permissive* view assigns a healthy and moral value to masturbation under any circumstance. This view considers masturbation to be a harmless and positive method for increasing awareness and responsiveness in our sexual identity. The *moderate* view maintains that masturbation can be both healthy and morally appropriate but also suggests that it has the potential to be unhealthy and morally inappropriate.

The *moderate* view seems to be the most reasonable. Masturbation can be a healthy, enjoyable way for a person without a marital partner to experience sexual gratification. Since God has created humans as sexual beings, masturbation provides a way for individuals to experience their sexuality and meet their sexual needs. Many Christians battle feelings of guilt associated with masturbation and sexual repression. Freedom from sexual guilt and repression allows one to accept and affirm our God-given sexuality.

However, masturbation is not always psychologically and morally healthy. Compulsive masturbation, like compulsive eating or even compulsive sleeping, can be harmful. Compulsive sexual behavior can lead to destructive and devastating sexual addictions, spiraling out of control. During periods of stress, masturbation can be used to reduce anxiety or provide an emotional escape from an unpleasant task (Laumann et al. 1994). When used as a mechanism for coping with feelings of fear or inferiority, masturbation can be an anesthetic that keeps us from dealing with these real problems.

Within marriage, masturbation can be a negative factor if it deprives the other spouse of sexual fulfillment. Similarly, if a partner is using masturbation to avoid sexual problems in the marriage relationship, both the relationship and the partner can be affected negatively. On the other hand, when married partners have different desires regarding the frequency of intercourse, masturbation can be a helpful and loving way for dealing with differing needs. The relationship is always the priority. Couples need to confront sexual problems hindering intimacy in the relationship rather than escaping problems through masturbation.

Masturbation, lust and fantasy. Masturbation is often associated with lust. Jesus addresses the issue of lust in Matthew 5:27-28: "You have heard that it was said, 'You shall not commit adultery.' But I say to you that every one who looks at a woman lustfully has already committed adultery with her in his heart" (RSV). This passage addresses lust for a specific woman in thought or deed, which violates the boundaries set by God. Jesus warns that lust leads to adultery, and adultery is sin. However, lusting is not necessarily to be equated with all fantasies.

Fantasies about future possibilities are usually benign, and masturbating with one's spouse or future spouse in mind can be a way of creating a more personal context for an otherwise solitary act. Yet desiring a specific person, and dwelling on ways to fulfill that desire, can become a form of lust.

Fantasy can develop into lust. For example, pedophiles may masturbate and fantasize about sexual interactions with young children. Over time, boundaries between fantasy and lust can become blurry, and pedophiles may seek out a young victim to act out their fantasy. Obviously, engaging in sexual activity with a child is a sinful act, which can stem from a fantasy life without boundaries. Monitoring and regulating our fantasy life will help us remain within God's intended context for ourselves as sexual beings.

Destructive fantasies often stem from a need for power. Increasing awareness about needs met through fantasy clarifies any discrepancies between our motives and God's intended purpose. For example, a destructive fantasy disregards God's commandments to love others, not to covet and not to harm others. Similarly, viewing erotic pictures while masturbating incorporates an element of dehumanizing sexual exploitation that is outside God's intention for humanity. It is more a concern that destructive and distorted attitudes and beliefs about women and sex within the content of pornography become associated with sexual arousal and can lead ultimately to an increase in violent sexual attitudes and even behavior. The association of masturbation with pornography generally incorporates exposure to attitudes that contradict God's value to love and respect others.

One who seeks to be holy before God must learn to discern between what one is free to do in Christ, and what is good to do within the context of one's particular life circumstances and relationship with God and others. Only the individual can determine the appropriateness of their fantasy life and its effect on their beliefs and attitudes. Monitoring fantasy is similar to the processes we incorporate to monitor our thoughts concerning world affairs and societal and relationship issues. Fantasy can increase responsiveness and receptiveness in the relationship, but can also be used as a substitute for unmet needs in the marriage.

There are also issues that a single person must face in regard to fantasy. Fantasy can create an ideal that sabotages intimacy and the hope of relationship by creating an unrealistic expectation. However, within a healthy context, fantasy can perpetuate hope for a relationship with another in a God-centered marital commitment. Regardless of the images associated with one's fantasies, it is important to continually evaluate them and to be willing to change elements of them that are not within God's intention for what it means to be fully human.

Fantasy can evolve into lust, or it can be a way of nurturing an appropriate desire for an intimate relationship. A fantasy about a future mate may keep a young person from becoming sexually active with dating partners. In this case, fantasy reinforces a God-centered value about sexuality.

Not long ago we were at the wedding of a friend's son and noticed the special bond between the groom and his groomsmen. All four had lived together for four years in a dorm at a Christian university and had become extremely close. They had made a vow to each other to uphold celibacy till marriage as a God-given blessing. Dave was the first of the four to marry. The rehearsal dinner was a loving and festive celebration for the young couple. During the dinner, the entire wedding party gathered around them to pray God's blessing on their life. On the wedding day, Dave's friends gave him the "high five" sign after they were pronounced husband and wife. "Do us proud!" was their cheer. Smiling, the entire wedding party understood the meaning of that cheer. It meant, "Take this woman you love and gently love her with all the passion you have. Enjoy the one-flesh union you've patiently waited for, and be richly blessed." This was more than a fantasy: it was real life.

This chapter has focused upon solitary forms of sexuality. Reliance on pornography, and even masturbation, in the extreme can come to have an unhealthy control over an individual. Dependence on pornography and other forms of inauthentic sexuality have increasingly come to be to identified as sexual addiction. In the next chapter we seek an understanding of sexual addiction and what can be done for persons who come to be controlled by inauthentic forms of sexuality.

FOR FURTHER READING

Carnes, P., D. Delmonico, E. Griffin and J. Moriarity. 2004. *In the shadows of the net: Breaking free of online sexual behavior.* Center City, Minn.: Hazelden.

Crosse, C., R. Crosse and M. Tabb. 2005. *I surender all: Rebuilding a marriage broken by pornography.* Colorado Springs: NavPress.

Hall, L. 1996. *An affair of the mind: One woman's courageous battle to salvage her family from the devastation of pornography.* Colorado Springs: Focus on the Family.

Mielke, A. 1995. *Christians, feminists, and the culture of pornography.* Lanham, Md.: University Press of America.

15

Sexual Addiction

Beginning in 1983, the subject of sexual addiction was popularized by the writings of Patrick Carnes. He defined the sexual addict as someone who has a pathological relationship with a mood-altering chemical, and that chemical just happens to be sex. Carnes surmises that the euphoria accompanying a sexual activity alters the person's mood like an adrenaline high. He likens sexual addiction to athlete's foot of the mind: "It never goes away. It always is asking to be scratched, promising relief. To scratch, however, is to cause pain and intensify the itch" (1983:vii).

Unlike an addiction to alcohol or another chemical substance, the sex addict abuses the very core of who he or she is. Familiar with secrets and leading a double life, sex addicts feel like they are the only ones who know what pain is about. They tell themselves, "No one could ever understand what I am going through. What's the use in trying to explain it?" they despair.

DEFINITION

Sexual addiction has been defined by Goodman (1992) as a recurrent failure to control sexual behavior despite the significant harmful consequences it has on the person and others. The obsession with getting that "sexual fix" can have a lifelong hold on a person. As we noted in the previous chapter, there is some controversy about using the term "sexual addict" since labeling may reinforce the notion that a person has no control over the sexual acting-out behavior.

Psychology professionals believe the sexual acting out is secondary to the more comprehensive obsessive-compulsive disorder (Moser 1993). Those who oppose using the term *sexual addiction* prefer psychological descriptions such as hypersexuality, compulsive sexual behavior, out-of-control sexual behavior, sexual impulse control disorder, obsessive-compulsive disorder, or sexual compulsivity (Bancroft and Vukadinovic 2004:81).

Resistance to sexual addiction language comes out of a concern that such language unnecessarily pathologizes and medicalizes the problem (Birchard 2004:81). In an effort to emphasize the positive, the National Council on Sexual Addiction and Compulsivity, which began in 1995, changed its name to the Society for the Advancement of Sexual Health in 2004.

We are sympathetic with these expressed concerns and agree that it may be better to say that persons have a sexual preoccupation, sexual dependency or sexual compulsivity, which they *can* overcome. However, we also believe it is important to describe the concepts developed by Patrick Carnes (1989, 1991, 1992, 2005) in his sexual addition model dealing with the beliefs, behaviors and attempts to control those behaviors that become part of the repetitive, self-defeating cycle. He also indicates the relational aspect of sexual addictions and the treatment method that is based on Alcoholics Anonymous ten-step programs. The need to be accountable in small groups to work with a sponsor and surrender to God (Higher Power) are essential aspects in breaking the cycle and escaping the control/out-of-control double bind (R. Earle and M. Earle 1995).

There is accumulative evidence that, for many, sex is only one of the multiple addictions of that person. In his study of 1000 sex addicts, Carnes, Murray and Charpentier (2004) found that less than 13 percent had just one addiction. Eisenman, Dantzker and Ellis (2004) report that although among sex addicts males have more multiple addictions than females, female mutiple addictions are more likely to include such things as cigarettes, chocolate and food. In noting that both food and sex are essential for the continuation of human life, Power (2005) reports six forms of eating disorders and ten types of sexual addictions. Grant and Steinberg (2005) report that 20 percent of those disgnosed with compulsive sexual behavior were also addicted to *gambling*, with the symptoms of sexual compulsion preceding the onset of pathological gambling in 70 percent of their subjects.

Sexual addiction affects not only the addict but also his or her significant relationships. There are some noteworthy corollaries of sexual addiction, including the tendency to engage in sexual activity in response to stressful situations, low self-esteem, and negative emotions such as anxiety, sadness and loneliness. Weiss (2004) reports that rates of depression are more than twice as high in a sample of male sexual addicts than in the general population (28 versus 12 percent). In addition, the effect of disclosure on the wife of the sexual addict is traumatic and sometimes a crisis, resulting in related distress. There is also evidence that successful sustained recovery is possible only when all addictions are addressed. Carnes, Murray and Charpentier (2004) report that the biggest factors in relapse are multiple addictions and the interactions among them.

In speculating about why a person becomes trapped in compulsive sexual addictions, researchers acknowledge possible *biological* leanings, yet most explanations focus primarily on sociocultural and family factors.

Biological factors. Evidence of the connection between the brain and the physiological system is just beginning to emerge. Coleman (2005) has documented that various types of neuroanatomical dysregulations cause compulsive sexual behavior. He gives neurochemical explanations of how addictions affect the brain, suggesting that *all addictive disorders* have a similar impact on the brain.

Recognizing the possible neurochemical dimensions of an addiction, Laaser and Gregoire (2003) recommend a period of total abstinence from all sexual activity for thirty to ninety days in their treatment model.

The addictive society. At the sociocultural level, sexual addiction can be understood as the product of living in an addictive society. The twentieth century has been labeled the age of anxiety. Distrust, isolation, abandonment, value confusion, lack of meaning, search for easy solutions, loneliness and a quick-fix mentality are part of modern culture, which make one vulnerable to addictive behaviors.

The person searches for meaning or comfort wherever it can be found, and sex is presented as the ultimate experience that brings personal satisfaction, a commodity that offers release. Contemporary culture places confidence in technology, where fast, easy solutions are promoted. In our microwave age with its quick-fix mentality, one looks for convenient and instant solutions. Many people use over-the-counter or prescribed drugs to soothe problems of life. The television bombards us with a host of commercials promoting relief for every imaginable irritation, from headaches to hangovers. An advertisement for a well-known brand of aspirin boasts relief "when you haven't got time for the pain!" Our society and culture also promote sex as another quick-fix way to deal with anxiety, distrust, isolation, abandonment, value confusion and meaninglessness.

The fast pace of life within modern technological society tempts one to find relief through anything that can reduce tension or soothe the effect of life stresses. The competitive emphasis on getting ahead, fragmentation of families, impersonal nature of relationships, and loss of involved community also make for a climate of exploitation. Needless to say, the commodification of sex proves to be a highly profitable product in an addiction-prone society.

The ever-changing and competing values of modern society, the general lack of meaning, and personal disenfranchisement often lead to value confusion and personal disillusionment.

Family factors. The cumulative research on unstable, fragmented families provides clues about particular types of families that may make an individual prone to various kinds of addictions. Two important characteristics of family interaction are cohesion and adaptability (Olson et al. 1979).

Cohesion represents the degree of emotional connectedness or separateness between family members. Effective families are characterized by a sufficient degree of cohesion, in which there is a satisfying emotional connection as well as respect for individual autonomy. In homes where members are not respected, there is often insufficient provision for rules concerning expressions of affection. For example, when sexual behaviors between members cause discomfort, the children do not feel that they have the right to express objections. Also, the unspoken and sometimes spoken message is, "Never to tell anyone outside the family about anything that goes on inside the family," for to do so is an unforgivable act of disloyalty. The no-talk rule keeps others out while covert and overt sexual abuse may be going on inside the home.

The opposite of overconnection is underconnection, where there is a serious lack of emotional cohesion between family members. In these homes, family members are unable to make a satisfying connection, so everyone learns to fend for themselves. Features of disengaged families include emotional abandonment, inability to talk about sexual feelings and behaviors, tensions around sexual matters, lack of physical or sexual affirmation, and isolation that leads to sexual evasion. The emotional distance between family members also makes it difficult for children to learn how to relate in meaningful ways to others outside the home.

Adaptability represents the degree of structure and flexibility in a family. Again, effective families are characterized by appropriate structure as well as the ability to adapt to needed change throughout the family life stages. When a family lacks structure, it can be extremely chaotic in the sense that there are vast discrepancies between values and behavior. The discrepancies often result in inconsistent sexual standards and discipline. Common patterns include sexual unmanageability for both parents and children as well as frequent role reversals in which children take on parental responsibility or even become sexual objects. Children are placed in a double bind, being told one thing about sex but experiencing another reality.

Low adaptability is expressed in rigid values. Parents are uncompromising and extremely strict about moral standards. The features of rigid homes include unreachable expectations about sexuality, black-and-white moral standards, extreme efforts to control a child's sexual behavior, and severe punishment of the child's sexual behavior. Children in rigid families find the unrealistic sexual standards frustrating and experience a sense of shame and inadequacy about sexuality. For example, children who are severely reprimanded for touching their genitals tend to reject their sexual self.

Most families fluctuate on the cohesion/adaptability dimensions at different times throughout the various life stages, but families at the extremes are particularly vulnerable to distortions about sexuality. To develop an authentic sexuality, a family must respect individual boundaries as well as establish reasonable and appropriate structures to safeguard a member's sexuality. To develop a strong sense of self as a sexual person, a child needs the secure love and connection of family members, as well as a clear affirmation of sexuality and relational strength.

Low self-esteem is a major component in the sexual acting-out patterns of the sex addict. Sex is often used to validate one's femininity or masculinity in a basic, raw manner. Not being affirmed by their family, sex addicts seek a substitute for what is lacking in their personal life.

SEXUAL VULNERABILITY FOR MINISTERS

Although there is little evidence that clergy are more vulnerable to pornography or other addictions than laypersons, clergy sexual indiscretion is more likely to gain media attention. Stack, Wasserman and Kern (2004) found that religious bonds had a negative influence on cyberporn use. Holding clergy up on a pedestal combined with an inherent incongruence between being a spiritual leader and a sexual person brings tension. Pressures to be above temptations may lead a pastor to "split off" aspects of their sexuality. Male clergy in particular may be vulnerable to Internet sex especially because it can be done in secret. A leader held in high esteem may be prone to narcissitic thinking; a leader isolated may not have a place to honestly share human frailties; a leader threatened by denominational authorities for accountability may feel trapped.

Based on his treatment of pastors who desire recovery from out-of-control use of Internet pornography, Birchard (2004) suggests that a treatment plan must begin with an understanding about an interlocking cycle of religious behavior and sexual addiction. The Christian notion that the flesh is bad and spirit is good may contribute to a splitting in the pastor's mind. The cycle of shame (all bad) and repentance (all good) is typical of the compulsive cycle we will discuss in more detail in the next section.

The pastor must see how this cycle has been perpetuated in his life. Only then can the recovery phase begin in which a "culture of recovery" is created. Borrowing from twelve-step strategies, the pastor must acknowledge helplessness and reliance on God and accountable peer support. Psychotherapeutic restructuring is also needed to repair narcissistic damage. Finally, structural changes must be made to fill the inner void by replacing "the anesthetizing functions of the addiction with enduring structures and sources of solace" (Birchard 2004:86).

Laaser and Gregoire (2003) believe that clergy Internet addicts also benefit from assistance in spiritual maturity. A spiritual director or mentor can help them practice being spiritual disciples as they learn new ways to connect with God and others.

How pastors and Christian leaders are dealt with after sexual indiscretion varies. Most often, the person is removed from the leadership position immediately after disclosure. The church or denomination mandates a time of rehabilitation and counseling before making a decision about being reinstated. The nature of the indiscretion will certainly be taken into consideration in the treatment mandate and ultimate decision making.

Though grace underlies the process, justice and firmness is also in order. Especially in cases such as pedophilia, where evidence for cure is minimal, decisions must be made in light of protecting innocent victims in present and future. In a lesser offense, such as comsumption of Internet pornography, which has less direct influence on others, the person may be able to retain the leadership position while they are in rehabilitation and therapy. In most cases, those who oversee the rehabilitation process will work with the individual, their family members, and the congregation in making final determination of whether one permanently resigns a position or can be reinstated.

UNDERSTANDING THE SEXUAL ADDICTION CYCLE

(*Note:* Both men and women struggle with sexually addictive behaviors, but since most sexual addicts are male, we will use masculine pronouns in this section.)

Our discussion of sexual addiction is greatly influenced by the work of Patrick Carnes (1983, 1989, 1992, 2005). In diagramming the addictive cycle, he was the first to point out the importance of the perceptions or "mistaken beliefs" that addicts bring into the addictive cycle. Treatment must begin here and continue with behavioral interventions throughout the repetitive, compulsive cycle to eventually change the self-defeating underlying belief system of the sexual addict.

Belief system. The core belief of the addict goes something like this: "I'm basically a bad, unworthy person, and no one wants me as I am. I must find another way to meet my needs, so I focus on sexual pleasure, which helps relieve my self-incriminating thoughts." Carnes (2005) points out that the sexual behaviors engaged in are often quite against the addict's own value system, leaving him with further feelings of shame and regret after engaging in the addictive behavior. The self-condemning behavior after acting out makes him feel even worse about himself than before. He is disgusted with himself for what he has done and makes promises to himself that he will never do it again. However, the negative beliefs keep coming back, ringing louder and louder in his mind. To drown out these negative messages, he focuses on sexual thoughts and certain sexual behaviors that he believes will numb the pain of these negative messages.

Compulsivity. The compulsion stage involves obsessive, persistent, repetitive thoughts. The addict now becomes preoccupied with sexual thoughts in such a strong way that it actually interferes with his life and relationships. It is not an occasional fantasy, but one that occupies hours of time and interferes with everything the person does. The tenacious thoughts take control of the addict, and life now revolves around the desire to get the fix (that is, act out the behavior). He will do almost anything to fulfill his goal. With unimaginable denial in full swing, the addict is completely oblivious to any negative consequences of his actions. The compulsive thoughts have taken control, and now he moves into the ritual phase of the cycle.

Ritualized behaviors. Ritualized behaviors include such things as making a phone call to a prostitute, getting in the car to cruise a red-light neighborhood, or anything else that starts the process of capturing the high. The power themes of conquest, breaking taboos, and taking risks can add to the addict's risk-taking at this point. The addict anticipates the mounting excitement of going through the elaborate routines, which intensify and prolong arousal, eventually leading to the sexual act. Once the ritual has started, the addict becomes increasingly focused on doing what it takes to get the sexual high. The ritualized actions and trancelike focus on the goal reduce the self-loathing beliefs. Sex, the drug of choice, anesthetizes these negative thoughts. J. Schneider and others (2005) point out that *ritualization and reinforcement* are two common themes of multiple addiction.

Impaired thinking. Once he has his mind on the sexual fix, impaired thinking takes over. Major denial keeps him from dealing forthrightly with his problems. He blames others for his plight and rationalizes his compulsive sexual desires away. He distorts reality, believes his own lies, lives a secret double life filled with suspicion and paranoid feelings about being found out. This is particularly true for those who have a moral and religious public life.

His distorted reality leads to risk-taking behaviors. For example, he puts himself and others at lethal risk when, in denial, he fails to take necessary precautions against contracting a sexually transmitted disease. Years can go by before he realizes he has been infected (and may have infected others) with HIV, for example. Impaired thinking gives him a false sense of power that keeps him from considering the actual life-threatening consequences of what he is about to do.

The fix. The unacceptable beliefs about himself and the impaired thinking are now transferred to the unacceptable behavior. He engages in the specific sexual behavior that is the final goal of his obsessions. Although the fix provides temporary relief from his incessant thoughts, the ugly shaming cycle kicks in immediately after he acts out, and profound feelings of remorse become a huge burden. The shaming cycle verifies what he already believes about himself: that he is inherently bad and can never change. Then the negative beliefs begin the cycle again.

CONTROL/OUT-OF-CONTROL PATTERN

One clue in identifying an addictive problem is the pattern of trying to control behavior on one hand and being totally out of control on the other hand. This control/out-of-control pattern overarches the entire cycle of negative beliefs, preoccupation with the fix, premeditated rituals, impaired thinking, getting the fix, feelings of remorse, and the adamant promises never to do it again. The in-control periods can last for quite a long time in the beginning, but as time goes by, it becomes increasingly difficult to maintain long periods of control. The period of time before negative beliefs enter in and trigger the intense out-of-control part of the cycle also becomes shorter and shorter. Figure 15.1 gives a summary depiction of this vicious cycle, which intensifies over time.

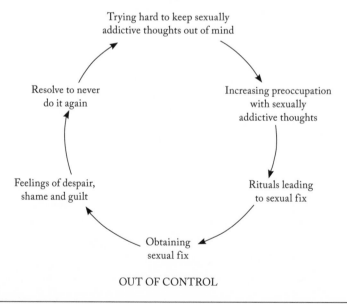

IN CONTROL

Trying hard to keep sexually
addictive thoughts out of mind

Resolve to never
do it again

Increasing preoccupation
with sexually
addictive thoughts

Feelings of despair,
shame and guilt

Rituals leading
to sexual fix

Obtaining
sexual fix

OUT OF CONTROL

Figure 15.1. The cycle of sexual addiction. This figure is based on models developed by Patrick Carnes (1983, 1989) and Fossum and Mason (1989).

A vicious cycle. The compulsive nature and out-of-control repetitive quality of the sexual action is what drives the sex addict, according to Travin (1995). While the addict is in an acting-out mode, everything else becomes secondary; the job, the wife, the deadlines, even the color of the stoplights seem to take a back seat to the addict's "need" for sex, his need for sexual validation. At times, he feels as though in a trance, driving around for hours and looking for sex. Bancroft and Vukadinovic found that 45 percent of the sex addicts in their study described a type of dissociation from reality while acting out (2004:230). Many addicts report that they have been in accidents because they were so completely unaware of their surroundings. All senses seem to be impaired by the person's fixation on finding sex. And once this process begins, it is difficult for sex addicts to pull themselves out of the trance and return to reality. During the act itself, the addict usually feels good because his addiction is being fed and his feelings of inadequacy are numbed for the moment. Unfortunately for the addict, like any addiction, one cannot stay on this high forever. Even though sexual bingeing can sometime last for days, there is a huge letdown after it is over. Then, it is not long before the entire cycle repeats itself.

Dangerous choices. Dodge and others (2004) report an association between sexual compulsivity and participation in a variety of high-risk sexual behaviors. Because the addict's senses are impaired, the addiction places his life in grave danger. The addiction takes the sexual addict to risky, acting-out locations. He may find himself in the midst of drug addicts and prostitutes as he tries to get his sexual fix. Deep in his addiction, unaware of his surroundings, the sexual addict does not realize that he could be set up for a police sting. All of a sudden, while engaging in anonymous sex at a urinal, he is arrested by an undercover cop for lewd conduct. In fact, most of the men arrested in public restrooms, parks, truck stops or porn shops are married and have families. In one afternoon, a secret he has kept for years can be out in the open in a matter of minutes. The out-of-control phase might cost him his job, his marriage and children, his good name and his reputation.

Eventually, the addict returns to reality and is left to deal not only with the pain and consequences of acting out, but also the lack of inner peace regarding his self-esteem issues. The void is still present; the negative, self-loathing feelings taunt him once again; and he inevitably returns to the compulsive behavior unless the vicious abuse cycle is broken. Though the fix offers some sexual gratification, it lasts only a brief time before the shaming messages hit even harder than before. The addict is now left alone to face himself again. He looks in the mirror and sees someone he knows well, a hopeless wretch of a person who is "bad to the core of his very being." He sees himself as a weak, out-of-control person who is unable to help himself. At this point the addict promises himself he will reform and moves into the control phase. Since he believes he is despicable, he tries harder than ever before to control his desires and sexual behaviors. His negative view of himself continues, and he becomes haunted by the idea that sex is the only remedy for his pain. So once again, sex is set up as the false idol that promises to numb the self-defeating thoughts but gives nothing except pain in return.

TREATMENT

The ultimate goal of treatment is to help sexual addicts to (1) recognize and understand the false beliefs; (2) commit to relinquishing the compulsive thoughts, ritualized behavior and sexual acts; (3) look to a Higher Power to transform their beliefs and empower them to change; and (4) develop a capacity for emotional intimacy with significant persons in their life. During treatment, denial is a major factor that keeps sexual addicts from taking these steps. The best efforts at breaking the sexual addiction cycle entail a personal commitment to change, combined with support from a group and a personal relationship with God. Twelve-step programs such as Sexaholics Anonymous (SA), Sex Addicts Anonymous (SAA) or Sexual Compulsives Anonymous (SCA) have been especially helpful for many sex addicts. Each group's focus is somewhat different, but the overriding goal is to stop compulsive sexual behaviors.

By the time a sex addict walks into his first twelve-step meeting, he may have two thoughts simultaneously running through his head. "I sure don't want to be here!" and "I really need to be here!" Soon, as he sits with his anxiety and listens to others describe the different characteristics of sexual addiction, he can personally relate to what is being said. As he looks around the room, he sees men and women, all there for the same reason. They all have a problem with using sex to validate unresolved feelings. As the addict hears others share their stories and talk about their recovery, he begins to realize that he too could have a life of recovery.

A core aspect of twelve-step recovery groups is the need to look to a

Higher Power to achieve recovery. For so long, the addict has tried to change and control behavior on his own efforts, but he must admit he cannot do it without God's help. This humility keeps a sex addict depending on God each step of the way toward recovery.

Sponsors are a wonderful part of the program. A sponsor is a person in the program who has achieved sobriety and becomes a mentor to the sex addict. As a fellow addict in recovery, a mentor routinely makes contact with the new member to help him develop a plan to stop the vicious cycle of addiction. For example, if compulsive masturbation is the problem, the sponsor and the addict will define realistic goals and work out a plan of sobriety for this behavior. Because sexual addiction is intertwined with the addict's past, personal therapy is recommended to help an addict understand the issues underlying the addictive behaviors.

The most effective treatment for a sexual addict is a combination of therapy and participation in a sexual addiction recovery group. In a comprehensive guidebook *A Gentle Path Through the Twelve Steps,* Patrick Carnes (1991) gives direction and tools to help people reach a successful recovery. Many sexual addiction intervention programs utilize a combination of strategies for all types of sexual addiction, including programs for an addiction to cybersex (Bingham and Piotrowski 1996).

Cognitive-behavioral programs include behavior therapy, social skills training, modification of distorted cognition, and relapse prevention. Relapse prevention is designed to help the addict anticipate and cope with potential relapses. Efective treatment focuses on the addictive behavior, thought processes and management.

Spiritual help consists of activities like writing in a journal, spending time in meditative prayer, reciting the serenity prayer, and being part of a small caring group and faith community. By grabbing hold of the powerful truth that God and others love them unconditionally, by receiving Christ's grace and forgiveness, and by drawing on the Holy Spirit for strength and empowerment, sex addicts discover their true self. These experiences help construct a new way of thinking and feeling about oneself and others.

When married, recovery from sexual addiction can be aided by conjoint marital therapy. In their work with husbands recovering from addictive use of pornography, Zitzman and Butler (2005:311) report that conjoint couple therapy helps couples to "organize the relationship to sponsor recovery while also promoting essential relationship and individual healing for both spouses." Couples therapy can increase marital trust and confidence, allow for a "mutual softening" in coming to terms with the addiction, and identify key strategies in facilitating recovery. Mark Laaser reports that sexual addiction can best be dealt with in a couple's therapy when the couple share a faith or spiritual perspective (2004).

Helpful principles might be expressed as follows:

- We acknowledge that we can take action to stop being dependent on sex for our self-esteem by trusting in the living God and the Holy Spirit, who empowers us.

- Our inner healing comes from the source of all healing, Jesus Christ, who is acquainted with our grief and, though tempted in every way, was victorious over sin.

- We make a decision to become authentic sexual selves as designed by our Creator God and by trusting in the power of God's word.

- We willingly relinquish shame, guilt and any behaviors that prevent God from working in our lives so that we can be all that we are intended to be as sons and daughters of Christ.

- We admit we have made serious mistakes and engaged in behaviors that are not in accord with God's design for authentic sexuality. We confess to those we have harmed in the process and will take steps to make amends.

- We seek to find our inward calling and develop the will to follow in God's way. We look to the Holy Spirit to convict, guide and empower us as we continue our life's journey.

- We express gratitude to the people who have come alongside us in our walk, have shown us unconditional love and acceptance, and have helped us develop our God-given strengths, talents and gifts.

A CHRISTIAN RESPONSE TO SEXUAL ADDICTION

Given the destructiveness of sexually addictive behavior, it is good once again to reaffirm sex as a good gift from God. Unfortunately, what God has given for good can be deeply distorted. As we noted in chapters seven and fourteen, 1 Corinthians 6:12-13 says that sex becomes destructive when it has mastery over a person. The basic problem of sexual addiction is that one is enslaved by sexual compulsions. The excesses and repetitive cycles hold the addict captive to ongoing self-destructive beliefs and behaviors.

One of our foundational assertions for building a theology of sexuality is to affirm that we are created in God's image and therefore meant to reflect the relationality of God. Sexual addiction/compulsion distorts the journey of moving toward this goal of relational wholeness. At the very core of the sexual addict is a limited capacity to develop and maintain healthy relationality when caught in the sex-focused cycle. Sexual addiction is a sin against the *self*, since sexual addiction is a *self*-reinforcing behaivor. Caught in the cycle, relationships with significant others are neglected. The emotional, psychological and sexual energy that should be drawing the addict to their loved ones is actually taking that person in the opposite direction.

Since the term *addiction* has become commonplace in modern society, it is necessary to examine whether this merely replaces the notion of *sin*. Christians might understandably be suspicious of using the term *addiction* too freely because it seems to fly in the face of the biblical emphasis on individual choice and personal accountability. The fear that this may lead to blatant sin, more denial, and an unwillingness to take responsibility for one's actions is certainly an important concern.

Romans 1:24-28 offers a perspective on this point. Verse 24 says, "God gave them over in the sinful desires of their hearts to sexual impurity for the degrading of their bodies with one another." Verse 26 reports, "God gave them over to shameful lusts." And verse 28 states, "[God] gave them over to a depraved mind, to do what ought not to be done." In this little phrase, "gave over," Richard Mouw (1988) believes we have the basis for a theology of addiction, which he describes as rebellion against God, suppression of the truth, and giving in to unrighteousness.

Note that the statement "God gave them over" is preceded by the word *therefore*. Quite clearly, God gave them over only *after* they volitionally rejected and sinned against God. In our thinking about sexual addiction, we must recognize that the addiction begins with a willful act on the part of the addict. Then, after repeating this act over and over, it becomes an addiction. A person must be held accountable, even though the compulsive nature seems to render one incapable of accountability. This is the very reason treatment involves such a strong emphasis on changing the addict's beliefs and breaking that cycle.

We certainly must balance a compassionate understanding along with a clear expectation of intentional choice. Treatment is effective as long as a person continues to be accountable to others and seeks strength from God to overcome. Those who do not believe in an all-powerful, all-loving and forgiving God will find it incredibly difficult to change destructive thinking patterns and recover in their own strength. And in the more extreme cases, repeat sex offenders often *sear* their consciences to the extent that they feel no guilt or remorse for their crimes. They have "hardened their hearts" (cf. Ex 9:34) and may never seek change or treatment. The only thing that works in this case is the threat of being caught and sent to jail. To be released from the prison of addiction and the compulsive bondage of sexual sin, the addict needs to turn to the One who promises wholeness and freedom from the derogatory stigma, pain and shame of the abusive cycle. Philippians 3:10-14 provides promise of hope in Christ:

> I want to know Christ and the power of his resurrection and the fellowship of sharing in his sufferings, becoming like him in his death, and so, somehow, to attain to the resurrection from the dead. Not that I have already obtained this, or have already been made perfect, but I press on to take hold of that for which Christ Jesus took hold of me. Brothers, I do not consider myself yet to have taken hold of it. But one thing I do: Forgetting what is behind and straining toward what is ahead, I press on toward the goal to win the prize for which God has called me heavenward in Christ Jesus.

FOR FURTHER READING

Carnes, P. 2005. *Facing the shadow: Starting sexual and relationship recovery.* Carefree, Ariz.: Gentle Path.

Carnes, P., D. Delmonico, E. Griffin and J. Moriarity. 2004. *In the shadows of the net: Breaking free of online sexual behavior.* Center City, Minn.: Hazelden.

Laaser, M. 2004. *Healing the wounds of sexual addiction.* Grand Rapids: Zondervan.

DMOZ Open Directory Project. 2007. Society: Sexuality: Sexual addiction. Listing of online sexual addiction resources. http://www.dmoz .org/Society/Sexuality/Sexual_Addiction/.

Weiss, Doug. Christian sexual addiction resources. http://www.sexaddict .com/Resource.html.

Willingham, R. 1999. *Breaking free: Understanding sexual addiction and the healing power of Jesus.* Downers Grove, Ill.: InterVarsity Press.

PART 4

Conclusion

16

The Sexually Authentic Society

Our investigation of human sexuality has been guided by a search for authenticity. Our journey has led to the consideration of a variety of factors that contribute to the formation of an authentic sexuality. Based on an understanding of psychological, sociological, cultural and biological factors affecting the development of one's sexuality, we have sought a deeper meaning through the Holy Scriptures as a way of understanding human sexual authenticity. In the meaning of being created sexual, we make sense of what it is to be an authentic sexual person.

As we come to the end of this discourse on human sexuality, we must stand back and take a broader bird's-eye view of the societal and cultural context within which individuals live out their lives as sexual beings. Clearly the development and nurturing of authentic sexuality does not exist in a vacuum; it is part of a larger social system, which can either promote or distort sexuality as God intended it to be.

Individualism and personal autonomy are among the strongest values in modern Western society. Although these values have freed individuals from being dominated and controlled by the collective will of the group, individuals within modern society are in danger of losing two very important correctives that give balance from a wider social system. To live consistently sexually authentic lives, individuals need both *support* and *accountability* from social structures. Whereas some forms of inauthentic sexuality are expressed in inauthentic sexual relationships (see chapters eleven to thirteen), other forms are expressed in more solitary ways, such

as pornographic consumption and sexual addiction. Support and accountability from sexually authentic social structures are the two important
ingredients lacking in all forms of inauthentic sexuality.

In chapter eleven the metaphor of an onion was used to suggest how
sexual harassment could be understood in terms of layers of explanation.
In a similar way, sexuality is influenced by the fabric of society, which
consists of many interwoven layers within which people live, find their
identity, seek support, and are held accountable. These several layers of
social structure can be conceptualized as forming increasingly inclusive
concentric circles around an individual's life. Figure 16.1 represents three
different layers of social structure, along with a biblically prescribed ideal
for each.

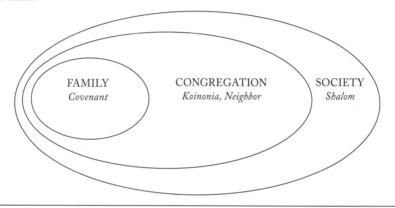

**Figure 16.1. The sexually authentic society: Levels of social structure and biblically
prescribed ideals**

For most people the family is the central arena in which sexual behavior and norms are taught and modeled. The *covenant* is the biblically
prescribed basis for family relationships, as we have discussed throughout
this book.

Beyond the family is the local church or fellowship in which Christian believers find their identity, support and accountability. While there
is much in Scripture to suggest that a church/fellowship should resemble family relationships, the biblically prescribed ideal is that of *koinonia*
(*koinōnia*, fellowship, close mutual relationship). The congregation, as the
people of God, are called not only to be a fellowship for each other but
also to reach out to the needs of others in their surrounding neighborhood
and community. *Neighbor* is the biblically prescribed ideal for believers'

relationships with people in their community. Finally, the most inclusive level is society. Here millions of people share identity through common membership in a nation-state that establishes formal laws and informal norms about sexuality. The biblically prescribed ideal here is *shalom* (peace, friendship, welfare, wholeness). We shall present a description of what authentic sexuality might be on the familial, local church/fellowship and societal levels.

AUTHENTIC FAMILY SEXUALITY

In chapter three we drew upon the writings of James Maddock to give a picture of family sexual health, which serves as the basis for our discussion. Healthy family sexuality was defined as "the balanced expression of sexuality in the life of the family, in ways that enhance the personal identities and sexual health of individual family members and the organization of the family as a system, functioning effectively within its social and material environment" (Maddock and Larson 1995:52-53).

The basic unit in society, both sociologically and theologically, is the family. Sociologically, the family is the unit into which individuals are born, find their sexual identity, and are socialized as male or female sexual beings. Theologically, the relationship principles of covenant, grace, empowerment and intimacy are supremely applicable to family relationships. The family is meant to be an intimate environment where persons can be themselves without fear of violation or rejection.

Family life is to be a place of security where members experience the faithful, unconditional love of family members through mutual care and regard. For husband and wife, this means offering oneself in body, mind and spirit. In becoming "one flesh," the couple grows through a relationship of mutual desire, vulnerability and responsiveness (1 Cor 7:5). For children, the family provides security through an unconditional love that puts their best interests as the priority. When children make mistakes, they are forgiven rather than shamed. Children who are valued know how to value themselves as sexual persons.

Children of empowering parents thrive in an atmosphere of nurture and guidance that builds them up rather than tears them down. Effective parents respect sexual boundaries through nonerotic physical touch, verbal support, and affirmation of gender and sexuality. Children learn to freely express their unique personalities rather than be confined by rigidly imposed gender roles. Both parents will have the ability to establish emotional bonds with male and female children.

The intimacy principles of sexually authentic family life ensure that members are able to be emotionally naked and not ashamed (Gen 2:25). It is a place where they can be themselves, free from the demanding requirements of the outside world. In an accepting atmosphere, family members are comfortable with themselves as sexual persons because they are supported and encouraged to be themselves. Home is a place where family members do not hide their feelings because feelings and opinions are honored. It is a place where members listen to and encourage each other to talk openly about sex and gender. There is no distrust in relationships because appropriate boundaries provide safety. Authentic family living affirms sexuality for what it is meant to be.

Unfortunately, not all families are as balanced as this ideal. The family is so often plundered on one side by the demands and intrusions of mass society and on the other by an individualistic emphasis that pulls members away from needed support and accountability of the family group. This is especially true when activities outside the home put such time demands on each member that they have little opportunity for family interaction. As children move through their formative years, they are deprived of strong family connections that contribute to authentic sexual and gender identities.

Family life needs to be reconstructed as a secure emotional holding environment that keeps effective boundaries against the bombardment of negative external influences. The family must protect itself from the intrusion of a multitude of inauthentic sexual messages and forces that sap it of vitality. When family members have a central place where they learn to be accountable to one another, they will know how to be responsible citizens outside the home.

With regard to the idea that a family functions most effectively within a social environment, there is need for a new understanding of biblical family life. In contrast to our individualistic emphasis, Israel held a strong sense of corporate solidarity and identity within the wider community. An analysis of families in ancient Israel concludes that they were formed, shaped and sustained by a core of corporate identity and responsibility (Perdue et al. 1997). The family household was not separate from but an essential part of wider society. Israelites learned to look at their "social world and the world of creation as a household or a village of households, in which members took up residence and dwelt, nurtured and protected one another, and provided care for the poor person, who was the 'sibling' or the 'neighbor' to be loved as the self" (p. 254). Although it is unlikely that we will return to these large household units of the past, we believe that the local church can and should be a place where individuals and families find a community of faith that upholds, nurtures, supports, guides, protects and develops people of authentic sexual character.

THE LOCAL CHURCH AS AN AUTHENTIC SEXUAL COMMUNITY

People in most societies are members of and find a sense of identity and social support from primary groups that exist beyond the family itself. Examples of such groups are churches, clubs, fellowships, and recreational and common interest groups.

Sociologically, a primary group serves as a mediating structure between the isolated, private world of the family and faceless remote societal structures. However, an increasing number of people in modern society are unable to locate supportive primary groups. Along with a decline in significant group accountability comes the loss of effective social control. Our families are more vulnerable today due to moral laxity. A type of impersonal social environment has caused an increasing number of persons to feel like they belong to a *lonely crowd*.

Some social scientists believe that networking has become the modern substitute for primary groups. Serving as mediating structures, friendship, occupational and religious networks provide for some needs. However, because these networks are individualized, they are subject to change and lack foundational group-based values like commitment and a sense of secure belonging.

Response to the disintegration of primary-group relationships is varied. There is one trend that promotes an extreme individualism and avoids significant dependence on or commitment to anyone else. Some people try a variety of groups based on interests such as economic sharing, hobbies or religious devotion. Some search for community in institutional contexts like suburban housing developments and take on names that indicate commonality and identity like Homewood, Pleasantville, Community Heights. In our mass society, primary-group identity and relationships are desperately sought out, yet often prove to be exceedingly difficult to achieve.

The local church as koinonia. The local church serves as a primary group for Christian believers. Sometimes described as a "family of families," the church gives members a source of identity, support and accountability. If the church is to become a supportive plausibility structure for faith, it must be a place where persons find a sexual identity that is supported and a belief system that is authentic.

The church is to serve as God's transforming agent in the lives of its believers. Peter Selby (1996) points out that "an understanding of the church as a 'family' has its origin in the determination of the New Testament to speak of the human situation in terms of relationship, and of the transformation of that situation by the grace of Christ in terms of transformed relationship." We must "recognize that the language of family and kinship is there in relation to church not for the purpose of encouraging some of the [inauthentic] attributes which we have seen to be associated with the concept of family in our time. Rather, it is there to emphasize that character of the transformation which has taken place in the relationships which human beings have to each other and to God in the light of God's grace" (p. 165).

The key to understanding God's ideal with regard to social and sexual relationships within a local church context is found in the New Testament concept of *koinonia*. Scripture used this term in order to refer to a group in which persons were united in identity and purpose by way of a voluntary sharing of all of their possessions. During New Testament times, people associated themselves with two main types of groups: *politeia*, or civic life, and *oikonomia*, or family life. *Koinonia* came to represent a new type of group situated between the inclusive, impersonal state and the exclusive, blood-based community of the household (R. Banks 1994).

One of the metaphors that the apostle Paul uses to describe the church is family. Christians are to see themselves as members of a divine family, the head of which is God the Father. Thus Paul, quoting from the Old Testament, writes, "I will receive you, I will be a Father to you, and you will be my sons and daughters" (2 Cor 6:18). We are also told that "God has sent the Spirit of his Son into our hearts, crying 'Abba! Father!'" (Gal 4:6 NRSV). And Ephesians 2:19 states, "You are no longer strangers and aliens, but you are citizens with the saints and also members of the household of God" (NRSV).

God desires that strong family relationships not simply be ends in themselves but also exemplary of how we are to care for each other in the local church. Jesus' attitude toward the inclusiveness of the family is clearly shown in Mark 3:31-35. While speaking to a crowd, he is informed that his mother and brothers have arrived. He replies, "'Who are my mother and my brothers?' And looking at those who sat around him, he said, 'Here are my mother and brothers! Whoever does the will of God is my brother and sister and mother'" (NRSV). The common membership we have in the body of Christ binds all believers to Christ and to one another as family, and our relationships are to be based upon covenant, grace, empowerment, intimacy and koinonia. The concept of *koinonia* provides us with a model of the church as a primary support and accountability community.

The decline of primary groups in modern society has more to do with the nature of contemporary mass society, with its forces of impersonalization, urbanization, industrialization, rationalization, dehumanization, bureaucratization and secularization than it does with the absence of Christianity. In the face of these societal changes, Christian churches that practice koinonia can be a witness to how God intends persons to relate in primary groups. Sociologically, a primary group other than a Christian fellowship might function as a koinonia-type group. For this to happen, however, this primary group will at the very least need to share common beliefs, values, ideals and goals. Nevertheless, we argue that the New Testament example of koinonia provides us with the best model for how all human beings may live meaningful lives in harmony with themselves, others and their Creator.

The local church as neighbor. To this point we have argued that the church needs to be a social unit in which persons and families find support and accountability for their sexual values and behavior. But in addition, the church needs to reach out into society in two important ways if it is to be a sexually authentic community. First, as a community of believers, the church needs the courage to play a prophetic role by challenging the sexually unhealthy and inauthentic aspects of society. The church is to faithfully preach the kingdom by exposing the sexual lies, manipulations and illusions perpetuated by elements in society that deny the light of God's redemption in Jesus Christ. Second, the people of God are also called to minister to the sexually wounded and hurting in the community.

In the parable of the good Samaritan, Jesus set forth the concept of *neighbor* as the normative model of all community-based relationships.

Luke 10:25-37 records this parable as follows:

> On one occasion an expert in the law stood up to test Jesus. "Teacher," he asked, "what must I do to inherit eternal life?"
>
> "What is written in the Law?" he replied. "How do you read it?"
>
> He answered: "'Love the Lord your God with all your heart and with all your soul and with all your strength and with all your mind'; and, 'Love your neighbor as yourself.'"
>
> "You have answered correctly," Jesus replied. "Do this and you will live."
>
> But he wanted to justify himself, so he asked Jesus, "And who is my neighbor?"
>
> In reply Jesus said: "A man was going down from Jerusalem to Jericho, when he fell into the hands of robbers. They stripped him of his clothes, beat him and went away, leaving him half dead. A priest happened to be going down the same road, and when he saw the man, he passed by on the other side. So too, a Levite, when he came to the place and saw him, passed by on the other side. But a Samaritan, as he traveled, came where the man was; and when he saw him, he took pity on him. He went to him and bandaged his wounds, pouring on oil and wine. Then he put the man on his own donkey, took him to an inn and took care of him. The next day he took out two silver coins and gave them to the innkeeper. 'Look after him,' he said, 'and when I return, I will reimburse you for any extra expense you may have.'
>
> "Which of these three do you think was a neighbor to the man who fell into the hands of robbers?"
>
> The expert in the law replied, "The one who had mercy on him."
>
> Jesus told him, "Go and do likewise."

How convenient it would have been for Jesus to make a clear distinction between those who are our neighbors and those who are not. Instead, he made the startling assertion that every individual is a potential neighbor: neighbor-type relationships are created when one person comes to the aid of another. Moreover, each of us is capable of both being a neighbor and having a neighbor. Thus, when I meet the needs of another, I am being a neighbor to that person. But when someone else serves me, then I have a neighbor.

The parable of the good Samaritan is a vivid illustration of Jesus' command to "love your neighbor as yourself" (Mt 19:19). In our own lives, this commandment may be observed by our actions in developing ministries for victims of rape and sexual violence, in providing small groups for those troubled by sexual addictions or identity issues, in responding to unwed mothers who need emotional, social and financial support in order to give birth to a child rather than have an abortion. The church can also be instrumental in establishing homeless shelters for runaway children, who are the prime targets for sexual predators, or developing twelve-step groups for persons who struggle with sexual violence or sexual addiction. Church families can open up their homes as places of temporary refuge for sexually abused children. In all these ways, we can come to the aid of others just as God in Christ has come to our aid.

When the call to be a neighbor is from God, the resultant action is an empowering one. In this regard Frazier (1986) comments: "A distinction must be made between the kind of aid that takes over and the kind that enables the recipient to continue the task. To take up the cause of another is not to give aid in the first sense. It is not to judge the other incompetent or weak or inadequate, and to set one's own self up as the morally superior deliverer of the sexually wounded. Rather it is to discern that point at which the other must be enabled to carry on a task, and to give that aid regardless of its seeming insignificance or lack of permanent value" (p. 268).

There is no promise that being a neighbor will result in having the other as a neighbor. But regardless of whether or not such neighborliness is reciprocated, God calls us to serve those who are sexually broken.

AUTHENTIC SOCIETAL SEXUALITY

At its broadest level, every society has a more or less agreed-upon view of what constitutes acceptable and unacceptable sexual behavior. While there is generally consensus about sexuality in traditional societies, there is considerably less consensus in modern industrialized societies. The brief historical perspective in chapter one reported that from the landing of the first Puritans up to the present time, there has been an enduring tension between an emphasis on sexual repression and sexual liberation. In the contemporary public debate over sexuality, terms such as "puritanical" and "Victorian" have come to be used as derogatory references to persons holding negative attitudes about sex. Over the past several hundred years, the sexual climate has changed from sexual repression to sexual liberation, with modernist and postmodernist thinking influencing changes in attitudes.

Modernist and postmodernist influences. Sexual attitudes and values in society have traditionally been based on the religious beliefs held by a people. In most industrialized and technologically oriented societies, the religious anchors are being ripped from their moorings. The major reason for this is that technology is based on a scientific worldview, which offers an alternative basis for beliefs. This challenges traditional religious systems, which before the scientific revolution had been the main source for foundational values. Modernization begins to challenge the religious sphere by seeking to replace traditional religious belief systems with secularized belief systems based on scientific rationalism.

To further complicate things, it can be argued that modernity itself is now being replaced by postmodernist thought. Rejecting both the moral certainty given by traditional religious systems, and the certainty of scientifically based modernist thinking, this approach embraces the potential good and usefulness of a variety of alternative sexual moralities. Postmodernity represents a radical response to the excessive emphasis on rationalism found in modernity and sees many flavors of truth, depending on one's personal experiences and collective perspective. Postmodernity can be a useful corrective to the certainties of modernity, which promoted human reason as the basis for constructing sexual morality, but it too can be problematic when taken to the extreme of holding that there is no reality except what is constructed by one's experience.

Postmodernists reject the general laws of nature as grounds for accepting or rejecting sexual morality, because reality is viewed as multilayered, with many ways of knowing. While a Christian perspective is acknowledged as one view, there are equally acceptable ways of knowing, and therefore it is just one of many plausible structures. In the postmodern view, there is danger in accepting one system of morality over the myriad of other options. To do so is to be judged as restrictive and intolerant. A strict postmodernist view leaves one with little ground upon which to evaluate the moral superiority of one system of sexual morality over another since all reality and alternative forms are acceptable. The problem is how to respond to the dehumanizing, degrading and abusive forms of sexual behavior that some may defend on the basis of their subjective system of morality. We must stand for a morality that recognizes the potential for evil as well as good in individuals and social systems.

While modernity seeks to construct a sexual ethic and morality on the basis of scientific and naturalistic assumptions, postmodernity is open to any cultural form that can collectively be argued as defensible. To avoid the modernist pitfall of idealizing a particular cultural form of sexual morality, postmodernity can go to the opposite extreme by rejecting any criteria for assessing the rightness or wrongness of sexual behavior.

There is a reality that the Christian community must seek to uphold, but to do so effectively demands a good understanding of both the potential benefits and the destructiveness of modern and postmodern thinking toward a biblical sexual morality. To embrace modernity and postmodernity uncritically leaves one in the position of merely choosing human perspectives over God's perspective. We believe that Christians must recognize the positive and negative forces of both modernity and postmodernity in order to make a biblically based, proactive response to the current cultural views of sexual morality.

Shalom as a model for a sexually authentic society. Having addressed the reasons why it might be difficult to assess the sexual authenticity of modern society, we suggest that the Old Testament concept of *shalom* is a theologically appropriate way to describe a sexually authentic society. In most modern translations of the Bible, this term *shalom*, which is used 250 times in the Hebrew Scriptures, is usually translated as "peace." Peace in Western cultures connotes the absence of conflict. However, in Scripture and Hebrew culture, shalom is not seen as the mere absence of conflict but rather that which promotes human welfare in both its material and spiritual aspects. It denotes a culture characterized by justice, holiness and righteousness. For shalom to exist, there must be justice, holiness and righteousness in the ethical structures of society; there must be fairness and respect in the way human beings treat each other at each social structural level. Such a situation is poignantly described in Isaiah:

> The wolf shall live with the lamb, and the leopard shall lie down with the kid, the calf and the lion and the fatling together; and a little child shall lead them. The cow and the bear shall graze, their young shall lie down together; and the lion shall eat straw like the ox. The nursing child shall play over the hole of the asp, and the weaned child shall put its hand on the adder's den. (Is 11:6-8 NRSV)

Shalom carries with it a holistic connotation of societal well-being. It is "the human being dwelling at peace in all his or her relationships: with God, with self, with fellows, with nature" (Wolterstorff 1983:69). When any one of these relationships is out of focus, disrupted, in tension or hurting, then shalom is not present.

One important sign that shalom is present in a society is evidence that public space is sexual safe space. To the extent to which a person, female or male, feels sexually unsafe while participating in the various arenas of life, to that extent shalom is absent. In the sexually authentic society, social space will be safe from sexual predators of both the less dangerous (sexual harassment) and more dangerous (rapists) variety. In such a society a woman would feel safe walking alone on a neighborhood street, and parents would be able to let their children play in a park or leave their child at a daycare center with full trust in the caretakers.

For shalom to be present in society, there must be an affirmation of the goodness of sexuality and a climate of openness and comfort in dealing with sexual content. When authentic sexuality is present, there will be a noticeable absence of inauthentic expressions of sexuality, such as what happens at the extremes when sex is either repressed or excessively expressed. There will probably always be some tension between sexual repression and sexual expression. Although there are subcultural pockets of sexual repression today, in North American society we would have to go back nearly one hundred years, when modesty was the order of the day, to find the strongest examples of societal repression of sexuality. At the present time we seem to be struggling much more against the tendencies toward excessive expressions of sexuality.

Excessive expressions of sexuality can most notably be found in the form of the *sexualization* or *eroticization* of nonsexual aspects of life and social relationships. Sexualization can be seen in the present-day use of sex in advertising, and the overreliance on sex and sexually suggestive content in the media. Possibly in reaction to former sexual repression, the present mood seems to be a preoccupation with the sexual.

When relationships are eroticized, it becomes difficult for persons of the opposite sex to develop noneroticized friendships. The evidence that men more than women eroticize relationships is true of nearly all types of social relationships for which we have data. When compared with women, men engage in sex with more partners, engage in a greater variety of sexual practices, have more fantasizing and thoughts about sex, and are more likely to masturbate. Further, the tendency for men more than women to eroticize relationships is true regardless of sexual orientation.

This observation is supported by the extensive research reported in *The Social Organization of Sexuality* (Laumann et al. 1994). These researchers found that men report having their first sexual experience because they are curious or because of peer pressure, while "love and affection motivate the initiation of sex for women and is the key motivation force that keeps sexual relationships going" (p. 547).

Perhaps most disturbing are the higher rates of involvement by men than women in the various forms of inauthentic sexual activities. Men more than women have higher rates of premarital sexual involvement, sexual promiscuity, extramarital sex, sexual abuse of children, sexual harassment, consumption of pornography, sexual addiction, rape and other violent sexual offenses. This evidence seems to indicate that men more than women are susceptible to depersonalized forms of sexual activity.

Sociobiologists argue that these differences between men and women are a result of an evolutionary process in which the genetic selection process was different for men than for women. They argue that the goal of human behavior has been to increase the chances that genetic lines will survive. Given the differential contribution of males and females to the reproductive process, members of each gender tried to protect their genetic packages in different ways. Since females have only a few eggs to be fertilized, investment in any conception is great; they therefore sought to save themselves for a strong, dependable male likely to care for their children. Males, on the other hand, had an unlimited number of sperm, so they could diversify their investments. People today, the theory concludes, are descendants of strong, promiscuous males and choosy females.

We believe, however, that much of the difference in sexual behavior between males and females results from unhealthy aspects in the traditional definition of masculinity. To the extent that real manhood is defined in terms of being sexually aggressive and of proving manhood through sexual conquests, men will continue to struggle with inauthentic forms of sexual behavior. Based on their research, Laumann et al. (1994) conclude: "It is clear that men's normal socialization and roles in the sexual encounter undermine their ability to recognize limits set by their female partners. . . . Men and women interpret these violations quite differently" (p. 547).

We believe that these found differences between men and women have important implications for ministry, especially one that focuses specifically on men and their sexual lives. The current Christian men's movement needs to include male sexuality as part of its emphasis in working with men. Hopefully, men's ministry will take root in the local church, and as it does we pray that male sexuality will be a topic that is directly addressed.

A proactive response to inauthentic societal sexuality. Given the evidence for the increased rates of premarital and extramarital sex, the explicit sanctioning of these behaviors in television and movies, and the multibillion-dollar industry in phone sex and cybersex via the Internet, a case can be made that we are now living in the postsexual revolution. In other words, the sexual revolution has taken place, and these pervasive and invasive forms of sexualized media are becoming normalized and standardized. Being a Christian at this time, perhaps as much as any time in history, means one is living out a minority sexual standard. How can a biblical standard of sexual morality be modeled and effectively advocated in the face of alternative and often contradictory standards of sexual morality?

The most noticeable response by the Christian community is reacting to unwholesome expressions of sexuality in society. Much of the activity in the so-called culture wars is symptomatic of this reactionary approach: boycotting products of companies that sponsor sexually offensive television programs or boycotting movies or music with objectionable sexual messages. There is a place for this type of response by the Christian community, and we applaud the attempts to combat the corroding effects of pornography and dishonest treatment of sex as they impact public sexual morality.

However, we believe a *reactive* response to sexual immorality needs to be bolstered by a *proactive* response. An effective proactive response allows for the Christian community to set the agenda rather than merely being opposed to an agenda set by another interest group. Making a reactive response to circumstances means one merely responds to the agenda presented in secular society. Picture the movement of a group of balls on a pool table after they have been struck by the cue ball. The force of the cue ball sends all the other balls colliding off each other and against the sides of the pool table. In a reactive model, the persons or things (pool balls) simply make adjustments to pressures (cue ball); while this is good, it is not good enough. Living in the sexual climate of the postsexual revolution, it is easy to feel controlled by damaging forces in society.

While reactivity responds to the actions of an undesirable element in society, proactivity is a form of acting that takes the initiative, and in the process it forces the undesirable element to respond. With proactive responses to circumstances, one takes intentional steps toward changing rather than merely reacting to external forces. One seeks a new understanding or a new posture toward a situation. With a proactive response, there is hope that one can be liberated from the sexual pollutant. A proactive response seeks control over the playing field, as it were, over the circumstances that are the source of degrading norms of sexual morality.

An example of a proactive response would be to educate Christians to the subtle and not-so-subtle ways in which popular culture is dishonest in its depiction of sexual content. We need to train our children to be experts in detecting the dishonest and destructive ways popular culture treats sex. This would involve teaching persons to critically analyze the sexual context in popular culture on the basis of how honestly it treats human sexuality. As a start, such theological categories as creation, the Fall and redemption could be used in the analysis. A mark of dishonest treatment of sex in films is the failure to show the negative consequences of premarital, extramarital or promiscuous sexual behavior. Viewers need to recognize when, for instance, comedy is used to avoid an honest portrayal of the negative consequences of promiscuous sexual involvement. The point is to move Christians beyond automatically rejecting a film, television program or music video or recording because it includes sexual content, moving them toward evaluating the content in terms of its theological correctness and honesty.

Although telling youths to "just say no" to sex is a reactive response, bringing a strong rationale for practicing sexual abstinence is a proactive response. The proactive approach involves developing a rationale for abstinence before marriage that integrates social science and biblically based truths. By calling women and men to be faithful to their spouses and to model justice, purity and righteousness to their children and to others, the Christian men's movement is a proactive example since it can set an agenda capable of making a significant difference.

An even more radical proactive response is for Christians to become involved in the creation of popular art and culture in which sex is handled responsibly. Perhaps the Christian community needs to be more open to the good that can be done by artists who cross over from singing "Christian" music to "secular" music. We need to affirm artists for treating love and sex honestly even as it is packaged as a secular product. C. S. Lewis once said that we do not need more books about Christianity, but rather more secular books written by Christians. Perhaps the same is true regarding Christian involvement in the production of popular culture. We need more Christians in the production of secular popular culture who will treat sex in a way that reflects biblical values.

Developing proactive responses to inauthentic societal expressions of sexuality takes effort. Sometimes the Christian community responds reactively because it is easier. This is not enough. When so much is at stake, the Christian community needs to develop clear rationales that affirm reasons for a biblically based sexuality. The producers of popular culture have often done their homework better than the church in knowing how sex can be used as a means for earning lots of money, especially from youth. The Christian community must be at least as knowledgeable and sophisticated in exposing the dishonest portrayal of sex when it occurs.

CONCLUSION

We have suggested that sexual authenticity will develop in a social environment that supports and holds members accountable at the *familial, congregational* and *societal* levels. We have used the biblical concepts *covenant love, koinonia* and *neighbor,* and *shalom* as descriptors of ideal social structures that would characterize each of these three levels. When authentic sexuality exists at all levels, each will mutually reinforce the sexual authenticity of the other and of the individuals within them.

We have shown that one's sense of an authentic expression of sexuality can be confused in what seems to be an enduring tension between a tendency to either *repress* or *excessively express* sexuality. When the authentic expression of sexuality is challenged at any level, the Christian church, as a called-out community, needs to be the *salt* of the earth by responsibly modeling authentic sexuality and to be willing to take a prophetic role as the *light* of the world by voicing God's call for authentic expressions of sexuality. This can be a perilous task, sabotaged by either timidity on one hand or self-righteousness on the other. It is our prayer that this book presents a challenge to the community of Christian believers, who are called to sexually authentic living at the beginning of this new millennium, through the power of the Holy Spirit and the life of our Lord Jesus Christ, who taught and modeled for us how to be salt and light to the world.

FOR FURTHER READING

Grenz, S. 1997. *Sexual ethics: An evangelical perspective.* Louisville, Ky.: Westminster John Knox.

Laumann, E., et al. 1994. *The social organization of sexuality: Sexual practices in the United States.* Chicago: University of Chicago Press.

Thatcher, A., and E. Stuart. 1996. *Christian perspectives on sexuality and gender.* Grand Rapids: Eerdmans. See sec. 1, Sexuality and the Christian tradition, pp. 1-51.

References

Alderson, J., A. Madill and A. Balen. 2004. Fear of devaluation: Understanding the experience of intersexed women with androgen insensititivity syndrome. *British Journal of Health Psychology* 9:81-101.

Allen, B., and D. Baucom. 2004. Adult attachment and patterns of extradyadic involvement. *Family Process* 43:467-88.

Allen, E., D. Atkins, D. Snyder, G. K. Gordon and S. Glass. 2005. Intrapersonal, interpersonal, and contextual factors in engaging in and responding to extramarital involvement. *Clinical Psychology: Science and Practice* 12:101-30.

Allen, M., D. D'Alessio and K. Brezgel. 1995. A meta-analysis summarizing the effects of pornography: II. Aggression after exposure. *Journal of Human Communication Research* 22 (2): 258-83.

Allen, M., T. Emmers, L. Gebhardt, and M. Giery. 1995. Exposure to pornography and acceptance of rape myths. *Journal of Communication* 45:5-26.

Amato, P., and S. Rogers. 1997. A longitudinal study of marital problems and subsequent divorce. *Journal of Marriage and Family* 59:612-24.

American Academy of Pediatrics, Committee on Public Education. 2001. Sexuality, contraception, and the media. *Pediatrics* 107:191-94. http://aappolicy.aappublications.org/cgi/content/full/pediatrics;107/1/191.

Anderson, I., and A. Lyons. 2005. The effect of victims' social support on attributions of blame in female and male rape. *Journal of Applied Social Psychology* 35:1400-1417.

Anderson, R. 1982. *On being human: Essays in theological anthropology.* Grand Rapids: Eerdmans.

————. 2004. Why can't a woman be more like a man. *The Semi.* Nov. 1-5. pp. 1 & 9. Fuller Theological Seminary, Pasadena, Calif.

Antecol, H. 2003. Does sexual harassment training change attitudes? A view from the federal level. *Social Science Quarterly* 84:826-42.

Archer, J. 1996. Sex differences in social behavior: Are the social role and evolutionary explanations compatible? *American Psychologist* 51:909-17.

Aronson, S., and A. Huston. 2004. The mother-infant relationship in single, cohabiting, and married families: A case for marriage? *Journal of Family Psychology* 18:5-18.

Atkins, D. C. 2003. Infidelity and marital therapy: Initial findings from a randomized clinical trial. Ph.D. diss., University of Washington.

Atkins, D. C., D. Baucom and N. Jacobson. 2001. Understanding infidelity: Correlates in a national random sample. *Journal of Family Psychology* 15:735-49.

Atkins, D. C., K. Eldridge, D. Baucom and A. Christiansen. 2005. Infidelity and behavioral couple therapy: Optimism in the face of betrayal. *Journal of Consulting and Clinical Psychology* 73:144-50.

Attwood, F. 2005. Fashion and passion: Marketing sex to women. *Sexualities* 8:392-406. http://sexualities.sagepub.com/cgi/content/abs tract/8/4/392.

Atwater, L. 1982. *The extramarital connection: Sex, intimacy, and identity.* New York: Irvington.

Atwood, J. D. 2006. Mommy's little angel, daddy's little girl: Do you know what your pre-teens are doing?" *American Journal of Family Therapy* 34:447-67.

Axinn, W., and J. Barber. 1997. Living arrangements and family formation attitudes in early adulthood. *Journal of Marriage and Family* 59:595-611.

Axinn, W., and A. Thornton. 1992. The relationship between cohabitation and divorce: Selectivity or causal influence? *Demography* 29:357-74.

Bailey, J. M., and A. P. Bell. 1993. Familiarity of female and male homosexuality. *Behavior Genetics* 23 (4): 313-20.

Bailey, J. M., and R. Pillard. 1991. A genetic study of male sexual orientation. *Archives of General Psychiatry* 48:1089-96.

Bailey, J. M., L. Willerman and C. Parks. 1991. A test of the maternal stress theory of human male sexuality. *Archives of General Psychiatry* 48:1089-96.

Balswick, J. K., and J. O. Balswick. 1994. *Raging hormones: What to do when you suspect your teen may be sexually active.* Grand Rapids: Zondervan.

————. 2003. *Relationship-empowered parenting.* Grand Rapids: Baker.

————. 2006. *A model for marriage: Covenant, grace, empowering and intimacy.* Downers Grove, Ill.: InterVarsity Press.

———. 2007. *The family: A Christian perspective on the contemporary home.* 3rd ed. Grand Rapids: Baker. Esp. see chaps. 1 and 5.

Balswick, J. O. 1992. *Men at the crossroads: Beyond traditional roles and modern options.* Downers Grove, Ill.: InterVarsity Press.

Balswick, J. O., P. King and K. Reimer. 2005. *The reciprocating self: Human development in theological perspective.* Downers Grove, Ill.: InterVarsity Press.

Bancroft, J., and Z. Vukadinovic. 2004. Sexual addition, sexual compulsivity, sexual impulsivity, or what? Toward a theoretical model. *The Journal of Sex Research* 41:225-34.

Bandura, A. 1974. Behavior theory and the models of man. *American Psychologist* 29:859-69.

———. 1978. The self system in reciprocal determinism. *American Psychologist* 33:344-58.

———. 1998. Exercise of agency in personal and social change. In *Behavior and cognitive therapy today: Essays in honor of Hans J. Eysenck,* edited by E. Sanavic. Oxford: Pergamon.

Banks, A., and N. K. Gartrell. 1995. Hormones and sexual orientation: A questionable link. Special issue: Sex, cell, and same-sex desire: The biology of sexual preference. *Journal of Homosexuality* 28 (3-4): 247-68.

Banks, R. 1994. *Paul's idea of community: The early churches in their cultural settings.* Rev. ed. Peabody, Mass.: Hendrickson.

Barbaree, H. E., and W. L. Marshall. 1991. The role of male sexual arousal in rape: Six models. *Journal of Consulting and Clinical Psychology* 20:268-70.

Barth, K. *Church Dogmatics 3/4.* Edinburgh: T & T Clark.

Baumeister, R. 2000. Gender difference in erotic plasticity: The female sex drive as socially flexible and responsive. *Pcychological Behavior* 126:347-74.

Bearman, P., and H. Bruckner. 2001. Promising the future: Virginity pledges and first intercourse. *American Journal of Sociology* 106:856-912.

———. 2002. Opposite-sex twins and adolescent same-sex attractions. *American Journal of Sociology* 107:1179-1205.

Beeghley, L., and C. Sellers. 1986. Adolescents and sex: A structural theory of premarital sex in the United States. *Deviant Behavior* 7 (4): 313-36.

Bell, A., M. Weinbert, and K. Hammersmith. 1981. *Sexual preference: Its development in men and women.* Bloomington: Indiana University Press.

Bem, D. 1996. Exotic becomes erotic: A developmental theory of sexual orientation. *Psychological Review* 103 (2): 320-35.

Ben-David, S., and O. Schneider. 2005. Rape perceptions, gender role attitudes, and victim-perpetrator acquaintance. *Sex Roles* 53:385-99.

Bentler, P., and M. Newcomb. 1978. Longitudinal study of marital success and failure. *Journal of Consulting and Clinical Psychology* 46 (5): 1053-70.

Berdahl, J., V. Magley and C. Waldo. 1996. The sexual harassment of men? Exploring the concept with theory and data. *Psychology of Women Quarterly* 20:527-47.

Berdahl, J., and C. Moore. 2006. Workplace harassment double jeopardy for minority women. *Journal of Applied Psychology* 9:426-36.

Bergen, H., G. Martin, A. Richardson, S. Allison and L. Roeger. 2003. Sexual abuse and suicidal behavior: A model constructed from a large community sample of adolescents. *Journal of the American Academy of Child and Adolescent Psychiatry* 42:1301-9.

Berliner, P. 2006. Doubly victimized: First by the abuser, then by the "helpers." *PsycCRITIQUES* 51, no. 6.

Bermant, G. 1995. To speak in chords about sexuality: Hormonal and neural modulation of physiological and behavioral function. *Neuroscience and Biobehavioral Reviews* 19 (2): 343-48.

Bieber, I. 1962. *Homosexuality.* New York: Basic Books.

———. 1976. Psychodynamics and sexual object choices: A reply to Dr. Richard C. Friedman's paper. *Contemporay Psychoanalysis* 12:366-69.

Bigner, J., and F. Bozett. 1989. Parenting by gay fathers. *Marriage and Family Review* 14:155-75.

Bilezikian, G. 2006. *Beyond sex roles: What the Bible says about a woman's place in church and family.* Grand Rapids: Baker Books

Billy, J., K. Tanfer, W. Grady and D. Klepenger. 1993. The sexual behavior of men in the United States. *Family Planning Perspectives* 25:52-60.

Bingham, J., and C. Piotrowski. 1996. Online sexual addition: A contemporary enigma. *Psychological Reports* 79:257-58.

Binstock, G., and T. Arland. 2003. Separation, reconciliation, and living apart in cohabiting and marital unions. *Journal of Marriage and Family* 65:432-43.

Birchard, T. 2004. "The snake and the seraph"—sexual addiction and religious behavior. *Counseling Psychology Quarterly* 17:81-88.

Blader, J., and W. Marshall. 1989. Is assessment of sexual arousal in males worthwhile? *Clinical Psychology Review* 9:569-87.

Blair, R. 2008. Review of *Ex-gays? A longitudinal study of religiously mediated change in sexual orientation. Review: A Quarterly of Evangelicals Concerned, Inc.* 33 (1).

Blanchard, R., J. M. Cantor, A. F. Bogaert, S. M. Breelove and L. Ellis. 2006.

Interaction of fraternal birth order and handedness in the development of male homosexuality. *Hormones and Behavior* 49:405-14.

Bleeker, E., and S. Muren. 2005. Fraternity membership, the display of degrading sexual images of women, and rape myth acceptance. *Sex Roles* 5:487-93.

Blow, A., and K. Hartnett. 2005. Infidelity in committed relationships I: A methodological review. II: A substantive review. *Journal of Marital and Family Therapy* 31:183-216, 217-34.

Bogaert, A. F. 2006. Biological versus nonbiological older brothers and men's sexual orientation. *Proceedings of the National Academy of Sciences of the United States of America* 103:10771-74.

Bohner, G., C. I. Jarvis, F. Eyssel and F. Seibler. 2005. The causal impact of rape myth acceptance on men's rape proclivity: Comparing sexually coercive and noncoercive men. *European Journal of Social Psychology* 35:819-28.

Booth, A., and J. Dabbs. 1993. Testosterone and men's marriages. *Social Forces* 72:463-77.

Booth, A., and D. Johnson. 1988. Premarital cohabitation and marital success. *Journal of Family Issues* 9:255-72.

Borawski, E., E. Trapl, L. Lovegreen, N. Colabianchi and T. Block. 2005. Effectiveness of abstinence-only intervention in middle school teens. *American Journal of Health Behavior* 29:423-34.

Boswell, J. 1980. *Christianity, social tolerance, and homosexuality.* Chicago: University of Chicago Press.

Bowen, M. 1978. *Family therapy in clinical practice.* New York: Aronson.

Brady-Rogers, Cissy. 2007. *E-Quality* [a publication of Christians for Biblical Equality]. Winter. http://www.cbeinternational.org/new/E-Journal/2007/07winter/07winterrogers.html.

Brecklin, L. R., and S. E. Ullman. 2005. Self-defense or assertiveness training and women's responses to sexual attacks. *Journal of Interpersonal Violence* 20:738-62.

Breulin, D. 1988. Oscillation theory and family development. In *Family transitions: Continuity and change over the life cycle,* ed. C. Falicov, pp. 133-55. New York: Guilford.

Brewis, A., and M. Meyer. 2005. Marital coitus across the life course. *Journal of Biosocial Science* 37:499-518.

Brookings, J., A. McEvoy and M. Reed. 1994. Sexual assault recovery and male significant others. *Families in Society: The Journal of Contemporary Human Services* 75:295-99.

Brooks, D. 2003. Love, Internet style. *New York Times.* November 8. http://query.nytimes.com/gst/fullpage.html?res=9F0DEFD61239F93BA35752C1 A9659C8B63.

Brown, J., and G. Warne. 2005. Practical management of the intersex infant. *Journal of Pediatric Endocrinology and Metabolism* 18:3-23.

Brown, S., L. Sanchez, S. Nock and J. Wright. 2006. Links between premarital cohabitation and subsequent marital quality, stability, and divorce: A comparison of covenant versus standard marriages. *Social Science Research* 35:454-70.

Brown, W. S., N. Murphy and H. N. Maloney, eds. 1998. *Whatever happened to the soul? Scientific and theological portraits of human nature.* Minneapolis: Fortress.

Bruckner, H., and P. Bearman. 2005. After the promise: The STD consequences of adolescent virginity pledges. *Journal of Adolescent Health* 36 (April): 271-78. http://www.yale.edu/ciqle/PUBLICATIONS/AfterThePromise.pdf.

Bruderl, J., A. Dickman and H. Engelhardt. 1997. Premarital cohabitation and marital stability? An empirical study with the family survey. *Kolner Zeitschrift fur Soziologie und Sozialpsychologie* 49 (2): 205-22.

Brunswig, K., and W. O'Donohue. 2002. *Relapse prevention for sexual harassers.* New York: Kluwer Academic/Plenum.

Buddie, A. M., and M. Testa. 2005. Rates and predictors of sexual aggression among students and nonstudents. *Journal of Interpersonal Violence* 20:713-24.

Buechner, F. 1992. *Listening to your life: Daily meditations with Frederick Buechner.* San Francisco: HarperSanFrancisco.

Buhrich, N., M. Bailey and N. G. Martin. 1991. Sexual orientation, sexual identity, and sex-dimorphic behaviors in male twins. *Behavior Genetics* 21 (1): 75-97.

Bumpass, L., and H. Lu. 2000. Trends in cohabitation and implications for children's family contexts in the U.S. *Population Studies* 54:29-41.

Burns, J. 1992. *Radical respect: A Christian approach to love, sex, and dating.* Eugene, Ore.: Harvest House.

Buss, D., and D. Schmitt. 1993. Sexual strategies theory: An evolutionary perspective on human mating. *Psychological Review* 100:204-32.

Butler, A. 2000. Trends in same-gender sexual partnering, 1988-1998. *Journal of Sex Research* 37:333-43.

Buunk, B., and P. Dijkstra. 2004. Gender differences in rival characteristics that evoke jealousy in response to emotional versus sexual infidelity. *Personal Relationships* 11:395-408.

Byne, W. 1994. The biological evidence challenged. *Scientific American* 270 (May): 50-55.

Byne, W., and B. Parsons. 1993. Human sexual orientation: The biological theories reappraised. *Archives of General Psychiatry* 50:228-39.

Cadwallader, M. 1966. Marriage as a wretched institution. *Atlantic Monthly* 218:62-66.

Calderone, M. 1983. Fetal erection and its message to us. *SEICUS Report* 11 (5/6):9-10.

Cameron, K., L. Salazar, J. Bernhardt, N. Burgess-Whitman, G. Wingood and R. DiClemente. 2005. Adolescents' experience with sex on the Web: Results from online focus groups. *Journal of Adolescence* 28:535-40.

Cameron, P., and K. Cameron. 1996. Homosexual parents. *Adolescence* 31:757-76.

Carnes, P. 1983. *Out of the shadows: Understanding sexual addiction.* Minneapolis: CompCare. 2nd ed., 1992. 3rd ed., Center City, Minn.: Hazelden, 2001.

———. 1989. *Contrary to love: Helping the sexual addict.* Minneapolis: CompCare.

———. 1991. *A gentle path through the twelve steps.* Minneapolis: CompCare.

———. 1992. *Don't call it love: Recovery from sexual addiction.* New York: Bantam Books.

———. 2005. *Facing the shadow: Starting sexual and relationship recovery.* Carefree, Ariz.: Gentle Path.

Carnes, P., D. Delmonico, E. Griffin and J. Moriarity. 2004. *In the shadows of the net: Breaking free of compulsive online sexual behavior.* Center City, Minn.: Hazelden.

Carnes, P., R. E. Murray and L. Charpentier. 2004. Addiction interaction disorder. In *Handbook of addictive disorders: A practical guide to diagnosis and treatment,* edited by R. H. Combs, pp. 31-59. Hoboken, N.J.: John Wiley & Sons, 2004.

Carr, D. 2003. *Sexuality, spirituality, and the Bible.* Oxford: Oxford University Press.

Carruthers, M. 1997. *Maximising manhood: Beating the male menopause.* London: HarperCollins.

Cassidy, L., and R. M. Hurrell. 1995. The influence of victim's attire on adolescents' judgments of date rape. *Journal of Adolescence* 30 (118): 319-23.

Cebulko, S. S. 2006. The experiences of women whose husbands use Internet pornography. *Dissertation Abstracts International, Section A: Humanities and Social Sciences* 66:2721.

Cecil, H., and S. C. Matson. 2005. Differences in psychological health and family dysfunction by sexual victimization type in a clinical sample of African American adolescent women. *Journal of Sex Research* 42:203-14.

Chaney, M. P., and C. Y. Chang. 2005. A trio of turmoil for Internet sexually addicted men who have sex with men: Boredom proneness, social connectedness, and dissociation. *Sexual Addiction and Compulsivity* 12:3-18.

Chau, P., and J. Herring. 2002. Defining, assigning, and designing sex. *International Journal of Law, Policy, and the Family* 16:327-68.

Chesire, D. 2006. Test of an integrated model for high school sexual harassment. *Dissertation Abstracts International* 66:6331.

Chicago Statistics. 1994. Contemporary sexuality. *American Association of Sex Educators, Counselors and Therapists Newsletter* 28 (11): 1.

Chodorow N. 1999. *The reproduction of mothering: Psychoanalysis and the sociology of gender.* Updated ed. Berkeley: University of California Press.

Clarkberg, M., R. Stolzenberg and L. Waite. 1995. Attitudes, values, and entrance into cohabitational versus marital unions. *Social Forces* 74:609-32.

Cochran, S., and V. Mays. 2000. Relationship between psychiatric syndromes and behaviorally defined sexual orientation in a sample of the US population. *American Journal of Epidemiology* 151:516-23. http://aje.oxfordjournals.org/cgi/reprint/151/5/516.pdf.

Coleman, E. 2005. Neuroanatomical and neurotransmitter dysfunction and compulsive sexual behavior. In *Biological substrates of human sexuality,* edited by J. S. Hyde, pp. 147-69. Washington, D.C.: American Psychological Association.

Collins, F. 2006. *The language of God: A scientist presents evidence for belief.* New York: Free Press.

Colopinto, J. 2000. *As nature made him: The boy who was raised as a girl.* New York: HarperCollins.

Comiskey, A. 1989. *Pursuing sexual wholeness: How Jesus heals the homosexual.* Lake Mary, Fla.: Creation House.

———. 2003. *Strength in Weakness: Overcoming sexual and relational brokenness.* Downers Grove, Ill.: Inter Varsity Press.

Cook, J., A. Boxer and G. Herdt. 1989. First homosexual and heterosexual experiences reported by gay and lesbian youth in an urban community. Paper presented to the American Sociological Association.

Court, J., and N. Whitehead. 1994. The ten percent solution: Homosexuality then and now. Paper presented at the 23rd International Congress of Applied Psychology.

Cox, J. 2002. *Human intimacy: Marriage, the family, and its meaning.* 9th ed. Belmont, Calif.: Wadsworth.

Crosse, C., R. Crosse and M. Tabb. 2005. *I surrender all: Rebuilding a marriage broken by pornography.* Colorado Springs: NavPress.

Dannecker, M. 1983. Towards a theory of homosexuality: Socio-historical perspective. *Journal of Homosexuality* 9 (4): 7.

Danzinger, C. 1976. Unmarried heterosexual cohabitation. Ph.D. diss., Rutgers University. *Unmarried heterosexual cohabitation.* San Francisco: R&E Research Associates, 1978.

Dawn, M. J. 1993. *Sexual character: Beyond technique to intimacy.* Grand Rapids: Eerdmans.

Deblinger, A., and A. Heflin. 1996. *Treating sexually abused children and their nonoffending parents.* Thousand Oaks, Calif.: Sage.

De Gaston, J. F., L. Jensen and S. Weed. 1995. A closer look at adolescent sexual activity. *Journal of Youth and Adolescence* 24 (4): 465-79.

De Gaston, J. F., S. Weed and L. Jensen. 1996. Understanding gender differences in adolescent sexuality. *Adolescence* 31 (121): 217-31.

DeKeseredy, W., and C. Joseph. 2006. Separation and/or divorce sexual assault in rural Ohio: Preliminary results of an exploratory study. *Violence Against Women* 12:301-11.

DeLeire, T., and K. Kalil. 2005. How do cohabiting couples with children spend their money? *Journal of Marriage and Family* 67:286-95.

DeMaris, A., and W. MacDonald. 1993. Premarital cohabitation and marital instability: A test of the unconventionality hypothesis. *Journal of Marriage and Family* 55:399-407.

Deveny, K., et al. 2003. We're not in the mood. *Newsweek,* June 30, 40-46.

Diamond, M. 1997. Sexual identity and sexual orientation in children with traumatized or ambiguous genitalia. *Journal of Sex Research* 32:199-211.

DMOZ Open Directory Project. 2007. Society: Sexuality: Sexual addiction. Listing of online sexual addiction resources. http://www.dmoz.org/Society/Sexuality/Sexual_Addiction/.

Dodge, B., M. Reece, S. Cole and T. Sandfort. 2004. Sexual compulsivity among heterosexual college students. *Journal of Sex Research* 41:343-50.

Doell, R. G. 1995. Sexuality in the brain. Special issue: Sex, cell and same-sex desire. Part 2: The biology of sexual preference. *Journal of Homosexuality* 28 (3-4): 345-54.

Donnelly, D. A. 1993. Sexually inactive marriages. *Journal of Sex Research* 30 (2): 171-79.

Donovan, C. 1996. Young people, alcohol and sex: Taking advantage. *Youth and Policy* 52 (Spring): 30-37.

Draucker, C. B. 1996. Family-of-origin variables and adult female survivors of childhood sexual abuse: A review of the research. *Journal of Child Sexual Abuse* 5 (4): 35-63.

Duncan, K. 2004. *Healing from the trauma of childhood sexual abuse: The journey for women*. Westport, Conn.: Praeger.

Duncombe, J. A., and D. Marsden. 1994. Whose orgasm is this anyway? "Sex work" and "emotion work" in long-term couple relationships. Annual meeting of the American Sociological Association.

Durfield, R. C., and R. Durfield. 1991. *Raising them chaste*. Minneapolis: Bethany House.

Eagly, A., and W. Wood. 1999. The origins of sex differences in human behavior: Evolved dispositions versus social roles. *American Psychologist* 54:408-23.

Earle, R., and M. Earle. 1995. *Sex addiction: Case studies and management*. New York: Brunner/Mazel.

Ehrensaft, D. 1990. *Parenting together: Men and women sharing the care of children*. Urbana: University of Illinois Press.

Eisenman, R., M. L. Dantzker and L. Ellis. 2004. Self ratings of dependency/addiction regarding drugs, sex, love, and food: Male and female college students. *Sexual Addiction and Compulsivity* 11:115-27.

Ellen, J. M., S. Cahn, S. L. Eyre and C. B. Boyer. 1996. Types of adolescent sexual relationships and associated perceptions about condom use. *Journal of Adolescent Health* 18 (6): 417-21.

Ellens, J. H. 2006. *Sex in the Bible: A new consideration*. Westport, Conn.: Praeger.

Ellis, B., J. Bates, K. Dodge, D. Fergusson, L. Horwood, G. Pettit, et al. 2003. Does father absence place daughters at special risk for early sexual activity and teenage pregnancy? *Child Development* 74:801-21.

Ellis, L. 1991. A synthesized (biosocial) theory of rape. *Journal of Consulting and Clinical Psychology* 59:631-42.

Ellis, L., and M. Ames. 1987. Neuro-hormonal functioning and sexual orientation: A theory of homosexuality-heterosexuality. *Psychological Bulletin* 101:233-58.

Equal Employment Opportunity Commission. 1980. Guidelines on discrimination because of sex under title VII of the civil rights act, as amended adoption of interim interpretive guideline. Title 29-labor, chap. 14, part 1604. April. Washington, D.C.: Government Printing Office.

Erikson, Erik. 1968. *Childhood and society*. New York: W. W. Norton.

————. 1982. *The life cycle completed.* New York: Norton.

Erzen, T. 2006. *Straight to Jesus: Sexual and Christian conversion in the ex-gay movement.* Berkeley: University of California Press.

Eyre, S., N. Read and S. Millstein. 1997. Adolescent sexual strategies. *Journal of Adolescent Health* 20 (4): 286-93.

Faust, J., M. K. Runyon and M. C. Kenny. 1995. Family variables associated with the onset and impact of intrafamilial childhood sexual abuse. Special issue: The impact of the family on child adjustment and psycho-pathology. *Clinical Psychology Review* 15 (5): 443-56.

Federal Bureau of Investigation. 1984. *Uniform crime reports for the United States.* Washington, D.C.: Department of Justice.

————. 1990. *Uniform crime reports for the United States.* Washington, D.C.: Department of Justice.

Fergusson, D. 1999. *Childhood sexual abuse: An evidence-based perspective.* Thousand Oaks, Calif.: Sage.

Ferree, M. 2003. Women and the web: Cybersex activity and implications. *Sexual and Relationship Therapy* 18 (3): 385-93.

Finkelhor, D. 1997. The victimization of children and youth. In *Victims of Crime,* edited by R. C. Davis, A. J. Lurigio and W. G. Skogan, pp. 86-107. 2nd ed. Thousand Oaks, Calif.: Sage.

————. 2007. Prevention of sexual abuse through educational programs directed toward children. *Pediatrics.* 120:540-645

Finkelhor, D., and L. Jones. 2004. Explanations for the decline in child sexual abuse. *Juvenile Justice Bulletin.* January. http://www.ncjrs.gov/pdffiles1/ojjdp/199298.pdf.

Firestone, R., L. Firestone and J. Catlett. 2006. *Sex and love in intimate relationships.* Washington, D.C.: American Psychological Association.

Firth, M. 1997. Male partner of female victims of child sexual abuse: Treatment issues and approaches. *Journal of Sexual and Marital Therapy* 12 (2): 159-71.

Fischer, G. 1996. Deceptive, verbally cohesive college males: Attitudinal predictors and lies told. *Archives of Sexual Behavior* 25:527-33.

Fisher, H. 2004. *Why we love: The nature and chemistry of romantic love.* New York: Henry Holt.

Fisher, W., and A. Barak. 2001. Internet pornography: A social psychological perspective on Internet sexuality. *Journal of Sex Research* 38:312-24.

Fitzgerald, L., and S. Shullman. 1993. Sexual harassment: A research analysis agenda for the 1990s. Special issue: Sexual harassment in the workplace. *Journal of Vocational Behavior* 42:5-27.

Foote, W., and J. Goodman-Delahunty. 2005. *Evaluating sexual harassment: Psychological, social, and legal considerations in forensic examinations.* Washington, D.C.: American Psychological Association.

Ford, C. A., and F. J. Donis. 1996. The relationship between age and gender in workers' attitudes toward harassment. *Journal of Psychology* 130 (6): 627-33.

Ford, C. S., and F. Beach. 1951. *Patterns of sexual behavior.* New York: Harper & Row.

Forman, D., and C. Chilvers. 1989. Sexual behavior of young and middle aged men in England and Wales. *British Medical Journal* 298:138-48.

Forste, R., and T. Heaton. 1988. Initiation of sexual activity among female adolescents. *Youth and Society* 19:250-68.

Fortune, M. 1996. *Sexual abuse prevention: A study for teenagers.* New York: United Church Press.

———. 2001. *Sexual violence: The unmentionable sin.* New York: Pilgrim.

———. 2005. *Sexual violence: The sin revisited.* Cleveland: Pilgrim.

Forward, S., and J. Torres. 1986. *Men who hate women and the women who love them.* Toronto and New York: Bantam Books.

Fossum, M., and M. Mason. 1989. *Facing shame: Families in recovery.* New York: W. W. Norton.

Freud, S. 1953. *Three essays on the theory of sexuality.* Authorized translation by James Strachey. London: Imago/Hogarth. (Orig. pub. 1905.)

Friedrich, W. N., et al. 1991. Normative sexual behavior in children. *Pediatrics* 88:456-64.

Friesen. L. 1989. *Sexuality: A biblical model in historical perspective.* D.Min. dissertation. Fuller Theological Seminary.

Fromm, E. 1956. *The art of loving.* New York: Bantam Books.

Gagnon, R. 2002. *The Bible and homosexual practice: Texts and hermeneutics.* Nashville: Abingdon.

———. 2005. Scriptural perspectives on homosexuality and sexual identity. *Journal of Psychology and Christianity* 24:293-303.

———. 2005. Why the disagreement over the biblical witness on homosexual practice? A response to David G. Myers and Letha Dawson Scanzoni, *What God Has Joined Together? Reformed Review* 59 (Autumn): 19-130. http://www.westernsem.edu/files/westernsem/gagnon_autm05_0.pdf.

Gallagher, B. J., J. A. McFalls and C. N. Vreeland. 1993. Preliminary results from a national survey of psychiatrists concerning the etiology of male homosexuality. *Journal of Psychology: A Journal of Human Behavior* 30:1-3.

Gardner, C. 2001. Tangled in the worst of the web. *Christianity Today,* March 15, 43-49.

Giedd, J. 1999. Brain development during childhood and adolescence: A longitudinal MRS study. *Nature Neuroscience.* 2:861-63.

Gildner, J. 2006. Acceptance of acquaintance rape: Attitude and personality characteristics of athletes. *Dissertation Abstracts International, Section B: The Sciences and Engineering* 66:3947.

Giordano, P., M. Longmore and W. Manning. 2006. Gender and the meaning of adolescent romantic relationships: A focus on boys. *American Sociological Review* 71:260-87.

Glass, S. 2003. *Not "just friends": Protect your relationship from infidelity and heal the trauma of betrayal.* New York: Free Press.

Glass, S., and T. Wright. 1997. Justifications for extramarital relationships. In *Clinical handbook of marriage and couples interventions,* edited by W. Halford and H. Markman, pp. 471-507. New York: Wiley.

Goldenberg, J., M. Landau, T. Pyszeznski, C. Cox, J. Greenberg, S. Solomon and H. Dunnam. 2003. Gender-typical responses to sexual and emotional infidelity as a function of mortality salience induced self-esteem striving. *Personality and Social Psychology Bullentin* 29:1585-95.

Goleman, D. 1985. Study lists ways to deter rapists. [Study by R. Prentky and A. Burgess.] *New York Times,* May 5, 1985, p. 35.

Goodman, A.. 1992. Sexual addiction: Designation and treatment. *Journal of Sex and Marital Therapy* 18:303-14.

Goodman, P. 1960. *Growing up absurd.* New York: Vintage.

Goodson, B., and D. McCormack. 2000. Sex on the Internet: College students' emotional arousal when viewing sexually explicit materials on-line. *Journal of Sex Education and Therapy* 25:252-61.

Grant, J. E., and M. A. Steinberg. 2005. Compulsive sexual behavior and pathological gambling. *Sexual Addiction and Compulsivity* 12:235-44.

Grenz, S. 1990. *Sexual ethics: An evangelical perspective.* Louisville, Ky.: Westminster John Knox.

———. 1997. *Sexual ethics: An evangelical perspective.* Louisville, Ky.: Westminster John Knox.

———. 2001. *The social God and the relational self: A trinitarian theology of the imago Dei.* Louisville, Ky.: Westminster John Knox.

Griffiths, M. 2003. Internet abuse in the workplace: Issues and concerns for employers and employment counselors. *Journal of Employment Counseling* 40:87-96.

Gross, A. M., A. Winslett, M. Roberts and C. L. Gohm. 2006. An examination of sexual violence against college women. *Violence Against Women* 12:288-300.

Grunbaum, J., et al. 2002. Youth risk behavior surveillance—United States, 2001. *Morbidity and Mortality Weekly Report* 5:1-62.

Grunebaum, H. 1997. Thinking about romantic/erotic love. *Journal of Marital and Family Therapy* 23:295-307.

Gunther, A. C. 1995. Overrating the X-rating: The third-person perception and support for censorship of pornography. *Journal of Communication* 45:138.

Gunton, C. 1990. *The one, the three and the many: God, creation and the culture of modernity.* Cambridge: Cambridge University Press.

Gwartney-Gibbs, P. 1986. The institutionalization of premarital cohabitation: Estimates from marriage license applications, 1970 and 1980. *Journal of Marriage and Family* 48:423-34.

Hall, D. R. 1996. Marriage as a pure relationship: Exploring the link between premarital cohabitation and divorce in Canada. *Journal of Comparative Family Studies* 27 (1): 1-12.

Hall, L. 1996. *An affair of the mind: One woman's courageous battle to salvage her family from the devastation of pornography.* Colorado Springs: Focus on the Family.

Hamer, D. H. 1993. A linkage between DNA markers on the X chromosome and male sexual orientation. *Science* 261:321-27.

Harley, W., Jr., and J. H. Chalmers. 1998. *Surviving an affair.* Grand Rapids: Revell.

Harry, J. 1988. Parental physical abuse and sexual orientation in males. Paper presented to the American Sociological Association in Atlanta.

Hart, A. 1995. *The sexual male.* Waco, Tex.: Word.

Hart, A., C. Weber, and D. Taylor. 1998. *Secrets of Eve.* Waco, Tex.: Word.

Haynes, J. D. 1995. A critique of the possibility of genetic inheritance of homosexual orientation. Special issue: Sex, cells, and same-sex desire: The biology of sexual preference. *Journal of Homosexuality* 28:91-113.

Hays, K., and S. Stanley. 1996. The impact of childhood sexual abuse on women's dental experience. *Journal of Child Sexual Abuse* 5:65-74.

Hays, R. 1996. *The moral vision of the New Testament.* San Francisco: Harper-Collins. Esp. see chap. 16, "Homosexuality," pp. 379-406.

Hazen, C. 2003. The essential nature of couple relationship. In *Attachment proc-*

esses in couple and family therapy, edited by S. M. Johnson and V. Whiffen, pp. 43-64. New York: Guildford.

Heitritter, L., and J. Vought. 2006. *Helping victims of sexual abuse.* Minneapolis: Bethany House.

Henderson-King, D. H., and J. Veroff. 1994. Sexual satisfaction and marital well-being in the first years of marriage. *Journal of Social and Personal Relationships* 11:509-34.

Herrn, R. 1995. On the history of biological theories of homosexuality used to justify homosexuality. Special issue: Sex, cells, and same-sex desire: The biology of sexual preference. *Journal of Homosexuality* 28:31-56.

Heuveline, P., and J. Timberlake. 2004. The role of cohabitation in family formation: The United States in Comparative Perspective. *Journal of Marriage and Family* 66:1214-30.

Hiebert, P. 1994. *Anthropological reflections on missiological issues.* Grand Rapids: Baker Academic.

Hirshfield, M. 1935. *Sex in human relationships,* translated by J. Rodker. London: John Lane.

Hite, S. 2006. *The Shere Hite report reader: New and selected readings on sex, globalization, and private life.* New York: Seven Stories Press.

Holcomb, D. R., P. D. Sarvela, K. A. Sondag and L. H. Holcomb. 1993. An evaluation of a mixed-gender date rape prevention workshop. *Journal of American College Health* 41:159-64.

Holzman, C. 1994. Multicultural perspectives on counseling survivors of rape. *Journal of Social Distress and the Homeless* 3:81-97.

Houston, S., and N. Hwang. 1996. Correlates of the objective and subjective experiences of sexual harassment in high school. *Sex Roles* 34:189-204.

Howes, R., R. Rupp and S. Simpson. 2007. *What wives wish their husbands knew about sex: A guide for Christian men.* Grand Rapids: Baker Books.

Huerta, M., L. Cortina, J. Pang, C. Torges and V. Magley. 2006. Sex and power in the academy: Modeling sexual harassment in the lives of college women. *Personality and Social Psychology Bulletin* 32:616-28.

Humphreys, T., and E. Herold. 1996. Date rape: A comparative analysis and integration of theory. *Canadian Journal of Human Sexuality* 5:69-82.

Hunt, M. 1959. *The natural history of love.* New York: Grove.

Hunter, J. 1990. Violence against lesbian and gay male youths. *Journal of Interpersonal Violence* 5:295-300.

Hunter, J., and M. Rosario. 1994. Suicidal behavior and gay-related stress among gay and bisexual male adolescents. *Journal of Adolescent Research* 9:498-508.

Hyde, J. 1994. *Understanding human sexuality.* 5th ed. New York: McGraw-Hill.

Hyde, J., and J. DeLamater. 2002. *Understanding human sexuality.* New York: McGraw-Hill.

Jacoby, S. 1999. Great sex: What's age got to do with it? *Modern Maturity* 32 (September-October): 56-64.

Jacques, M., and K. Chason. 1979. Cohabitation: Its impact on marital success. *Family Coordinator* 28:35-39.

Jankowiak, W. 2006. Sexual desire and emotional intimacy: The individual's and the culture's dilemma. Paper presented at the annual meeting of the Society for the Scientific Study of Sexuality. Las Vegas, Nev.

Janssen, E. 1995. Understanding the rapist's mind. *Perspectives in Psychiatric Care* 31:9-13.

Javaid, G. 1993. The children of homosexual and heterosexual single mothers. *Child Psychiatry and Human Development* 23:235-48.

Jewett, P. K. 1976. *Man as male and female.* Grand Rapids: Eerdmans.

Jewkes, R., L. Peen-Kekana and H. Rose-Junius. 2005. "If they rape me, I can't blame them": Relections on gender in the social context of child rape in South Africa and Namibia. *Social Science and Medicine* 61:1809-20.

Johnson, R., A. Nahmins and L. Madger. 1989. A seroepidemiologic survey of the prevalence of herpes simplex versus type 2 infection. *New England Journal of Medicine* 321:7-12.

Johnson, S. 2002. *Emotionally focused couple therapy with trauma survivors: Strengthening attachment bonds.* New York: Guilford.

Jones, C. 2006. Drawing boundaries: Exploring the relationship between sexual harassment, gender and bullying. *Women's Studies International Forum* 29:147-58.

Jones, S. 2006. *A study guide and response to Mel White's "What the Bible says—and doesn't say—about homosexuality."* http://www.wheaton.edu/CACE/resources/booklets/StanJonesResponsetoMelWhite.pdf.

Jones, S., and M. Yarhouse. 2007. *Ex-gays? A longitudinal study of religiously mediated change in sexual orientation.* Downers Grove, Ill.: IVP Academic.

Jones, S. L., and B. B. Jones. 1993. *How and when to tell your kids about sex.* Colorado Springs: NavPress. 2nd ed. 2007.

Joy, D. M. 1986. *Re-bonding: Preventing and restoring damaged relationships.* Waco, Tex.: Word.

Kahn, J. R., and K. A. London. 1991. Premarital sex and the risk of divorce. *Journal of Marriage and Family* 53:845-55.

Kaiser, W. 1983. *Toward Old Testament ethics.* Grand Rapids: Zondervan.

Kallman, F. 1952. Twin and sibship study of overt male homosexuality. *American Journal of Human Genetics* 4:136-47.

Kerr, M., and M. Bowen, M. 1988. *Family evaluation.* New York: W. W. Norton.

King, B. 2005. *Human sexuality today.* 5th ed. Upper Saddle River, N.J.: Prentice Hall.

King, B., and J. Lorusso. 1997. Discussions in the home about sex: Different recollections by parents and children. *Journal of Sex and Marital Therapy* 23 (1): 52-60.

King, V., and M. Scott. 2005. A comparison of cohabiting relationships among older and younger adults. *Journal of Marriage and Family* 67:271-85.

Kinsey, A., W. Pomeroy, and C. Martin. 1948. *Sexual behavior in the human male.* Philadelphia: W. B. Saunders.

———. 1953. *Sexual behavior in the human female.* Philadelphia: W. B. Saunders.

Kliever, D. Managing sexual feeling in the Christian community. *Journal of Pastoral Counseling* 5:51.

Kroeger, C., and N. Nason-Clark. 2001. *No place for abuse: Biblical and practical resources to conteract domestic violence.* Downers Grove, Ill.: InterVarsity Press.

Ku, L., et al. 1998. Understanding changes in sexual activity among young metropolitan men: 1979-1995. *Family Planning Perspectives* 30:256-62.

Laaser, M. 2004. *Healing the wounds of sexual addiction.* Grand Rapids: Zondervan.

Laaser, M., and L. Gregoire. 2003. Pastors and cybersex addiction. *Sexual and Relationship Therapy* 10:395-404.

La Fond, J. 2005. *Preventing sexual violence: How society should cope with sex offenders.* The law and public policy: Psychology and the social sciences. Washington, D.C.: American Psychological Association.

Lammers, C., M. Ireland, M. Resnick and R. Blum. 2000. Influences on adolescents' decision to postpone onset of sexual intercourse: A survival analysis of virginity among youths aged 13 to 18 years. *Journal of Adolescent Health* 26:42-48.

Langberg, D. 2003. *Counseling survivors of sexual abuse.* Fairfax, Va.: Xulon.

Langevin, R., and S. Curnoe. 2004. The use of pornography during the commision of sexual offenses. *International Journal of Offender Therapy and Comparative Criminology* 48:572-86.

Laumann, E., J. Gagnon, R. Michael and S. Michaels. 1994. *The social organi-*

zation of sexuality: Sexual practices in the United States. Chicago: University of Chicago Press.

Lebowitz, L., and S. Roth. 1994. "I felt like a slut": The cultural context and women's response to being raped. *Journal of Traumatic Stress* 7:363-89.

Lenhard, S. 2004. *Clinical aspects of sexual harassment and gender discrimination: Psycholgical consequences and treatment interventions.* New York: Brunner-Routledge.

Levant, R., and G. Brooks. 1997. Nonrelational sexuality in men. In *Men and Sex: New Psychological Perspectives,* edited by R. Levant and G Brooks. New York: J. Wiley & Sons.

LeVay, S. 1991. A difference in hypothalamic structure between heterosexual and homosexual men. *Science* 253:1034-37.

LeVay, S. 2003. Can gays become straight? *New Scientist* 180:19.

Levinson, D. J., with J. D. Levinson. 1978. *The seasons of a man's life.* New York: Knopf.

———. 1996. *The seasons of a woman's life.* New York: Knopf.

Lewis, C. S. 1960. *Mere Christianity.* New York: Macmillan.

———. 1963. *The Four Loves.* London: Collins/Fontana.

Levy, J. 1994. Sex and sexuality in later life stages. In *Sexuality across the life span,* edited by A. Rossi, pp. 287-309. Chicago: University of Chicago Press.

Lindsey, B., and W. Evans. 1927. *Companionate marriage.* New York: Boni & Liverwright.

Lisak, D., and C. Ivan. 1995. Deficits in intimacy and empathy in sexually aggressive men. *Journal of Interpersonal Violence* 10:296-308.

Loader, W. 2005. *Sexuality and the Jesus tradition.* Grand Rapids: Eerdmans.

Loe, M. 1996. Working for men: At the intersection of power, gender and sexuality. *Sociological Inquiry* 66:399-421.

Loftus, E. 1993. False memory syndrome. *Family Therapy Networker* 17 (5): 27.

Long, E., R. Cate, D. Fehsenfelt and K. Williams. 1996. A longitudinal assessment of a measure of premarital conflict. *Family Relations* 45:302-8.

Lottes, I. L. 1997. Sexual coercion among university students: A comparison of the United States and Sweden. *Journal of Sex Research* 34:67-76.

Luo, T. Y. 1996. Sexual harassment in the Chinese workplace: Attitudes toward and experiences of sexual harassment among workers in Taiwan. *Violence Against Women* 2:284-301.

Maccoby, E. 1998. *The two sexes: Growing up apart, coming together.* Cambridge, Mass.: Harvard University Press.

MacKay, P. 1974. *The clockwork image.* Downers Grove, Ill.: InterVarsity Press.

Madanes, C. 1990. *Sex, love, and violence: Strategies for transformation.* New York: W. W. Norton.

—————. 1995. *The violence of men: New techniques for working with abusive families; A therapy of social action.* San Francisco: Jossey-Bass.

Maddock, J. 1975. Sexual health and health care. *Postgraduate Medicine* 58:52-58.

Maddock, J., and N. Larson. 1995. *Incestuous families: An ecological approach to understanding and treatment.* New York: W. W. Norton.

Magnacca, D. 2004. *Love and infertility: Survival strategies for balancing infertility, marriage, and life.* Washington, D.C.: Lifeline Press.

Maguen, S., and L. Armistead. 2006. Abstinence among female adolescents: Do parents matter above and beyond the influence of peers? *American Journal of Orthopsychiatry* 76:260-64.

Malamuth, N. 1981. Rape proclivity in males. *Journal of Social Issues* 37 (4): 138-57.

—————. 1984. Aggression against women: Cultural and individual causes. In *Pornography and sexual aggression,* edited N. Malamuth and E. Donnerstein. New York: Academic.

—————. 1996. Sexually explicit media, gender differences, and evolutionary theory. *Journal of Communication* 46 (3): 8-31.

Malamuth, N., M. Heim and S. Feshback. 1980. Sexual responsiveness of college students to rape depictions: Inhibitory and disinhibitory effects. *Journal of Personality and Social Psychology* 38:399-408.

Malamuth, N., R. J. Sockloskie, M. P. Koss and J. S. Tanaka. 1991. Characteristics of aggressors against women: Testing a model using a national sample of college students. *Journal of Consulting and Clinical Psychology* 59:670-781.

Malamuth, N., T. Addison and M. Koss. 2000. Pornography and sexual aggresssion: Are there reliable effects and can we understand them? *Annual Review of Sex Research* 11:26-91.

Manning, J. 2005. Pornography's impact on marriage and the family. Testimony of Jill C. Manning Before the Subcommittee on the Constitution, Civil Rights and Property Rights Committee on Judiciary, United States Senate, November 9, 2005. The Heritage Foundation. http://www.heritage.org/Research/Family/tst111405a.cfm.

—————. 2006. The impact of Internet pornography on marriage and the family: A Review of the research. *Sexual Addiction and Compulsivity* 13:131-65.

Manning. W., M. Longmore and P. Giordano. 2007. The changing institution of marriage: Adolescents' expectations to cohabit and to marry. *Journal of Marriage and Family* 69:559-75.

Markowski, E. M., and M. J. Johnston. 1980. Behavior, temperament and idealization of cohabiting couples who married. *International Journal of Sociology of the Family* 10:115-25.

Masters, W. H., and V. E. Johnson. 1966. *Human sexual response*. Boston: Little, Brown.

———. 1979. *Homosexuality in perspective*. New York: Bantam.

Masters, W. H., V. E. Johnson and R. C. Kolodny. 1994. *Heterosexuality*. New York: HarperCollins.

Matta, C. 2005. Ambiguous bodies and deviant sexualities: Hermaphrodites, homosexuals, and surgery in the United States, 1850-1904. *Perspectives in Biology and Medicine* 48:74-84.

McCabe, M., and L. Hardman. 2005. Attitudes and perceptions of workers to sexual harrassment. *Journal of Social Psychology* 145 (6): 719-40.

McCann, J. T., and M. K. Biaggio. 1989. Sexual satisfaction in marriage as a function of life meaning. *Archives of Sexual Behavior* 18 (1): 59-72.

McCarthy, B. 1999. Relapse prevention strategies and techniques for inhibited sexual desire. *Journal of Sex & Marital Therapy* 25:297-303.

McCarthy, B., R. Ginsberg and L. Fucito. 2006. Resilient sexual desire in heterosexual couples. *Family Journal: Counseling and Therapy for Couples and Families* 14:59-64.

McLean, S. 1984. The language of covenant and a theology of the family. Paper presented at seminar, Consultation on a Theology of the Family. Fuller Theological Seminary, November 19-20.

McMinn, Lisa. 2000. *Growing strong daughters: Encouraging girls to become all they're meant to be*. Grand Rapids: Baker Books. Rev. ed., 2007.

———. 2004. *Sexuality and holy longing: Embracing intimacy in a broken world*. San Francisco: Jossey-Bass.

McRae, S. 1997. Cohabitation: A trial run for marriage? *Sexual & Marital Therapy*. 12:259-73.

Mead, M. 1966. Marriage in two steps. *Redbook* 127:48-49.

Messiah, A., et al. 1995. Sociodemographic characteristics and sexual behavior of bisexual men in France: Implications for HIV prevention. *American Journal of Public Health* 85:1543-46.

Metz, M., and M. Miner. 1998. Psychosexual and psychosocial aspects of male aging and sexual health. *The Canadian Journal Human Sexuality* 7:245-59.

Mielke, A. 1995. *Christians, feminists, and the culture of pornography.* Lanham, Md.: University Press of America.

Miles, A., with foreword by M. Fortune. 2002. *Violence in families: What every Christian needs to know.* Minneapolis: Augsburg.

Miller, B., and K. Moore. 1990. Adolescent sexual behavior, pregnancy, and parenting: Research through the 1980s. *Journal of Marriage and Family* 51:1025-44.

Miller, B., and T. Olson. 1988. Sexual attitudes and behavior of high school students in relation to background and contextual factors. *Journal of Sex Research* 24:194-200.

Miller, B. C., and T. Heaton. 1991. Age at first sexual intercourse and the timing of marriage and childbirth. *Journal of Marriage and Family* 53 (3): 719-32.

Miller, L. L. 1997. Not just weapons of the weak: Gender harassment as a form of protest for army men. *Social Psychology Quarterly* 60 (1): 32-51.

Milner, R., and S. Webster. 2005. Identifying schemas in child molesters, rapists, and violent offenders. *Sexual Abuse: Journal of Research and Treatment* 17:425-39.

Mitchell, K., D. Finkelhor and J. Wolak. 2007. Youth internet users at risk for the most serious online sexual solicitations. *American Journal of Preventive Medicine* 32:532-37.

Moberly, Elizabeth. 1983a. *Homosexuality: A new Christian ethic.* Greenwood, S.C.: Attic Press. New York: Robson Books, 1997.

———. 1983b. *Psychogenesis.* London: Routledge & Kegan Paul.

Moeller, I., and J. Sherlock. 1981. Making it legal: A comparison of previously cohabiting and engaged newlyweds. *Journal of Sociology and Social Welfare* 8:97-110.

Mohler, R. A., Jr. 2005. A Christian case for gay marriage? R. Albert Mohler Jr., President of Southern Baptist Theological Seminary, Louisville, Kentucky, on the Albert Mohler Program, Salem Radio Network. August 26. http://www.crosswalk.com/blogs/mohler/1347782/.

Monahan, B. A., J. A. Marolla and D. G. Bromley. 2005. Constructing coercion: The organization of sexual assault. *Journal of Contemporary Ethnography* 34:284-316.

Money, J. 1975. Ablatio penis: Normal male infant sex-reassigned as a girl. *Archives of Sexual Behavior* 4:65-72.

———. 1987. Sin, sickness, or status? *American Psychologist* 42 (4): 384-99.

————. 1995. *Arguing about sex: The rhetoric of Christian sexual morality.* Albany, N.Y.: SUNY Press.

Moore, D., and C. Travis. 2000. Biological models and sexual politics. In *Sexuality, society, and feminism,* edited by C. Travis and J. White, pp. 299-319. Washington, D.C.: American Psychological Association.

Moser, C. 1993. A response to Aviel Goodman's "Sexual addiction": Designation and treatment. *Journal of Sex and Marital Therapy* 19 (3): 220-24.

Mott, S. 1982. *Biblical ethics and social change.* New York: Oxford University Press.

Mouw, R. 1988. Toward a theology of social change. Paper presented at the second IFACS Sociology Conference at Wheaton College, Wheaton, Ill.

Muehlenhard, C. L., P. A. Harney and J. M. Jones. 1992. From "victim-precipitated rape" to "date rape": How far have we come? *Annual Review of Sex Research* 3:219-53.

Mullen, P., J. Martin, J. Anderson, S. Romans and G. Herbison. 1996. The long-term impact of the physical, emotional and sexual abuse of children: A community study. *Child Abuse and Neglect* 20:7-21.

Mustanski, B., and J. Bailey. 2003. A therapist's guide to the genetics of human sexual orientation. *Sexual and Relationship Therapy* 18:429-36.

Mustanski, B., M. Chivers and J. Bailey. 2002. A critical review of recent biological research on human sexual orientation. *Annual Review of Sex Research* 13:89-140.

Myers, D., and L. Dawson Scanzoni. 2005. *What God has joined together? A Christian case for gay marriage.* New York : HarperSanFrancisco.

Nagel, B., H. Matsuo, K. P. McTintyre and N. Morrison. 2005. Attitudes toward victims of rape: Effects of gender, race, religion, and social class. *Journal of Interpersonal Violence* 20:725-37.

National Women's Health Network. 2002. *The truth about hormone replacement therapy: How to break free from the medical myths of menopause.* Roseville, Calif.: Prima Lifestyles.

Neal, C. J., and M. W. Mangis. 1995. Unwanted sexual experiences among Christian college women: Saying no on the inside. *Journal of Psychology and Theology* 23 (3): 171-79.

Nelson, J., and S. Longfellow. 1994. *Sexuality and the sacred: Sources for theological reflection.* Louisville, Ky.: Westminster John Knox.

Newfield, E., S. Hart, S. Dibble and L. Kohler. 2006. Female-to-male transgender quality of life. *Quality of Life Research.* 15:1447-57.

Nicolosi, J. 1991. *Reparative therapy of male homosexuality: A new clinical approach.* Northvale, N.J.: Jason Aronson. Softcover ed., 1997.

Nicolosi, J., and L Nicolosi. 2002. *A parent's guide to preventing homosexuality.* Downers Grove, Ill.: InterVarsity Press.

Nishith, P., R. Nixon and P. Resick. 2005. Resolution of trauma-related guilt following treatment of PTSD in female rape victims: A result of cognitive processing therapy targeting comorbid depression? *Journal of Affective Disorders* 86 (2): 259-65.

Nock, S. 1994. A comparison of marriages and cohabiting relationships: Commitment, relationship quality, intergenerational integration and ideal fertility. *Journal of Family Issues* 16:53-76.

Norwood, R. 1985. *Women who love too much: When you keep wishing and hoping he'll change.* New York: Simon & Schuster.

O'Byrne, R., M. Rapley and S. Hansen. 2006. "You couldn't say 'no,' could you?" Young men's understandings of sexual refusal. *Feminism and Psychology* 16:133-54.

Oddone-Paolucci, E., M. Genuis and C. Violato. 2000. A meta-analysis of the published research on the effects of pornogrpahy. In *The Changing Family and Child Development,* edited by C. Violato, E. Oddone-Paoluci and M. Genuis, pp. 48-59. Aldershot, U.K.: Ashgate.

O'Donohue, W., and A. Bowers. 2006. Pathways to false allegations of sexual harassment. *Journal of Investigative Psychology and Offender Profiling* 3 (1): 47-74.

Oliver, M., and J. Hyde. 1993. Gender differences in sexuality: A meta-analysis. *Psychological Bulletin* 114:29-51.

Olson, D., D. Sprenkle and C. Russell. 1979. Circumplex model of marital and family systems: Cohesion and adaptability dimensions, family types, and clinical applications. *Family Process* 18:3-28.

Olson, M., C. Russell, M. Higgins-Kessler and R. Miller. 2002. Emotional processes following disclosure of an extramarital affair. *Journal of Marital and Family Therapy* 28:423-34.

Olthuis, J. 1975. *I pledge you my troth: A Christian view of marriage, family, friendship.* New York: Harper and Row.

Omot, A., and H. Kurtzman, eds. 2006. *Sexual orientation and mental health: Examining identity and development in lesbian, gay, and bisexual people.* Washington D.C.: American Psychological Association.

Orbach, S. 2004. The body in clinical practice. In *Touch: Attachment and the body;*

The John Bowlby memorial conference monograph 2003, edited by K. White, pp. 17-47. London: Kanac.

Orten, J. 1990. Coming up short: The physical, cognitive, and social effects of Turner's Syndrome. *Health and Social Work* 15 (2): 100-106.

Pallard, P. 1995. Pornography and sexual aggression. *Current Psychology* 14:200-221.

Paludi, M., and C. Paludi Jr., eds. 2003. *Academic and workplace sexual harassment*. Westport, Conn.: Praeger.

Paul, J. P. 1993. Childhood cross-gender behavior and adult homosexuality: The resurgence of biological models of sexuality. Special issue: If you seduce a straight person, can you make them gay? Issues in biological essentialism versus social constructionism in gay and lesbian identities. *Journal of Homosexuality* 24 (3-4): 41-54.

Payne, L. 1984. *The healing of the homosexual*. Westchester, Ill.: Crossway Books.

Penner, C., and J. Penner. 2003. *The gift of sex: A guide to sexual fullfillment*. Nashville: W Publishing Group.

Perdue, L., J. Blenkinsopp, J. Collins and C. Meyers. 1997. *Families in ancient Israel*. Louisville, Ky.: Westminster John Knox.

Peterman, D. J. 1975. Does living together before marriage make for a better marriage? *Medical Aspects of Human Sexuality* 9:39-41.

Peters, D., and L. Range. 1995. Childhood sexual abuse and current suicidality in college women and men. *Journal of Child Abuse and Neglect* 19:335-41.

Petersen, J., A. Kretchmer, B. Nellis, K. Lever and R. Hertz. 1983. *The Playboy readers' sex survey*, parts 1 and 2. *Playboy*, January, 108; March, 90.

Philaretou, A., A. Mahfouz and K. Allen. 2005. Use of Internet pornography and men's well-being. *International Journal of Men's Health* 4:149-69.

Phillps, J., and M. Sweeney. 2005. Premarital cohabitation and marital disruption among white, black, and mexican american women. *Journal of Marriage and Family* 67:296-314.

Pinello, D. 2006. *America's struggle for same-sex marriage*. Cambridge: Cambridge University Press.

Pittman, F. 1987. *Turning points: Treating families in transition and crisis*. New York: W. W. Norton.

———. 1989. *Private lies: Infidelity and the betrayal of intimacy*. New York: W. W. Norton.

Pittman, F., and T. Wagers. 1995. Crises of infidelity. In *Clinical handbook of couple therapy,* edited by N. Jacobson and A. Gurman, pp. 295-316. New York: Guilford.

Pleck, J. 1995. The gender role strain paradigm: An update. In *A new psychology of men,* edited by R. Lavant and W. Pollack. New York: Basic Books.

Pollack, W. 1998. *Real boys: Rescuing our sons from the myths of boyhood.* New York: Henry Holt.

Popenoe, D., and B. Whitehead. 2002. *Should we live together? What young adults need to know about cohabitation before marriage; A comprehensive review of recent research.* 2nd ed. Piscataway, N.J.: National Marriage Project. Executive summary, http://marriage.rutgers.edu/Publications/SWLT2%20TEXT.htm.

———. 2007. *The state of our unions 2007.* http://marriage.rutgers.edu/publications/SOOU2007.pdf.

Poulin, C. 2005. The causes of rape: Understanding individual differences in male propensity for sexual agression. *Canadian Psychology* 46:254-56.

Power, C. 2005. Food and sex addiction: Helping the clinician recognize and treat the interaction. *Sexual Addiction & Compulsivity* 12:219-34.

Prins, K. S., B. P. Buunk and N. W. Van Yperen. 1993. Equity, normative disapproval and extramarital relationships. *Journal of Social and Personal Relationships* 10 (1): 39-53.

Quinsey, V., and T. Chaplin. 1984. Stimulus control of rapists and non-sex offender's sexual arousal. *Behavioral Assessment* 6:169-76.

Rahman, Q., and G. Wilson 2003. Born gay? The psychobiology of human sexual orientation. *Personality and Individual Differences* 34:1337-82.

RAINN: Rape, Abuse and Incest National Network. 2006. Website with statistics and a national sexual assault hotline number. http://www.rainn.org/statistics.

Raviv, M. 1993. Personality characteristics of sexual addicts and pathological gamblers. *Journal of Gambling Studies* 9 (1): 17-30.

Rector, R., K. Johnson and J. Marshall. 2004. Teens who make virgnity pledges have substantially improved life outcomes. Retrived January 3, 2008, from http://www.heritage.org/Research/abstinence/cda0.4-07.cfm.

Regan, P. C., and E. Berscheid. 1997. Gender differences in characteristics desired in a potential sexual and marriage partner. *Journal of Psychology and Human Sexuality* 9 (1): 25-37.

Reid, K. G., with foreword by M. Fortune. 1994. *Preventing child sexual abuse: A curriculum for children ages five through eight.* New York: United Church Press.

Reid, K. S., R. Wampler and D. K. Taylor. 1996. The "alienated" partner: Responses to traditional therapies for adult sex abuse survivors. *Journal of Marital and Family Therapy* 22 (4): 443-53.

Reiner, W. 2005. Gender identity and sex-of-rearing in children with disorders of sexual differentiation. *Journal of Pediatric Endocrinology and Metabolism.* 18:549-53.

Reiner, W., and J. Gearhart. 2004. Sex determination, differentiation, and identity. *New England Journal of Medicine* 350:2204-6.

Reisman, J., E. Eichel, J. Court and J. Muir. 1990. *Kinsey, sex, and fraud: The indoctrination of a people.* Lafayette, Ind.: Huntington House.

Reiss, I. 1960. *Premarital sexual standards in the United States.* New York: Free Press.

———. 1986. *Journey into sexuality.* Englewood Cliff, N.J.: Prentice Hall.

———. 2006. *An insider's view of sexual science since Kinsey.* Lanham, Md.: Rowman & Littlefield.

Reiss, I., R. Anderson, and G. Sponaugle. 1980. A multivariate model of the determinants of extramarital sexual permissiveness. *Journal of Marriage and Family* 42:395-411.

Remafedi, G., M. Resnick, R. Blum and L. Harris. 1992. Demography of sexual orientation in adolescents. *Pediatrics* 89:714-21.

Resick, P. 1993. The psychological impact of rape. *Journal of Interpersonal Violence* 8:223-55.

Rhoades, G., S. Stanley, and H. Markman. 2006. Pre-engagement cohabitation and gender asymmetry in marital commitment. *Journal of Family Psychology* 20:553-60.

Rich, A. 1986. *Of woman born.* New York: W. W. Norton.

Ricoeur, P. 1967. *The symbolism of evil,* translated by E. Buchanan. New York: Harper & Row.

———. 1994. *Oneself as another,* translated by Kathleen Blarney. Chicago: University of Chicago Press.

Ridley, C., D. Peterman and A. Avery. 1978. Cohabitation: Does it make for a better marriage? *Family Coordinator* 27:130-44.

Risman, B., C. Hill, R. Zick and L. Peplau. 1981. Living together in college. *Journal of Marriage and Family* 43:77-83.

Rogers, J. B. 2005. *Jesus, the Bible, and homosexuality.* Louisville, Ky.: Westminster John Knox.

Rogers, J. K., and K. D. Henson. 1997. "Hey, why don't you wear a shorter skirt?" Structural vulnerability and the organization of sexual harassment in temporary clerical employment. *Gender and Society* 11 (2): 215-37.

Rogers, S., and C. Turner. 1991. Male-male sexual contact in the U.S.A.: Findings from five sample surveys, 1970-1990. *Journal of Sex Research* 28:491-519.

Romano, E., and R. V. DeLuca. 1996. Characteristics of perpetrators with histories of sexual abuse. *International Journal of Offender Therapy and Comparative Criminology* 40 (2): 147-56.

Romans, S. E., J. L. Martin, J. C. Anderson and M. L. O'Shea, et al. 1995. Factors that mediate between child sexual abuse and adult psychological outcome. *Psychological Medicine* 25 (1):127-42.

Roosa, M., J. Tein, C. Reinholt and P. Angelini. 1997. The relationship of childhood sexual abuse to teenage pregnancy. *Journal of Marriage and Family* 59:131-42.

Rosenbaum, E., and D. B. Kandel. 1990. Early onset of adolescent sexual behavior and drug involvement. *Journal of Marriage and Family* 52 (3): 783-98.

Rosenbaum, J. 2006. Reborn a virgin: Adolescents' retracting of virginity pledges and sexual histories. *American Journal of Public Health* 96:1098-1103.

Ross, L. F. 1996. Adolescent sexuality and public policy: A liberal response. *Politics and the Life Sciences* 15 (1): 13-21.

Rossi, A. 1994. *Sexuality across the life course.* Chicago: University of Chicago Press.

Rotundo, M., D. Nquyen, and P. Sackett. 2001. A meta-analytic review of gender differences in perception of sexual harasssment. *Journal of Applied Psychology* 86:914-22.

Rousenau, D. 2005. *A celebration of sex for newlyweds.* Nashville: Thomas Nelson.

Rousseau, M., and C. Gallagher. 1986. *Sex is holy.* Amity, N.Y.: Amity House.

Russell, D. E. H. 1986. The incest legacy: Why today's abused children become tomorrow's victims of rape. *The Sciences* 26 (2): 28-32.

Sanday, P. 1981. The socio-cultural context of rape: A cross-cultural study. *Journal of Social Issues* 37:5-27.

Sandfort, T. 2003. Studying sexual orientation change: A methodological review of the Spitzer study, "Can some gay men and lesbians change their sexual orienation?" *Journal of Gay and Lesbian Psychotherapy.* 2003:15-29.

Sandfort, T., F. Bakker, I. Vanwesenbeeck and F. Schellevis. 2006. Sexual orientation and mental and physical health status: Findings from a Dutch population survey. *American Journal of Public Health* 96:1119-25.

Sandnabba, N., P. Santilla, M. Wannas and K. Krook. 2003. Age and gender specific sexual behaviors in children. *Child Abuse and Neglect* 27:579-605.

Sarkar, N., and R. Sarkar. 2005. Sexual assault on woman: Its impact on her life and living in society. *Sexual and Relationship Therapy* 20:407-19.

Saunders, R. M., and P. J. Naus. 1993. The impact of social content and audience factors on responses to sexually explicit videos. *Journal of Sex Education and Therapy* 19 (2): 117-30.

Scanzoni, L., and V. R. Mollenkott. 1978. *Is the homosexual my neighbor?* New York: Harper & Row.

Schaumberg, H., and H. Schaumberg. 1997. *False intimacy: Understanding the struggle of sexual addiction.* Colorado Springs: NavPress.

Schewe, P. A., and W. O'Donohue. 1996. Rape prevention with high-risk males: Short-term outcome of two interventions. *Journal of Archives of Sexual Behavior* 25 (5): 455-71.

Schlinger, H. 2002. *The science of romance: Secrets of the sexual brain.* Amherst, N.Y.: Prometheus Books.

Schmitt. D. 2003. Universal sex differences in the desire for sexual variety: Tests from 52 nations, 6 continents, and 13 islands. *Journal of Personality and Social Psychology* 85:85-104.

———. 2006. Sociosexuality from Argentina to Zimbabwe: A 48-nation study of sex, culture and strategies of human mating. *Behavioral & Brain Sciences* 28:247-75.

Schnarch, D. 1991. *Constructing the sexual crucible.* New York: W. W. Norton.

———. 1993. Treating affairs in the sexual crucible. *American Association of Sex Educators, Counselors and Therapists Newsletter* 27 (9): 1-4.

———. 1997. *The passionate marriage.* New York: W. W. Norton.

Schnarch, D., and J. Maddock. 2002. *Resurrecting sex: Resolving sexual problems and rejuvenating your relationship.* San Fransico: HarperCollins.

Schneider, H. J. 1996. Violence in the mass media. *Journal on Studies of Crime and Crime Prevention* 5 (1): 59-71.

Schneider, J. P. 2003. The impact of compulsive cybersex behaviors on the family. *Sexual & Relationship Therapy* 18:329-57.

———. 2005. Addiction is addiction is addiction. *Sexual Addiction and Compulsivity* 12:75-77.

Schneider, J. P., R. Irons and D. Corley. 1999. Disclosure of extramarital sexual activities by exploitive professionals and other persons with addictive or compulsive sexual disorders. *Journal of Sex Education and Therapy* 24:277-87.

Schneider, J. P., J. Sealy, J. Montgomery and R. Irons. 2005. Ritualization and reinforcement: Keys to understanding mixed addiction involving sex and drugs. *Sexual Addiction and Compulsivity* 12:121-48.

Schuklenk, U., and M. Ristow. 1996. The ethics of research into the causes of homosexuality. *Journal of Homosexuality* 31 (3): 5-30.

Schultz, Q., R. Anker, J. Bratt, W. Romanowski, J. Worst and L. Zuidervaart. 1991. *Dancing in the dark: Youth, popular culture and the electronic media.* Grand Rapids: Eerdmans.

Scriven, M. 1968. Putting the sex back into sex education. *Phi Delta Kappan* 49:485-89.

Senn, C., and S. Desmarais. 2004. Impact of interaction with a partner or friend on the exposure effects of pornography and erotica. *Violence and Victims* 19 (6): 645-58.

Selby, P. 1996. Is the church a family? In *The family in theological perspective,* edited by S. Barton, pp. 151-68. Edinburgh: T&T Clark.

Serbin, L., and J. Karp. 2004. The intergenerational transfer of psychosocial risk: Mediators of vulnerability and resilience. *Annual Review of Psychology.* 55:333-63.

Sex Addicts Anonymous. *Sex as an addiction.* Northbrook, Ill.: Sex Addicts Anonymous. Cf. http://saa-recovery.org/.

Sheldon-Keller, A., E. Lloyd–McGarvey, M. West and R. Canterbury. 1994. Attachment and assessment of blame in date rape scenarios. *Social Behavior and Personality* 22:313-18.

Shults, F. LeRon. 2003. *Reforming theological anthropology: After the turn to rationality.* Grand Rapids: Eerdmans.

Silny, A. 1993. Sexuality and Aging. In *Handbook of human sexuality,* edited by B. Wolman and J. Money, pp. 123-46. Northvale, N.J.: Jason Aronson.

Smedes, L. B. 1994. *Sex for Christians: The limits and liberties of sexual living.* Rev. ed. Grand Rapids: Eerdmans. (1st ed., 1976.)

Smith, A., and J. Minson. 1997. Discipline. *Economy and Society* 26 (2): 191-210.

Smock, P. 2000. Cohabitation in the United States. *Annual Review of Sociology* 26:1-26.

Song, J., M. Bergen, and W. Schumm. 1995. Sexual satisfaction among Korean-American couples in the midwestern United States. *Journal of Sex and Marital Therapy* 21:147-58.

Spanier, G. 1983. Married and unmarried cohabitation in the United States: 1980. *Journal of Marriage and Family* 45:277-88.

Spear, L. 2000. Neurobehavioral changes in adolescence. *Current Directions in Psychological Science* 9:111-14.

Spitzer, R. L. 2003. Can some gay men and lesbians change their sexual orientation? 200 participants reporting a change from homosexual to heterosexual orientation. *Archives of Sexual Behavior* 32:403-17.

Spong, J. S. 1988. *Living in sin? A bishop rethinks human sexuality.* San Francisco: Harper & Row.

Stacey, J., and E. Saewyc. 2006. Reversal of findings (Focus on the Family). *Gay and Lesbian Review Worldwide* 13:9.

Stack, S., I. Wasserman, and R. Kern. 2004. Adult social bonds and use of Internet pornography. *Social Science Quarterly* 85:75-88.

Stanley, S., G. Rhoades and H. Markman. 2006. Sliding versus deciding: Inertia and the premarital cohabitation effect. *Family Relations* 55:499-509.

Stanley, S., and G. Smalley. 2005. *The power of commitment: A guide to active, lifelong love* . San Francisco: Jossey-Bass.

Steele, T. 1992. Lesbian identity and childhood abuse: Facts and fallacies. Paper presented to the American Sociological Association in Pittsburgh.

Sternberg, R. 1987. A triangular theory of love. *Psychological Review* 93:119-35.

Stets, J. E., and M. A. Straus. 1989. The marriage license as a hitting license: A comparison of assaults in dating, cohabiting, and married couples. *Journal of Family Violence* 4 (2): 161-80.

Stets, J. 1993. The link between past and present intimate relationships. *Journal of Family Issues* 14:236-60.

Storms, M. 1981. A theory of erotic orientation development. *Psychological Review* 88:340-53.

Stott, J. 1998. *Same-sex partnerships: A Christian perspective.* Grand Rapids: Baker.

Strong, B., and R. Reynolds. 1982. *Understanding our sexuality.* St. Paul, Minn.: West. 2nd ed., 1988.

Strouse, J., M. Goodwin, and B. Roscoe. 1994. Correlates of attitudes toward sexual harassment among early adolescents. *Sex Roles* 31:559-77.

Surra, C. 1990. Research and theory on mate selection and premarital relationships in the 1980s. *Journal of Marriage and Family* 52:844-65.

Tanfer, K. 1987. Patterns of premarital cohabitation among never-married women in the United States. *Journal of Marriage and Family* 49:483-95.

Tangri, S., M. Burt, and L. Johnson. 1982. Sexual harassment at work: Three explanatory models. *Journal of Social Issues* 384:33-54.

Tangri, S., and S. Hayes. 1997. Theories of sexual harassment. In *Sexual harassment: Theory, research, and treatment,* edited by W. O'Donohue, pp. 99-111. Boston: Allyn & Bacon.

Tannahill, R. 1980. *Sex in history.* New York: Stein & Day.

Tasker, F., and S. Golombok. 1995. Adults raised as children in lesbian families. *American Journal of Orthopsychiatry* 65:203-15.

Teachman, J. 2003. Premarital sex, premarital cohabitation, and the risk of subsequent marital disruption among women. *Journal of Marriage and Family.* 65:444-55.

Thacker, R. A. 1996. A descriptive study of situational and individual influences upon individuals' responses to sexual harassment. *Human Relations* 49:1105-22.

Thatcher, A. 1993. *Liberating sex: A Christian theology.* London: SPCK.

Thatcher, A., and E. Stuart. 1996. *Christian perspectives on sexuality and gender.* Grand Rapids: Eerdmans. See sec. 5, Sexuality and spirituality.

Thomson, E., and U. Colella. 1992. Cohabitation and marital stability: Quality or commitment? *Journal of Marriage and Family* 54:259-67.

Thornton, A., W. Axinn and J. Teachman. 1995. The influence of school enrollment and accumulation on cohabitation and marriage in early adulthood. *American Sociological Review* 24:323-40.

Thornton, A., and D. Camburn. 1987. The influence of the family on premarital sexual attitudes and behavior. *Demography* 24:323-40.

———. 1989. Religious participation and adolescent sexual behavior. *Journal of Marriage and Family* 51:641-53.

Tomasson, R. 1998. Modern Sweden: The declining importance of marriage. *Scandinavian Review* 86 (August): 83-89.

Travin, S. 1995. Compulsive sexual behaviors. *Clinical Sexuality* 18 (Special issue): 155-69.

Treas, J. 2000. Sexual infidelity among married and cohabiting Americans. *Journal of Marriage and Family* 62:48-60.

Trepper, T., and M. Barrett. 1989. *Systemic treatment of incest: A theraputic handbook.* New York: Brunner/Mazel.

Trible, P. 1987. *God and the Rhetoric of Sexuality.* Philadelphia: Fortress.

Trobisch, W. 1968. *Essays on love: A HIS reader on love and the Christian view of marriage.* Downers Grove, Ill.: InterVarsity Press.

Trost, J. 1975. Married and unmarried cohabitation: The case of Sweden, with some comparison. *Journal of Marriage and Family* 37:677-82.

Truman, D. M., D. M. Tokar and A. R. Fischer. 1996. Dimensions of masculinity: Relations to date rape supportive attitudes and sexual aggression in dating situations. *Journal of Counseling and Development* 74 (6): 555-62.

Tubman, J. G., M. Windle and R. C. Windle. 1996. Cumulative sexual intercourse patterns among middle adolescents: Problem behavior precursors and concurrent health risk behaviors. *Journal of Adolescent Health* 18 (3): 182-91.

Udry, J. R. 1988. Biological predispositions and social control in adolescent sexual behavior. *American Sociological Review* 53:709-22.

Ullman, S. E., H. H. Filipas, S. M. Towsend and L. L. Starzynski. 2006. Correlates of comorbid PTSD and drinking problems among sexual assault surviors. *Addictive Behaviors* 31 (January): 128-32.

U.S. Equal Employment Opportunity Commission. 2007. "Sexual harassment." http://www.eeoc.gov/types/sexual_harassment.html.

U.S. Public Health Service. 1992. *Latest facts about AIDS, American Red Cross, U.S. Public Health Service.* Washington, D.C.

Ussher, J., and C. Dewberry. 1995. The nature and long-term effects of childhood sexual abuse: A survey of adult women survivors in Britain. *British Journal of Clinical Psychology* 34 (2): 177-92.

Van Leeuwen, M. S. 1984. Sexual values in a secular age. *Radix Magazine,* November/December, 4-11.

———. 1990. *Gender and grace: Love, work and parenting in a changing world.* Downers Grove, Ill.: InterVarsity Press.

———. 2002. *My brothers keeper: What social sciences do and don't tell us about masculinity.* Downers Grove, Ill.: InterVarsity Press.

Van Leeuwen, M. S., A. Knoppers, M. Koch, D. Schuurman and H. Sterk. 1993. *After Eden: Facing the challenge of gender reconciliation.* Grand Rapids: Eerdmans.

Veniegas, R., and T. Conley. 2000. Biological research on women's sexual orientations: Evaluating the scientific evidence. *Journal of Social Issues* 56:267-82.

Vicary, J., L.Klingaman and W. L. Harkness. 1995. Risk factors associated with date rape and sexual assault of adolescent girls. *Journal of Adolescence* 18:289-306.

Volf, M. 1996. *Exclusion and embrace: A theological exploration of identity, otherness, and reconciliation.* Nashville: Abingdon.

———. 1998. *After our likeness: The church as the image of the Trinity.* Grand Rapids: Eerdmans.

Vukovich, M. 1996. The prevalence of sexual harassment among female family practice residents in the United States. *Violence and Victims* 11:175-80.

Waite, L., and K. Joyner. 2001. Emotional satisfaction and physical pleasure in marital unions: Time horizons, sexual behavior, and sexual exclusivity. *Journal of Marriage and Family* 63:247-63.

Walker, A. 1982. *The color purple*. New York: Washington Square Press.

Walker, J., J. Archer, and M. Davies. 2005. Effects of male rape on psychological functioning. *British Journal of Clinical Psychology*. 44:445-51.

Walp, G. 2006. The missing link between pornography and rape: Convicted rapists respond with validated truth. *Dissertation Abstracts International, Section A: Humanities and Social Sciences* 66:2734.

Warren, R. C., and M. T. Green. 1995. Challenging the current paradigm amidst a culture of denial: Transformative treatment of sex offenders. *Canadian Journal of Human Sexuality* 4 (4): 299-309.

Weiss, D. Christian sexual addiction resource. http://www.sexaddict.com/Resource.html.

Weiss, R. 2004. Treating sex addiction. In *Handbook of addictive disorders: A practical guide to diagnosis and treatment*, edited by R. H. Combs, pp. 233-72. Hoboken, N.J.: John Wiley & Sons.

Welsh, S., J. Carr, B. Macquarrie and A. Huntley. 2006. "I'm not thinking of it as sexual harassment": Understanding harassment across race and citizenship. *Gender and Society*. 20:87-107.

Whatley, M. A. 2005. The effect of participant sex, victim dress, and traditional attitudes on causal judgments for marital rape victims. *Journal of Family Violence* 20:191-200.

Whitam, F., C. Daskalos and C. T. Mathy. 1995. A cross-cultural assessment of familial factors in the development of female homosexuality. *Journal of Psychology and Human Sexuality* 7:59-76.

White, J. 1993. *Eros redeemed: Breaking the stranglehold of sexual sin*. Downers Grove, Ill.: InterVarsity Press.

White, M. 1994. *Stranger at the gate: To be gay and Christian in America*. New York: Simon & Schuster.

———. 2002. *What the Bible says—and doesn't say—about homosexuality*. Lynchburg, Va.: Soulforce. http://www.soulforce.org/article/homosexuality-bible.

———. 2006. *Religion gone bad: The hidden dangers of the Christian right*. New York: J. P. Tarcher/Penguin.

Whitehead, Neil E. 1996. What can sociological surveys contribute to the understanding of the causation of homosexuality? *Journal of Psychology and Christianity* 15 (4): 322-35.

Whitty, M. T. 2003. Pushing the wrong buttons: Men's and women's attitudes toward online and offline infidelity. *CyberPsychology and Behavior* 6 (6): 569-79.

Wiederman, M. W., and E. R. Allgeier. 1996. Expectations and attributions regarding extramarital sex among young married individuals. *Journal of Psychology and Human Sexuality* 8 (3): 21-35.

Willingham, R. 1999. *Breaking free: Understanding sexual addiction and the healing power of Jesus.* Downers Grove, Ill.: InterVarsity Press.

Winner, L. 2005. *Real sex: The naked truth about chastity.* Grand Rapids: Brazos.

Wistow, F. 1988. The facts of life. *Family Therapy Networker* 12 (2): 20-31.

Wolfe, L. 1981. *The Cosmo report.* New York: Arbor House.

Wolff, C. 1971. *Love between women.* New York: St. Martin's Press.

Wolterstorff, N. 1983. *Until justice and peace embrace.* Grand Rapids: Eerdmans.

Worthen, A., and B. Davies. 1996. *Someone I love is gay: How family and friends can respond.* Downers Grove, Ill.: InterVarsity Press.

Wright, D., L. Williamson and M. Henderson. 2006. Parental influences on young people's sexual behaviour: A longitudinal analysis. *Journal of Adolescence* 29:473-94.

Wu, Z. 1995. Premarital cohabitation and postmarital cohabiting union formation. *Journal of Family Issues* 16 (2):212-32.

Wylie, M. 1993. The shadow of a doubt. *Family Therapy Networker* 17 (5): 18-29, 70-73.

Xu, N., C. Hudspeth and J. Bartkowski. 2006. The role of cohabitation in remarriage. *Journal of Marriage and Family* 68:261-74.

Yapko, M. 1993. The seductions of memory. *Family Therapy Networker* 17 (5): 31-37.

Ybarra, M., and K. Michell. 2005. Exposure to Internet pornography among children and adolescents: A national survey. *CyberPsychology and Behavior* 8:473-86.

Yoder, J., and P. Aniakudo. 1996. When pranks become harassment: The case of African American women firefighters. *Sex Roles* 35 (5-6): 253-70.

Yoder, V., T. Virden and K. Amin. 2005. Internet pornography and loneliness: An association? *Sexual Addiction and Compulsivity* 12:19-44.

Young, E. B. 1996. A psychoanalytic approach to addiction: The formation and use of a precocious paranoid schizoid depressive organization. *Melanie Klein and Object Relations* 14 (2): 177-95.

Zillmann, D., and J. Bryant. 1988. Effects of prolonged consumption of pornography on family values. *Journal of Family Issues* 9 (4): 518-44.

Zitzman, S., and M. Butler. 2005. Attachment, addiction, and recovery: Conjoint marital therapy for recovery from a sexual addiction. *Sexual Addiction and Compulsivity* 12:311-37.

Subject Index

Scripture Index